TONAL HARMONY

with an Introduction to Twentieth-Century Music

Second Edition

TONAL HARMONY
with an Introduction to Twentieth-Century Music

Second Edition

Stefan Kostka
The University of Texas at Austin

Dorothy Payne
The University of Connecticut at Storrs

Consulting Editor in Music
ALLAN W. SCHINDLER
Eastman School of Music

McGraw-Hill, Inc.
New York St. Louis San Francisco Auckland Bogotá
Caracas Lisbon London Madrid Mexico Milan
Montreal New Delhi Paris San Juan Singapore
Sydney Tokyo Toronto

This book is printed on recycled paper containing a minimum of 50% total recycled fiber with 10% postconsumer de-inked fiber.

Second Edition

910 HDHD 99876543
TONAL HARMONY, 2e

Library of Congress Cataloging-in-Publication Data

Kostka, Stefan.
 Tonal harmony, with an introduction to twentieth-century music.
 Includes indexes.
 1. Harmony. I. Payne, Dorothy. II. Schindler, Allan.
 III. Title.
MT50.K85   1989   781.3   88-32848

ISBN 0–07–557016–5

PREFACE

Tonal Harmony, with an Introduction to Twentieth-Century Music deals with the resources and practice of Western music from the seventeenth century to the present day. The second edition retains those features that the users of this text have found the most useful:

A single-volume format, with accompanying Workbook.

Illustrative musical examples from a broad spectrum of styles and performing media.

Self-Tests for individual and in-class work.

Abundant Workbook exercises, ranging from objective drills to creative writing assignments for class performance and discussion.

A thorough introduction to historic and contemporary twentieth-century resources.

An approach to musical understanding that is authoritative and consistent, but flexible in application. The emphasis is on actual practice, rather than rules or formulas.

Principal changes and additions in the second edition include:

Streamlining and consolidation of related topics. Examples include Chapters 3 and 12 in the present edition, each of which had formerly occupied two chapters.

Occasional re-sequencing of topics to facilitate continuity of presentation. Examples include names of scale degrees, which have been moved to Chapter 1, and the chapter on levels of harmony, which now appears later in the text (Chapter 15).

Inclusion of a number of new musical examples in addition to or in place of examples found in the first edition.

Expanded twentieth-century coverage.

Theory curricula vary considerably from one institution to another. Some courses are structured around the traditional study of harmony, while at other schools such topics as counterpoint, form, jazz, and popular music are incorporated in basic theory studies. Ear training work, keyboard harmony, and other practical musicianship skills may be integrated with the study of harmony, or treated in separate courses. With these different approaches in mind, the authors have designed *Tonal Harmony* to be both flexible in usage and broad in its stylistic range and applications.

The text provides students with a comprehensive but accessible and highly practical set of tools for the understanding of music. Actual musical practice is stressed more than rules or prohibitions. Principles are explained and illustrated, and exceptions are noted.

In its presentation of harmonic procedures, the text introduces students to the most common vocal and instrumental textures encountered in tonal music. Traditional four-part chorale settings are used to introduce many concepts, but three-part instrumental and vocal textures are also presented in illustrations and drill work, along with a variety of keyboard styles. To encourage the correlation of writing and performing skills, we have included musical examples in score and reduced-score formats, as well as charts on instrumental ranges and transpositions. Some of the assignments ask the student to write for small ensembles suitable for performance in class. Instructors may modify these assignments to make them most appropriate for their particular situations.

The text employs a variety of techniques to clarify underlying voice leading, harmonic structure, and formal procedures. These include textural reductions, accompanying many of the examples, which highlight chordal motion. Our goal has been to elucidate tonal logic at the phrase and section level as well as from one chord to the next. Abundant musical illustrations, many with commentaries, serve as a springboard for class discussion and individual understanding.

The book provides an extensive series of learning aids. A large portion of the text is devoted to Self-Tests, consisting of student-graded drills in chord spelling, part writing, and analysis, with suggested answers given in Appendix B. The Self-Tests can be used for in-class drill and discussion, in preparation for the Workbook exercises, or for independent study. Periodic Checkpoints enable students to gauge their understanding of the preceding material.

Exercises in the Workbook are closely correlated with the corresponding chapters of the text. In each chapter, the Workbook exercises begin with problems similar to those found in the Self-Tests, but also incorporate more creative types of compositional problems for those instructors who include this type of work.

ORGANIZATION

Part One (Chapters 1-4) begins the text with a thorough but concise overview of the fundamentals of music, divided into one chapter each on pitch and rhythm. Chapters 3 and 4 introduce the student to triads and seventh chords in various inversions and textures, but without placing them yet in their tonal contexts.

Part Two (Chapters 5-11) opens with an exposition of the principles of voice leading, with practice limited to root position triads. Chapter 6 follows with a systematic discussion of normative tonal progressions. Subsequent chapters deal with triads in inversion (Chapters 7 and 9), basic elements of musical form (Chapter 8), and non-chord tones (Chapters 10 and 11).

Part Three (Chapters 12-15) is devoted almost entirely to diatonic seventh chords, moving from the dominant seventh in root position and inversion (Chapter 12) through the supertonic and leading-tone sevenths (Chapter 13) to the remaining diatonic seventh chords (Chapter 14). The final chapter of this section introduces the concept of levels of harmony, the basis for techniques of reductive analysis.

Part Four begins the study of chromaticism with secondary functions (Chapters 16-17) and modulation (Chapters 18-19), concluding in Chapter 20 with a discussion of binary and ternary forms. Chromaticism continues to be the main topic in Part Five (Chapters 21-26), which covers mode mixture, the Neapolitan, augmented sixth chords, and enharmonicism. Some further elements, ninth chords and altered dominants among them, are the subject of the final chapter of this section.

The final part of the text, "Late Romanticism and the Twentieth Century," begins in Chapter 27 with a discussion of the developments and extensions in tonal practice that occurred in later nineteenth-century music. The concluding chapter provides an extensive introduction to major twentieth-century practices.

ACKNOWLEDGEMENTS

Many colleagues and friends provided assistance and encouragement during the development of the first edition of this text, notably Professors Douglass Green, Jerry Grigadean, and Janet McGaughey. Reviewers of the manuscript contributed many helpful suggestions; our sincere thanks are extended to Judith Allen, University of Virginia; Michael Arenson, University of Delaware; B. Glenn Chandler, Central Connecticut State College; Herbert Colvin, Baylor University; Charles Fligel, Southern Illinois University; Roger Foltz,

University of Nebraska, Omaha; Albert G. Huetteman, University of Massachusetts; Hanley Jackson, Kansas State University; Marvin Johnson, University of Alabama; Frank Lorince, West Virginia University; William L. Maxson, Eastern Washington University; Leonard Ott, University of Missouri; John Pozdro, University of Kansas; Jeffrey L. Prater, Iowa State University; Russell Riepe, Southwest Texas State University; Wayne Scott, University of Colorado; Richard Soule, University of Nevada; James Stewart, Ohio University; William Toutant, California State University at Northridge; John D. White, University of Florida.

We are also grateful to those who contributed to the development of this second edition: James Bennighof, Baylor University; Richard Devore, Kent State University; Lora Gingerich, Ohio State University; Kent Kennan, University of Texas at Austin; James W. Krehbiel, Eastern Illinois University; Frank Lorince, West Virginia University (retired); Donald Para, Western Michigan University; Marian Petersen, University of Missouri at Kansas City; Donald Peterson, University of Tennessee; John Pozdro, University of Kansas.

Finally, we would express gratitude to Marilyn Kostka for her years of patience and support, and to Bill Penn for his unfailing encouragement.

Stefan Kostka
Dorothy Payne

TO THE STUDENT

HARMONY IN WESTERN MUSIC

One thing that distinguishes Western art music from many other kinds of music is its preoccupation with harmony. In other words, just about any piece that you are apt to perform will involve more than one person playing or singing different notes at the same time—or, in the case of a keyboard player, more than one finger pushing down keys. There are exceptions, of course, such as works for unaccompanied flute, violin, and so on, but an implied harmonic background is often still apparent to the ear in such pieces.

In general, the music from cultures other than our own European-American culture is concerned less with harmony than with other aspects of music. Complexities of rhythm or subtleties of melodic variation, for example, might serve as the focal point in a particular musical culture. Even in our own music, some compositions, such as those for nonpitched percussion instruments, may be said to have little or no harmonic content, but they are the exception.

If harmony is so important in our music, it might be a good idea if we agreed on a definition of it. What does the expression *sing in harmony* mean to you? It probably conjures up impressions of something on the order of a barbershop quartet, or a chorus, or maybe just two people singing a song, one with the melody, the other one singing the harmony. Since harmony began historically with vocal music, this is a reasonable way to begin formulating a definition of harmony. In all of these examples, our conception of harmony involves more than one person singing at once, and the *harmony* is the sound that the combined voices produce.

> Harmony is the sound that results when two or more pitch classes* are performed simultaneously. It is the vertical aspect of music, produced by the combination of the components of the horizontal aspect.

While this book deals with harmony and with chords, which are little samples taken out of the harmony, it would be a good idea to keep in mind that musical lines (vocal or instrumental) produce the harmony, not the reverse.

*Pitch class: Notes an octave apart or enharmonically equivalent belong to the *same* pitch class (all C's, B♯'s, and D♭♭'s, for example). There are twelve pitch classes in all.

Sing through the four parts in Example 1. The soprano and tenor lines are the most melodic. The actual melody being harmonized is in the soprano, while the tenor follows its contour for a while and then ends with an eighth-note figure of its own. The bass line is strong and independent but less melodic, while the alto part is probably the least distinctive of all. These four relatively independent lines combine to create harmony, with chords occurring at the rate of approximately one per beat.

Example 1.   Bach, "Herzlich lieb hab' ich dich, o Herr"

The relationship between the vertical and horizontal aspects of music is a subtle one, however, and it has fluctuated ever since the beginnings of harmony (about the ninth century). At times the emphasis has been almost entirely on independent horizontal lines, with little attention paid to the resulting chords—a tendency easily seen in the twentieth century. At other times the independence of the lines has been weakened or is absent entirely. In Example 2 the only independent lines are the sustained bass note and the melody (highest notes). The other lines merely double the melody at various intervals, creating a very nontraditional succession of chords.

Example 2.   Debussy, "La Cathédrale engloutie," from *Preludes,* Book I

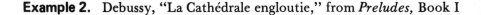
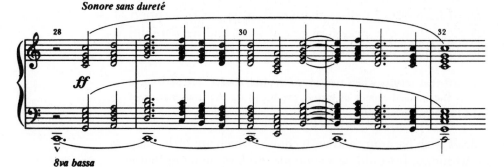
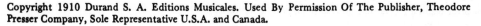

TONAL HARMONY DEFINED

The kind of harmony that this book deals with primarily is usually called *tonal harmony*. The term refers to the harmonic style of music composed during the period from about 1650 to about 1900. This would include such composers as Purcell, Bach, Handel, Haydn, Mozart, Beethoven, Schubert, Schumann, Wagner, Brahms, Tchaikovsky, and all of their contemporaries. Not that these composers all sound the same—they don't. They use different textures, timbres, ranges, rhythms, and ensembles, among other things. Even their harmonic styles differ in certain details. Yet they were all composers of tonal harmony.

And tonal harmony is not really limited to the period 1650-1900. It began evolving long before 1650, and it is still around today. Turn on your radio, go to a nightclub, listen to the canned music in the supermarket—it's almost all tonal harmony. Then why do we put the demise of tonal harmony at 1900? Because from about that time, most composers of "serious," or "legitimate," or "concert" music have been more interested in nontonal harmony than in tonal harmony. This does not mean that tonal harmony ceased to exist in the real world or in music of artistic merit.

Much of today's popular music is based on tonal harmony, just as Bach's music was, which means that both types have a good deal in common. First, both make use of a *tonal center,* a key pitch class that provides a center of gravity. Second, both types of music make use almost exclusively of major and minor scales. Third, both use chords that are tertian in structure. *Tertian* means "built of thirds," so a tertian chord might be C/E/G, a nontertian one C/F/B. Fourth, and very important, is that the chords built on the various scale degrees relate to each other and to the tonal center in fairly complex ways. Because each chord tends to have more or less standard roles, or functions, within a key, this characteristic is sometimes referred to as *functional* harmony. The details of these relationships between chords will be discussed more fully in the text; but to get an idea of what it's all about, play the chord of Example 3 on the piano.*

Example 3.

---

*If you cannot arrange to be at a piano while reading this book, try to play through the examples just before or right after reading a particular section or chapter. Reading about music without hearing it is not only dull, it's uninformative.

Play it several times. Arpeggiate it up and down. The "function" of this chord is clear, isn't it? Somehow, you know a lot about this chord without having to read a book about it. Play it again, and listen to where the chord "wants" to go. Then play Example 4, which will seem to follow Example 3 perfectly. This is an example of what is meant by the relationships between chords in tonal harmony and why we sometimes use the term *functional harmony.*

Example 4.

It is important to realize that not all music with a tonal center makes use of functional harmony—especially a good deal of the music of the twentieth century—music by composers such as Bartók and Hindemith, for example.

From our discussion we can formulate this definition of tonal harmony:

Tonal harmony refers to music with a tonal center, based on major and/or minor scales, and using tertian chords that are related to each other and to the tonal center in various ways.

USING THIS TEXT

The information in this text is organized in the traditional chapter format, but there are several additional features of which you should be aware.

Self-Tests.

Most chapters contain one or more such sections. These Self-Tests contain questions and drill material for use in independent study or classroom discussion. Suggested answers to all Self-Test problems appear in Appendix B. In many cases more than one correct answer is possible, but only one answer will be given in Appendix B. If you are in doubt about the correctness of your answer, ask your instructor.

Exercises.

After each Self-Test section, we refer to a group of Exercises to be found in the Workbook. Most of the Workbook Exercises will be similar to those in the preceding Self-Test, so refer to the Self-Test if you have questions concerning completion of the Exercises. However, the Workbook will also often contain more creative compositional problems than appeared in the Self-Test, since it would be impossible to suggest "answers" to such problems if they were used as Self-Tests.

Checkpoints.

You will occasionally encounter a Checkpoint section. These are intended to jog your memory and to help you review what you have just read. No answers are given to Checkpoint questions.

CONTENTS

Preface   v

To the Student   ix

PART ONE: FUNDAMENTALS   1

Chapter One
Elements of Pitch   3

    The Keyboard and Octave Registers   3
    Notation on the Staff   4
    The Major Scale   6
    The Major Key Signatures   9
    Minor Scales   13
    Minor Key Signatures   14
    Scale Degree Names   18
    Intervals   19
    Perfect, Major, and Minor Intervals   20
    Augmented and Diminished Intervals   22
    Inversion of Intervals   23

Chapter Two
Elements of Rhythm   26

    Rhythm   26
    Durational Symbols   26
    Beat and Tempo   27
    Meter   27
    Division of the Beat   30
    Simple Time Signatures   31

Compound Time Signatures   32
Time Signatures Summarized   34
More on Durational Symbols   35

Chapter Three
Introduction to Triads and Seventh Chords   **41**

Introduction   41
Triads   41
Seventh Chords   44
Inversion of Chords   46
Inversion Symbols and Figured Bass   47
Recognizing Chords in Various Textures   51

Chapter Four
Diatonic Chords in Major and Minor Keys   **56**

Introduction   56
The Minor Scale   56
Diatonic Triads in Major   59
Diatonic Triads in Minor   60
Diatonic Seventh Chords in Major   63
Diatonic Seventh Chords in Minor   64

PART TWO: DIATONIC TRIADS   **67**

Chapter Five
Principles of Voice Leading   **69**

Introduction   69
The Melodic Line   70
Notating Chords   72
Voicing a Single Triad   73
Parallels   76
Root Position Part Writing with Repeated Roots   82
Root Position Part Writing with Roots a 5th (4th) Apart   83
Root Position Part Writing with Roots a 3rd (6th) Apart   86
Root Position Part Writing with Roots a 2nd (7th) Apart   88
Instrumental Ranges and Transpositions   92

Chapter Six
Harmonic Progression   **94**

Introduction   94
Sequences and the Circle of Fifths   95
The I and V Chords   98
The II Chord   99
The VI Chord   100
The III Chord   101
The VII Chord   102
The IV Chord   103
Common Exceptions   104
Differences in the Minor Mode   105
Conclusion   106

Chapter Seven
Triads in First Inversion   **111**

Introduction   111
Bass Arpeggiation   112
Substituted First Inversion Triads   113
Parallel Sixth Chords   115
Part Writing First Inversion Triads   117

Chapter Eight
Cadences, Phrases, and Periods   **126**

Musical Form   126
Cadences   126
Motives and Phrases   132
Mozart: "An die Freude"   134
Period Forms   136

Chapter Nine
Triads in Second Inversion   **148**

Introduction   148
Bass Arpeggiation and the Melodic Bass   149
The Cadential Six-Four   150

The Passing Six-Four   152
The Pedal Six-Four   154
Part Writing for Second Inversion Triads   156

Chapter Ten
Non-Chord Tones 1   160

Introduction   160
Classification of Non-Chord Tones   161
Passing Tones   162
Neighboring Tones   164
Suspensions and Retardations   165
Figured Bass Symbols   170
Embellishing a Simple Texture   171

Chapter Eleven
Non-Chord Tones 2   175

Appoggiaturas   175
Escape Tones   177
The Neighbor Group   177
Anticipations   178
The Pedal Point   180
Special Problems in the Analysis of Non-Chord Tones   181
Summary of Non-Chord Tones   184

PART THREE: DIATONIC SEVENTH CHORDS   189

Chapter Twelve
The V⁷ Chord   191

Introduction   191
General Voice-Leading Concerns   192
The V⁷ in Root Position   193
The V⁷ in Three Parts   196
Other Resolutions of the V⁷   198
The Inverted V⁷ Chord   202
The V$\substack{6\\5}$ Chord   202

The V$^4_3$ Chord   204
The V$^4_2$ Chord   205
The Approach to the 7th   206

Chapter Thirteen
The II^7 and VII^7 Chords   210

Introduction   210
The II^7 Chord   211
The VII^7 Chord in Major   213
The VII^7 Chord in Minor   215

Chapter Fourteen
Other Diatonic Seventh Chords   224

The IV^7 Chord   224
The VI^7 Chord   227
The I^7 Chord   229
The III^7 Chord   231
Seventh Chords and the Circle-of-Fifths Sequence   231

Chapter Fifteen
Levels of Harmony   237

English Grammar and Tonal Harmony   237
Levels of Harmony   238
Examples from a Chorale   241
Conclusion   245

PART FOUR: CHROMATICISM 1   247

Chapter Sixteen
Secondary Functions 1   249

Chromaticism and Altered Chords   249
Secondary Functions   250
Secondary Dominant Chords   250
Spelling Secondary Dominants   252

Recognizing Secondary Dominants   253
Secondary Dominants in Context   254

Chapter Seventeen
Secondary Functions 2   266

Secondary Leading-Tone Chords   266
Spelling Secondary Leading-Tone Chords   268
Recognizing Secondary Leading-Tone Chords   268
Secondary Leading-Tone Chords in Context   270
Sequences Involving Secondary Functions   276
Deceptive Resolutions of Secondary Functions   280
Other Secondary Functions   281

Chapter Eighteen
Modulations Using Diatonic Common Chords   289

Modulation and Change of Key   289
Modulation and Tonicization   290
Key Relationships   292
Common-Chord Modulation   295
Analyzing Common-Chord Modulation   297

Chapter Nineteen
Some Other Modulatory Techniques   306

Altered Chords as Common Chords   306
Sequential Modulation   307
Modulation by Common Tone   310
Monophonic Modulation   314
Direct Modulation   315

Chapter Twenty
Binary and Ternary Forms   323

Formal Terminology   323
Binary Forms   323

Ternary Forms   326
Rounded Binary Forms   330
Other Formal Designs   333

PART FIVE: CHROMATICISM 2   339

Chapter Twenty-One
Mode Mixture   341

Introduction   341
Borrowed Chords in Minor   341
The Use of ♭6̂ in Major   342
Other Borrowed Chords in Major   345
Modulations Involving Mode Mixture   348

Chapter Twenty-Two
The Neapolitan Chord   357

Introduction   357
Conventional Use of the Neapolitan   357
Other Uses of the Neapolitan   360

Chapter Twenty-Three
Augmented Sixth Chords 1   368

The Interval of the Augmented Sixth   368
The Italian Augmented Sixth   369
The French Augmented Sixth   370
The German Augmented Sixth   372

Chapter Twenty-Four
Augmented Sixth Chords 2   383

Introduction   383
Other Bass Positions   383
Resolutions to Other Scale Degrees   385

Resolutions to Other Chord Members   386
Other Types of Augmented Sixth Chords   388

Chapter Twenty-Five
Enharmonic Spellings and Enharmonic Modulations   392

Enharmonic Spellings   392
Enharmonic Reinterpretation   395
Enharmonic Modulations Using the
    Major-Minor Seventh Sonority   396
Enharmonic Modulations Using the
    Diminished Seventh Chord   398

Chapter Twenty-Six
Further Elements of the Harmonic Vocabulary   406

Introduction   406
The Dominant with a Substituted 6th   406
The Dominant with Raised 5th   409
Ninth, Eleventh, and Thirteenth Chords   412
The Common-Tone Diminished Seventh Chord   414
Simultaneities   418
Coloristic Chord Successions   420

**PART SIX: LATE ROMANTICISM AND
   THE TWENTIETH CENTURY   429**

Chapter Twenty-Seven
Tonal Harmony in the Late Nineteenth Century   431

Introduction   431
Counterpoint   433
Sequence   437
Shifting Keys   440
Treatment of Dominant Harmony   444
Expanded Tonality   448

Chapter Twenty-Eight
An Introduction to Twentieth-Century Practices   453

Introduction   453
Impressionism   453
Scales   454
Chord Structure   462
Parallelism   472
Pandiatonicism   477
Set Theory   479
The Twelve-Tone Technique   483
Total Serialization   492
Rhythm and Meter   495
Aleatory or Chance Music   507
Texture and Expanded Instrumental Resources   513
Electronic Music   523

Appendix A
Instrumental Ranges and Transpositions   529

Appendix B
Answers to Self-Tests   531

Index of Music Examples   623

Subject Index   628

PART ONE

FUNDAMENTALS

CHAPTER ONE

ELEMENTS OF PITCH

THE KEYBOARD AND OCTAVE REGISTERS

Pitch in music refers to the highness or lowness of a sound. Pitches are named by using the first seven letters of the alphabet: A, B, C, D, E, F, and G. We will approach the notation of pitch by relating this pitch alphabet to the piano keyboard, using C's as an example. The C nearest the middle of the keyboard is called *middle C* or C4. Higher C's (moving toward the right on the keyboard) are named C5, C6, and so on. Lower C's (moving left) are named C3, C2, and C1. All the C's on the piano are labeled in Example 1-1.

Example 1-1.

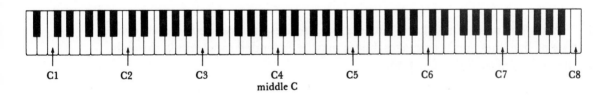

| C1 | C2 | C3 | C4 | C5 | C6 | C7 | C8 |

middle C

From any C up to or down to the next C is called an *octave*. All the pitches from one C up to, but not including, the next C are said to be in the same *octave register*. As Example 1-2 illustrates, the white key above C4 would be named D4, because it is in the same octave register, but the white key below C4 would be named B3.

Example 1-2.

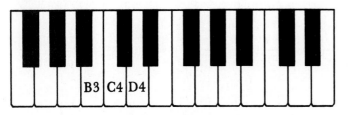

NOTATION ON THE STAFF

Our system of musical notation is similar to a graph in which time is indicated on the X axis and pitch is shown on the Y axis. In Example 1-3 R occurs before S in time and is higher than S in pitch.

Example 1-3.

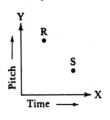

A *staff* is used in music to indicate the precise pitch desired. A staff consists of five lines and four spaces, but it may be extended indefinitely through the use of *ledger lines* (Ex. 1-4).

Example 1-4.

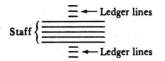

A *clef* must appear at the beginning of the staff in order to indicate which pitches are to be associated with which lines and spaces. The three clefs commonly used today are shown in Example 1-5, and the position of C4 in each is illustrated. Notice that the C clef appears in either of two positions.

Example 1-5.

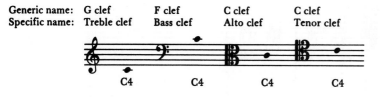

The clefs in Example 1-5 are shown in the positions that are in common use today, but you may occasionally find them placed differently on the staff in some editions. Wherever they appear, the design of the G clef circles G4, the dots of the F clef surround F3, and the C clef is centered on C4.

The *grand staff* is a combination of two staves joined by a *brace,* with the top and bottom staves using treble and bass clefs, respectively. Various pitches are notated and labeled on the grand staff in Example 1-6. Pay special attention to the way in which the ledger lines are used on the grand staff. For instance, the notes C4 and A3 appear twice in Example 1-6, once in relation to the top staff and once in relation to the bottom staff.

Example 1-6.

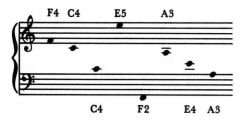

SELF-TEST 1-1
(Answers begin on page 531.)

A. Name the pitches in the blanks provided, using the correct octave register designations.

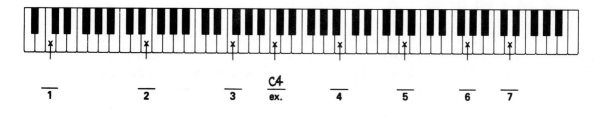

B. Notate the indicated pitches on the staff in the correct octave.

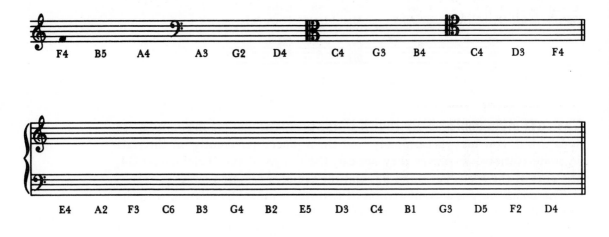

| F4 | B5 | A4 | A3 | G2 | D4 | C4 | G3 | B4 | C4 | D3 | F4 |

| E4 | A2 | F3 | C6 | B3 | G4 | B2 | E5 | D3 | C4 | B1 | G3 | D5 | F2 | D4 |

EXERCISE 1-1. See Workbook.

THE MAJOR SCALE

The *major scale* is a specific pattern of small steps (called half steps) and larger ones (called whole steps) encompassing an octave. A *half step* is the distance from a key on the piano to the very next key, white or black. Using only the white keys on the piano keyboard, there are two half steps in each octave (Ex. 1-7).

Example 1-7.

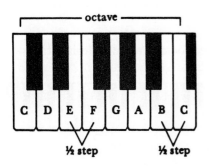

A *whole step* skips the very next key and goes instead to the following one. Using only the white keys on the piano keyboard, there are five whole steps in each octave (Ex. 1-8).

Example 1-8.

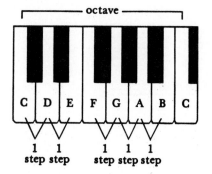

The major scale pattern of whole and half steps is the same as that found on the white keys from any C up to the next C. In the diagram below, the numbers with carats above them (1̂, 2̂, etc.) are scale degree numbers for the C major scale.

You can see from this diagram that half steps in the major scale occur only between scale degrees 3̂ and 4̂ and 7̂ and 1̂.* Notice also that the major scale can be thought of as two identical, four-note patterns separated by a whole step.

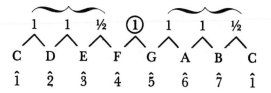

*Throughout this book we will refer to major keys with upper-case letters—for example, A major or A—and minor keys with lower-case letters—for example, a minor or a.

If we examine the steps on the white keys of a G-to-G octave, as in Example 1-9, we do not find the same pattern of whole and half steps that occurred in the C-to-C octave. In order to play a G major scale, we would need to skip the F key and play the black key that is between F and G. We will label that key with an *accidental,* a symbol that raises or lowers a pitch by a half or whole step. All the possible accidentals are listed in this table.

Symbol	Name	Effect
✕	Double sharp	Raise a whole step
♯	Sharp	Raise a half step
♮	Natural	Cancel a previous accidental
♭	Flat	Lower a half step
♭♭	Double flat	Lower a whole step

Example 1-9.

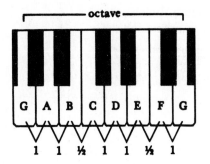

We can make our G scale conform to the major scale pattern by adding one accidental, in this case a sharp.

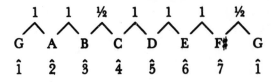

The scale is written on the staff in Example 1-10.

Example 1-10.

Notice that when we write or say the names of notes and accidentals, we put the accidental last (as in F♯ or F-sharp), but in staff notation the accidental always *precedes* the note that it modifies (as in Ex. 1-10).

THE MAJOR KEY SIGNATURES

One way to learn the major scales is by means of the pattern of whole and half steps discussed in the previous section. Another is by memorizing the key signatures associated with the various scales. The term *key* is used in music to identify the first degree of a scale. For instance, *the key of G major* refers to that major which begins on G. A *key signature* is a pattern of sharps or flats that appears at the beginning of a staff and indicates that certain notes are to be consistently raised or lowered. There are seven key signatures using sharps. In each case, the name of the major key can be found by going up a half step from the last sharp (Ex. 1-11).

Example 1-11.

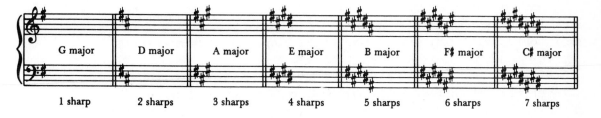

G major	D major	A major	E major	B major	F♯ major	C♯ major
1 sharp	2 sharps	3 sharps	4 sharps	5 sharps	6 sharps	7 sharps

There are also seven key signatures using flats. Except for the key of F major, the name of the major key is the same as the name of the next-to-last flat (Ex. 1-12).

Example 1-12.

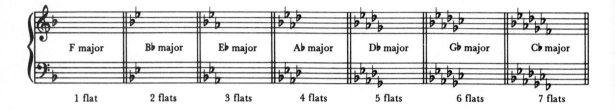

F major	Bb major	Eb major	Ab major	Db major	Gb major	Cb major
1 flat	2 flats	3 flats	4 flats	5 flats	6 flats	7 flats

You may have noticed that there are three pairs of major keys that would sound exactly the same—that is, they would be played on the very same keys of the piano keyboard.

$$B \text{ major} = Cb \text{ major}$$
$$F\sharp \text{ major} = Gb \text{ major}$$
$$C\sharp \text{ major} = Db \text{ major}$$

Notes that are spelled differently but sound the same are said to be *enharmonic;* so B major and Cb major, for example, are *enharmonic keys.* If two major keys are not enharmonic, then they are *transpositions* of each other. To *transpose* means to write or play music in some key other than the original.

The key signatures in Examples 1-11 and 1-12 must be memorized—not only the number of accidentals involved, but also their placement upon the staff. Notice that the pattern of placing the sharps on the staff changes at the fifth sharp for both the treble and the bass clefs.

Some people find it easier to memorize key signatures if they visualize a *circle of fifths,* which is a diagram somewhat like the face of a clock. Reading clockwise around the circle of fifths below, you will see that each new key begins on $\hat{5}$ (the fifth scale degree) of the previous key.

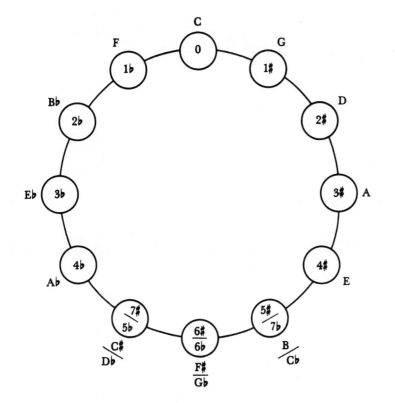

SELF-TEST 1-2
(Answers begin on page 532.)

A. Notate the specified scales using accidentals, *not* key signatures. Show the placement of whole and half steps, as in the example.

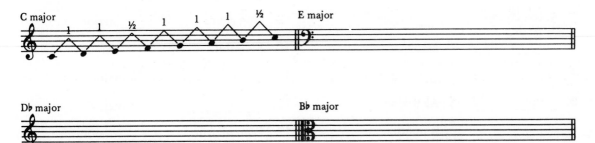

C# major   A major

F major   F# major

B. Identify these major key signatures.

<u>C</u> major ___ major ___ major ___ major ___ major ___ major ___ major ___ major
ex.   1   2   3   4   5   6   7

C. Notate the specified key signatures.

A major   Db major   F# major   Bb major   B major   Cb major   D major   C major

D. Fill in the blanks.

	Key signature	*Name of key*		*Key signature*	*Name of key*
1.	Three flats	___ major	**8.**	_____	Bb major
2.	Seven sharps	___ major	**9.**	One sharp	___ major
3.	_____	D major	**10.**	Five flats	___ major
4.	One flat	___ major	**11.**	_____	F# major
5.	_____	Ab major	**12.**	_____	Cb major
6.	_____	B major	**13.**	Four sharps	___ major
7.	Six flats	___ major	**14.**	_____	A major

EXERCISE 1-2. See Workbook.

MINOR SCALES

Musicians traditionally memorize and practice three minor scale formations, although they are not used with equal frequency, as we shall see in a later chapter. One of these is the *natural minor scale.* You can see from the illustration below that the natural minor scale is like a major scale with lowered $\hat{3}$, $\hat{6}$, and $\hat{7}$.

C major	C	D	E	F	G	A	B	C
Scale degree	$\hat{1}$	$\hat{2}$	$\hat{3}$	$\hat{4}$	$\hat{5}$	$\hat{6}$	$\hat{7}$	$\hat{1}$
c natural minor	C	D	Eb	F	G	Ab	Bb	C

Another minor scale type is the *harmonic minor scale,* which can be thought of as major with lowered $\hat{3}$ and $\hat{6}$.

C major	C	D	E	F	G	A	B	C
Scale degree	$\hat{1}$	$\hat{2}$	$\hat{3}$	$\hat{4}$	$\hat{5}$	$\hat{6}$	$\hat{7}$	$\hat{1}$
c harmonic minor	C	D	Eb	F	G	Ab	B	C

The third type of minor scale is the *melodic minor scale,* which has an ascending form and a descending form. The ascending form, shown below, is like major with a lowered $\hat{3}$.

C major	C	D	E	F	G	A	B	C
Scale degree	$\hat{1}$	$\hat{2}$	$\hat{3}$	$\hat{4}$	$\hat{5}$	$\hat{6}$	$\hat{7}$	$\hat{1}$
c ascending melodic minor	C	D	Eb	F	G	A	B	C

The descending form of the melodic minor scale is the same as the natural minor scale.

The three minor scale types are summarized in Example 1-13. The scale degrees that differ from the major are circled. Notice the arrows used in connection with the melodic minor scale in order to distinguish the ascending $\hat{6}$ and $\hat{7}$ from the descending $\hat{6}$ and $\hat{7}$.

Example 1-13.

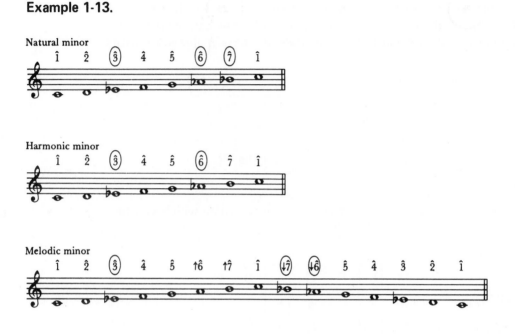

MINOR KEY SIGNATURES

Minor key signatures conform to the natural minor scale, no matter which minor scale type is actually in use. Looking back at Example 1-13, you can see that the natural minor scale on C requires three accidentals: B♭, E♭, and A♭. The key signature of c minor, then, is the same as the key signature of E♭ major; c minor and E♭ major are said to be *relatives*, since they share the same key signature. The $\hat{3}$ of any minor key is $\hat{1}$ of its relative major and the $\hat{6}$ of any major key is $\hat{1}$ of its relative minor. If a major scale and a minor scale share the same $\hat{1}$, as do C major and c minor, for example, they are said to be *parallels*. We would say that C major is the parallel major of c minor.

The circle of fifths is a convenient way to display the names of the minor keys and their *relative* majors, as well as their key signatures.

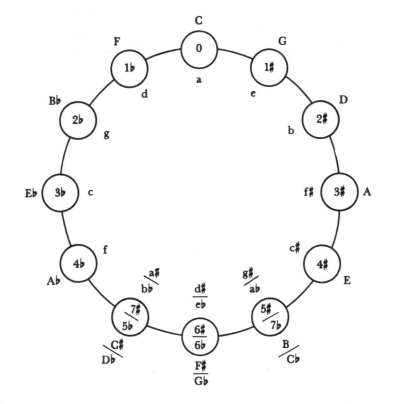

You may find it easier to learn the minor scales in terms of their relative majors, as in the circle-of-fifths diagram above, than in terms of their parallel majors, which is how minor scales were introduced on pages 13-14. If you do use the relative major approach, remember that the key signature for any minor scale conforms to the *natural* minor scale and that accidentals must be used in order to spell the other forms. Example 1-14 illustrates the spellings for the related keys of F major and d minor.

Example 1-14.

F major scale

Relative minor, natural form

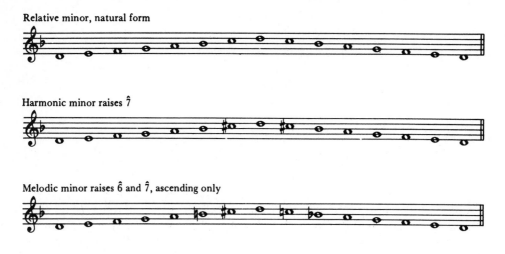

Harmonic minor raises $\hat{7}$

Melodic minor raises $\hat{6}$ and $\hat{7}$, ascending only

It is very important to practice faithfully all of the major and minor scales on an instrument until they become memorized patterns. An intellectual understanding of scales cannot substitute for the secure tactile and aural familiarity that will result from those hours of practice.

SELF-TEST 1-3
(Answers begin on page 533.)

A. Notate the specified scales using accidentals, *not* key signatures. Circle the notes that differ from the *parallel* major scale. The melodic minor should be written both ascending and descending.

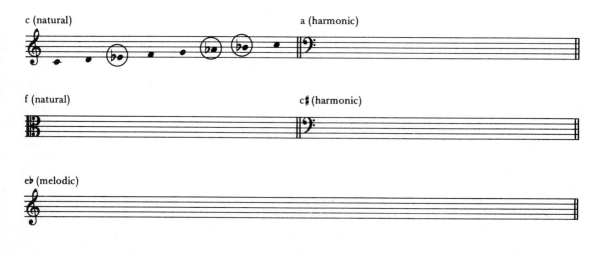

c (natural)   a (harmonic)

f (natural)   c♯ (harmonic)

e♭ (melodic)

bb (natural)

g# (harmonic)

f# (melodic)

B. Identify these minor key signatures.

a minor   ___ minor   ___ minor   ___ minor   ___ minor   ___ minor   ___ minor   ___ minor
ex.   1   2   3   4   5   6   7

C. Notate the specified minor key signatures.

b   d   g#   c   f#   a   bb   a#

D. Fill in the blanks.

	Key signature	Name of key		Key signature	Name of key
1.	_____	d minor	**8.**	Two flats	___ minor
2.	Six flats	___ minor	**9.**	_____	f minor
3.	Four sharps	___ minor	**10.**	_____	b minor
4.	_____	f# minor	**11.**	Three flats	___ minor
5.	Six sharps	___ minor	**12.**	_____	ab minor
6.	_____	bb minor	**13.**	One sharp	___ minor
7.	_____	a# minor	**14.**	Five sharps	___ minor

SCALE DEGREE NAMES

Musicians in conversation or in writing often refer to scale degrees by a set of traditional names rather than by numbers. The names are shown in Example 1-15. Notice that there are two names for $\hat{7}$ in minor, depending upon whether it is raised or not.

Example 1-15.

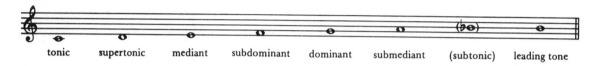

| tonic | supertonic | mediant | subdominant | dominant | submediant | (subtonic) | leading tone |

The origin of some of these names is not what you would probably expect from studying Example 1-15. For example, *subdominant* does not mean "below the dominant," as the chart below illustrates.

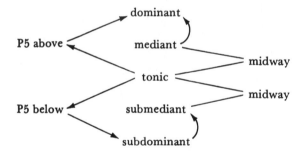

CHECKPOINT

Now is the time to start learning the scale degree names, if you do not know them already. Here are a couple of exercises that will help.

1. Translate these numbers aloud to scale degree names as fast as possible. Repeat as often as necessary until speed is attained.

$\hat{1}$ $\hat{2}$ $\hat{3}$ $\hat{4}$ $\hat{5}$ $\hat{6}$ $\hat{7}$ $\hat{1}$ $\hat{7}$ $\hat{6}$ $\hat{5}$ $\hat{4}$ $\hat{3}$ $\hat{2}$ $\hat{1}$

$\hat{3}$ $\hat{5}$ $\hat{7}$ $\hat{6}$ $\hat{4}$ $\hat{2}$ $\hat{1}$ $\hat{6}$ $\hat{3}$ $\hat{7}$ $\hat{2}$ $\hat{5}$ $\hat{4}$ $\hat{3}$ $\hat{1}$

$\hat{5}$ $\hat{2}$ $\hat{7}$ $\hat{4}$ $\hat{6}$ $\hat{3}$ $\hat{1}$ $\hat{2}$ $\hat{7}$ $\hat{5}$ $\hat{6}$ $\hat{4}$ $\hat{1}$ $\hat{3}$ $\hat{2}$

2. Call out or sing the scale degree names contained in each example below.

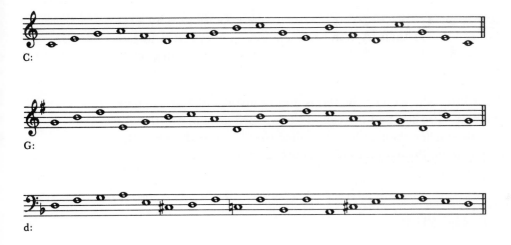

INTERVALS

An *interval* is the measurement of the distance in pitch between two notes. A *harmonic interval* results if the notes are performed at the same time, while a *melodic interval* occurs when the notes are played successively (Ex. 1-16). The method of measuring intervals is the same for both harmonic and melodic intervals.

Example 1-16.

Harmonic intervals   Melodic intervals

There are two parts to any interval name: the numerical name and the modifier that precedes the numerical name. As Example 1-17 illustrates, the numerical name is a measurement of how far apart the notes are vertically on the staff, regardless of what accidentals are involved.

Example 1-17.

In speaking about intervals, we use the terms *unison* instead of 1 and *octave* (8ve) instead of 8. We also say 2nd instead of "two," 3rd instead of "three," and so on. Intervals smaller than an 8ve are called *simple intervals,* while the larger intervals (including the 8ve) are called *compound intervals.*

SELF-TEST 1-4
(Answers begin on page 534.)

Provide the numerical names of the intervals by using the numbers 1 through 8.

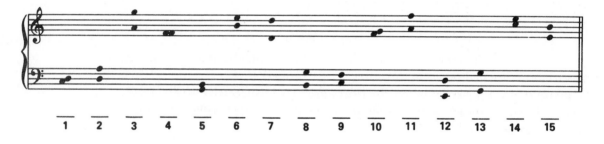

EXERCISE 1-4.   See Workbook.

PERFECT, MAJOR, AND MINOR INTERVALS

One way to begin learning intervals is by relating them to the intervals contained in the major scale, specifically the intervals from 1̂ up to the other scale degrees. This method can then be applied in any context, whether or not the major scale is actually being used.

The term *perfect* (abbreviated P) is a modifier used only in connection with unisons, 4ths, 5ths, 8ves, and their compounds (11ths, and so on). As Example 1-18 illustrates, a P1, P4, P5, and P8 can all be constructed by using 1̂ in the major scale as the *bottom* note.

Example 1-18.

If we want to spell one of these intervals above E♭, for example, we need only to think of scale steps $\hat{1}$, $\hat{4}$, and $\hat{5}$ of the E♭ major scale. If the bottom note does not commonly serve as $\hat{1}$ of a major scale (such as D♯), remove the accidental temporarily, spell the interval, and then apply the accidental to both notes (Ex. 1-19).

Example 1-19.

Usually, 2nds, 3rds, 6ths, and 7ths are modified by the terms *major* (M) or *minor* (m). The intervals formed by $\hat{1}$-$\hat{2}$, $\hat{1}$-$\hat{3}$, $\hat{1}$-$\hat{6}$, and $\hat{1}$-$\hat{7}$ in the major scale are all major intervals, as Example 1-20 illustrates.

Example 1-20.

If a major interval is made a half step smaller without altering its numerical name, it becomes a minor interval (Ex. 1-21).

Example 1-21.

SELF-TEST 1-5
(Answers begin on page 534.)

A. All the intervals below are unisons, 4ths, 5ths, or 8ves. Put "P" in the space provided *only* if the interval is a perfect interval.

B. All of the intervals below are 2nds, 3rds, 6ths, or 7ths. Write "M" or "m" in each space, as appropriate.

C. Notate the specified intervals above the given notes.

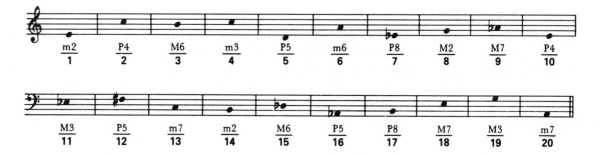

EXERCISE 1-5. See Workbook.

AUGMENTED AND DIMINISHED INTERVALS

If a perfect or a major interval is made a half step larger without changing the numerical name, the interval becomes *augmented* (abbreviated +). If a perfect or a minor interval is made a half step smaller without changing its numerical name, it becomes *diminished* (abbreviated °). These relationships are summarized below.

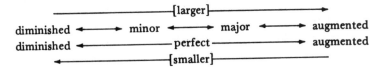

Doubly augmented and doubly diminished intervals are also possible, but they seldom occur. *Tritone* is a term used for the +4 or its enharmonic equivalent, the °5.

INVERSION OF INTERVALS

Descending intervals, especially large ones, are easier to spell and identify through the use of *interval inversion*. We invert an interval by putting the bottom pitch above the top one; for example, the interval D-A inverts to A-D. When we invert an interval, the new numerical name is always different from the old one. The new numerical name can be calculated by subtracting the old numerical name from 9.

Constant value of 9	9	9	9	9	9	9
Minus old numeric name	−2	−3	−4	−5	−6	−7
Equals new numeric name	7	6	5	4	3	2

You can see that an inverted 2nd becomes a 7th, a 3rd becomes a 6th, and so on (Ex. 1-22).

Example 1-22.

2	7	3	6	4	5	5	4	6	3	7	2

The modifier also changes when an interval is inverted, with the exception of perfect intervals.

Old modifier	m	M	P	+	°
New modifier	M	m	P	°	+

As an example of the usefulness of inversion, suppose you wanted to know what note lies a m6 below G3. Invert the m6 down to a M3 up, as in Example 1-23, transpose the B3 down an 8ve, and you find that the answer is B2.

Example 1-23.

Fluency with intervals, as with scales, is necessary for any serious musician and will provide a solid foundation for your further study. As you did with scales, you will benefit from finding out how various intervals sound and feel on a musical instrument.

SUMMARY

Below is an outline of some of the concepts discussed in this chapter. If any are unfamiliar, go back and reread the appropriate discussions.

Pages	Concepts
3-4	Pitch; middle C; octave registers; the piano keyboard
4-5	Staff; ledger lines; clefs; grand staff
6-9	Major scale; half step; whole step; accidentals
9-11	Major key signatures; enharmonic keys; transposition
13-14	Minor scales
14-16	Minor key signatures; relative keys; parallel keys
18	Scale degree names
19-20	Harmonic interval; melodic interval; compound and simple intervals
20-21	Perfect, major, and minor intervals
22-23	Diminished and augmented intervals
23-24	Interval inversion

SELF-TEST 1-6
(Answers begin on page 534.)

A. Most of the intervals below are either augmented or diminished. Label each interval.

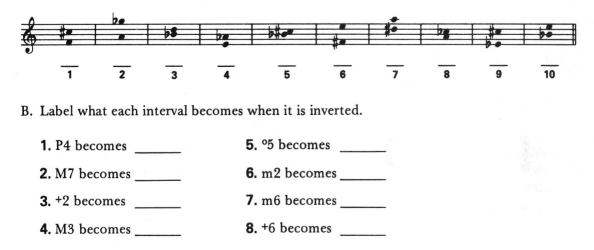

B. Label what each interval becomes when it is inverted.

1. P4 becomes _____

2. M7 becomes _____

3. +2 becomes _____

4. M3 becomes _____

5. °5 becomes _____

6. m2 becomes _____

7. m6 becomes _____

8. +6 becomes _____

C. Notate the specified interval *below* the given note. (You may find it helpful to invert the interval first in some cases.)

D. Label each interval in this melody (from Wagner's *Götterdämmerung*).

EXERCISE 1-6. See Workbook.

CHAPTER TWO

ELEMENTS OF RHYTHM

RHYTHM

This chapter is concerned with the time aspect of music—how sounds are notated so that they will occur at a predictable moment and in a predetermined pattern. *Rhythm* is a general term used to refer to the time aspect of music, as contrasted with the pitch aspect.

DURATIONAL SYMBOLS

Durations are notated by using symbols that are organized so that each symbol is twice the duration of the next shorter symbol and half the duration of the next longer symbol. The table below lists a number of these symbols.

Value	Note	Rest
Breve	𝆷 = o + o	𝄻 = 𝄺 + 𝄺
Whole	o = ꝺ + ꝺ	𝄻 = 𝄼 + 𝄼
Half	ꝺ = ♩ + ♩	𝄼 = 𝄽 + 𝄽
Quarter	♩ = ♪ + ♪	𝄽 = 𝄾 + 𝄾
Eighth	♪ = ♬ + ♬	𝄾 = 𝄿 + 𝄿
Sixteenth	♬ = 𝅘𝅥𝅯 + 𝅘𝅥𝅯	𝄿 = 𝅀 + 𝅀

The same series could be continued to thirty-seconds, sixty-fourths, and so on. Durations other than these must be indicated through the use of ties, dots, or other symbols. A *tie* is a curved line that connects two durational symbols, creating a new duration that is equal to their sum. A *dot* always adds to the duration one-half the value of the note or dot that precedes it.

For example, $\.=\,+\,\flat$, and $\..=\,+\,\flat+\,\flat$. When notated on the staff, a dot is never placed on a staff line. If the notehead itself is on a staff line, the dot is put to the right of the note but in the space *above* it.

BEAT AND TEMPO

The *beat* is the basic pulse of a musical passage. To determine the beat of a passage you are listening to, tap your foot to the music or try to imagine the way a conductor would conduct the passage—the conductor's arm movement. The resulting steady pulse is called the beat, and the rate at which the beats occur is called the *tempo*.

A composer commonly specifies the tempo of a passage by one of two methods—sometimes by both. The first method uses words, often in Italian, to describe the tempo.

Italian	*English*	*German*	*French*
Grave	Solemn	Schwer	Lourd
Largo	Broad	Breit	Large
Lento	Slow	Langsam	Lent
Adagio	Slow	Langsam	Lent
Andante	Moderately slow	Gehend	Allant
Moderato	Moderate	Mässig	Modéré
Allegretto	Moderately fast	Etwas bewegt	Un peu animé
Allegro	Fast	Schnell	Animé
Vivace	Lively	Lebhaft	Vif
Presto	Very fast	Eilig	Vite

The second method is more exact, since it shows precisely how many beats are to occur in the space of one minute. For example, if the desired tempo would result in seventy-two quarter notes in one minute, the tempo indication would be $\quarternote = 72$ or M.M. $\quarternote = 72$. The M.M. stands for Maelzel's metronome, after the nineteenth-century man who promoted the device.

METER

Beats tend to be grouped into patterns that are consistent throughout a passage; the pattern of beats is called the *meter*. Groups of two, three, and four beats are the most common, although other meters occur. Incidentally, a group of four beats could often also be interpreted as two groups of two beats each, and vice versa. In any case, the groups of beats are called *measures* (abbreviated m. or mm.), and in notation the end of a measure is always indicated by a vertical line through the staff called a *bar line*. The words *duple, triple,* and *quadruple* are used to refer to the number of beats in each measure, so we have *duple meter, triple meter,* and *quadruple meter.* These terms are summarized below, along with the pattern of stresses usually found in each meter (referred to as *metric accent*).

Grouping	Meter type	Metric accent pattern
Two-beat measure	Duple	Strong-weak
Three-beat measure	Triple	Strong-weak-weak
Four-beat measure	Quadruple	Strong-weak-less strong-weak

The meter of many passages is clear and easily identified, but in other cases the meter may be ambiguous. For example, sing "Take Me Out to the Ball Game" quite slowly while you tap your foot or conduct, then decide upon the meter type. Now sing it again, but very fast. The first time you probably felt the meter was triple, but at a faster tempo you should have identified the meter as duple (or quadruple). Between those extreme tempos are more moderate tempos, which two listeners might interpret in different ways—one hearing a faster triple meter, the other a slower duple meter. Both listeners would be correct, because identifying meter is a matter of interpretation rather than of right and wrong.

SELF-TEST 2-1
(Answers begin on page 535.)

A. Show how many notes of the shorter duration would be required to equal the longer duration.

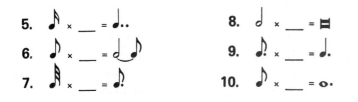

5. ♪ × __ = ♩...

6. ♪ × __ = ♩♩♪

7. ♪ × __ = ♪.

8. ♩ × __ = 𝅗𝅥𝅗𝅥

9. ♪. × __ = ♩.

10. ♪ × __ = 𝅝.

B. Sing aloud each of the songs listed below. Then identify the meter type of each, using the terms *duple, triple,* and *quadruple.*

1. "Silent Night" (slow tempo) _____

2. "Jingle Bells" _____

3. "America the Beautiful" _____

4. "Seventy-Six Trombones" _____

5. "Home on the Range" _____

C. Scale review. Given the key and the scale degree, supply the note name. Assume the *melodic minor* form for each minor key.

ex. f♯: $\hat{4}$ **B** ___

1. D♭: $\hat{6}$ ___

2. f: $\hat{3}$ ___

3. A: $\hat{5}$ ___

4. B: $\hat{3}$ ___

5. g: ↑$\hat{6}$ ___

6. c♯: ↓$\hat{7}$ ___

7. E♭: $\hat{5}$ ___

8. B♭: $\hat{4}$ ___

9. c: ↓$\hat{6}$ ___

10. e: $\hat{4}$ ___

11. A♭: $\hat{7}$ ___

12. F♯: $\hat{2}$ ___

13. b♭: $\hat{5}$ ___

14. E: $\hat{6}$ ___

15. d: ↑$\hat{7}$ ___

EXERCISE 2-1. See Workbook.

DIVISION OF THE BEAT

In most musical passages we hear durations that are shorter than the beat. We call these shorter durations *divisions of the beat*. Beats generally divide either into two equal parts, called *simple beat*, or into three equal parts, called *compound beat*. Be careful not to confuse beat type, which refers to how the *beat* divides (simple or compound), with meter type, which refers to how the *measure* divides (duple, triple, or quadruple). The common beat and meter types can be combined with each other in six possible ways.

	Meter		
Beat	Duple	Triple	Quadruple
Simple	Simple duple	Simple triple	Simple quadruple
Compound	Compound duple	Compound triple	Compound quadruple

For example, sing "Take Me Out to the Ball Game" quickly in duple meter, as you did in the discussion of meter on page 28. You can hear that the beats divide into thirds, so this is an example of compound duple. Do the same with "I Don't Know How to Love Him" (from *Jesus Christ Superstar*), and you will find that it is simple quadruple (or simple duple).

SELF-TEST 2-2
(Answers begin on page 536.)

Sing aloud each of the songs listed below. Then identify the beat and meter types of each, using the terms simple duple, and so on.

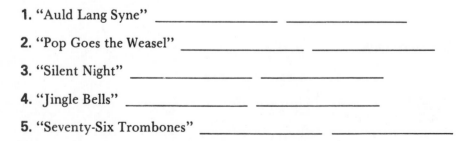

1. "Auld Lang Syne" _____ _____

2. "Pop Goes the Weasel" _____ _____

3. "Silent Night" _____ _____

4. "Jingle Bells" _____ _____

5. "Seventy-Six Trombones" _____ _____

SIMPLE TIME SIGNATURES

A *time signature* is a symbol that tells the performer how many beats will occur in each measure, what note value will represent the beat, and whether the beat is simple or compound. A time signature for simple beat has 2, 3, or 4 as the top number. The top number indicates the number of beats in the measure; the bottom number indicates the beat note (2 = 𝅗𝅥, 4 = ♩, 8 = ♪, and so on). Some typical simple time signatures are listed in the following table.

Time signature	Beats per measure	Beat note	Division of the beat
$\frac{2}{4}$	2	♩	♫
$\frac{2}{2}$ or ¢	2	𝅗𝅥	♩ ♩
$\frac{3}{16}$	3	♬	♬♬
$\frac{3}{4}$	3	♩	♫
$\frac{4}{8}$	4	♪	♫
$\frac{4}{4}$ or C	4	♩	♫

Example 2-1 illustrates how some of the songs we have been considering might be notated. The beat values were chosen arbitrarily; "Jingle Bells," for example, could also be notated correctly in $\frac{2}{2}$ or $\frac{2}{8}$ or any other simple duple time signature.

Example 2-1.

"Jingle Bells"

"America the Beautiful"

"Home on the Range"

COMPOUND TIME SIGNATURES

If the beat divides into thee equal parts, as in compound beat, the note value representing the beat will be a dotted value, as shown below.

Beat note	Division of the beat
𝅗𝅥.	♩♩♩
♩.	♫♪
♪.	♬♪
♪.	♬♪

Dotted values present a problem where time signatures are concerned. For example, if there are two beats per measure, and the beat note is ♩., what would the time signature be? $\frac{2}{4\frac{1}{2}}$? $\frac{2}{4+8}$? $\frac{2}{8+8+8}$? There is no easy solution, and the method that survives today is the source of much confusion concerning compound beat. Simply stated, a compound time signature informs the musician of the *number of divisions* of the beat contained in a measure and what the *division duration* is. This means that the top number of a compound time signature will be 6, 9, or 12, because two beats times three divisions equals six, three beats times three divisions equals nine, and four beats times three divisions equals twelve. Some examples are given in the table below.

Time signature	Beats per measure	Beat note	Division of the beat
$\frac{6}{8}$	2	♩.	♫♫♫
$\frac{6}{4}$	2	𝅗𝅥.	♩♩♩
$\frac{9}{16}$	3	♪.	♬♬♬
$\frac{9}{8}$	3	♩.	♫♫♫
$\frac{12}{8}$	4	♩.	♫♫♫
$\frac{12}{4}$	4	𝅗𝅥.	♩♩♩

Example 2-2 illustrates some familiar tunes that use compound beat. As before, the choice of the actual beat note is an arbitrary one.

Example 2-2.

"Take Me Out to the Ball Game"

"Down in the Valley"

"Pop Goes the Weasel"

You can see from this discussion that compound time signatures do *not* follow the rule, so often learned by the student musician, that "the top number tells how many beats are in a measure, and the bottom number tells what note gets the beat.'' Of course, there are some pieces in $\frac{6}{8}$, for example, that really do have six beats to the measure, but such a piece is not really in compound duple. A measure of $\frac{6}{8}$ performed in six does not sound like compound duple; instead, it sounds like two measures of simple triple, or $\frac{3}{8}$. To be compound duple, the listener must hear two compound beats to the measure, not six simple beats. In the same way, a slow work notated in $\frac{2}{4}$ might be conducted in four, which would seem to the listener to be simple quadruple. In both cases, the usual division value has become the beat value.

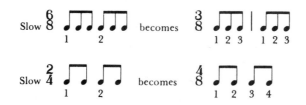

The reverse also occurs—that is, the usual beat value sometimes becomes the actual division value. For instance, a fast waltz or scherzo is almost always notated as simple triple, usually as $\frac{3}{4}$. But the aural effect is of one beat per measure, for which we might use the term *compound single*. If you didn't know the metric convention of such pieces, you would probably assume on hearing them that they were in compound duple.

TIME SIGNATURES SUMMARIZED

There are two types of beat, simple and compound, and three common meters, duple, triple, and quadruple, which can be combined in a total of six ways. For each of these six combinations there is a number that will always appear as the top part of the time signature.

	Meter type		
Beat type	*Duple*	*Triple*	*Quadruple*
Simple	2	3	4
Compound	6	9	12

A listener can usually recognize the beat and meter types of a passage without seeing the music. Therefore, you can usually say what the top number of the time signature is (except that duple and quadruple are often indistinguishable). However, to know what the bottom number of the time signature is, you have to look at the music, since any number representing a note value can be used for any meter.

Bottom number	Simple beat duration	Compound beat duration
1	𝅝	𝅝﹒
2	𝅗𝅥	𝅝﹒
4	𝅘𝅥	𝅘𝅥﹒
8	𝅘𝅥𝅮	𝅘𝅥﹒
16	𝅘𝅥𝅯	𝅘𝅥𝅮﹒

MORE ON DURATIONAL SYMBOLS

When rhythms are notated, it is customary to use beams, ties, and dots in such a way that the metric accent is emphasized rather than obscured. Several incorrect and correct examples are notated below.

Of course, it is correct to notate rhythms so as to obscure the metric accent when that is the desired result. *Syncopations* (rhythmic figures that contradict the prevailing beat or meter) are frequently notated in that way, as below.

More involved figures, such as the following, are especially common in twentieth-century music.

A *grouplet* refers to the division of an undotted value into some number of equal parts other than two, four, eight, and so on, or the division of a dotted value into some number of equal parts other than three, six, twelve, and so on, as you can see below.

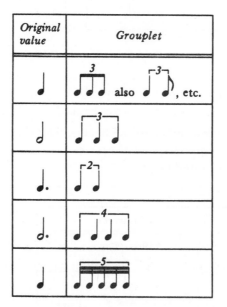

Original value	Grouplet

Of all the possibilities, the superimposition of triplets on a simple beat is the most common.

When a single-stem note is notated on the staff, the stem should go up if the note is below the middle line and down if the note is above the middle line. A note on the middle line may theoretically have its stem point in either direction, but most professional copyists consistently put a downward stem on notes that occur on the middle line (Ex. 2-3).

Example 2-3.

Beams are used to connect durations shorter than a quarter note when the durations occur within the same beat. The stem direction of beamed notes is decided by the note that is farthest from the middle line. That is, if the note that is farthest from the middle line is below it, then all the stems that are to be beamed together will point upward (Ex. 2-4).

Example 2-4.

SUMMARY

Here is a list of some of the terms and concepts discussed in this chapter. If any of them are unfamiliar to you, go back to the appropriate section.

Pages	Concepts
26	Rhythm
26-27	Durational symbols; ties; dotted notes
27	Beat; tempo; foreign terms for tempos; metronome markings
27-28	Meter; measure; duple, triple, and quadruple meter; metric accent
30	Divisions of the beat; simple beat; compound beat
31-32	Time signature; simple time signatures
32-34	Compound time signatures
35-37	Grouplets; beams; stem direction

SELF-TEST 2-3
(Answers begin on page 536.)

A. Fill in the blanks.

	Beat and meter type	Beat value	Division value	Time signature
1.				$\frac{4}{4}$
2.	Compound triple	♩.		
3.				$\frac{2}{8}$
4.	Compound duple		♩	
5.			♩	3
6.			♪	12

B. Each measure below is incomplete. Add one or more rests to the end of each to complete the measure.

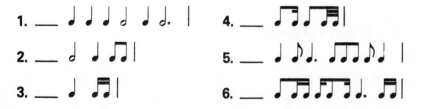

C. Provide the best time signature for each exercise. In some cases there may be more than one correct answer possible.

D. Each passage below is notated so that placement of the beats is obscured in some fashion. Rewrite each one to clarify the beat placement.

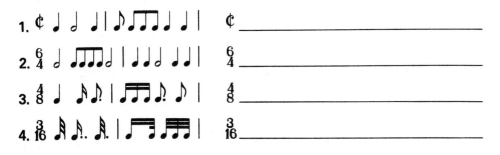

E. Add stems as required.

1. Each duration is a quarter note.

2. Each duration is an eighth note. Beam them in groups of three.

F. Listen to a recording of the beginning of each of the five movements of Beethoven's Symphony No. 6, Op. 68, and identify the beat and meter types of each. Then name three time signatures that *could* have been used to notate the movement. (Note that movements I and V begin with slow introductions; wait until the allegro portions before making any decision.)

Movement	Beat type	Meter type	Possible time signatures
I	_____	_____	_____
II	_____	_____	_____
III	_____	_____	_____
IV	_____	_____	_____
V	_____	_____	_____

G. Scale review. Given the scale degree, the note, and whether the key is major or minor, supply the name of the key. Assume melodic minor for all minor key examples.

ex. ↑6̂ is C♯ in __e__ minor

1. 4̂ is B♭ in ____ minor   8. 5̂ is B♭ in ____ major
2. 3̂ is B in ____ major   9. ↑6̂ is G♯ in ____ minor
3. ↑7̂ is B♯ in ____ minor   10. 5̂ is C in ____ major
4. 6̂ is F♯ in ____ major   11. 3̂ is B♭ in ____ minor
5. 4̂ is E♭ in ____ major   12. ↓7̂ is E in ____ minor
6. 5̂ is G in ____ minor   13. 7̂ is D♯ in ____ major
7. 6̂ is B in ____ major   14. 2̂ is B♭ in ____ major

H. Interval review. Notate the specified interval above the given note.

I. Interval review. Notate the specified interval below the given note.

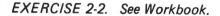

EXERCISE 2-2. See Workbook.

CHAPTER THREE

INTRODUCTION TO TRIADS
AND SEVENTH CHORDS

INTRODUCTION

In this chapter we begin working with chords, the basic vocabulary of tonal harmony. We will not be concerned at this stage with how chords are used compositionally or even what kinds of chords occur in the major and minor modes, although we will get to these topics soon enough. First we have to learn how to spell the more common chord types and how to recognize them in various contexts.

TRIADS

In "To the Student" (pp. ix-xiii), we explained that tonal harmony makes use of *tertian* (built of 3rds) chords. The fundamental tertian sonority is the *triad,* a three-note chord consisting of a 5th divided into two superimposed 3rds. There are four possible ways to combine major and minor 3rds to produce a tertian triad.

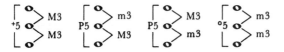

The names and abbreviations for these four triad types are given in Example 3-1.

Example 3-1.

Play these triads at the piano and compare the way they sound. You might be able to guess from listening to them that in tonal music the major and minor triads are found the most often, the augmented the least often. There are also names (in addition to note names) for the members of a triad (Ex. 3-2).

Example 3-2.

Study the preceding diagram and examples very carefully before going on.

CHECKPOINT

1. Which triad types contain a m3 as the bottom interval? As the top interval?

2. Which triad types contain a M3 as the top interval? As the bottom interval?

3. Which triad types contain a P5 between the root and the 5th? a °5? a +5?

SELF-TEST 3-1
(Answers begin on page 538.)

A. Spell the triad, given the root and type. (As with keys, upper-case letters indicate major and lower-case letters indicate minor; augmented triads are represented by upper-case letters followed by a "+," and diminished by lower-case letters followed by a "°.")

1.	b♭	_____	**7.** A	_____
2.	E	_____	**8.** d	_____
3.	g°	_____	**9.** G♭	_____
4.	f°	_____	**10.** B	_____
5.	c	_____	**11.** a♭	_____
6.	D+	_____	**12.** c♯	_____

B. Notate the triad, given the root and type.

C. Fill in the blanks.

	ex.	1.	2.	3.	4.	5.	6.	7.	8.	9.	10.
Fifth	F	__	__	__	D♯	__	__	__	__	G♯	B
Third	D	A	G♭	__	__	__	F♯	C♯	__	__	__
Root	B♭	__	__	B	__	C♭	__	__	F	__	__
Type	M	+	m	m	+	M	°	M	°	m	M

D. Given the chord quality and one member of the triad, notate the remainder of the triad, with the root as the lowest tone.

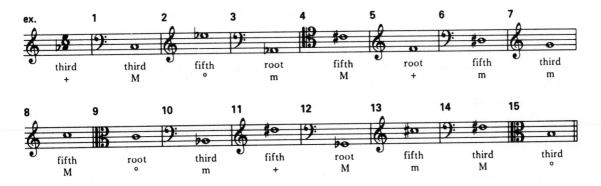

EXERCISE 3-1. See Workbook.

SEVENTH CHORDS

If we extend a tertian triad by adding another 3rd on top of the 5th of the triad, the result is a four-note chord. Because the interval between this added note and the root is some kind of 7th (major, minor, or diminished), chords of this sort are called *seventh chords.*

Since it would be possible to use more than one kind of 7th with each triad type, there are many more seventh-chord types than triad types. However, tonal harmony commonly makes use of only five seventh-chord types (Ex. 3-3). Below each chord in Example 3-3 you will find the commonly used name for the chord and the symbol used as an abbreviation. Also given is the technical name, which is constructed by naming the triad type and the 7th type and putting a hyphen in between. Be sure to play Example 3-3 to familiarize yourself with the sound of these chords.

Example 3-3.

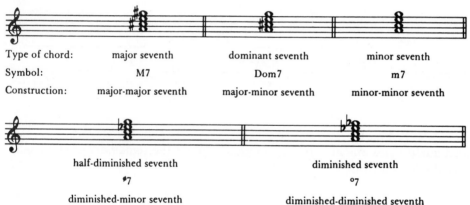

Type of chord:	major seventh	dominant seventh	minor seventh
Symbol:	M7	Dom7	m7
Construction:	major-major seventh	major-minor seventh	minor-minor seventh

half-diminished seventh	diminished seventh
ø7	°7
diminished-minor seventh	diminished-diminished seventh

Quite soon we will begin composition exercises using triads. While seventh chords will not be used in composition exercises for some time, you will nevertheless be able to start becoming familiar with them from an analytical standpoint through examples and analysis assignments.

CHECKPOINT

1. Which seventh-chord types have a diminished triad on the bottom?

2. Which ones have a M3 between the 5th and the 7th of the chord?

3. Which ones have a m3 between the 3rd and the 5th of the chord?

4. Which ones contain at least one P5? Which contain two?

SELF-TEST 3-2
(Answers begin on page 539.)

A. Identify the type of each seventh chord, using the abbreviations given in Example 3-3 (M7, Dom7, m7, °7, °7).

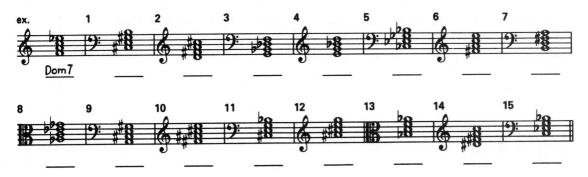

B. Notate the seventh chord, given the root and type.

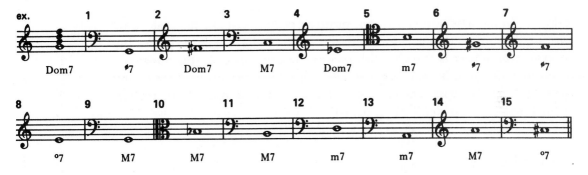

C. Given the seventh chord quality and one member of the chord, notate the rest of the chord.

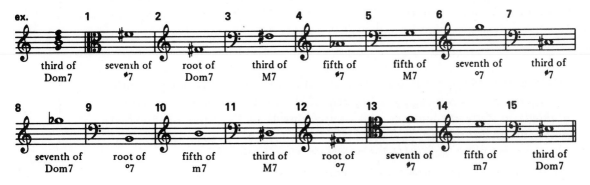

EXERCISE 3-2. **See Workbook.**

INVERSIONS OF CHORDS

Up to now, we have been notating all chords with the root as the lowest tone. But in a musical context, any part of a chord might appear as the lowest tone. The three possible *bass positions* of the triad are illustrated in Example 3-4.

Example 3-4.

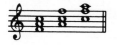

The bass position that we have been using, with the root as the lowest tone (or "in the bass"), is called *root position.* You might assume that "third position" would be the term for a chord with the 3rd as the lowest tone, but musical terminology is fraught with inconsistencies. Instead, this position is called *first inversion.* Reasonably enough, *second inversion* is used for chords with the 5th in the bass. The term *inversion* is used here to mean the transfer of the lowest note to some higher octave.

Example 3-5.

root first second
position inversion inversion

Notice that the upper notes of the chord can be spaced in any way without altering the bass position. Also, any of the notes can be duplicated (or *doubled*) in different octaves. All of the chords in Example 3-6 are first inversion F major triads.

Example 3-6.

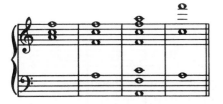

The inversion of seventh chords works just like the inversion of triads, except that three inversions (four bass positions) are possible (Ex. 3-7).

Example 3-7.

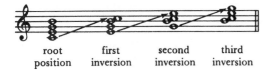

root position   first inversion   second inversion   third inversion

INVERSION SYMBOLS AND FIGURED BASS

In analyzing music we often use numbers to indicate the bass positions of chords. Instead of using 1 for first inversion, 2 for second inversion, and so on, we use numbers derived from the Baroque system called *figured bass* or *thoroughbass*. During the Baroque period (approximately 1600-1750), the keyboard player in an ensemble read from a part consisting only of a bass line and some symbols indicating the chord to be played. This is strikingly similar to the lead sheet system used today in popular music, in which the musician reads a melody line and pop symbols.

In the Baroque system, the symbols consisted basically of numbers representing *intervals above the bass* to be formed by the members of the chord, but the notes could actually be played in any octave above the bass. Notice that the system dealt only with intervals, not with roots of chords, because the theory of chord roots had not been devised when figured bass was first developed.

The table below illustrates the figured bass symbols for root position and inverted triads and seventh chords.

Sonority desired							
Complete figured bass symbol	5 3	6 3	6 4	7 5 3	6 5 3	6 4 3	6 4 2
Symbol most often used		6	6 4	7	6 5	4 3	4 2

In the figured bass system, the number 6 designates a 6th above the bass. Whether it is a M6 or a m6 depends upon the key signature. If the Baroque composer wished to direct the keyboard player to raise or lower a note, there were several methods that could be used, including the following three.

1. An accidental next to an arabic numeral in the figured bass could be used to raise or lower a note.

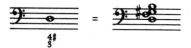

2. An accidental by itself always referred to the 3rd above the bass and could be used to alter that note.

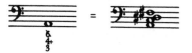

3. A slash or plus sign in connection with an arabic numeral meant to raise that note.

Example 3-8 illustrates a portion of an actual figured bass part from the Baroque period, along with a possible *realization*. Some keyboard players may have added embellishments not shown in this realization. Bach included the numeral 5 at several places to remind the player to play a root position triad.

Example 3-8. Bach, *Easter Oratorio*, II

The realization of figured basses is still considered to be an effective way to learn certain aspects of tonal composition, and we will occasionally use exercises of this kind in the text.

The inversion symbols that we use today are summarized in the table below. These symbols are usually used with a roman numeral (as in I^6 or V^6_5) as part of a harmonic analysis. Notice that when a seventh chord is inverted, the 7 is replaced by the appropriate inversion symbol.

Bass position	Triad symbol	Seventh chord symbol
Root position	(none)	7
First inversion	6	$^6_5$
Second inversion	$^6_4$	$^4_3$
Third inversion	(none)	$^4_2$ or 2

SELF-TEST 3-3
(Answers begin on page 540.)

A. Identify the root and type of each chord, and show the correct inversion symbol.

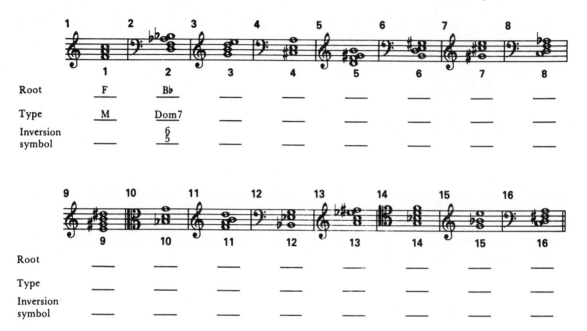

	1	2	3	4	5	6	7	8
Root	F	B♭	__	__	__	__	__	__
Type	M	Dom7	__	__	__	__	__	__
Inversion symbol	__	6/5	__	__	__	__	__	__

	9	10	11	12	13	14	15	16
Root	__	__	__	__	__	__	__	__
Type	__	__	__	__	__	__	__	__
Inversion symbol	__	__	__	__	__	__	__	__

B. The bottom staff of this recitative is played on bassoon and keyboard, the keyboard player (the "continuo") realizing the figured bass. Fill in each blank below the bass line with the root and type of the chord to be played at that point.

Bach, *Easter Oratorio,* II

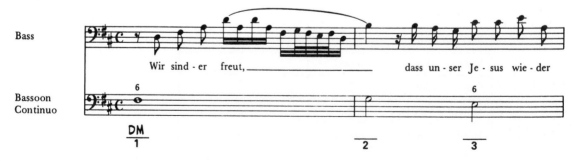

lebt, und un-ser Herz, so erst in Trau-rig-keit zer-flos-sen und ge - schwebt, ver-gisst den Schmerz und

sinnt auf Freu - den - lie - der; denn un - ser Hei - land le - bet wie - der.

EXERCISE 3-3. *See Workbook.*

RECOGNIZING CHORDS IN VARIOUS TEXTURES

Some people, especially those without much keyboard experience, find it difficult at first to analyze a chord that is distributed over two or more staves, as in Example 3-9.

Example 3-9.

One procedure to follow with the chord is to make an inventory of all the *pitch classes** found in the chord (B♭, G, and D) and to notate the chord with each pitch class in turn as the lowest note. The other notes should be put as close to the bottom note as possible. The version that consists only of stacked 3rds is in root position. We can see from Example 3-10 that the chord in Example 3-9 is a g minor triad in first inversion.

Example 3-10.

The chord in Example 3-11 contains the pitch classes E, A, C♯, and G, which allows four bass positions.

Example 3-11.

Example 3-12 tells us that the chord in Example 3-11 is an A dominant seventh chord in second inversion.

Example 3-12.

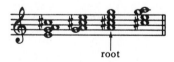

You may already be able to carry out this process in your head, which will speed things up considerably. If not, you will learn to do so with practice.

---

*The term *pitch class* is used to group together all pitches that have an identical sound or that are identical except for the octave or octaves that separate them. For example, all B♯'s, C's, and D♭♭'s belong to the same pitch class, no matter what octave they are found in.

CHECKPOINT

1. What is the symbol for the first inversion of a triad?

2. Of a seventh chord?

3. Explain $\frac{4}{2}$, $\frac{6}{4}$, and $\frac{4}{3}$.

4. Which bass position for which chord type requires no symbol?

SELF-TEST 3-4
(Answers begin on page 540.)

A. Identify the root, type, and inversion symbol for each chord. All the notes in each exercise belong to the same chord. The lowest note is the bass note for the purpose of analysis.

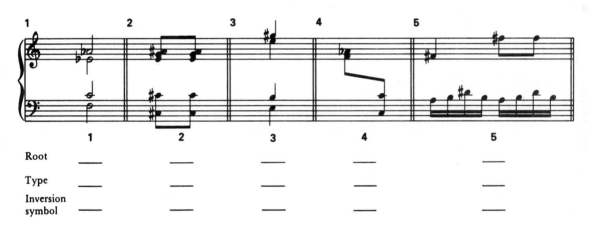

	1	2	3	4	5
Root	___	___	___	___	___
Type	___	___	___	___	___
Inversion symbol	___	___	___	___	___

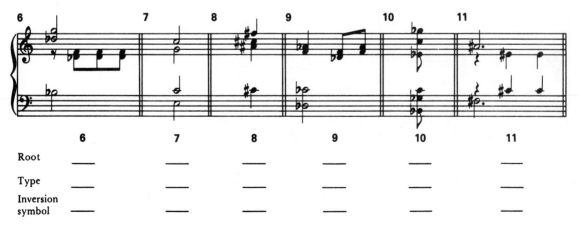

	6	7	8	9	10	11
Root	___	___	___	___	___	___
Type	___	___	___	___	___	___
Inversion symbol	___	___	___	___	___	___

B. The excerpts below are to be analyzed in a similar fashion. Each chord is numbered. Put your analysis of each chord in the numbered blanks below the excerpt.

1. Schubert, *Moment Musical,* Op. 94, No. 6

Root   ___ ___ ___   ___ ___   ___ ___   ___ ___ ___   ___ ___

Type   ___ ___ ___   ___ ___   ___ ___   ___ ___ ___   ___ ___

Inversion
symbol ___ ___ ___   ___ ___   ___ ___   ___ ___ ___   ___ ___

2. Byrd, *Psalm LIV*

The 8 under the treble clef on the tenor staff (third staff from the top) means that the notes are to be sung an 8ve lower than written.

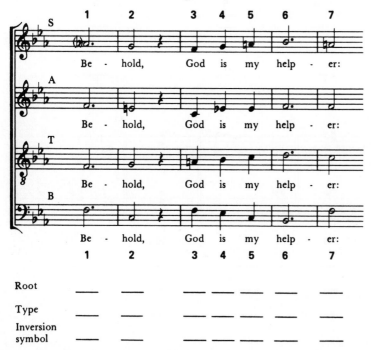

Root   ___ ___   ___ ___ ___ ___ ___

Type   ___ ___   ___ ___ ___ ___ ___

Inversion
symbol ___ ___   ___ ___ ___ ___ ___

3. Fischer, "Blumen-Strauss"

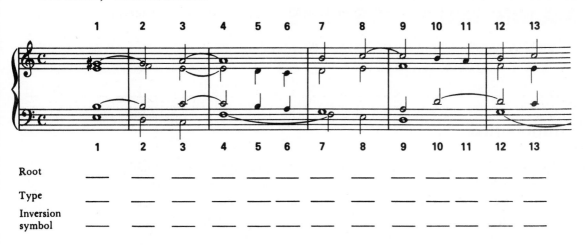

	1	2	3	4	5	6	7	8	9	10	11	12	13
Root	—	—	—	—	—	—	—	—	—	—	—	—	—
Type	—	—	—	—	—	—	—	—	—	—	—	—	—
Inversion symbol	—	—	—	—	—	—	—	—	—	—	—	—	—

EXERCISE 3-4. See Workbook.

CHAPTER FOUR

DIATONIC CHORDS IN MAJOR AND MINOR KEYS

INTRODUCTION

Now that we have presented the four triad types and the five common seventh-chord types, we can begin to look at how they are used in tonal music. Most chords in tonal music are made up only of notes from the scale on which the passage is based. That is, if a passage is in G major, most of the chords contain only notes found in the G major scale. Chords of this kind are called *diatonic* chords. All other chords—those using notes not in the scale—are called *altered* chords. We will get to them later. At this point we are not going to worry about how you might *compose* music using diatonic chords, although that will come up soon. For now, we are going to concentrate on spelling and recognizing diatonic chords in various keys.

THE MINOR SCALE

Before we can begin talking about diatonic chords, we have to return to the problem of the minor scale. Because instrumentalists are taught to practice natural, harmonic, and melodic minor scales, we sometimes assume that the tonal composer had three independent minor scale forms from which to choose. But this is not how the minor mode works in tonal music.

We can make the following generalization about the three minor scales: there is, in a sense, one minor scale that has two scale steps, $\hat{6}$ and $\hat{7}$, that are variable. That is, there are two versions of $\hat{6}$ and $\hat{7}$, and both versions will usually appear in a piece in the minor mode. All of the notes in Example 4-1 are diatonic to e minor. Notice the use of ↑$\hat{6}$ and ↑$\hat{7}$ to mean raised $\hat{6}$ and $\hat{7}$ and ↓$\hat{6}$ and ↓$\hat{7}$ to mean unaltered $\hat{6}$ and $\hat{7}$.

Example 4-1.

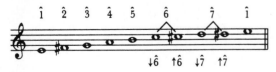

How do composers decide which versions of $\hat{6}$ and $\hat{7}$ to use? Melodically, the most graceful thing for ↑$\hat{6}$ and ↑$\hat{7}$ to do is to ascend by step, while ↓$\hat{6}$ and ↓$\hat{7}$ tend naturally to descend by step; these tendencies conform to the melodic minor scale. Example 4-2 provides a good illustration of the use of the minor scale. If you look closely at Bach's treatment of $\hat{6}$ and $\hat{7}$ (circled notes), you will see that all of the motion is stepwise, with two exceptions. The first leap is from the Gb4 in m. 2. Here the eventual goal is F, not A, so the ↓$\hat{6}$ form is used. The other leap occurs in the bass in m. 4. Here the goal of the line is Bb, not Gb, so the ↑$\hat{7}$ form is used.

Example 4-2.   Bach, *Well-Tempered Clavier*, Book II, Prelude 22

If a $\hat{6}$ or $\hat{7}$ is left by leap instead of by step, there will generally be an *eventual* stepwise goal for that scale degree, and the $\hat{6}$ and $\hat{7}$ will probably be raised or left unaltered according to the direction of that goal, as in Example 4-2. In the next excerpt, Example 4-3, the Ab4 in m. 1 (↓$\hat{6}$) is left by leap to the C5. But the eventual stepwise goal of the Ab4 is the G4 in the next measure, so the descending form of the melodic minor is used. Still, the use of the melodic minor is just a rule of thumb, not a law. It is not difficult to find passages in minor where ↑$\hat{6}$ and ↑$\hat{7}$ lead downward (Ex. 4-3, m. 3).

Example 4-3.   Bach, *Well-Tempered Clavier*, Book I, Fugue 2

In some cases, ↓6̂ and ↓7̂ lead upward (Ex. 4-4).

Example 4-4.   Bach, *Well-Tempered Clavier,* Book I, Prelude 10

In other instances, ↑7̂ and ↓6̂ appear next to each other, forming a harmonic minor scale (Ex. 4-5).

Example 4-5.   Beethoven, Sonata Op. 2, No. 2, III, Trio

The reasons for such exceptions to the melodic minor scale are usually harmonic. As we will see later in this chapter, the underlying harmonies generally conform to the harmonic minor scale.

CHECKPOINT

1. What is the term for chords that contain no notes outside of the scale? What about chords that do contain such notes?

2. Individual lines in tonal music tend to conform most closely to which of the three traditional minor scales?

3. Name the five common seventh-chord types.

DIATONIC TRIADS IN MAJOR

Triads may be constructed using any degree of the major scale as the root. Diatonic triads, as we have mentioned, will consist only of notes belonging to the scale. To distinguish the triads built upon the various scale degrees from the scale degrees themselves, we use roman numerals instead of arabic numerals (for example, V instead of $\hat{5}$). The triad type is indicated by the form of the roman numeral itself.

ART

Triad type	Roman numeral	Example
Major	Upper case	V
Minor	Lower case	vi
Diminished	Lower case with a °	vii°
Augmented	Upper case with a +	III⁺

Taking C major as an example, we can discover the types of diatonic triads that occur on each degree of the major scale.

Example 4-6.

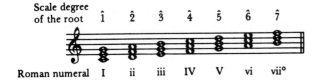

You should memorize the following table.

Diatonic triad types in major	
Major	I, IV, and V
Minor	ii, iii, and vi
Diminished	vii°
Augmented	none

DIATONIC TRIADS IN MINOR

The construction of triads is somewhat more involved in the minor mode than in major. Since $\hat{6}$ and $\hat{7}$ are variable, and because nearly all triads contain $\hat{6}$ or $\hat{7}$, more diatonic triads are possible in minor. Nonetheless, there are seven triads in minor (one for each scale degree) that occur more frequently than the others, and these are the ones we will use in our exercises for now. The roman numerals of the more common diatonic triads are circled in Example 4-7.

Example 4-7.

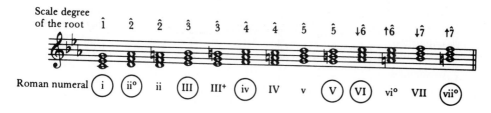

Notice that the *roots* of the triads circled above all belong to the *harmonic* minor scale. In fact, all of the notes of the circled triads belong to the harmonic minor scale, with the exception of the 5th of the III chord. Here is the table of minor-key triads, which you should also memorize.

Common diatonic triads in minor	
Major	III, V, and VI
Minor	i and iv
Diminished	ii° and vii°
Augmented	none

CHECKPOINT

1. In a major key which triads are minor?

2. In a minor key which triads are major?

3. The triads on which two scale degrees are the same type in both major and minor?

4. Which of the four triad types occurs least often in tonal music?

SELF-TEST 4-1
(Answers begin on page 541.)

A. Given the key and the triad, supply the roman numeral. Be sure your roman numeral is of the correct type (upper case, and so on). Inversion symbols, where required, go to the upper right of the roman numeral (as in I⁶).

d: i   B: ___   b: ___   Ab: ___   e: ___   F#: ___   a: ___   Db: ___

bb: ___   G: ___   d#: ___   C: ___   A: ___   c#: ___   Bb: ___   g: ___

B. In the exercises below you are given the name of a key and a scale degree number. *Without using key signatures,* notate the triad on that scale degree and provide the roman numeral. In minor keys be sure to use the triad types circled in Example 4-7.

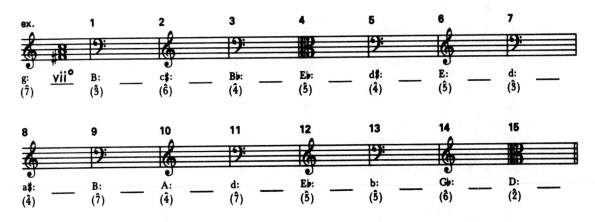

g: vii°   B: ___   c#: ___   Bb: ___   Eb: ___   d#: ___   E: ___   d: ___
(7̂)   (3̂)   (6̂)   (4̂)   (5̂)   (4̂)   (5̂)   (3̂)

a#: ___   B: ___   A: ___   d: ___   Eb: ___   b: ___   Gb: ___   D: ___
(4̂)   (7̂)   (4̂)   (7̂)   (5̂)   (5̂)   (6̂)   (2̂)

C. Analysis. Write roman numerals in the spaces provided, making sure each roman numeral is of the correct type and includes an inversion symbol if needed. The tenor line sounds an octave lower than notated.

Brahms, "Ach lieber Herre Jesu Christ"

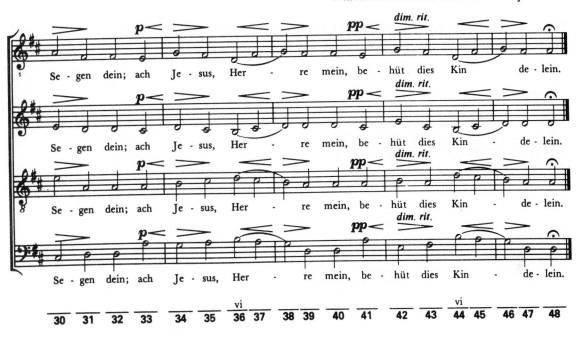

EXERCISE 4-1. See Workbook.

DIATONIC SEVENTH CHORDS IN MAJOR

In the next chapter we will begin simple composition exercises using triads, but seventh chords will not be used compositionally until Chapter 12. Nevertheless, we will continue to work with seventh chords in spelling exercises and in analysis in order to build a solid foundation for those later chapters.

The triads on each scale degree in major can be extended by the addition of a 7th above the root. The roman numeral system for seventh chords is similar to that for triads, as you will see in the following table.

Seventh chord type	Roman numeral	Example
Major seventh	Upper case with M7	I^{M7}
Dominant seventh	Upper case with a 7	V^7
Minor seventh	Lower case with a 7	vi^7
Half-diminished seventh	Lower case with ∅7	$ii^{\varnothing 7}$
Diminished seventh	Lower case with °7	$vii^{\circ 7}$

Four of the five seventh-chord types occur as diatonic seventh chords in major keys.

Example 4-8.

You should learn the following table, which summarizes major-key seventh chords.

Diatonic seventh chords in major	
M7	I^{M7} and IV^{M7}
Dom7	V^7
m7	ii^7, iii^7, and vi^7
$\emptyset7$	$vii^{\emptyset7}$
$°7$	none

DIATONIC SEVENTH CHORDS IN MINOR

Because of the variability of $\hat{6}$ and $\hat{7}$, there are sixteen possible diatonic seventh chords in minor. Example 4-9 shows the most commonly used seventh chords on each scale degree. The others will be discussed in later chapters. Notice that most of the notes in Example 4-9 belong to the harmonic minor scale.

Example 4-9.

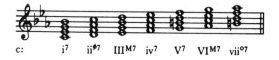

Here is the last chord table to learn.

Common diatonic seventh chords in minor	
M7	III^{M7} and VI^{M7}
Dom7	V^7
m7	i^7 and iv^7
⌀7	ii$^{⌀7}$
°7	vii$^{°7}$

Remember that the inversion symbols for seventh chords are $\frac{6}{5}$, $\frac{4}{3}$, and $\frac{4}{2}$. This means that the V^7 in first inversion is symbolized as V$\frac{6}{5}$, *not* as V$\frac{7}{6}$.

CHECKPOINT

1. Most of the five common seventh-chord types appear diatonically in both major and minor. Which one type does not?

2. Does the m7 chord occur on more scale steps in minor than in major?

3. The seventh chords on most scale steps are different qualities in major and minor. Which chord is the exception to this?

SELF-TEST 4-2
(Answers begin on page 542.)

A. Given the key and the seventh chord, supply the roman numeral. Be sure your roman numeral is the correct type and includes inversion if applicable.

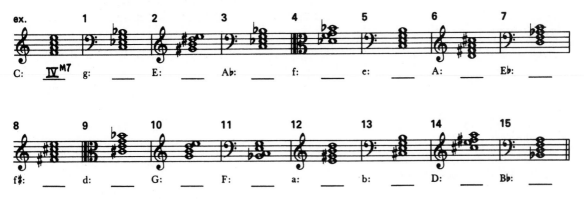

B. In the exercises below you are given the name of a key and a scale degree number. *Without using key signatures,* notate the seventh chord on that scale degree and provide the roman numeral. In minor keys be sure to use the chord types shown in Example 4-9.

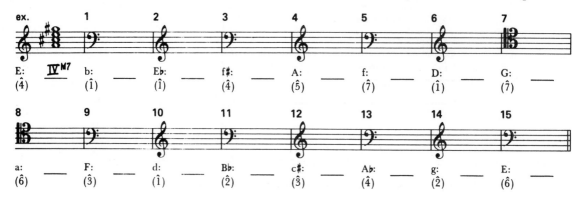

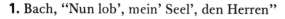

C. Analysis. Put roman numerals in the spaces provided, making sure each roman numeral is of the correct type and includes an inversion symbol if needed.

1. Bach, "Nun lob', mein' Seel', den Herren"

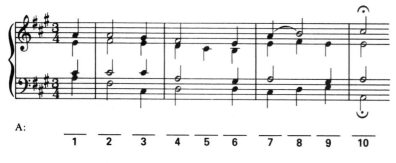

2. Schumann, *Chorale,* Op. 68, No. 4

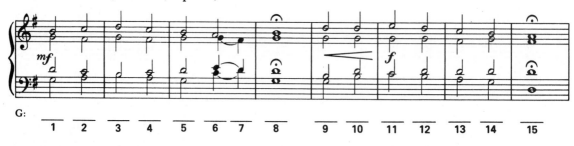

EXERCISE 4-2. See Workbook.

PART TWO

DIATONIC TRIADS

CHAPTER FIVE

PRINCIPLES OF VOICE LEADING

INTRODUCTION

The compositional process, being a creative one, is not entirely understood. It is reasonable to assume that a composer thinks of several aspects more or less simultaneously—melody, harmony, rhythm, and so forth. Naturally, a complete analysis of a composition must take all of these factors into account. For the most part, however, this text concentrates upon questions relating to the harmonic aspect of tonal music, since it is this aspect that most clearly delineates tonal music from other types.

We could say that the basic vocabulary of tonal harmony consists of triads and seventh chords and that its grammar involves the ways in which these chords are selected (harmonic progression) and connected (voice leading). In this chapter we will concentrate upon some of the basics of the voice-leading aspect: how does a composer write out a given succession of chords for some combination of performers? How can he or she decide in which direction each vocal or instrumental line should go?

Voice leading (or *part writing*) may be defined as the ways in which chords are produced by the motions of individual musical lines. A closely related term is *counterpoint,* which refers to the combining of relatively independent musical lines. Naturally, the style of voice leading will depend upon the composer, the musical effect desired, and the performing medium (for example, it is easier to play a large melodic interval on the piano than it is to sing it). But there are certain voice-leading norms that most composers follow most of the time, and our study will concentrate upon these norms.

For various reasons, many theory texts have based their approach to voice leading upon the style of the four-voice chorale harmonizations by J. S. Bach. While the Bach chorales epitomize the late Baroque approach to choral writing, most musicians today feel the need to study other textures and styles as well. To answer this need, our study of voice leading will deal with a variety of textures in both vocal and instrumental styles.

THE MELODIC LINE

Our beginning exercises will make use of short and simple melodies in vocal style, in order to avoid for now the complications involved with more ornate vocal and instrumental melodies. The following procedures should be followed for Chapters 5 through 9.

1. *Rhythm.* Keep the rhythm simple, with most durations being equal to or longer than the duration of the beat. The final note should occur on a strong beat.

2. *Harmony.* Every melody note should belong to the chord that is to harmonize it.

3. *Contour.* The melody should be primarily *conjunct* (stepwise). The shape of the melody should be interesting but clear and simple, with a single *focal point,* the highest note of the melody.

Example 5-1a is a good example of the points discussed so far. Example 5-1b is not as good because it has an uninteresting contour. Example 5-1c, while more interesting, lacks a single focal point and contains one unharmonized tone (E5).

Example 5-1.

4. *Leaps*
   a. Avoid augmented intervals, 7ths, and intervals larger than a P8. Diminished intervals may be used if the melody changes direction by step immediately after the interval.

b. A melodic interval larger than a P4 is usually best approached and left in the direction *opposite* to the leap.

c. When smaller leaps are used consecutively in the same direction, they should outline a triad.

5. *Tendency tones.* In tonal music $\hat{7}$ has a strong tendency to move up to $\hat{1}$. An exception to this is the scalewise line descending from $\hat{1}$: $\hat{1}$-$\hat{7}$-$\hat{6}$-$\hat{5}$. The only other tendency tone that needs to be considered is $\hat{4}$, which often moves down to $\hat{3}$, but not with the regularity with which $\hat{7}$ goes to $\hat{1}$.

Example 5-2a illustrates a good melody in the restricted style we are beginning with. Example 5-2b, on the other hand, breaks all of rule 4 as well as rule 5.

Example 5-2.

SELF-TEST 5-1
(Answers begin on page 543.)

A. Criticize each melody in terms of the rules for simple melodies discussed under "The Melodic Line" on pages 70-71.

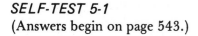

B. Compose simple melodies that will conform to the given progressions. Slashes represent bar lines, and every chord except the last takes one beat.

1. D: I V I / IV I I / vi ii V / I /

2. e: i iv i i / V V i i / iv V i /

3. F: I V vi IV / I IV ii V / I /

EXERCISE 5-1. See Workbook.

NOTATING CHORDS

A *musical score* is a tool used by a composer, conductor, or analyst. A score shows all of the parts of an ensemble arranged one above the other, enabling the experienced reader to "hear" what the composition will sound like. In a *full score* all or most of the parts are notated on their own individual staves. Any musician should be able both to read and to prepare a full score, and some of your theory exercises should be done in full score. But a *reduced score,* notated at concert pitch upon as few staves as possible, may be more practical for daily theory exercises. Your choice of full or reduced score will depend partly upon the sort of musical texture that the exercise will use. That is, if you are composing for four parts in chorale style, two staves will probably suffice. On the other hand, four active and independent instrumental lines might require four staves.

When you are notating more than one part upon a single staff, be sure that the stems of the top part always point up and those of the bottom point down, even if the parts have crossed. Example 5-3 illustrates some common notational errors. The score in this case is the familiar SATB (Soprano, Alto, Tenor, Bass) reduced score.

Example 5-3.

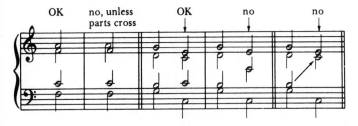

VOICING A SINGLE TRIAD

Once you have settled upon what combination of instruments and voices you are writing for and have selected the opening chord, the next consideration is *voicing:* how the chord is to be distributed or spaced. The way in which a chord is spaced has a great deal of influence upon its aural effect. To convince yourself of this, play Example 5-4 at the piano. Each chord in the example contains five parts and covers the same range, but the aural effects are quite different. An even wider variety of effects could be contained by playing Example 5-4 on various combinations of instruments. While each of these spacings might be appropriate under certain circumstances, the spacing in Example 5-4e is the least commonly used because of its "muddy" effect.

Example 5-4.

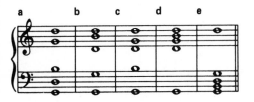

Because so much attention has been paid to four-part textures by authors of theory texts, a terminology concerning the voicing of chords in four-part textures has been developed.

Close structure: less than an octave between soprano and tenor

Open structure: an octave or more between soprano and tenor

Example 5-5 illustrates these spacings in traditional hymn style.

Example 5-5. "Old One Hundredth" (Protestant hymn)

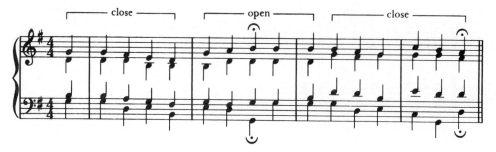

In your beginning part-writing exercises, it would be advisable for you to follow two simple conventions concerning spacing.

1. Do not allow any part to cross above the soprano or below the bass, or the essential soprano/bass counterpoint may become unclear.

2. When writing for three or more parts, avoid muddy sonorities by keeping *adjacent upper parts* (excluding the bass) within an octave of each other. For example, in a four-part texture there should not be more than a P8 between soprano and alto or between alto and tenor, although there might be more than a P8 between tenor and bass.

After you have gained some experience in composing, you may begin to experiment with exceptions to these conventions.

When you are composing for vocal ensembles, use the ranges given in Example 5-6.

Example 5-6.

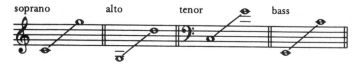

SELF-TEST 5-2
(Answers begin on page 544.)

A. Analyze the excerpt from a Bach chorale below, using roman numerals. Then show beneath each roman numeral the structure of the chord by writing "O" or "C" for open or close structure. The note in parentheses in m. 3 is not part of the chord and should be ignored for the purpose of harmonic analysis.

Bach, "Wo soll ich fliehen hin"

g: ___ ___ ___ ___ ___ ___ ___ ___ ___

B. Review the two conventions concerning spacing on page 74. Then point out in the example below any places where those conventions are not followed.

C. Fill in the circled missing inner voice(s) to complete each root position triad, being sure that each note of the triad is represented. Follow the spacing conventions and stay within the range of each vocal part.

EXERCISE 5-2. See Workbook.

PARALLELS

One of the basic goals of voice leading in tonal music is to maintain the relative independence of the individual parts. Because of this, voices moving together in parallel motion must be given special attention. Look at Example 5-7, and you will see that it consists of three versions of the i-V-i progression in the key of b. Each version uses the same chords, and each version contains parallel voice leading (indicated by the diagonal lines in the example). But only one version, Example 5-7c, would be considered acceptable by a composer of tonal music.

Example 5-7.

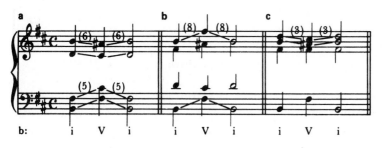

The reason Examples 5-7a and 5-7b are unacceptable in the tonal style is that they contain parallel 5ths and 8ves. Composers of tonal music generally followed the convention, dating from around 1450, of avoiding parallel 5ths and 8ves, as well as their octave equivalents, such as 12ths and unisons. Note that this does *not* rule out the *duplication* of a line at the 8ve, which was common in orchestral writing, for example (see Ex. 6-8 on p. 99, in which the bass line is doubled at the 8ve, because the double basses sound a P8 lower than written). The reason for avoiding parallel 5ths and 8ves has to do with the nature of counterpoint. The P8 and P5 are the most stable of intervals, and to link two voices through parallel motion at such intervals interferes with their independence much more than would parallel motion at 3rds or 6ths. We can deduce a rule of parallel motion:

> *Objectionable parallels* result when two parts that are separated by a P5 or a P8 or by their octave equivalents move to new pitch classes that are separated by the same interval.

If you apply this rule to the three parts of Example 5-8, you will find that all of them are acceptable. In Example 5-8a the soprano and tenor do not move to new pitch classes, while in Example 5-8b the parallels do not occur between the same pair of parts. Finally, the parallel 4ths in Example 5-8c are allowed, even though a P4 is the inversion of a P5.

Example 5-8.

Consecutive 5ths and 8ves by contrary motion were also generally avoided, at least in vocal music. This means that the composer usually did not "correct" parallels (Ex. 5-9a) by moving one of the parts up or down an octave (Ex. 5-9b).

Example 5-9.

D: V   I   V   I

Octaves by contrary motion are occasionally found at cadences in instrumental music and in some vocal writing, when both melody and bass outline $\hat{5}$-$\hat{1}$. You will see that this occurs in Example 5-10, below the arrow, but the listener probably understands that A4 and G4 are the basic notes of the melody in m. 7-8, while the D4 is only a quick arpeggiation. Notice also in

Example 5-10 that some of the notes are in parentheses. In many of the examples in this book, notes that do not belong to the chord are put in parentheses. Non-chord tones will be discussed in more detail in Chapters 10 and 11.

Example 5-10.   Haydn, Quartet Op. 64, No. 4, II

The term *unequal 5ths* refers to a P5 followed by a °5, or the reverse. Apparently, some tonal composers avoided unequal 5ths above the bass line, and others used P5-°5 but not °5-P5, yet neither of these restrictions holds true for tonal music in general. For the purposes of our part-writing exercises, we will consider unequal 5ths acceptable *unless* they involve a °5-P5 above the bass. Several sets of unequal 5ths are illustrated in Example 5-11, with all but the last being acceptable.

Example 5-11.

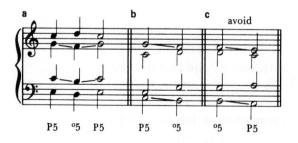

Direct or *hidden 5ths* and *8ves* occur when the *outer* voices move in the same direction into a P5 or P8, with a leap in the soprano part. The aural result is similar to parallel 5ths and 8ves. In Examples 5-12a and 5-12b the interval of a P5 or P8 between the outer voices is approached from the same direction with a leap in the soprano. In Example 5-12c the 5th involves the bass and alto, not the bass and soprano, while in Example 5-12d the soprano moves by step, not by leap. Both Examples 5-12c and 5-12d are correct.

Example 5-12.

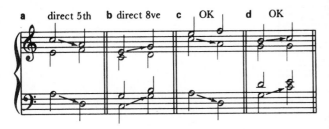

The avoidance of parallels of all types was somewhat less strictly maintained in instrumental than in vocal music. In piano writing, for instance, accompaniment figures have frequently outlined 5ths or 8ves, as in Example 5-13.

Example 5-13. Mozart, Sonata K. 284, III

In most cases, such instances of parallels are confined to those textures and instrumental lines in which they are not obvious to the ear. When you attempt to compose tonal music, you should use parallel 5ths and 8ves very sparingly, if at all, and in such a way that the listener's attention will not be drawn to them. Parallels involving both of the outer parts are especially rare and should be avoided. The few instances of such parallels, such as in Example 5-14, do not contradict the general validity of the rule. Possibly Beethoven was trying to evoke a rustic, unsophisticated atmosphere through the use of the parallels—the example is, after all, from the beginning of the *Pastoral* Symphony.

Example 5-14.   Beethoven, Symphony No. 6, Op. 68, I

SELF-TEST 5-3
(Answers begin on page 545.)

A. Label the chords in the excerpt below with roman numerals. Then label any examples of parallelism (objectionable or otherwise) that you can find.

Bach, "Ermuntre dich, mein schwacher Geist"

B. Find and label the following errors in this example:

1. Parallel 8ves
2. Parallel 5ths
3. Direct 5ths
4. 5ths by contrary motion
5. Spacing error (review pp. 73-74)

C. Find and label the following errors in this example:

1. Parallel 8ves
2. Parallel 5ths
3. Direct 8ves
4. 8ves by contrary motion
5. Unacceptable unequal 5ths
6. Spacing error

EXERCISE 5-3. See Workbook.

ROOT POSITION PART WRITING WITH REPEATED ROOTS

In this and the following three sections, some other conventions followed in writing for three and four parts are discussed. In each section the traditional four-part texture will be discussed first.

When we refer to a note being *doubled* or *tripled,* we mean that two or three of the parts are given that pitch class, although not necessarily in the same octave. For example, look at the Bach excerpt in Part A of Self-Test 5-3 (p. 80). The root of the first chord, G, is tripled in the alto, tenor, and bass. The root of the second chord, C, is doubled in the soprano and bass.

Four-part textures

1. All members of the triad are usually present. The final I chord is sometimes incomplete, consisting of a 3rd and a tripled root.
2. The root is usually doubled. The leading tone ($\hat{7}$) is almost never doubled.

Three-part textures

1. The 5th of the triad is often omitted. The final I chord may consist only of a tripled root.
2. An incomplete triad will usually have the root doubled. The leading tone ($\hat{7}$) is almost never doubled.

When a root position triad is repeated, the upper voices may be arpeggiated freely, as long as the spacing conventions are followed (review discussion of voicing a single triad, pp. 73-74). The bass may arpeggiate an octave. Example 5-15 illustrates appropriate part writing for repeated roots.

Example 5-15.

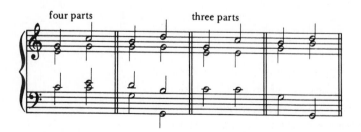

SELF-TEST 5-4   Using repeated roots.
(Answers begin on page 546.)

Test your understanding of the preceding section by filling in the inner voice or voices in the second chord of each pair. The key is C major throughout.

EXERCISE 5-4.   See Workbook.

ROOT POSITION PART WRITING
WITH ROOTS A 5TH (4TH) APART

As you will learn in the next chapter, one of the most fundamental root movements in tonal music is that of the descending P5 (or ascending P4). The part-writing principles involved in this root movement are identical to those concerned with the ascending P5 (or descending P4). Other principles that must always be kept in mind are those concerning spacing, parallelism, and the resolution of $\hat{7}$ to $\hat{1}$ when $\hat{7}$ occurs in the melody.

Four-part textures

1. One method for writing this root relationship in four parts is to keep in the same voice the tone that is common to both chords, while the remaining two upper parts move by step. The stepwise motion will be ascending for a root movement of a P5 down (Ex. 5-16a) and descending for a root movement of a P5 up (Ex. 5-16b).

Example 5-16

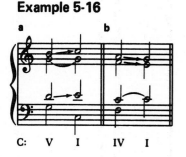

C: V I IV I

2. A second method moves all three upper parts in the same direction, with no leaps larger than a 3rd. The motion will be descending for a root movement of a P5 down (Ex. 5-17a) and ascending for a root movement of a P5 up (Ex. 5-17b).

Example 5-17.

C: I IV I V

3. A third method, while not as smooth as the first two, is useful for changing between close and open structures. Here we again keep in the same voice the tone that is common to both chords, while the voice that has the 3rd in the first chord leaps to provide the 3rd of the second chord. The remaining voice moves by step.

Example 5-18.

C: I IV I V

Three-part textures

The more flexible nature of three-part writing makes it impossible to distill a few conventional methods. Remember that each chord must contain at least a root and 3rd, and observe conventions concerning spacing and parallelism (Ex. 5-19).

Example 5-19.

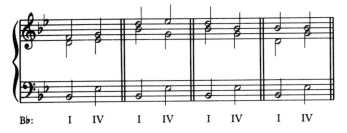

Bb: I   IV   I   IV   I   IV   I   IV

SELF-TEST 5-5   Using roots a 5th (4th) apart.
(Answers begin on page 547.)

A. Add alto and tenor parts to each exercise below. Each progression involves roots a P5 (P4) apart. Use one of the three methods outlined on pages 83-84 in each case, and state which you have used.

d: i   iv   A: vi   ii   V   I   Bb: ii   V   I   IV

e: V   i   iv   i   F: I   IV   I   V   Bb: I   V   I   IV   I

B. Add an alto part to each example. Be careful to observe conventions concerning spacing, parallels, and doubling. Each triad should include at least a root and a 3rd.

G: I   V   I   IV   I   Eb: vi   ii   V   I   d: i   iv   i

EXERCISE 5-5. See Workbook.

ROOT POSITION PART WRITING
WITH ROOTS A 3RD (6TH) APART

The voice leading that involves root position triads a 3rd or 6th apart is often quite smooth, because the two triads will always have two tones in common.

Four-part textures

Assuming that the first of the two root position triads has a doubled root, only one of the upper voices will need to move. The two upper voices that have tones in common with the second chord remain stationary, while the remaining voice moves by step. The stepwise motion will be upward for roots a descending 3rd apart (Ex. 5-20a), and downward for roots an ascending 3rd apart (Ex. 5-20b).

Example 5-20.

Three-part textures

Commonly encountered part-writing situations are more diverse in three-part textures. Some possibilities are illustrated in Example 5-21. Especially tricky is the ascending root movement. In that case, you should not omit the 5th of the second chord, for the listener may assume that the music has progressed only from a root position triad to an inverted form of the same triad (Exx. 5-21c and 5-21d).

Example 5-21.

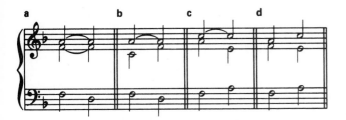

SELF-TEST 5-6 Using roots a P5th (P4th) and 3rd (6th) apart.
(Answers begin on page 548.)

A. Add alto and tenor parts to each exercise. Use the smoothest voice leading in each case.

Bb: vi   IV   ii   V   f#:   i   VI   iv   i   G: I   iii   vi   ii   V   —   I

B. Add an alto part to each exercise. Be careful to observe the conventions concerning parallels, spacing, and doubling.

A: I   iii   vi   IV   d: i   III   VI   iv   i   Bb: I   vi   IV   I   V   I

EXERCISE 5-6.   See Workbook.

ROOT POSITION PART WRITING
WITH ROOTS A 2ND (7TH) APART

Two triads with roots a 2nd (or 7th) apart have *no* tones in common, so every part must move from the first chord to the second. In this discussion we will assume that the bass moves by 2nd rather than by 7th, but voice leading is the same for a 7th down, for example, as it is for a 2nd up.

Four-part textures

If the root is doubled in the first chord, as is usually the case, then the voice leading is usually quite simple: if the bass moves up, the upper voices move down to the next chord tone (Ex. 5-22a), while if the bass moves down, the upper voices move up to the next chord tone (Ex. 5-22b).

Example 5-22.

The progression V-vi (or V-VI) presents some special problems. In most cases the 3rd is doubled in the vi chord in this progression. This results when only two of the three upper voices (the voices containing $\hat{2}$ and $\hat{5}$) move down, while $\hat{7}$ follows its usual tendency to resolve up to $\hat{1}$. Example 5-23 illustrates the V-vi progression with the 3rd doubled in the vi chord.

Example 5-23. Bach, "O Ewigkeit, du Donnerwort"

On the other hand, if $\hat{7}$ is in an inner voice in the V chord, its need to resolve is not so apparent to the ear, and it may move *down* by step to $\hat{6}$ in the V-vi progression. This is not practicable in minor, however, because of the awkward +2 that results. All three situations are illustrated in Example 5-24. The voice leading away from a triad with a doubled 3rd must be handled carefully, since the conventions discussed in this chapter all assumed doubled roots.

Example 5-24.

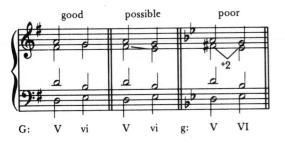

Three-part textures

The smoothest voice leading will find a complete triad followed by a triad with two roots and a 3rd (Exx. 5-25a and 5-25b) or a triad consisting of two roots and a 3rd followed by a complete triad (Exx. 5-25c and 5-25d). In other words, with roots a 2nd apart, the sequence will usually be complete to incomplete or incomplete to complete. Remember to resolve $\hat{7}$ to $\hat{1}$ in the V-vi progression—with the possible exception of cases in which $\hat{7}$ is in the inner voice in a major key.

Example 5-25.

SELF-TEST 5-7 Using all root relationships.
(Answers begin on page 548.)

A. Complete each progression. Make two versions of each, one for three parts and one for four parts.

G: I vi IV   d: i iv V   A: I vi ii   e: i V VI   Bb: iii vi V

B. Fill in alto and tenor parts in these two exercises.

C. Analyze the chords specified by these figured basses. Then compose a good melody line for each. Finally, fill in alto and tenor parts to make a four-part texture.

EXERCISE 5-7. See Workbook.

INSTRUMENTAL RANGES AND TRANSPOSITIONS

Before you begin composing a theory exercise, you must consider the performing medium you are writing for. While many of your exercises may require only a piano, a classroom situation makes it possible to compose exercises for various ensembles. You should try to get to know the performing capabilities of the individual class members and the capabilities of their instruments. Range is probably the most important element to keep in mind.

Instrumental ranges are apt to vary a great deal from one performer to the next, and the capabilities of your fellow class members should not be exceeded. Appendix A gives suggested ranges for some instruments, but remember that in many cases the high and low extremes require special handling. The *written range* in Appendix A refers to the transpositions that must be made for some instruments when copying out the individual parts from a score notated at concert pitch. For example, the lowest tone in the B♭ clarinet's range would be notated in the clarinet player's part as an E3, but the sounding pitch would be a D3.

One procedure to use when writing for an ensemble is this:

1. Notate the sounding ranges of the performers at the top of your page of manuscript paper.

2. Compose the exercise in the form of a reduced score upon as few staves as practicable. Keep an eye on the ranges.

3. Provide enough copies for the ensemble so that players will not have to huddle around a single stand. Instrumental parts should be copied onto separate sheets using correct transpositions.

SELF-TEST 5-8
(Answers begin on page 550.)

A. Notate the chords below for the specified instruments. Each chord is written at concert pitch, so transpose as needed for the performers. Use the correct clef for each instrument. Note that the instruments are listed in *score order,* the order used in Appendix A, which is not always the same as order by pitch.

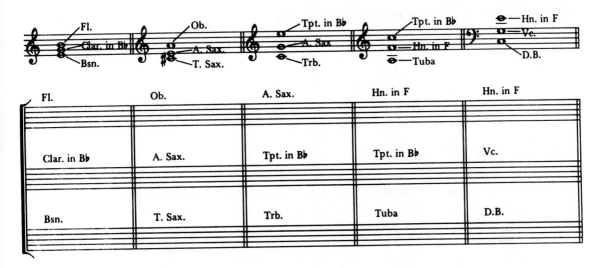

B. Here is a short chord progression to use in these exercises:

F: I   vi   ii   V   I

1. Make an arrangement for two alto saxophones and one tenor saxophone. Copy out the parts, using correct transpositions.

2. Make a four-part arrangement for SATB chorus.

EXERCISE 5-8. See Workbook.

CHAPTER SIX

HARMONIC PROGRESSION

INTRODUCTION

Before you can begin to compose convincing tonal music or to learn anything from harmonic analyses, you must learn which chord successions are typical of tonal harmony and which ones are not. Why is it that some chord successions seem to "progress," to move forward toward a goal, while others tend to wander, to leave our expectations unfulfilled? Compare the two progressions in Example 6-1. The first was composed following the principles that will be discussed in this chapter, but the chords for the second were selected through rolling a die. While the random example has a certain freshness to it, there is no doubt that the first one sounds more typical of tonal harmony. This chapter will explore this phenomenon, but first we must turn to a topic that concerns melody as well as harmony.

Example 6-1.

SEQUENCES AND THE CIRCLE OF FIFTHS

One of the important means of achieving unity in tonal music is through the use of a *sequence,* a pattern that is repeated immediately in the same voice but begins on a different pitch class. A *diatonic sequence* will keep the pattern in a single key, which means that modifiers of the intervals (major, minor, and so forth) will probably change, as in Example 6-2a. A *modulating sequence,* as in Example 6-2b, transposes the pattern to a new key. Modulating sequences will be discussed in more detail in a later chapter.

Example 6-2.

Four sequences occur in 7½ measures in Example 6-3. Sequences A, B, and D are modified sequences, because the pattern is not identical in each "leg" of the sequence. Sequence C is a true sequence, because the pattern is maintained exactly.

Example 6-3.   Bach, Partita No. 2, Gigue

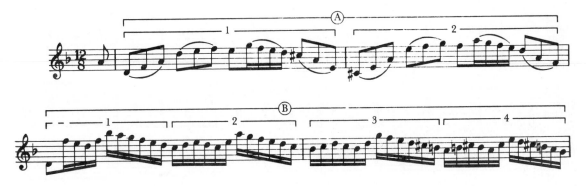

All of the sequences in Example 6-3 are descending—that is, the pattern is lower in pitch with each occurrence. Ascending sequences certainly do occur, as in Example 6-4.

Example 6-4. Handel, *Messiah,* "For Unto Us a Child Is Born"

The sequence in the Handel excerpt involves not just the melody, but the harmony as well. The harmonic sequence is:

I - IV - ii - V - iii - vi - IV - V

A sequence may be melodic or harmonic or both. One common sequential harmonic pattern is:

I - V - vi - iii - IV - I

This forms the basis of the famous Pachelbel "Canon."

Example 6-5. Pachelbel, Canon in D

D: I   V   vi   iii   IV   I   IV   V

But a sequential harmonic pattern that is far more significant to this chapter is the *circle-of-fifths progression,* which consists of roots related by descending 5ths (and ascending 4ths). While most of the 5ths (and 4ths) will be perfect, if the progression goes on long enough, a °5 (or +4) will appear (Ex. 6-6).

Example 6-6.

Progressions of this sort often appear in connection with melodic sequences, as in Example 6-7.

Example 6-7. Vivaldi, Concerto Grosso Op. 3, No. 11, I (soloists only)

While the chords in Example 6-7 are all in root position, if some or all of them were inverted, the progression would still contain a circle-of-fifths harmonic sequence.

Because the root progression of a 5th down (or 4th up) is so basic to tonal harmony, we will use the circle-of-fifths progression to show how diatonic chords are used in tonal music. We begin with the strongest of all such progressions, the V-I progression.

THE I AND V CHORDS

The ultimate harmonic goal of any tonal piece is the tonic triad, and this triad is often also the goal of many of the formal subdivisions of a composition. The tonic triad is most often preceded by a V (or V^7) chord, and it would be safe to say that $V^{(7)}$ and I together are the most essential elements of a tonal work. It is not difficult to find examples in which the harmony for several measures consists only of I and V chords, as in Example 6-8, which Mozart composed at the age of fifteen.

Example 6-8. Mozart, Symphony K. 114, III

THE II CHORD

If we extend our circle-of-fifths progression backward one step from the
V chord, we have the following progression:

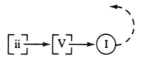

This diagram illustrates the normal function of ii to progress to V and of V to progress to I. The dotted line after the I indicates that if the piece continues, the I chord might be followed by anything.

Many phrases contain only a I-ii-V-I progression. Example 6-9 shows a typical soprano/bass framework for such a progression.

Example 6-9.

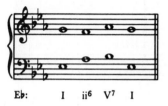

E♭:   I   ii⁶   V⁷   I

Play Example 6-9 and then compare it with Beethoven's version of this progression in Example 6-10. Here Beethoven uses a ii$^6_5$ instead of a ii⁶.

Example 6-10. Beethoven, Minuet

E♭:   I   ii$^6_5$ V⁷   I

THE VI CHORD

One more step in the circle of fifths brings us to the vi chord.

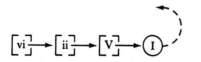

Put in root position, this progression illustrates an ostinato (repeated) bass pattern often found in popular tunes. Play Example 6-11 and see whether it sounds familiar.

Example 6-11.

Bb: I   vi   ii   V

The same progression, but in minor, is seen in Example 6-12. As we will demonstrate in a later section, chord functions in minor are almost identical to those in major.

Example 6-12. Verdi, *La forza del destino,* Act II (piano-vocal score)

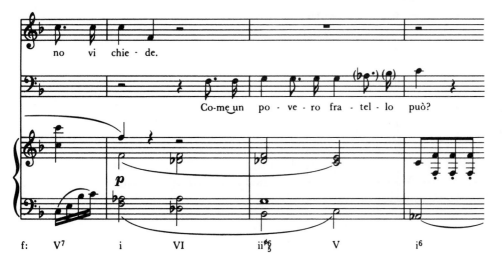

THE III CHORD

Another 5th backward brings us to the iii chord, far removed from the tonic triad.

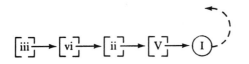

Beginning theory students often assume that the iii chord is frequently encountered and that they should be sure to include at least one iii chord in each exercise they write. This is not at all the case, at least not in the major mode. When $\hat{3}$ is found in a bass line, the chord above it is almost always a I⁶ rather than a iii. Similarly, a $\hat{7}$ in the melody is usually harmonized by V or vii° instead of iii. The iii chord does occur occasionally, of course. When it follows the natural descending 5ths progression, it will go to vi, as in Example 6-13. The use of the III chord in minor will be discussed on page 105.

Example 6-13. Bach, "O Ewigkeit, du Donnerwort"

F: I   vi   ii⁶   iii⁷   vi⁷   ii⁷ vii°⁶ I⁶   V

THE VII CHORD

Continuing the circle of fifths backward from iii brings us to vii°. While the vii°-iii progression does occur in sequential passages, the vii° usually acts instead as a substitute for V. Therefore, the customary goal of vii° outside of circle-of-fifths sequences is not iii, but the I chord.

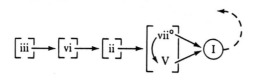

If vii° and V are used next to each other, V will usually follow the vii°, since the V is the stronger sound.

The most common use of vii° is in first inversion between two positions of the tonic triad: I-vii°⁶-I⁶ or I⁶-vii°⁶-I (Ex. 6-14).

Example 6-14. Handel, *Messiah*

d: i   vii°⁶   i⁶

THE IV CHORD

Still missing from our diagram is the IV chord, which lies a P5 *below* the tonic. The IV is an interesting chord because it has three common functions. In some cases, IV proceeds to a I chord, sometimes called a *plagal* progression. More frequently, IV is linked with ii; IV can substitute for ii (going directly to V or vii°), or IV can be followed by ii (as in IV-ii-V). These three common uses of the IV are summarized in the chord diagram.

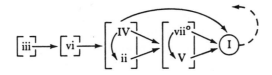

In Example 6-15 the IV appears in a plagal progression. The I$^6_4$ in the last measure indicates that the notes of the tonic triad are present at that point. However, the bracket with the V under it means that everything within the bracket functions as V. The I$^6_4$ is actually a kind of embellishment called a *cadential six-four,* which will be explained further in Chapter 9.

Example 6-15. Haydn, Sonata No. 35, II

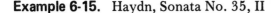

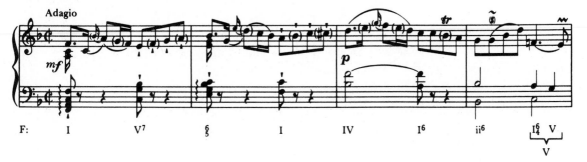

F: I   V⁷ $^6_5$ I   IV   I⁶   ii⁶   I$^6_4$ V
                                                                                                  V

Later on in the same sonata in which Example 6-15 appears, IV is used in its pre-dominant function (Ex. 6-16).

Example 6-16. Haydn, Sonata No. 35, III

COMMON EXCEPTIONS

The chord diagram on page 103 includes all of the diatonic triads and gives a reasonably accurate picture of the chord progressions most often found in tonal music. But to make our chart of chord functions more complete, we must include three commonly encountered exceptions to the norms discussed so far.

1. V-vi (the deceptive progression)
2. vi-V (skipping over IV or ii)
3. iii-IV (probably as common as iii-vi)

These additions are included in the diagram below, which may be considered complete for major keys. Remember that the dotted line after the I chord means that any chord may follow it.

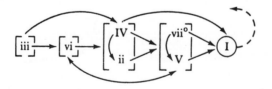

DIFFERENCES IN THE MINOR MODE

Most chords function the same way in minor as in major. However, the mediant triad, so seldom found in the major mode, is a common feature of the minor mode: it represents the relative major key, and minor-key music has a decided tendency to drift in that direction.

In addition, the variability of $\hat{6}$ and $\hat{7}$ will occasionally produce chords of different quality and function. The most important of these are the following:

1. The subtonic VII, sounding like the V in the key of the relative major—that is, a V of III.

2. The minor v, usually v^6, after which the $\downarrow\hat{7}$ will move to $\downarrow\hat{6}$, usually as part of a iv^6 chord.

The first of these possibilities is included in the chord diagram below.

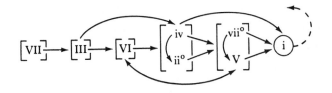

The second possibility, v^6-iv^6, is illustrated in Example 6-17.

Example 6-17. Bach, "Als vierzig Tag' nach Ostern"

CONCLUSION

The last two chord diagrams on pages 104-105 are somewhat complex, but both are based on the circle-of-fifths progression. Keep this in mind while you are learning them. At the same time, be aware that Bach and Beethoven did *not* make use of diagrams such as these. They lived and breathed the tonal harmonic style and had no need for the information the diagrams contain. Instead, the diagrams represent norms of harmonic practice observed by theorists over the years in the works of a large number of tonal composers. They do not represent rules; they are just guidelines for your use in analyzing and composing tonal music.

SELF-TEST 6-1
(Answers begin on page 551.)

A. Complete each progression to conform with the last two chord diagrams presented (pp. 104-105). The chord in the blank should be different from those on either side of it. In most cases there is more than one correct answer.

1. I   _?_   vi (___ or ___)   4. I   _?_   IV (___ or ___)
2. IV _?_ V (___ or ___)   5. vi _?_ V (___ or ___)
3. V _?_ IV (___ or ___)   6. vii° _?_ V (___)

B. Bracket any portions of these progressions that do not conform to the complete major and minor chord diagrams (pp. 104-105).

1. I V ii vii° I
2. i iv i VII i V i
3. I IV iii vi ii V I
4. I IV ii V vi ii V I

C. Analysis. Label all chords with roman numerals, and bracket any successions of chords that do not agree with the complete major and minor chord diagrams.

1. Bach, "O Herre Gott, dein göttlich Wort"

2. Vivaldi, Cello Sonata in G Minor, Sarabande*

In addition to labeling the chords, bracket any melodic sequences in the cello part. Non-chord tones in the solo part have not been put in parentheses, but the harmonic analysis can be done by concentrating upon the accompaniment. The key is g minor, in spite of what appears to be an incorrect key signature. Key signatures had not yet become standardized when this work was composed.

*Unfigured bass realization by S. Kostka.

D. Analyze the chords specified by these figured basses and add inner voices to make a four-part texture. Bracket all circle-of-fifths progressions, even those that contain only two chords.

E. Analyze this figured bass, then add a good soprano line and inner voices. Bracket all circle-of-fifths progressions.

F. Harmonize the melodies below by using root position major or minor (not diminished) triads in an acceptable progression. Try to give the bass a good contour while avoiding parallel and direct 5ths and 8ves with the melody. Be sure to include analysis. Finally, fill in one or two inner parts.

1

F:

2

e:

3

Eb:

4

d:

5

A:

G. Add an alto part (only) to mm. 1-2. Then compose a good soprano line for mm. 3-4 and fill in an alto part.

Bb: I   iii   IV   V   vi   ii   V   I   iii   vi   IV   ii   V   I

H. Review. Label the chords with roman numerals and inversion symbols (where needed).

F: vii°⁶   e: ___   A: ___   g: ___   Ab: ___   b: ___   G: ___   f: ___

c#: ___   D: ___   Eb: ___   f#: ___   E: ___   d: ___   Bb: ___   c: ___

EXERCISE 6-1. See Workbook.

CHAPTER SEVEN

TRIADS IN FIRST INVERSION

INTRODUCTION

Listen to the short phrase below, paying special attention to the bass line.

Example 7-1.

It's not bad, but it could be improved. The melody line is fine, having both shape and direction, but the bass seems too repetitive and too rigid. Compare Example 7-1 with Example 7-2.

Example 7-2. Haydn, Sonata No. 33, III

Now the bass line is improved through the use of inverted chords (indicated by circled bass notes in the example). Although the harmony is the same, the inverted chords have created a bass line with a more interesting contour and with more tonal variety.

Most phrases of tonal music contain at least one inverted chord, and the inversions usually serve the purposes that we have just demonstrated. We are not saying that a phrase without inverted chords is poorly composed—it just depends upon what effect the composer is after. For example, minuets from the Classical period often contain phrases with chords that are all in root position.

BASS ARPEGGIATION

One way in which first inversion triads often originate is simply through bass arpeggiation. If you look back at the first measure of Example 7-2, you will see that D4 is the primary bass note in the measure. The F#4 serves the dual purpose of providing the 3rd of the chord and of giving the bass some variety. A similar situation is found in the first two beats of the second measure. When you analyze a bass arpeggiation such as these, you should identify the arpeggiations only with arabic numerals (as in Ex. 7-2) or omit symbols altogether (as in Ex. 7-3).

Accompaniment figures in keyboard music often involve faster arpeggiations. Two examples by Haydn are shown below (Exx. 7-3 and 7-4). In both, the fundamental bass line is the one shown in the textural reduction. The other pitches played by the left hand should be considered as inner voices that are simply filling in the chords. They are not part of the bass line, so we would not consider these notes to be creating inversions at all.

Example 7-3.   Haydn, Sonata No. 43, I

Example 7-4. Haydn, Sonata No. 45, I

Textural reduction

Textural reductions such as those of Examples 7-3 and 7-4 appear throughout this text. Their purpose is to simplify the texture and make the voice leading easier to understand. Notice that in the reduction of Example 7-4 the E♭5 has been transposed up one octave from the original. The octave transposition helps clarify the essentially conjunct (stepwise) nature of the melodic line.

SUBSTITUTED FIRST INVERSION TRIADS

First inversion triads are often used as *substitutes* for root position triads, instead of coming about through bass arpeggiation. One reason for using such inversions is to improve the contour of the bass line. Another is to provide a greater variety of pitches in the bass line. A third reason is to lessen the importance of V and I chords that do not serve as goals of harmonic motion. Instances of this third type can be seen in Examples 7-3 and 7-4, where dominant chords are inverted. Example 7-5 contains a substituted inverted triad in the V6, which allows the ascending stepwise motion of the bass to continue. The I6 is an example of an arpeggiation following a structurally more important root position chord. The use of the I6 provides tonal variety and allows the bass to imitate the soprano figure from the previous beat.

Example 7-5. Bach, "Schmücke dich, o liebe Seele"

F: I   V   vi   (V⁶)   I   ⑥   V⁷   I

The diminished triad was used almost exclusively in first inversion through-out much of the tonal era. Earlier composers had considered a sonority to be acceptable only if all of the intervals above the *bass* were consonant, and, as the diagram illustrates, a dissonant °5 or +4 occurs above the bass of a diminished triad unless it is in first inversion.

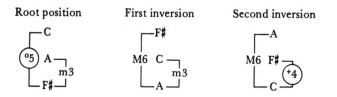

Tonal composers, while perhaps being unaware of the historical background, accepted for a time the tradition of using the diminished triad only in first inversion.

One first inversion triad that should *not* be freely substituted for the root position is vi⁶ (or VI⁶). A good rule to remember is that V in root position should not be followed by vi⁶. The reason for this can best be understood by playing Example 7-6 and comparing the effect of the V-vi and V-vi⁶ pro-gressions. The V-vi sounds fine—a good example of a deceptive progression—but the vi⁶ sounds like a mistake.

Example 7-6.

One common context for the vi⁶ chord is between a root position I and a root position ii, as in Example 7-7a. The vi⁶ will also occur occasionally as part of a sequential pattern, as in Example 7-7b.

Example 7-7.

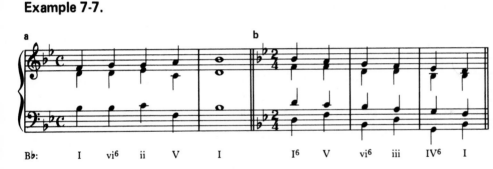

PARALLEL SIXTH CHORDS

Most passages use a reasonable balance of root position and first inversion triads, but there are many passages in which this is not true. Some styles call for a preponderance of root position chords. On the other hand, a whole series of parallel first inversion triads (or *sixth chords,* from figured bass symbols) is often found, especially in sequences. Chords used in parallel motion in this way generally do not function in the usual fashion. Instead, they serve as passing chords, connecting some chord at the beginning of the passage to some chord at the end of it. In Example 7-8 the parallel motion connects the root position I chord in m. 4 with another root position I chord in m. 7. The roman numerals in the sixth chord passage are in parentheses to show that the chords are not functioning in their usual manners.

Example 7-8. Haydn, Symphony No. 104, I

Textural reduction

In the textural reduction of Example 7-8 the line in mm. 2-3 connecting D3 to C♯4 shows that a simplified version of the bass line would have stepwise motion here (m2 down) instead of the leap. Notice also the parallel 5ths in mm. 5-7. Haydn disguised the 5ths in the original through the use of non-chord tones. The usual technique used to avoid parallel 5ths in a sixth-chord passage is to put the root of each chord in the melody, thus producing acceptable parallel 4ths instead of objectionable parallel 5ths (Ex. 7-9).

Example 7-9.

D: IV⁶   iii⁶   ii⁶   I⁶   vii°⁶

PART WRITING FIRST INVERSION TRIADS

Composition exercises using triads in first inversion as well as in root position are much more satisfying musically than are exercises restricted to root position only. Previous suggestions concerning spacing and voice leading still apply, of course, and should be considered together with those that follow.

Four-part textures

Inverted triads are nearly always complete in four-part textures. Since there are four voices and only three chord members, one of the members obviously will have to be doubled. The following suggestions should prove helpful.

1. In a contrapuntal texture—that is, in a texture consisting of relatively independent melodic lines—the doubling to use is the one that results from the best voice leading.

2. In a homophonic texture—that is, one that is primarily chordal or consists of a melody with chordal accompaniment—the doubling selected should be the one that provides the desired effect.

3. In any texture, it is usually best not to double the leading tone.

The first of these suggestions probably needs no further explanation. Concerning the second suggestion, you should play Example 7-10, listening carefully to the different sonorities produced. If possible, you should also hear the example sung and performed by several combinations of instruments. The four parts of the example are presented in what is generally considered the order of preference on the part of composers of tonal music. However, this ordering is not to be interpreted as a rule. The quality of the sonority is affected as much by spacing as it is by doubling, as you will discover by comparing the last two chords in Example 7-10.

Example 7-10.

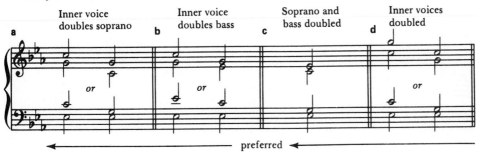

A doubled leading tone usually results in or implies parallel 8ves because of the strong tendency of $\hat{7}$ to resolve to $\hat{1}$. If you play Examples 7-11a through 7-11c, you will probably agree that Example 7-11c produces the most pleasing effect. Example 7-11a is obviously incorrect because of the parallel 8ves. But Example 7-11b, which avoids the parallels, still produces an unpleasant effect, probably because the parallels are still implied by the doubled leading tone.

Example 7-11.

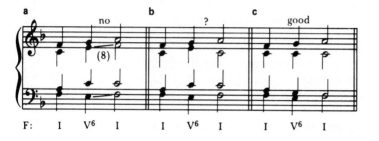

Three-part textures

Inverted triads are usually complete in three-part writing. While incomplete inverted triads do occur, they are not used with the same frequency as incomplete root position triads. If a member of the triad is omitted, it will almost always be the 5th. The omitted member obviously cannot be the 3rd, since that is the bass note. If the root is omitted, the resulting sonority may be heard *not* as an inverted triad, but as root position triad, as in Example 7-12.

Example 7-12.

Example 7-13 is from a composition for TTB (Tenor, Tenor, Bass) chorus. The tenor parts sound an octave lower than written. There are two incomplete I⁶ chords in this excerpt. In the first of these the 5th is omitted, as we would expect. In the second incomplete I⁶, however, the root is omitted, but the listener recognizes the sonority as representing a I⁶ because it follows a V chord. Notice also that the IV at the beginning of m. 46 could also be analyzed as a ii⁶, as in Example 7-12 above. All of the other inverted triads in the excerpt are complete.

Example 7-13. Schubert, "Bardengesang"

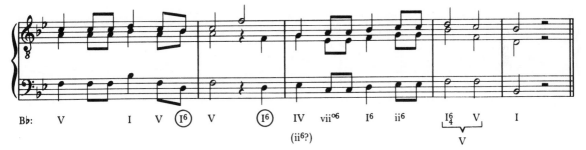

SUMMARY

1. Triads in inversion are not at all unusual in tonal music. In fact, most phrases contain at least one.

2. First inversions come about either as *arpeggiations* or *substitutions*.

3. They are used for variety, to improve the bass line, and to lessen the weight of some I and V chords, as well as for other reasons.

4. First inversion also allows the use of *diminished triads* (and sometimes augmented ones), since these are not commonly used in root position.

5. *Parallel sixth chords* is one term used for a passage that features first inversion triads in parallel motion.

6. If a tone must be omitted from a triad in first inversion, it should usually be the 5th. This would generally occur only in three-part textures.

7. If a tone is to be doubled, any tone but the leading tone will do. In four parts, the preferred doublings are soprano or bass with an inner voice.

SELF-TEST 7-1
(Answers begin on page 554.)

A. Analysis.

1. Bracket the longest series of complete parallel sixth chords you can find in this excerpt. Do not attempt a roman numeral analysis. Does the voice leading in the sixth-chord passage resemble more closely Example 7-8 or Example 7-9?

Mozart, Sonata K. 279, III

2. Label all chords with roman numerals. Then classify the doubling in each inverted triad according to the methods shown in Example 7-10.

Bach, "Herzliebster Jesu, was hast du"

3. Label all chords with roman numerals. Write out the contour of the bass line in quarter-note heads (without rhythm). Can you find part or all of the bass line hidden in the melody?

Beethoven, Sonata Op. 2, No. 1, I

B. The following excerpt is from Mozart's *Eine kleine Nachtmusik*. Supply the missing tenor line (viola part in the original), and then compare your result with Mozart's (in Appendix B).

G: V⁷   vi   ii⁶   V⁷   V   I⁶   V   I

C. Supply alto and tenor lines for the following excerpts.

Bb: I   6   V   e: i   V⁶   i   D: vi   ii⁶   V   vi
                                            ⁵₃

Eb: IV   V   I⁶   IV⁶   f#:   i   V⁶   i   iv   d: i⁶   iv⁶   V   i

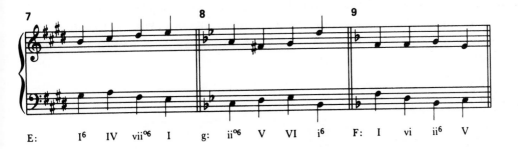

E: I⁶   IV   vii°⁶   I   g: ii°⁶   V   VI   i⁶   F: I   vi   ii⁶   V

G: V⁶   V   vi   ii⁶   b: i⁶   ii°⁶   V   VI   A: V   I⁶   IV   V

D. Using the first six problems from **Part C**, add an alto line to each to create a three-part texture.

E. Analyze the chords specified by these figured basses, then add alto and tenor parts.

F. The excerpt below is from the Gavotte from Bach's French Suite No. 5. Supply the missing alto line (only), and then compare your result with Bach's original three-part version (Appendix B). Since this is written for a keyboard instrument, you do not need to worry about the range of the alto part.

G: I   V⁶   vi   iii⁶   IV   ii⁶   V   (⁶₄   6   7)   I

G. Analyze the chords implied by the soprano and bass lines below, remembering to use only triads in root position and first inversion. Then add alto and tenor parts to make a four-part texture.

H. The following example is reduced from Beethoven's Sonata Op. 79, III. Analyze the implied harmonies (more than one good solution is possible) and add two inner parts, one on each staff.

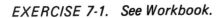

I. Continue your solution to Part E with a second four-measure segment, similar to the first.

EXERCISE 7-1. **See Workbook.**

CHAPTER EIGHT

CADENCES, PHRASES, AND PERIODS

MUSICAL FORM

Understanding tonal harmony requires more than the knowledge of how each chord tends to function harmonically and how the voice leading might bring the chord into being. We must also give some consideration to musical *form,* the ways in which a composition is shaped to create a meaningful musical experience for the listener.

A study of the forms of lengthy compositions is beyond the scope of this text. However, it will be helpful for you to learn something of the harmonic basis of the smaller building blocks that combine to produce those larger forms.

CADENCES

While the ultimate harmonic goal of a tonal composition is the final tonic triad, there will also be many interior harmonic goals found within the piece, some of them tonic triads and some of them not. These interior goals may be reached at a fairly regular rate (often every four measures); or sometimes their appearances may not form a pattern at all. We use the term *cadence* to mean a harmonic goal, specifically the chords used at the goal. There are several types of cadences commonly found in tonal music. Some cadences sound more or less conclusive, or final, while others leave us off balance, feeling a need for the music to continue.

Locating the cadences in a composition is easier to do than it is to explain. Remember that what you are listening for is a goal, so there will often be a slowing down through the use of longer note values, but even a piece that never slows down (a "perpetuum mobile") will contain cadences. As you listen to the examples in this chapter, you will realize that you are already aurally familiar with tonal cadences and that finding them is not a complicated process.

There is a standard terminology used for classifying the various kinds of cadences, and the terms apply to both major and minor keys. One very important type of cadence consists of a tonic triad preceded by some form of

V or vii°. This kind of cadence is called an *authentic cadence* (which is an unfortunate term, since it implies that all of the others are less than authentic). The *perfect authentic cadence* (abbreviated PAC) consists of a V-I (or V⁷-I) progression, with both the V and the I in root position and $\hat{1}$ in the melody over the I chord (Ex. 8-1). The PAC is the most final sounding of all cadences. Most tonal compositions end with a PAC, but such cadences may also be found elsewhere in a piece.

Example 8-1. Bach, *Well-Tempered Clavier,* Book II, Prelude 10

An *imperfect authentic cadence* (IAC) is usually defined simply as any authentic cadence that is not a PAC. However, it is useful to identify several subcategories, as follows.

1. *Root position IAC:* Like a PAC, but $\hat{3}$ or $\hat{5}$ is in the melody over the I chord (Ex. 8-2).

Example 8-2. Bach, *Well-Tempered Clavier,* Book II, Prelude 12

2. *Inverted IAC:* V⁽⁷⁾-I, but with either or both of the chords inverted (Ex. 8-3).

Example 8-3. Schumann, "Nachtlied," Op. 96, No. 1

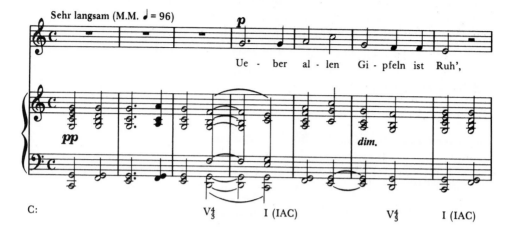

3. *Leading-tone IAC:* Some form of vii°-I, the vii° substituting for a V chord (Ex. 8-4).

Example 8-4. Bach, "Befiehl du deine Wege"

The root position IAC is certainly the most final sounding of the three IAC types, and you may find some compositions that end with such a cadence. The other types are limited almost exclusively to less important interior cadences.

Remember that not every V-I progression constitutes an authentic cadence. Only when the I chord seems to serve as the goal of a longer passage—usually at least a few measures—would we term a V-I progression a cadence. This same distinction also applies to the other cadence types.

A *deceptive cadence* (DC) results when the ear expects a V-I authentic cadence but hears V-? instead. The ? is usually a submediant triad, as in Example 8-5, but others are possible. A DC produces a very unstable feeling and would never be used to end a tonal work. Remember that V-vi involves special part-writing problems. Review Example 5-24.

Example 8-5. Haydn, Sonata No. 4, II

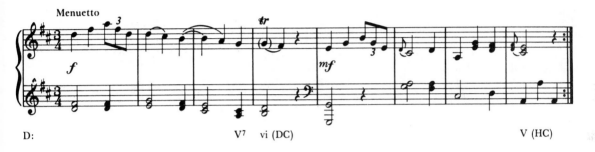

The *half cadence* (HC) is a very common type of unstable or "progressive" cadence. The HC ends with a V chord, which can be preceded by any other chord (Ex. 8-6).

Example 8-6. Haydn, Sonata No. 44, II

The *Phrygian half cadence* (Ex. 8-7) is a special name given to the iv⁶-V HC in minor. The name refers to a cadence found in the period of modal polyphony (before 1600), but it does not imply that the music is actually in the

Phrygian mode.* Notice, incidentally, that Example 8-7 contains a deceptive *progression* (V^7-VI), but not a deceptive *cadence,* since the goal of the passage is the V in m. 4, not the VI in m. 3.

Example 8-7.   Schumann, "Folk Song," Op. 68, No. 9

A *plagal cadence* (PC) typically involves a IV-I progression. While plagal cadences are usually final sounding, they are not as important in tonal music as the authentic cadence. In fact, a plagal cadence is usually added on as a kind of tag following a PAC. A familiar example of this is the "Amen" sung at the end of hymns, as in Example 8-8.

Example 8-8.   Dykes, "Holy, Holy, Holy!"

*Modal polyphony used a number of scalar patterns seldom employed by tonal composers. One of these was the Phrygian mode, which used a scale pattern the same as E to E with no accidentals.

The definitions of cadence types given above are standard, for the most part, and they will apply to most cadences found in tonal music. Exceptions will be found, however, in which cases the more general definition listed in the table below should be applied.

Cadence type	First chord	Second chord
Authentic	Contains leading tone	Tonic
Plagal	Does not contain leading tone	Tonic
Deceptive	Contains leading tone	Not tonic
Half	Does not contain leading tone	Not tonic

A still more general but useful method of classifying cadences puts them into two groups: *conclusive* (authentic and plagal) and *progressive* (deceptive and half).

CHECKPOINT

Match the cadence-type abbreviations with the definitions and examples.

Conclusive cadences

1. PAC _____

2. Root position IAC _____

3. Inverted IAC _____

4. Leading-tone IAC _____

5. PC _____

Progressive cadences

6. HC _____

7. Phrygian HC _____

8. DC _____

Definitions and examples

a. V-I, both in root position, with $\hat{3}$ or $\hat{5}$ in the melody over the I chord

b. IV-I

c. ?-V

d. V-vi

e. vii°6-I

f. V-I6

g. V-I, both in root position, with $\hat{1}$ in the melody over the I chord

h. iv6-V in minor

MOTIVES AND PHRASES

A *motive* is the smallest identifiable musical idea. A motive can consist of a pitch pattern or a rhythmic pattern, or both, as you can see below.

Of the two aspects of a pitch/rhythm motive, rhythm is probably the stronger and more easily identified when it reappears later in a composition. It is best to use *motive* only to refer to those musical ideas that are "developed" (worked out or used in different ways) in a composition.

A *phrase* is a relatively independent musical idea terminated by a cadence. A *phrase segment* is a distinct portion of a phrase, but it is not a phrase either because it is not terminated by a cadence or because it seems too short to be relatively independent. Phrases are usually labeled with lower-case letters (a, b, c, and so on), as in Example 8-9.

Example 8-9. Beethoven, Symphony No. 6, Op. 68, I

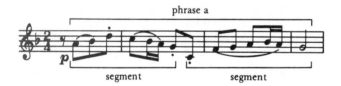

As you might guess from the definition of "phrase," there is a good deal of subjectivity involved in identifying phrases. What sounds like a phrase to one listener may be a phrase segment to another listener. The issue cannot be decided by finding cadences, because phrase segments frequently end with cadences. Also, phrases are often extended by means of a deceptive cadence followed by an authentic cadence, or they may be extended by repetition of the cadence, as in the "a" phrase of Example 8-10 (mm. 1-6). The final phrase of this minuet, marked "a," returns the "a" phrase with an added repetition of the first phrase segment, creating an eight-measure phrase. The "b" and "c" phrases also contain repetitions of their opening phrase segments, but with some variation in each case.

Example 8-10. Haydn, Sonata No. 15, II

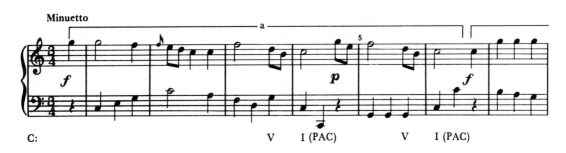

The last note of one phrase sometimes serves as the first note of the next one, a process referred to as *elision*. An even more extreme overlap can be seen by looking back at Example 8-3, where the fourth measure of the first phrase in the accompaniment serves also as the first measure of the first phrase of the song.

MOZART: "AN DIE FREUDE"

The concepts we have presented so far in this chapter are all well illustrated in Example 8-11. This deceptively simple song was composed by Mozart when he was eleven years old. The singer doubles the right hand of the piano part throughout, and a nice effect is obtained in performance if the left hand of the piano part is doubled by a cello or a bassoon.

Example 8-11. Mozart, "An die Freude," K. 53

Cadences occur regularly every four measures in this song, each cadence marking the end of a phrase. Since the texture contains only two lines, the chords are necessarily incomplete, but the implied harmonies at the cadences are clear enough and have been labeled for you. The cadences illustrate all of the types discussed in this chapter, with the exception of the PC. Notice that two cadences occur in the key of the dominant (C), and one occurs in the key of the supertonic (g). Since we do not lose track aurally of the key of F as we listen to the song, it would be appropriate to refer to mm. 13-24 as embellishments of V and ii, rather than as a true change of tonal center. All the cadences are listed in the following table.

Measure	Cadence type	Key
4	DC	F
8	Root position IAC	F
12	HC	F
16	DC	C
20	PAC	C
24	Inverted IAC	g
28	HC	F
32	Leading-tone IAC	F
36	DC	F
40	PAC	F

Many of the phrases in this song can be heard as consisting of two phrase segments. For instance, mm. 1-2 and mm. 3-4 are two segments that combine to make the first phrase. While most people would agree that the mm. 1-2 segment is too short to be a phrase, the distinction is not always clear, and it is perfectly possible for two informed musicians to disagree about this and other examples.

"An die Freude" also contains motives, of course. Two of the most important are primarily rhythmic: ♩. ♫ and ♫♫ . The grace note in m. 22 is performed as an eighth note on beat 1, so m. 22 is an instance of the second motive.

PERIOD FORMS

Phrases are often combined to form a larger structural unit called a *period*. A period typically consists of two phrases in an antecedent-consequent (or question-answer) relationship, that relationship being established by means of a stronger cadence at the end of the second phrase. The most commonly encountered patterns are the following:

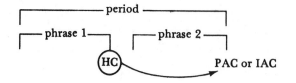

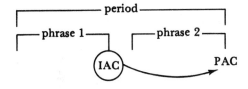

Notice that by definition the phrase endings in a period must be different. If both phrases are identical, the result is not a period but a *repeated phrase*. Repetition is important in tonal music, but it does not contribute to the growth of a musical form.

We use the term *parallel period* if both phrases *begin* with similar or identical material. Example 8-12 illustrates a parallel period.

Example 8-12. Schubert, "Am Meer"

A formal diagram of Example 8-12 would show the parallel relationship between the phrases by labeling them a and a′ (pronounced "a prime").

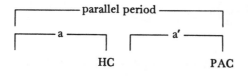

Sometimes the parallel relationship between phrases is not so obvious. In Example 8-13 the melody of the second phrase begins like the first, but it is a step higher. Still, the phrase beginnings are probably similar enough to call this a parallel period.

Example 8-13.   Mozart, Violin Sonata K. 377, III

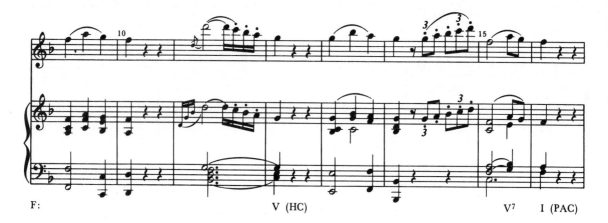

A period in which the phrase beginnings are not similar is called a *contrasting period*. Example 8-14 illustrates a contrasting period.

Example 8-14. Beethoven, Violin Sonata Op. 12, No. 1, III

While a period typically has two phrases, one an antecedent and one a consequent, some periods have more. One way of constructing a three-phrase period is illustrated by Example 8-15, in which the consequent phrase is repeated.

Example 8-15. Mozart, Sonata K. 283, I

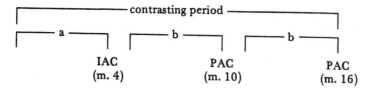

A *double period* consists typically of four phrases in two pairs, the cadence at the end of the second pair being stronger than the cadence at the end of the first pair.

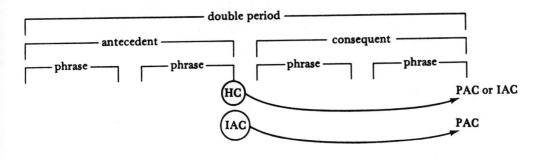

There are several things that should be pointed out about this diagram. First, notice that this structure is much like a period, with the only difference being that each half consists here of a pair of phrases instead of one phrase. Also notice that the first two phrases will probably not form a period according to our original definition. Finally, notice that a *repeated period* is not the same as a double period because a double period requires contrasting cadences.

Double periods are called *parallel* or *contrasting* according to whether or not the melodic material that begins the two halves of the period is similar. Example 8-16 illustrates a parallel double period, and its structure is outlined in the following diagram.

Example 8-16. Beethoven, Sonata Op. 26, I

V (HC)

V (HC)   V⁷   I (PAC)

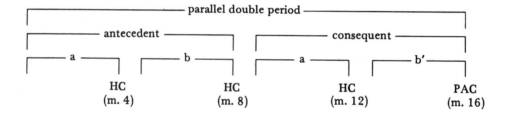

Because the first and third phrases have the same cadence, the third phrase in the diagram is labeled a, not a′, even though the original a is somewhat ornamented when it returns as the third phrase.

Often, several phrases will seem to constitute a formal unit other than a period or double period. The term *phrase group* is used for such situations. Before assigning this term, however, study the music (especially the cadences) closely to see whether a passage might be analyzed as a variant of some period form.

SUMMARY

The basic definitions of most of the concepts introduced in this chapter are given below.

Musical form: the ways in which a composition is shaped to create a meaningful musical experience for the listener.

Cadence: a harmonic goal; the chords used at a harmonic goal.

Authentic cadence: some form of V or vii° followed by I or I⁶.

Perfect authentic cadence (PAC): root position V or V⁷ followed by a root position I with $\hat{1}$ in the soprano over the I chord.

Imperfect authentic cadence (IAC): any authentic cadence that is not a PAC. The possibilities are root position IAC, inverted IAC, and leading-tone IAC.

Deceptive cadence (DC): V followed by something other than I, usually vi.

Half cadence: a cadence that ends on V.

Phrygian half cadence: iv⁶-V in minor.

Plagal cadence (PC): IV-I.

Motive: the smallest identifiable musical idea.

Phrase: a relatively independent musical idea terminated by a cadence.

Phrase segment: a distinct portion of a phrase.

Period: two phrases (sometimes more) in an antecedent-consequent relationship, that relationship being established by means of a stronger cadence at the end of the second phrase. Parallel or contrasting according to the beginnings of the phrases.

Double period: four phrases in two pairs, the cadence at the end of the second pair being stronger than the cadence at the end of the first pair. Parallel or contrasting according to the beginnings of the first and third phrases.

Repeated phrase or *period:* repetition, possibly with variation, but with the same cadences. Repetition of a formal unit does not produce a new kind of formal unit.

Phrase group: two or more phrases that seem to belong to the same formal unit, but not in period or double period form.

SELF-TEST 8-1
(Answers begin on page 559.)

A. Analysis. The cadence chords have been analyzed for you in each example.

1. Make a diagram of this excerpt similar to the diagrams used in the text. Include phrase labels (a, b, and so on), cadence types and measure numbers, and the form of the excerpt. In addition, label the first seven chords in the first phrase.

Beethoven, Sonata Op. 10, No. 3, III

2. Diagram the form of this excerpt. In addition, point out any *sequences* (review Chapter 6), either exact or modified, that occur in the melody.

Mozart, Sonata K. 284, II

3. There is certainly more than one way to interpret this famous theme. Most writers seem to prefer the three-phrase analysis shown here, the third phrase being an unusually long one (mm. 9-17). What would the form of the theme have been if it had ended in m. 8? Is there any way to hear the entire theme as an expansion of that form?

Beethoven, Sonata Op. 13, III

4. Diagram this excerpt. See if you can find an example of 8ves by contrary motion (review pp. 77-78) between the melody and bass.

Chopin, Mazurka Op. 33, No. 2

B. Aural analysis. Sing through the following tunes and try to imagine aurally the cadence chords, or play the tunes on the piano and try to play the cadence chords. Then make a formal diagram of each song.

1. "Daisy"

2. "Take Me Out to the Ball Game" (four phrases)

C. Review. Notate the chords in the keys and bass positions indicated.

EXERCISE 8-1. See Workbook.

CHAPTER NINE

TRIADS IN SECOND INVERSION

INTRODUCTION

It would be logical to assume that second inversion triads are used in tonal music just as first inversion triads are: as bass arpeggiations and as substitutes for the root position. However, this is only partly true. For while both first and second inversion triads are created through bass arpeggiations, second inversion triads are not used as substitutes for the root position. The reason is that the second inversion of a triad is considered to be a much less stable sonority than either of the other two bass positions. For centuries before the development of tonal harmony, the interval of a P4 had been considered a dissonance if the *lowest voice* in the texture was sounding the bottom pitch of the P4. While each of the sonorities in Example 9-1 contains a P4 (or a P4 plus a P8), the first two are considered to be consonant because the interval of a P4 does not involve the lowest voice. The other two sonorities are dissonant in the tonal style, although our twentieth-century ears may not readily hear the dissonance.

Example 9-1.

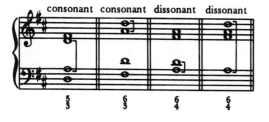

Notice that diminished and augmented $^6_4$ chords would also contain dissonant intervals above the bass—an +4 and a °4, respectively.

Because the composers of the tonal era recognized the instability of the $^6_4$ (six-four) chord (the only position in which there is a 4th above the bass), the chord is not used as a substitute for the more stable root position or first inversion sonorities. It is used in bass arpeggiations, as well as in several other contexts to be described below.

BASS ARPEGGIATION AND THE MELODIC BASS

The six-four chord may come about through a bass arpeggiation involving a root position triad, a first inversion triad, or both (Ex. 9-2).

Example 9-2.   Mendelssohn, Symphony No. 4, Op. 90, I

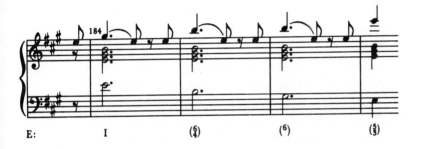

Your analysis of the "real" bass note will depend upon the context, taking into account such factors as metric placement, duration, and register. The figures in parentheses in Example 9-2 are often omitted when analyzing a passage employing an arpeggiated bass.

Another somewhat incidental way in which six-four chords may be formed is through a melodic bass. If the bass part has an important melodic line instead of fulfilling its usual supporting role, then any number of inverted chords may result. Since a melodic bass is no longer the harmonic foundation of the texture, inversions should not be indicated in such a passage. For instance, the bass melody in Example 9-3 is accompanied only by repeated A's and C's, implying the tonic harmony in F major. It would not be correct to analyze the excerpt as beginning with a I$^6_4$.

Example 9-3. Beethoven, String Quartet Op. 59, No. 1, I

THE CADENTIAL TONIC SIX-FOUR

Besides its appearance in a bass arpeggiation or a melodic bass, the six-four chord tends to be used in three stereotyped contexts. If you compare the two halves of Example 9-4 below, you can see that they have much in common. Both begin with a tonic triad and end with a perfect authentic cadence. In Example 9-4b, however, the movement from ii^6 to V is momentarily delayed by a I$^6_4$ in a *metrically stronger position*. This is a very typical illustration of the cadential six-four, the most familiar of all six-four uses.

Example 9-4.

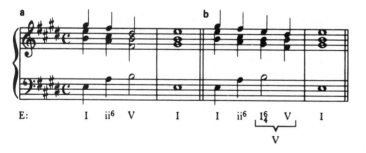

Examples from the literature of the cadential six-four may be seen in Example 6-15 (p. 103) and Example 7-13 (p. 119), as well as in later examples in this chapter.

Theorists have long debated whether it is better to analyze the cadential six-four as I$^6_4$-V or simply as V, treating $\hat{1}$ and $\hat{3}$ as non-chord tones. On the one hand, all the notes of the tonic triad *are* present, but on the other hand, the *function* of the cadential I$^6_4$ is clearly decorative: it does not substitute for the root position tonic. The analytical symbols used in Example 9-4 and throughout this text are a compromise and reflect the validity of both schools of thought.

The voice leading in the upper parts into and away from the cadential I$^6_4$ is usually smooth, as in Example 9-4. The most dramatic demonstration of the delaying character of the cadential I$^6_4$ is found at the cadenza of many solo concertos. In such cases, the orchestra usually stops on a I$^6_4$, after which the soloist performs the cadenza. No matter what the length of the cadenza, it eventually reaches V and, simultaneously with the return of the orchestra, resolves to I. In a cadenza played by a single-line instrument, the V chord will often be represented by a single tone or a trill, as in Example 9-5.

Example 9-5. Mozart, Violin Concerto K. 271a, III

One special use of the III+6 in minor is so similar to the cadential six-four that it will be discussed here. If you play the cadences in Example 9-6 and compare them, it will be obvious to you that the same principle—the momentary delay of the dominant—is operating in each case. The cadential III+6, which is not often used, is clearly a *linear event* and not part of a III+-V progression. A cadential iii6 in the major mode is also a possibility, but it is not often found.

Example 9-6.

THE PASSING SIX-FOUR

Second inversion triads are frequently encountered harmonizing the middle note of a three-note scalar figure in the bass. The figure may be ascending or descending. While any triad may be used as a passing six-four chord, those in Example 9-7 are the most common and are found in both major and minor modes. The passing six-four usually falls on a weak beat and typically features smooth voice leading, as in Example 9-7. As with the cadential six-four, some theorists prefer not to assign a roman numeral to passing six-fours because of their weak harmonic function. In this text we will indicate this weak function by putting such roman numerals in parentheses.

Example 9-7.

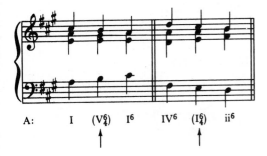

A: I   (V⁶₄)   I⁶   IV⁶   (I⁶₄)   ii⁶

Example 9-8 contains both a passing I⁶₄ (m. 25) and a cadential I⁶₄ (m. 27) in a three-part texture. The first inversion chords in mm. 24-26 are all substituted first inversions. Notice that the melody in mm. 24-27 is an embellished stepwise descent from A5 to B4.

Example 9-8.   Mozart, Sonata K. 309, III

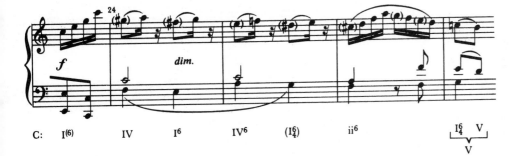

C: I⁽⁶⁾   IV   I⁶   IV⁶   (I⁶₄)   ii⁶   I⁶₄ V
                                                                      V

Textural reduction

Longer stepwise motions in the bass often use passing six-four chords, as in Example 9-9. The textural reduction shows that the melody is also essentially stepwise and moves for several measures in parallel 6ths with the bass.

Example 9-9.   Mozart, Symphony No. 40, K. 550, IV (piano score)

Textural reduction

THE PEDAL SIX-FOUR

One way of elaborating a static root position triad is to move the 3rd and 5th of the triad up by step then back down by step to their original positions. The sonority that results is a six-four chord (Ex. 9-10).

Example 9-10.

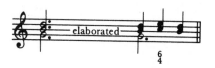

The next example shows the same elaboration in a more interesting musical context. Compare Example 9-10 with Example 9-11.

Example 9-11. Corelli, Concerto Grosso Op. 6, No. 8, Pastorale

Because this elaboration is similar to a pedal point (Chapter 11), it is called a *pedal six-four* (some theorists call it an embellishing or stationary six-four). The roman numeral beneath a pedal six-four is put in parentheses to indicate its weak harmonic function.

The pedal six-four typically falls on a weak beat and employs stepwise voice leading. While any chord might be embellished by a pedal six-four, the most common progressions are V-(I$^6_4$)-V and I-(IV$^6_4$)-I, as in Example 9-12.

Example 9-12.

The bass usually remains stationary after the pedal six-four chord, awaiting the return of the root position triad. However, this does not always happen. In Example 9-13 the IV$^6_4$ moves on to V^6 instead of back to I.

Example 9-13. Mozart, Quartet K. 465, I

PART WRITING FOR SECOND INVERSION TRIADS

In a four-part texture, the bass (5th of the chord) should be doubled. Exceptions to this are rarely encountered in tonal music. The other voices generally move as smoothly as possible—often by step—both into and out of the six-four chord. In a three-part texture, it is generally best to have all members of the triad present (Ex. 9-14a). But sometimes the root or 3rd is omitted, in which case the *5th* is doubled (Exx. 9-14b and 9-14c).

Example 9-14.

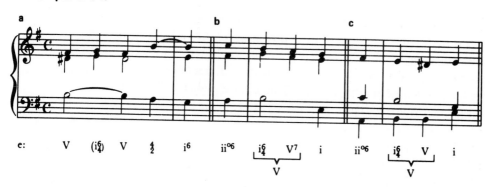

SUMMARY

Six-four chords may occur freely through bass arpeggiation or when the bass line is itself a melody. Other than these contexts, six-four chords tend to belong to one of three classifications.

1. *Cadential six-four:* A I$^6_4$ on an accented beat, delaying a V chord. In triple meter the accented beat for the I$^6_4$ will often be beat 2.

2. *Passing six-four:* A six-four chord on the second of three stepwise bass notes. Most common are I$^6_4$ and V$^6_4$, usually unaccented.

3. *Pedal six-four:* A six-four chord over a stationary bass. Most common are I$^6_4$ and IV$^6_4$, usually unaccented.

The voice leading is usually smooth in all parts, both into and away from the six-four chord. If a note is to be doubled, it is almost always the 5th of the chord (the bass note). If a chord member is to be omitted, it may be either the root or the 3rd.

SELF-TEST 9-1
(Answers begin on page 561.)

A. Analysis. In addition to the specific instructions for each example, label each six-four chord by type.

1. Label the chords with roman numerals. Be sure to include the F♯5 at the beginning of m. 69 and m. 70 as a chord member.

Mozart, Piano Sonata K. 333, III

2. Label the chords with roman numerals.

Schumann, "Little Morning Wanderer," Op. 68, No. 17

3. Label the chords with roman numerals and put non-chord tones in parentheses. The key of the excerpt is E major, even though the principal key of the work is A major.

Schumann, "Little Morning Wanderer," Op. 68, No. 17

B. Fill in one or two inner parts, as specified. Identify any six-four chords by type.

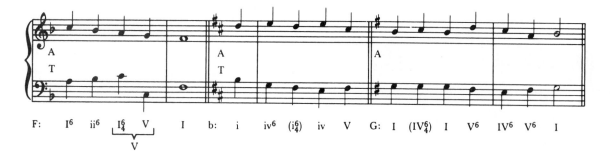

C. Realize these figured basses for three or four voices, as specified. Notice the frequent use of $\frac{5}{3}$ (or the equivalent, such as $\frac{5}{\sharp}$) to indicate a root position triad following an inverted chord. Analyze with roman numerals and label six-four types.

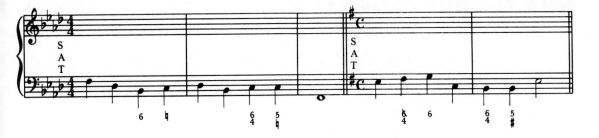

EXERCISE 9-1. *See Workbook.*

CHAPTER TEN

NON-CHORD TONES 1

INTRODUCTION

Many of the examples in the preceding chapters contain notes that do not belong to the chord as analyzed. In many of those examples these notes have been put in parentheses to emphasize the embellishing quality of such non-chord tones, as opposed to chord tones, which are structurally more important. But in order to understand tonal music we have to understand non-chord tones, since the vast majority of passages of tonal music contain at least a few of them.

A *non-chord tone* (abbreviated NCT) is a tone, either diatonic or chromatic, that is not a member of the chord. The tone might be an NCT throughout its duration, or, if the harmony changes before the tone does, the tone might be an NCT for only a portion of its duration.

Obviously, you have to analyze the chords before you can begin labeling NCTs, but the process is nearly simultaneous. In multipart music recognizing the chords and the NCTs is often quite simple, as in Example 10-1.

Example 10-1. Schubert, "Frühlingstraum," Op. 89, No. 11

Other textures and compositional techniques may make the separation of chords from NCTs more problematical. This will be discussed in greater detail at the conclusion of Chapter 11.

CLASSIFICATION OF NON-CHORD TONES

One way of classifying NCTs is according to the ways in which they are approached and left.* The table below presents the basic definitions of the various types, along with abbreviations. Those in the top half of the table will be discussed in detail in this chapter. The others are discussed in Chapter 11.

NCT name (and abbreviation)	Approached by	Left by
Passing tone (p)	Step	Step in same direction
Neighboring tone (n)	Step	Step in opposite direction
Suspension (s)	Same tone	Step down
Retardation (r)	Same tone	Step up
Appoggiatura (app)	Leap	Step
Escape tone (e)	Step	Leap
Neighbor group (n.gr)	(see pp.177-178)	
Anticipation (ant)	Step or leap	Same tone (or leap)
Pedal point (ped)	(see pp. 180-181)	

Example 10-2 provides illustrations of each of the NCT types in a three-part texture.

Example 10-2.

*NCT terminology is not standardized. However, the definitions given here are widely used.

In addition to the basic definitions given above, NCTs can be further classified as to their *duration* and relative degree of *accent*.

1. *Submetrical:* a fraction of a beat in duration and occurring on either *accented* or *unaccented portions* of the beat (Ex. 10-3a).

2. *Metrical:* one beat in duration and occurring on either *accented* or *unaccented beats* (Ex. 10-3b).

3. *Supermetrical:* more than one beat in duration (Ex. 10-3c).

Example 10-3.

C: vii°⁶   vii°⁶   vii°⁶

This terminology is admittedly cumbersome, but such considerations have much to do with the style and general effect of a passage. Remember that the beat in the definitions above is not always indicated by the bottom number of the meter signature.

Other terms used in the description of NCTs include *diatonic, chromatic, ascending, descending, upper,* and *lower.* These terms will be brought up in connection with the appropriate NCTs. The remainder of this chapter is devoted to a more detailed discussion of the NCT types that do not involve leaps: passing tones, neighboring tones, suspensions, and retardations.

PASSING TONES

The *passing tone* is used to fill in the space between two other tones. The two other tones may belong either to the same or to different chords, or they might be NCTs themselves. Usually the space between them is a 3rd, either up or down, and the passing tone is given whatever scale degree lies in between. In Example 10-1 the B4 in m. 6 is used to fill in the space between C♯5 and A4. The B4, then, is an *accented, submetrical, diatonic, descending passing tone.* You might think that this terminology is too detailed to be really useful, and you'd be right. Most of the time we would refer to the

B4 in Example 10-1 as a passing tone and let it go at that. But a good musician, while perhaps not consciously using all of the modifiers employed above, will still be aware of the possibilities and their influence upon the musical effect.

Occasionally a passing tone fills the space between two notes that are only a M2 apart. Look at Example 10-4, from the *Jupiter* Symphony. The G♯5 in m. 56 is a passing tone, but the two tones that it connects, G5 and A5, are only a M2 apart. The G♯5, then, is an *unaccented, metrical, chromatic, ascending passing tone,* as is the A♯3 in the bass line in m. 58.

Still referring to Example 10-4, look at the first violin part in m. 59. The tones G5 and D5, which are a P4 apart, are connected by two passing tones, F♯5 and E5. In m. 61 several passing tones appear in the first violin part. Technically, the A4, the D5, and the F♯5 are chord tones and the others are passing tones. In a functional sense, however, *all* of the tones after the A4 serve as passing tones filling in the m7 between A4 and G5, connecting the half cadence in m. 61 to the beginning of the next phrase.

(Note that the A♯3 in the second violin part in m. 58 is a passing tone, as analyzed. Two lines are being played simultaneously by the second violins.)

Example 10-4. Mozart, Symphony No. 41 (*Jupiter*), K. 551, I

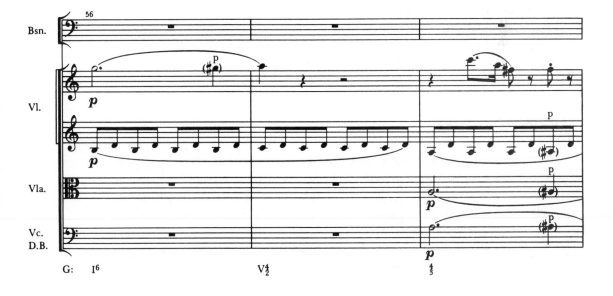

Textural reduction

NEIGHBORING TONES

The *neighboring tone* is used to embellish a single tone. It may appear above the main tone (upper neighbor) or below it (lower neighbor), and it may be diatonic or chromatic. Example 10-1 contains neighboring tones in the voice line; all of them are *unaccented, submetrical, diatonic, upper neighboring tones.* The neighbors in Example 10-5 are all *accented* and *submetrical.* The upper neighbors (the A's and the D) are *diatonic,* while the *lower neighbors* (the F#'s and the B) are *chromatic.*

Example 10-5. Schumann, Scherzo Op. 32

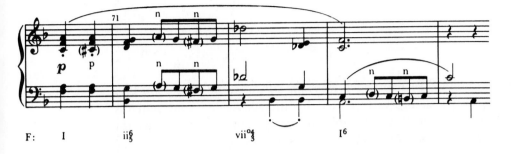

We can only guess about Schumann's reason for using the chromatic form of the lower neighboring tone here, since diatonic neighbors would have been possible. A chromatic neighbor lends more tonal color to a passage, and it tends to draw more attention to the pitch that it is embellishing. A chromatic lower neighbor, like those above, acts as a leading tone to the tone it ornaments. As an experiment, try playing Example 10-5 four ways: (1) all diatonic neighbors, (2) chromatic upper neighbors, (3) chromatic lower neighbors, and (4) all chromatic neighbors. Compare the results.

SUSPENSIONS AND RETARDATIONS

The *suspension* holds on to or suspends a chord tone after the other parts have moved on to the next chord. While the suspension may not seem more important than any other type of NCT, considerably more study has been devoted to it. Part of the reason for this is that the suspension is the primary source of dissonance on the *accented* beat in much tonal and pretonal music. Suspensions may be submetrical, metrical, or supermetrical, but in any case, they almost always fall upon accented beats or accented portions of beats.

A special terminology has developed concerning the suspension. The *preparation* is the tone preceding the suspension. The *suspension* itself may or may not be tied to its preparation. The *resolution* is the tone following the suspension and lying a 2nd below it. The preparation and resolution are usually chord tones (Ex. 10-6).

Example 10-6.

Suspension terminology also provides a means of categorizing suspensions according to the vertical intervals created by the suspended tone and the resolution. For instance, in Example 10-6, the vertical interval created by the suspension is a 7th and that created by the resolution is a 6th, so the entire figure is referred to as a 7-6 suspension.

Example 10-7 summarizes the common suspensions. Notice that the second number is larger than the first only in the 2-3 suspension, a type sometimes referred to as a *bass suspension*. In textures involving more than two parts, the vertical intervals are calculated between the bass and the suspended part. If the bass itself is suspended, the interval is calculated between the bass and the part with which it is most dissonant (generally a 2nd or 9th above in a 2-3 suspension). With the exception of the 9-8 suspension, the note of resolution should not be present anywhere in the texture when a suspension occurs.

Example 10-7.

The names of most suspensions remain constant, even if compound intervals are involved. For instance, even if the 4-3 is actually an 11-10, as in Example 10-7, it is still referred to as a 4-3. The exception to this is the 9-8. It is always called a 9-8 suspension unless it does *not* involve a compound interval, in which case it is labeled as a 2-1 suspension. The reason for this inconsistency is that the 2-1 suspension is found much less frequently than the 9-8, so it is appropriate that they have different labels.

When a suspension occurs in one of the upper voices, the bass will some-times move on to another chord tone at the same time as the suspension resolves. This device is referred to as a *suspension with change of bass.* In such a case a 7-6 suspension, for example, might become a 7-3 suspension because of the movement of the bass. It is also possible to move the upper part of the dissonance as the bass resolves in a 2-3 suspension, creating a 2-6 suspension (Ex. 10-8).

Example 10-8.

While most suspensions are dissonant, consonant suspensions do occur. Example 10-9 contains a suspension in the second measure, even though no dissonance is present.

Example 10-9.

Suspensions are very often embellished. That is, other tones, some of them chord tones and some not, may appear after the suspended tone but before the true resolution. In Example 10-10 there is an embellished 7-6 sus-pension at the beginning of the second measure. In other words, the G5 is a suspension that resolves to F5, but ornamenting tones are heard before the F5 is reached. A similar figure appears at the beginning of the next measure, but here the 7th is a chord tone, part of the G^7 chord. In this case, the F5 is a chord tone that is treated as a suspension. Such *suspension figures,* in which the suspension is actually a chord tone, are quite common. Notice also in this example the use of the minor v^6 as a passing chord between i and iv^6.

Example 10-10. Bach, French Suite No. 2, Sarabande

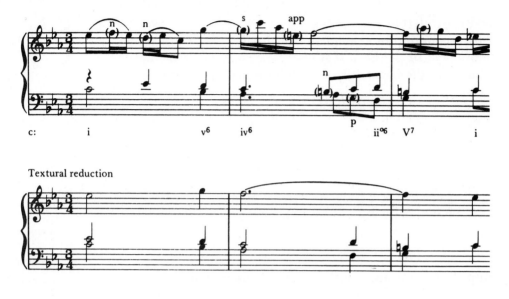

Textural reduction

When the resolution of one suspension serves as the preparation for another, the resulting figure is called a *chain of suspensions*.

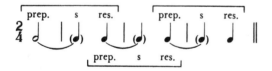

Example 10-10 above contains a chain suspension: the G5 is suspended, resolving to F5, which in turn is suspended (although not as an NCT), resolving to E♭5. A chain of 7-6 suspensions can be seen in Example 7-8 (p. 116).

Much of what has been said about the suspension applies also to the *retardation*, which is simply a suspension with an upward resolution. Retardations may occur anywhere in a passage, but they are especially common at cadences in Classical style, where they appear in combination with suspensions. As in Example 10-11, the retardation usually involves $\hat{7}$ resolving up to $\hat{1}$.

Example 10-11.

Ab: V⁷   I

Notice in this example that the I chord begins as soon as the tonic note is reached in the bass. It would be incorrect to consider the Ab to be an anticipation on the first beat underneath continuing dominant harmony.

As if to help us summarize the suspension, Bach has provided us with a chorale phrase containing all of the common suspensions as well as a less common one. In order to help you get the most out of Example 10-12, chord roots are provided along with the functional harmonic analysis. This is because the phrase *modulates* (changes key) from a to C and back again, and we have not yet presented the ways in which modulations are analyzed. After you understand the chords, follow each voice part through, looking at the NCTs and following the discussion below the example. Finally, play through Example 10-12 and listen to the effect of the suspensions.

Example 10-12. Bach, "Danket dem Herren, denn er ist sehr freundlich"

| roots: | A | A | E | A | G | C | C | G | A | E |

a: i   V⁶   i⌋   ⌈a: i
                     ⌊C: vi   V⁶   I   6   V⁽⁷⁾ vi⌋   V

Soprano

No NCTs

Alto

m. 1   The B4 is a submetrical 9-8 suspension. Its resolution, A4, becomes a submetrical 7-6 suspension on the next beat. Therefore, this is a chain of suspensions.

Tenor

m. 2   The D4 eighth note actually represents a metrical 9-8 suspension. The suspension is ornamented by the two sixteenth notes that follow it, one of them being a chord tone that anticipates the resolution, the other being a lower neighbor. Notice that by the time the "real" resolution arrives (beat 2), the bass has moved to another chord tone, so this is a 9-6 change of bass suspension.

       The B3 on beat 4 is an example of a relatively unusual suspension, the 2-1.

m. 3   The quarter note A3 represents a half note A3, which is a supermetrical 4-3 suspension. The suspension is ornamented with an augmentation of the figure used to ornament the suspended D4 in m. 2.

Bass

m. 1   The empty parentheses on beat 2 remind us that the A3 is still sounding but is no longer part of the chord. This is an example of a submetrical 2-3 suspension.

m. 3   The NCTs in this measure are unaccented, submetrical, ascending passing tones.

FIGURED BASS SYMBOLS

With the exception of suspensions, NCTs are generally not indicated in a figured bass. Suspensions are shown by the use of symbols identical or similar to the numbers we use to name suspension types. For example, a 7-6 suspension might appear as "7 6" or "⁷₃ 6," while a 4-3 suspension might be "4 3" or "4♯." Change of bass suspensions can be recognized by such combinations as "7 3" or "9 6" appearing over a moving bass.

EMBELLISHING A SIMPLE TEXTURE

One way to compose in the tonal style is to begin with a simple texture that has an interesting soprano/bass counterpoint and then embellish it. Two common types of NCT embellishments are the neighbor and the passing tone. Another type of embellishment, although it is not an NCT, is arpeggiation. We have seen bass arpeggiations in connection with inverted triads, but arpeggiations can be used in any part to create motion or a more interesting line.

Adding neighbors, passing tones, and arpeggiations to the texture is not difficult, but you must be careful not to create objectionable parallels in the process. Example 10-13a illustrates a simple texture without parallels. Example 10-13b shows the same music embellished, but each embellishment has created objectionable parallels. While parallels created by passing and neighboring tones may occasionally be found in tonal music, you should try to avoid them for now.

Example 10-13.

Adding suspensions to the texture does not usually create parallels, but it is still somewhat tricky at first. You may find the following suggestions helpful.

1. Find a step down in the bass. Is the harmonic interval between the bass and some upper voice over the second bass note a 3rd (or 10th)? If so, the 2-3 suspension will work.

2. Find in one of the upper voices a step down. Is the harmonic interval between the second note and the bass a 3rd, 6th, or 8ve? If so, the 4-3, 7-6, or 9-8 suspension, respectively, will work. Exception: do not use the 4-3 or 7-6 if the resolution of the suspension would already be present in another voice. The aural result is very disappointing.

Below is a simple two-voice example (Ex. 10-14). Possible locations for suspensions are shown with an *X*. The second part of Example 10-14 is an embellished version containing all of the embellishments discussed so far.

Example 10-14.

SUMMARY

Non-chord tones are classified chiefly by contour (p. 161), but terms relating to duration and accent are sometimes also applied (p. 162). The passing tone (pp. 162-164) is approached by step and left by step in the same direction. The neighboring tone (pp. 164-165) is approached by step and left by step in the opposite direction. The suspension (pp. 165-170) is an accented NCT prepared by the same tone and resolved by step downward. The common types are the 7-6, 4-3, 9-8, and 2-3 suspensions. Any but the 2-3 may occur with a change of bass. Only in the 9-8 is the resolution tone present in the texture at the point of suspension. The retardation (p. 168) is similar to the suspension, but it has an upward resolution.

SELF-TEST 10-1
(Answers begin on page 562.)

A. Analysis.

1. Go back to Example 6-10 (p. 100) which shows NCTs in parentheses, and identify the type of each NCT in the blanks below. Always show the interval classification (7-6, and so on) when analyzing suspensions.

Measure	Treble	Bass
1	_____	
2	_____	_____
3	_____	
4	_____	
5	_____	
6	_____	_____
7	_____	

2. Do the same with Example 8-4 (p. 128).

soprano: _____

alto: _____ _____

tenor: _____ _____ _____

3. Analyze chords and NCTs in this excerpt. Then make a reduction similar to those seen in this text by (1) removing all NCTs, (2) using longer note values or ties for repeated notes, and (3) transposing parts by a P8 when necessary to make the lines smoother. Study the simplified texture. Do any voice-leading problems appear to have been covered up by the embellishments?

Bach, "Schmücke dich, o liebe Seele"

B. After reviewing the discussion of embellishment (pp. 171-172), decide what *one* suspension would be best in each excerpt below. Then renotate with the suspension and at least one other embellishment. Remember to put parentheses around NCTs and to label NCTs and arpeggiations.

F: I⁶   V   vi   IV   f♯:   i   V⁶   i   VI   B♭:   I   V⁶   I   IV⁶   d: i   vii°⁶   i⁶   iv

C. The example below is a simplified excerpt from a Bach chorale harmonization. Analyze the chords with roman numerals and activate the texture with embellishments of various kinds. While many correct solutions are possible, it will be interesting to compare yours with Bach's, which may be found in Appendix B.

EXERCISE 10-1. See Workbook.

CHAPTER ELEVEN

NON-CHORD TONES 2

APPOGGIATURAS

All of the NCTs discussed so far are approached and left by step or by common tone. In most tonal music the majority of NCTs will be of the types already discussed. NCTs involving leaps (appoggiaturas, escape tones, neighbor groups, and some anticipations) are not rare, however, and they tend to be more obvious to the listener.

As a very general rule, *appoggiaturas* are accented, approached by ascending leap, and left by descending step. The Tchaikovsky theme in Example 11-1 (notice the transposition) contains two appoggiaturas that fit this description. The first, A4, might also be heard as a suspension from the previous measure.

Example 11-1. Tchaikovsky, Symphony No. 5, II

All appoggiaturas are approached by leap and left by step, but the sequence is not always ascending leap followed by descending step. In fact, Example 10-10 (p. 168) has already provided us with an example of an unaccented appoggiatura approached from above (the E5). Notice that it is also chromatic. Probably the only other generalization that could be made concerning the appoggiatura is that the appoggiatura, especially the supermetrical variety, is more typical of the nineteenth century than the eighteenth. As an illustration, consider Example 11-2. Four of the five NCTs in the phrase (not counting the A3s in m. 5, left hand, because they double the melody) are appoggiaturas, and two of the four are supermetrical. It is largely this aspect—though in combination with others (slow harmonic rhythm, disjunct melody, homophonic texture, wide range, and so on)—that gives this phrase its Romantic flavor.

Example 11-2. Chopin, Nocturne Op. 27, No. 2

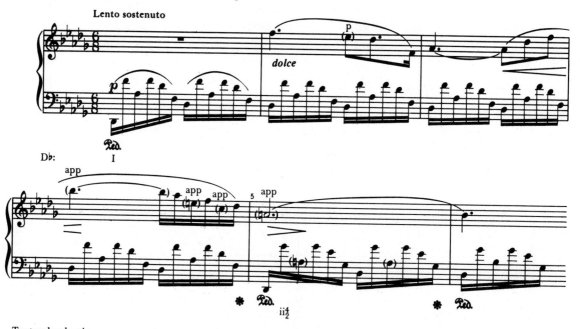

Textural reduction

The reduction of Example 11-2 shows that when we move from the surface of the piece to the background voice leading, our interpretation of the supermetrical appoggiaturas changes considerably.

ESCAPE TONES

The contour of the *escape tone* is the reverse of that of the appoggiatura, because the escape tone is approached by step and left by leap. Escape tones are usually submetrical, unaccented, and diatonic. They are often used in sequence to ornament a scalar line, as in mm. 59-60 of Example 10-4 (p. 163). Notice in Example 10-4 that while *escape tone figures* ornament the line D5-C5-B4, actual escape tones occur only two times.

The escape tone is also frequently used at cadences to ornament the scale degree progression $\hat{2}$-$\hat{1}$. An instance of this can be seen in Example 11-3.

Example 11-3.   Haydn, Sonata No. 35, I

All of the escape tones cited in this section have been *submetrical, unaccented,* and *diatonic;* these are all usually characteristic of the escape tone in tonal music.

THE NEIGHBOR GROUP

A common method of embellishing a single tone involves a combination of two NCTs in succession, the first being an escape tone, the second an appoggiatura. The figure is referred to as a *neighbor group.* As Example 11-4 illustrates, the neighbor group bears a resemblance to a neighboring tone figure.

Example 11-4.

ANTICIPATIONS

An *anticipation,* as the name implies, anticipates a chord that has not yet been reached. This NCT moves, by step or by leap, to some pitch that is contained in the anticipated chord but is not present in the chord that precedes it. For example, if the triad F/A/C were to proceed to the triad Bb/D/F, you could use either the note Bb or the note D to anticipate the Bb/D/F chord while the F/A/C chord is still sounding. The note F could not be used as an NCT, because it is common to both chords. Of the two notes Bb and D, the Bb is probably the better choice. In Example 11-5a the anticipated Bb4 forms a satisfying dissonance with the other pitches and is clearly an NCT, but in Example 11-5b the D5 forms no true dissonance with any other pitch.

Example 11-5.

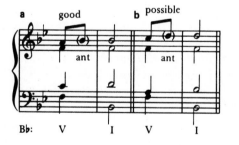

An anticipation very much like the one in Example 11-5a appears in Example 11-6.

Example 11-6. Bach, *Well-Tempered Clavier*, Book II, Fugue 22

Most anticipations are approached by step, but the approach by leap is not rare. In Example 11-7 there are three *anticipation figures,* each approached by leap and left by common tone, but only one figure, that in the bass, is an NCT.

Example 11-7. Schumann, "Little Morning Wanderer," Op. 68, No. 17

The least commonly encountered variety of NCT is the anticipation approached and *left* by leap. This is sometimes referred to as a *free anticipation.* Below is an example from Mozart, in which the bass anticipates the tonic triad before the dominant chord has resolved, allowing the bass in mm. 7-9 to imitate the soprano in mm. 5-7.

Example 11-8. Mozart, Sonata K. 332, I

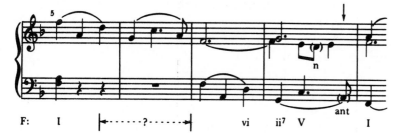

THE PEDAL POINT

The pedal point has been saved for last in the discussion of NCTs because it is really in a class by itself. The *pedal point* is a compositional device that begins as a chord tone, then becomes a NCT as the harmonies around it change, and finally ends up as a chord tone when the harmony is once more in agreement with it. The other NCTs are clearly decorative and are always dependent upon the harmony for their meaning. But the pedal point often has such tonal strength that the harmonies seem to be embellishing the pedal point, rather than the other way around. This sounds more complicated than it is. Look at Example 11-9, which shows the ending of a fugue by Bach.

Example 11-9. Bach, "Allein Gott in der Höh' sei Ehr"

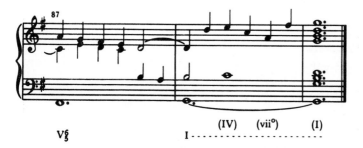

In one sense, the piece ends on beat 1 of m. 88 with the IAC. What follows that cadence is a short codetta, with the tonic note sustained in the bass beneath a IV-vii°-I progression in the upper voices. The chords above the tonic pedal are analyzed, but in a very real sense the pedal overpowers the upper parts and represents the tonic harmony. Incidentally, the relatively weak inverted IAC is used to end this work because the bass line is presenting the melody on which the piece is based.

You may have noticed that inversions above the pedal point are not indicated in Example 11-9. This is generally a good practice to follow in the analysis of such passages. The aural effect of inversion is altered by the pedal, and there are no conventional symbols to represent this alteration.

The term *pedal point* comes from the frequent use of the device in organ compositions. At any point in the composition, but most frequently at the end of the work, the organist will be called upon to sustain a single pitch with a pedal while continuing to play moving lines with the manuals (keyboards). Most frequently the sustained pitch is the tonic or the dominant, and the passage often includes the triad whose root is a P4 above the pedal point (hence the term *pedal six-four chord*). Therefore if the tonic pitch is the pedal, the IV chord will often be used above it (as in Ex. 11-9), and if the dominant pitch is the pedal, the I chord will often be used above it.

Pedal points occasionally occur in parts other than the bass, in which case they are referred to as *inverted pedal points*. Another possibility is for the pedal point to contain more than one pitch class (*double pedal point,* and so on), as in Example 11-10. While most pedal points are sustained, rearticulated pedal points, as in Example 11-10, are not uncommon.

Example 11-10. Schumann, "Reaper's Song," Op. 68, No. 18

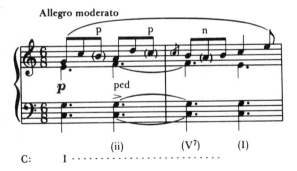

SPECIAL PROBLEMS IN THE ANALYSIS OF NON-CHORD TONES

In this section we will discuss three excerpts that demonstrate special problems that you may encounter from time to time in analyzing tonal music. First, the actual label that you assign to a tone may change as you reduce the passage. Such possibilities were mentioned in connection with Examples 11-1 and 11-2. For variety, we will do a reverse textural reduction of a similar passage. Example 11-11 shows two versions of a portion of a melody in E♭, the first melody being diatonic, the second incorporating chromatic and diatonic passing tones.

Example 11-11.

If we embellish each tone of Example 11-11b, we create the melody found in Example 11-12.

Example 11-12. Schubert, Impromptu Op. 90, No. 2

The labeling of the NCTs in Example 11-12 is problematical. For instance, the first E♮4 in m. 3 is, on the surface, a neighboring tone (E♭4-E♮4-D♯4). But Example 11-11b showed that the E♮4 in not a neighbor but a passing tone (E♭4-E♮4-F4). Probably the best solution is to label tones according to the level on which you are analyzing, remembering that other interpretations may be necessary at different levels.

Example 11-13 is our second problematical excerpt. It is very unlikely that you would be able to determine the harmonic background of this excerpt just from looking at it, and actually it involves too many advanced harmonic concepts to allow detailed discussion of the harmonies at this time. But if you play it slowly, you will discover that the right hand lags further and further behind the left. The cadence on f♯ in the right hand comes three eighth notes later than the cadence on f♯ in the left, and the cadences on A are four eighth notes apart. Both cadences are identified in the example.

Example 11-13. Brahms, *Variations on a Theme by Schumann*, Op. 9, Var. 2

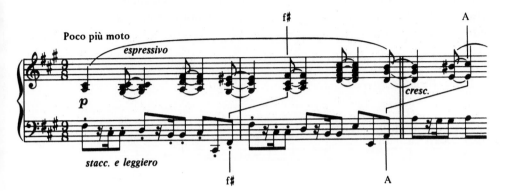

Once the two staves are "correctly" aligned, it becomes apparent that the texture contains no NCTs at all (except, perhaps, for the B♯4). Example 11-14 brings the right hand into alignment with the left. Play through both examples slowly and compare them.

Example 11-14.

Conventional NCT terminology is inadequate to explain a passage such as this. Instead, it is better to use an approach such as the one we have demonstrated.

Finally, we consider the problem of implied harmonies and the analysis of unaccompanied melodies. As a general rule, NCT analyses based upon melodies alone are arbitrary and uninformative. Nevertheless, the experienced musician can sometimes recognize the NCTs in an unaccompanied melodic line on the basis of implied harmonies alone. Example 11-15 shows one interpretation (others are possible) of the harmonies implied by a Bach fugue subject. The textural reduction shows that the melody is an elaboration of a simple stepwise line.

Example 11-15. Bach, *Well-Tempered Clavier*, Book II, Fugue 14

Textural reduction

SUMMARY OF NON-CHORD TONES

NCTs are most commonly classified by their contours. Stepwise NCTs (p, n, s, r, some anticipations) are somewhat more common than NCTs involving both steps and leaps (app, e, n.gr, some anticipations). NCTs involving only leaps (some anticipations) are quite rare. The pedal point has unique characteristics and is common throughout the tonal era. NCTs should also be considered in terms of their duration, relative metric accent, direction, and possible chromatic alteration. All have influence upon the musical effect of the NCT.

The analysis of chords and NCTs must always be carried out simultaneously. While most NCTs are clearly recognizable as being embellishments of the basic harmony, ambiguous cases will be encountered occasionally.

SELF-TEST 11-1
(Answers begin on page 564.)

A. Analysis.

1. Go back to Self-Test 7-1, Part F (p. 124), which shows NCTs in parentheses, and identify the type of each NCT in the blanks below. Always show the interval classification (7-6, and so on) when you analyze suspensions.

   m. 1 _____

   m. 3 _____ _____ _____

   m. 4 _____ _____

2. Analyze the NCTs in Example 9-8 (p. 153).

   m. 24 _____ _____

   m. 25 _____ _____

   m. 26 _____ _____ _____

3. Analyze the NCTs in Example 9-9 (p. 154).

   m. 72 _____ _____   m. 76 _____ _____

   m. 74 _____   m. 77 (melody) _____

   m. 75 _____ _____ _____   (alto) _____

4. Label the chords and NCTs in this excerpt. Then make a simplified version without NCTs. Comment upon the simplified version. Analyze two chords in m. 11, beat 3.

   Bach, "Ermuntre dich, mein schwacher Geist"

5. Follow the same instructions for this excerpt as for exercise 4. Try to make your reduction as simple as possible, even omitting arpeggiations. Assume that chords sustain through rests (in m. 6, for instance).

Mozart, Sonata K. 333, I

B. The example below is for three-part chorus. Analyze the chords with roman numerals. Then add the specified NCTs at the points indicated. Show the interval classification of each suspension.

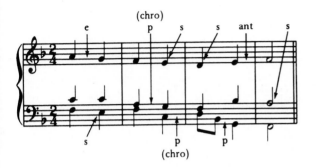

C. The excerpt below is a reduction of Mozart's Sonata K. 330, III, mm. 1-8. Use it as a framework for elaboration, employing arpeggiations and NCTs as you see fit. It is also possible to thicken the texture occasionally, if you wish.

EXERCISE 11-1. See Workbook.

DIATONIC SEVENTH CHORDS

CHAPTER TWELVE

THE V⁷ CHORD

INTRODUCTION

Diatonic seventh chords were introduced quite early in this text, in Chapter 4. Subsequent examples and exercises have included the analysis of many seventh chords, but we have not dealt with the details of how composers have used seventh chords in tonal music. The use of seventh chords is the subject of the next several chapters.

Before reading further, review the material on seventh chords on pages 63-65. In those sections you learned, among other things, that the five most common seventh-chord qualities are the major seventh, dominant seventh, minor seventh, half-diminished seventh, and diminished seventh chords. Of these types, the dominant seventh is by far the most frequently encountered. It is generally built on $\hat{5}$, with the result that the terms *dominant seventh* and V^7 are used more or less interchangeably.

Dominant seventh chords by definition are always major-minor sevenths—that is, when spelled in root position, they contain a major triad plus the pitch a m7 above the root. In major keys a seventh chord built on $\hat{5}$ will be automatically a major-minor seventh chord. But in minor keys *it is necessary to raise $\hat{7}$* in order to obtain the major-minor seventh quality. The seventh chord built on $\hat{5}$ without the raised $\hat{7}$ (v⁷ instead of V⁷) is not as common. It serves only as a passing chord, not as a true dominant, because it lacks the tonic-defining leading tone essential for a chord with a dominant function.

Example 12-1.

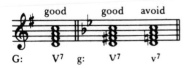

GENERAL VOICE-LEADING CONSIDERATIONS

The essential concept in the handling of *any* seventh chord involves the treatment of the 7th of the chord: *the 7th almost always resolves down by step.* We are naturally suspicious of generalizations, as we should be, but the downward resolution of the 7th as a general principle is extremely important. The 7th originated in music as a downward-resolving suspension or descending passing tone, and the downward resolution came to be the only one acceptable to the musical ear. To compare a 7th resolving down with one resolving up, listen to Example 12-2. The difference may or may not seem startling to you, but tonal music contains very few instances of the second resolution.

Example 12-2.

When you are working with the V⁷, you must also consider the leading tone: *when it is in an outer part, the leading tone almost always resolves up by step.* To convince yourself of the reason for this, play Example 12-3, and notice the disappointing effect of the cadence.

Example 12-3.

When you apply these two principles, remember not to confuse the 7th of the chord with the seventh scale degree. We will summarize what we have presented so far in this chapter.

1. The V⁷ chord is a major-minor seventh chord.

2. The 7th of the chord ($\hat{4}$) resolves down to $\hat{3}$.

3. The 3rd of the chord ($\hat{7}$) resolves up to $\hat{1}$, especially when it is in an outer part.

THE V⁷ IN ROOT POSITION

The resolution of the dominant seventh in root position to the tonic in root position is more difficult than that of any other combination. To master this technique, however, you need only to remember the principles we discussed earlier in this chapter.

1. The 7th must resolve *down* to $\hat{3}$.

2. The leading tone, when in the *top* part, must resolve *up* to $\hat{1}$.

Another way of looking at these principles is in terms of the resolution of the tritone: the +4 tends to resolve outward to a 6th (Ex. 12-4a), the °5 inward to a 3rd (Ex. 12-4b). If we follow these principles, we find that the tonic triad is incomplete—it has no 5th.

Example 12-4.

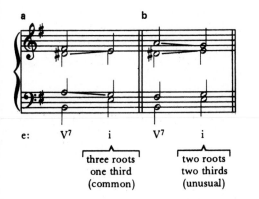

The resolution of V⁷ to an incomplete triad is not an "error" to be avoided and is, in fact, a very common occurrence, especially at final cadences. In

Example 12-5 the leading tone, even though it is not in the top voice, resolves up by step, resulting in an incomplete tonic triad.

Example 12-5. Schubert, Quartet (*Death and the Maiden*), Op. post., I

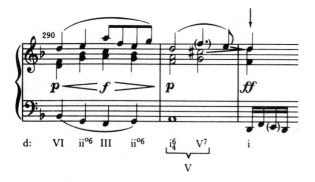

If you want to resolve the root position V⁷ in four parts to a complete tonic triad, either of these methods will work.

1. Use an incomplete V⁷, omitting the 5th (or, less commonly, the 3rd) and doubling the root.

2. Use a complete V⁷, but put the leading tone (3rd of the V⁷) in an *inner* part, and "frustrate" its natural resolution by taking it down a M3 to the 5th of the tonic triad.

The first solution works because the incomplete V⁷ is a perfectly usable sonority. The second method, which is the more common, succeeds by tucking away the leading tone in an inner voice, where its lack of resolution is not so apparent to the listener. Both options are summarized in Example 12-6.

Example 12-6.

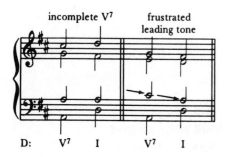

Illustrations of these two procedures from the literature are seen in the next two examples. In the first (Ex. 12-7) an incomplete V^7 (5th omitted) is used.

Example 12-7.   Bach, "Nun ruhen alle Wälder"

In the second (Ex. 12-8) Beethoven uses a complete V^7 but frustrates the leading tone.

Example 12-8.   Beethoven, Quartet Op. 18, No. 1, IV

You may have discovered by now that there *is* a way to resolve a complete V^7 in four parts to a complete tonic triad while still resolving both the leading tone and the 7th of the chord: if the 5th of the V^7 leaps to the 5th of the tonic triad, the complete tonic triad is obtained, but at the expense of parallel 5ths. This resolution is illustrated in Example 12-9.

Example 12-9.

A: V⁷   I

In instrumental music this solution is occasionally found when the 5ths are taken by contrary motion, as in Example 12-10. Notice how the rests in the lower parts and the continued activity in the first violin distract the listener's attention from the 5ths.

Example 12-10.   Haydn, Quartet Op. 76, No. 1, III (piano score)

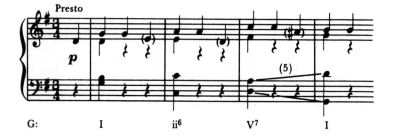

G: I   ii⁶   V⁷   I

THE V⁷ IN THREE PARTS

The V⁷ in a three-part texture will have to appear with one of the chord tones missing, unless one part articulates two pitches. Obviously, neither root nor 7th can be omitted without losing the flavor of the seventh chord. Of the two remaining members, the 5th is more commonly omitted, but examples with the 3rd omitted are not rare.

Example 12-11.

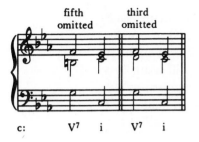

Example 12-12 illustrates the V⁷ with omitted 5th.

Example 12-12.   Bach, Sinfonia No. 9

A V⁷ with the 3rd omitted can be seen in Example 12-13.

Example 12-13.   Mozart, Sonata K. 570, III

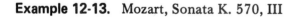

OTHER RESOLUTIONS OF THE V⁷

The V⁷ in root position often moves deceptively to the submediant triad. When the leading tone is present in the V⁷ (which it generally is), it usually resolves up to $\hat{1}$, even when it is in an inner voice, although $\hat{7}$-$\hat{6}$ in an inner voice is acceptable in *major* keys. In four parts this resolution will result in a doubled 3rd in the vi (or VI) chord. Some sample V⁷-VI progressions are given in Example 12-14. The voice leading would be the same in major. Notice that in every case it is only the bass that "deceives." That is, all of the other voices resolve as they normally would in an authentic cadence.

Example 12-14.

b: V⁷   VI   V⁷   VI   V⁷   VI   V⁷   VI

The only diatonic triads that commonly follow the V⁷ chord are the root position tonic and submediant triads. There are some altered chords that can embellish the deceptive progression and we will come upon these in later chapters, but for now you should probably restrict your exercises to V⁷-I(i) and V⁷-vi(VI). The V⁷-I⁶(i⁶) resolution, seen in Example 12-15, is *not* a good choice, because of the sound of the implied parallel 8ves.

Example 12-15.

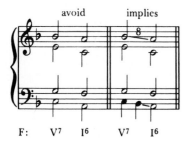

F: V⁷   I⁶   V⁷   I⁶

CHECKPOINT

1. In the resolution of any seventh chord, the 7th of the chord almost always moves (up/down) by (step/leap).

2. In the resolution of a V^7 chord, the 3rd of the chord ($\hat{7}$) usually moves (up/down) by (step/leap). This principle is sometimes not followed when the 3rd of the chord is in an (inner/outer) part, in which case it may leap down to $\hat{5}$.

3. If a member of the V^7 is to be omitted, it is usually the (3rd/5th).

4. If a member of the V^7 is to be doubled, it is usually the _____.

5. If the principles listed in questions 1 and 2 are followed in a four-part texture, the V^7-I progression will lead to (a complete/an incomplete) I chord.

6. Describe two good methods for attaining a complete I chord in a V^7-I progression in four parts.

7. Two good resolutions of the V^7 chord are V^7-___ and V^7-___ .

SELF-TEST 12-1
(Answers begin on page 566.)

A. The note given in each case is the root, 3rd, 5th, or 7th of a V^7 chord. Notate the chord in root position and name the major key in which it would be the V^7.

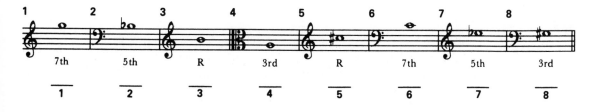

B. Go back to Self-Test 10-1, A. 3 on page 173. Study carefully the V^7 chords in mm. 1, 2, and 5, and comment on the voice leading. (Note: You may have analyzed the A♭3 in m. 1 as a passing tone, but it could also be considered as a 7th.)

C. Resolve each chord below to a root position I. (Note: *c* means complete chord, *i* means incomplete chord.)

D. Notate the key signature and the V⁷ chord, then resolve it.

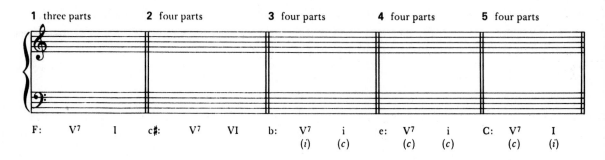

E. Analyze the harmonies implied by these soprano/bass frameworks. Then make four-part versions with embellishments and at least one root position V⁷.

F. Analyze the chords specified by this figured bass. Then make two harmonizations, one for SAB chorus and one for SATB chorus.

EXERCISE 12-1. See Workbook.

THE INVERTED V⁷ CHORD

The inversions of the V⁷ chord are actually easier to handle than the root position V⁷. However, none of the inversions of the V⁷ should be considered to be possible substitutions for the root position V⁷ at an important cadence. The voice-leading principles followed by composers in the resolution of inverted dominant sevenths are the following.

1. The 3rd ($\hat{7}$) resolves up by step to $\hat{1}$.

2. The 7th ($\hat{4}$) resolves down by step to $\hat{3}$.

The other members of the V⁷ have greater freedom, but they generally move by step ($\hat{2}$-$\hat{1}$) or are retained ($\hat{5}$-$\hat{5}$).

You will recall that the symbols used to indicate inverted seventh chords are these.

$\frac{6}{5}$	3rd in the bass
$\frac{4}{3}$	5th in the bass
$\frac{4}{2}$ (or 2)	7th in the bass

THE V⁶₅ CHORD

Example 12-16 illustrates the basic voice leading in the resolution of the V⁶₅.

Example 12-16.

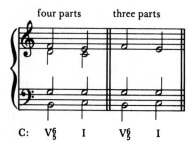

C: V⁶₅   I   V⁶₅   I

In practice, the V_5^6 is often used in a relatively weak position in the phrase. The example below is typical, with the V_5^6 harmonizing an F5 that is essentially a harmonized passing tone in the melody. The root position V that ends the passage has a much stronger effect than the V_5^6.

Example 12-17. Mozart, Sonata K. 309, III

Textural reduction 1

Textural reduction 2

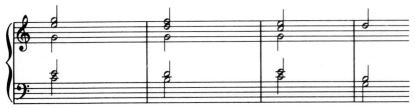

THE V⁴₃ CHORD

The V⁴₃ is often used in a fashion similar to that of the passing V⁶₄: to harmonize $\hat{2}$ in a $\hat{1}$-$\hat{2}$-$\hat{3}$ or $\hat{3}$-$\hat{2}$-$\hat{1}$ bass line. The V⁴₃ is seldom used in three-part textures, the V⁶₄ or vii°⁶ being used instead. Example 12-18 summarizes the treatment of the V⁴₃ in four parts.

Example 12-18.

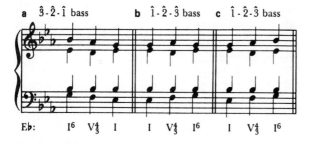

In the last progression above the 7th of the V⁴₃ moves *up* to $\hat{5}$, one of the few situations in which composers frustrated the normal resolution of the 7th. The unequal 5ths seen between the soprano and alto in Example 12-18c are acceptable. Example 12-19 gives an example from Haydn of the I-V⁴₃-I⁶ progression with an unresolved 7th (in the viola).

Example 12-19. Haydn, Quartet Op. 50, No. 6, II

THE V$^4_2$ CHORD

Because of the downward resolution of the 7th, the V$^4_2$ is almost always followed by a I^6 (Ex. 12-20). Generally avoid doubling the bass of the I^6 (or i^6) in this progression.

Example 12-20.

A less conventional but certainly effective treatment of the upper voices is seen in Example 12-21, in which the 5th of the V$^4_2$ leaps to the 5th of the I^6 chord.

Example 12-21.   Beethoven, Sonata Op. 13, II

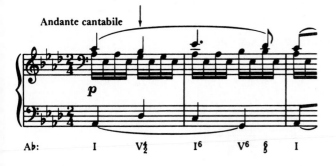

THE APPROACH TO THE 7TH

We have seen that the resolution of the 7th of the V^7 (or of any seventh chord) is usually down by step. The way in which the 7th is approached should also be considered in any detailed analysis, because different approaches have different musical effects. One way of doing this is to classify the contour of the voice that has the chord 7th. If the chord tone preceding the 7th is:

1. the same pitch class as the 7th, we use the term *suspension figure* (Ex. 12-22a);

2. a step above the 7th, we use the term *passing tone figure* (Ex. 12-22b);

3. a step below the 7th, we use the term *neighbor tone figure* (Ex. 12-22c);

4. none of the above, we use the term *appoggiatura figure* (Ex. 12-22d). This is historically the least common approach to the 7th. When used, the leap is almost always an ascending one.

Example 12-22.

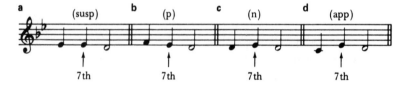

The contours defined above are put into context in Example 12-23.

Example 12-23.

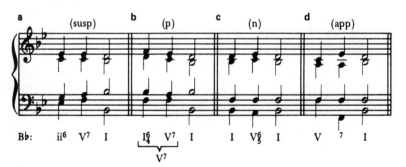

To be sure that you understand this section, look at the approach to the 7th in the examples listed below.

Example 12-7 (p. 195)	Suspension figure (true of both the ii^7 and the V^7).
Example 12-8 (p. 195)	Neighbor tone figure.
Example 12-17 (p. 203)	Passing tone figure. The line is G5-F5-E5.
Example 12-19 (p. 204)	Ascending passing tone figure. The passing tone figure usually descends, the I-V$^4_3$-I^6 progression being the only common exception.
Example 12-21 (p. 205)	Appoggiatura figure in the V$^4_2$, passing tone figure in the V$^6_5$.

SUMMARY

Learning to hear, spell, recognize, notate, and resolve the V^7 chord is essential in the study of tonal music. You should review the points outlined below and make sure that you understand them completely before proceeding to the exercises.

1. The 7th of the V^7 resolves down by step, except in the V$^4_3$-I^6 progression, where it may move up by step.

2. The leading tone resolves up by step. When it is in an inner part, it may leap down a 3rd, but this is uncommon in the inverted V^7.

3. Common resolutions of the dominant seventh chord are:

   V^7-I (or vi)   V$^6_5$-I   V$^4_3$-I (or I^6)   V$^4_2$-I^6

4. The 7th of the V^7 may be approached by:

   common tone, in a suspension figure;

   step, in neighbor and passing tone figures;

   ascending leap, in an appoggiatura figure.

SELF-TEST 12-2
(Answers begin on page 569.)

A. Notate the specified chords. Use accidentals instead of key signatures.

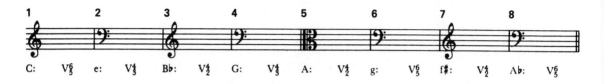

B. Comment on the resolution of the leading tone and both the approach to and the resolution of the 7th in the examples referred to below.

1. Self-Test 4-2, C. 1, p. 66 (V⁴₂).

2. Self-Test 4-2, C. 2, p. 66 (V⁴₃).

3. Example 6-16, p. 104 (V⁴₂).

C. Resolve each chord to a tonic triad (except as indicated). Analyze both chords.

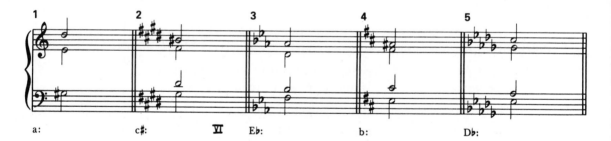

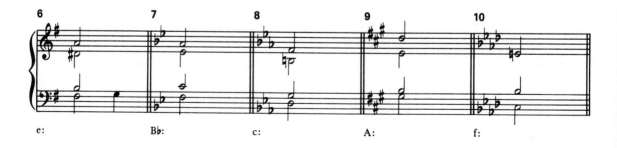

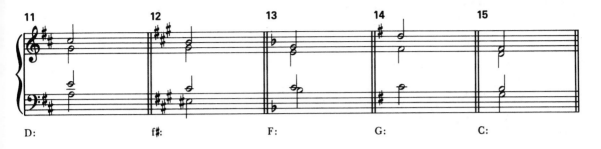

D: f#:   F: G: C:

D. Supply the key signature. Then notate and resolve the specified chord. Finally, begin the exercise with a chord that will allow good voice leading and provide the indicated approach to the 7th. Notate as quarter notes. Label all unlabeled chords.

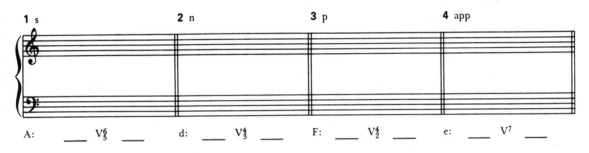

A: ____ V^6_5 ____   d: ____ V^4_3 ____   F: ____ V^4_2 ____   e: ____ V^7 ____

E. Review. Identify the following keys. If the chord occurs diatonically in both major and minor, name both keys.

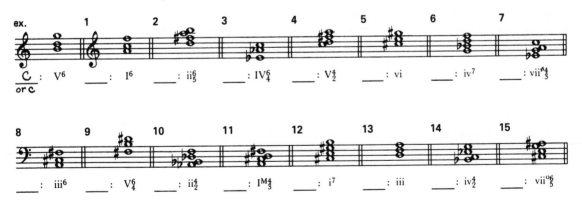

C: V^6 ____ : I^6 ____ : ii^6_5 ____ : IV^6_4 ____ : V^4_2 ____ : vi ____ : iv^7 ____ : vii^{M4}_3
or c

____ : iii^6 ____ : V^6_4 ____ : ii^4_2 ____ : I^{M4}_3 ____ : i^7 ____ : iii ____ : iv^4_2 ____ : vii^{o6}_5

EXERCISE 12-2. See Workbook.

CHAPTER THIRTEEN

THE II⁷ AND VII⁷ CHORDS

INTRODUCTION

Any diatonic triad may appear with a 7th added, but the various diatonic seventh chords do not occur with equal frequency in tonal music. In fact, the vast majority of seventh chords used are dominant sevenths, appearing either as the V^7 or as a secondary V^7 (to be discussed in Chapter 16). In the major mode, by far the most common seventh chord other than the V^7 is the ii^7. A ranking by frequency of the seventh chords in major would be approximately that shown below.

$$V^7 \quad ii^7 \quad vii^{\varnothing7} \quad IV^{M7} \quad vi^7 \quad I^{M7} \quad iii^7$$
$$\longleftarrow \text{------- more frequent} \longleftarrow \text{----------}$$

Because of the larger number of possible seventh chords in the minor (see p. 44) a corresponding diagram for minor would be difficult to produce. The leading-tone seventh is more frequently found in minor than in major, but the supertonic seventh is still the more common of the two in minor. At any rate, a diagram showing the order of frequency of seventh chords in minor would not differ radically from that shown for major. In this chapter and the next each of the diatonic seventh chords is illustrated and discussed briefly. This chapter covers only the supertonic and leading-tone seventh chords, the remainder being discussed in Chapter 12.

You will not find the voice-leading principles to be difficult. Actually, Chapter 12 presented the most formidable part-writing problems to be found in tonal harmony. Since the principles are not difficult, there are not separate sections dealing with the handling of each chord in three and four voices. Instead, the following principles apply throughout.

1. Incomplete chords must contain at least the root and the 7th.

2. Doubled tones would generally not be the chord 7th or the leading tone of the scale.

3. The 7th of the chord almost always resolves down by step.

4. The 7th of the chord may be approached in various ways (review p. 206). Especially smooth is the suspension figure.

THE II⁷ CHORD

By far the most common of nondominant diatonic seventh chords, supertonic sevenths may be found in most compositions of the tonal era. In major the ii⁷ is a minor seventh chord (Ex. 13-1a), while in minor keys the
ii⁰⁷ is almost always used (Ex. 13-1b). Another possibility in minor is the
ii⁷ chord created by a raised $\hat{6}$ (Ex. 13-1c); this chord is used rarely, since the
linear tendencies of both the ↑$\hat{6}$ and the chord 7th would usually resolve
to a doubled leading tone in the V chord.

Example 13-1.

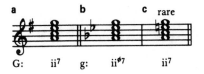

Like the supertonic triad, the supertonic seventh typically moves to V.
The root position V may be delayed by the appearance of a cadential I$_4^6$
chord, or the V may be represented by a vii⁰⁶ (see Ex. 13-2 for some typical resolutions).

Example 13-2.

Examples of all the cases above, as well as of others, are not difficult to find,
but the first inversion of the ii⁷ is the most common bass position. A ii$_5^6$-V⁷
progression in a three-part texture is illustrated in Example 13-3. Notice the
suspension figure that prepares the 7th of the ii$_5^6$.

Example 13-3.   Mozart, Symphony No. 41, K. 551, IV

C: I⁶   ii§   V⁷   vi

Textural reduction

A very familiar example of the ii$^4_2$-V$^6_5$ progression in a five-part texture occurs at the beginning of the *Well-Tempered Clavier*. Again the 7th is approached by means of a suspension figure.

Example 13-4.   Bach, *Well-Tempered Clavier*, Book I, Prelude 1

C: I   ii$^4_2$

V$^6_5$ I

Textural reduction

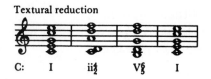

C: I   ii$^4_2$ V$^6_5$ I

A much less typical use of the supertonic seventh chord is as a substitute for a IV chord in a plagal cadence. In such cases, the ii⁷ is usually in first inversion, where its close resemblance to the IV is most obvious. In Example 13-5, which may be somewhat difficult to follow because of the clefs, Dvořák closes the phrase with a ii^ø⁶₅-i plagal cadence. The textural reduction makes the voice leading clearer and points out that most of the phrase is sequential.

Example 13-5. Dvořák, Symphony Op. 95 (*From the New World*), I

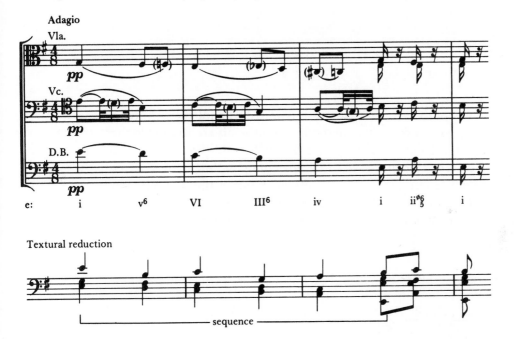

Perhaps a better explanation of the ii^ø⁶₅ in the example above is that it is a iv chord with an added 6th (the F♯3). This is especially convincing in that it accounts for the E3, which is otherwise an unresolved 7th in the ii^ø⁷ chord.

THE VII⁷ CHORD IN MAJOR

The leading-tone seventh in major is a half-diminished seventh chord,* possessing, as does the vii° triad, a dominant-like function. It normally resolves directly to the tonic, but it may first move to the V⁷ by simply taking

*The fully diminished vii°⁷ in major is discussed in Chapter 21.

6̂ (the 7th of the chord) down one step. Typical resolutions to tonic in four parts are demonstrated in Example 13-6. The third inversion, which is quite rare, is not shown, nor is vii°⁶₅-I, which would contain parallel 5ths.

Example 13-6.

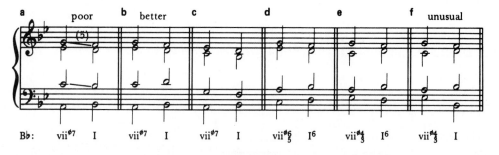

Notice that the root position vii°⁷-I progression must be handled carefully to avoid parallel 5ths (Ex. 13-6a). Two methods of doing this are to double the 3rd in the I chord (Ex. 13-6b) and to revoice the vii°⁷ chord (Ex. 13-6c). The progression in Example 13-6f, the vii°⁴₃-I, is not common, but it does occur. When used at an important cadence, it results in an interesting combination of the characteristics of both plagal and authentic cadences. This is illustrated in Example 13-7, which is from the ending of a composition for two four-part choruses.

Example 13-7.   Brahms, "Unsere Vater hofften auf dich," Op. 109, No. 1

As Example 13-6 showed, the root position vii°⁷ must be handled carefully in order to avoid parallel 5ths. In the Haydn example below (Ex. 13-8), parallel 3rds in the violins move in contrary motion to the parallel 10ths beneath. This allows a very natural resolution to the tonic triad with doubled 3rd.

Example 13-8.   Haydn, Quartet Op. 74, No. 3, III

G: ii   I   vii°⁷   I

Otherwise, the vii°⁷ poses no new problems. It should be remembered, however, that the vii°⁷ is much less common than the other chords with dominant functions—V, V⁷, and vii°⁽⁶⁾.

THE VII⁷ CHORD IN MINOR

In the minor mode, the leading-tone seventh (Ex. 13-9a) appears as a fully diminished seventh chord (vii°⁷). The subtonic seventh chord (Ex. 13-9b) generally is used in sequences, to be discussed in Chapter 14, or as a secondary dominant seventh (V⁷ of III), a usage that is explained in Chapter 16. The vii°⁷ is found more frequently and is discussed in the following paragraphs.

Example 13-9.

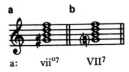

a: vii°⁷   VII⁷

The vii°⁷, whether in root position or inverted, tends to resolve to tonic. As with the vii⁰⁷, the vii°⁷ may move first to the V⁷ simply by moving the 7th of the chord down to $\hat{5}$. The resolution of vii°⁷ to i, however, requires more discussion.

The vii°⁷ contains two tritones. The tendency of the tritone is to resolve inward by step when spelled as a °5, outward by step when spelled as a +4. If these tendencies are followed in four parts, as in Example 13-10, the tonic triad will have a doubled 3rd.

Example 13-10.

Composers have not always cared to follow these tendencies, often taking $\hat{2}$ down to $\hat{1}$ instead of moving it up to $\hat{3}$ (compare Ex. 13-11a and b). In certain voicings, this can result in unequal 5ths (Ex. 13-11c).

Example 13-11.

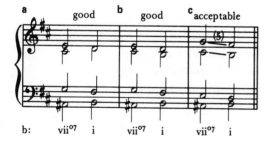

The 5ths, though acceptable, are often disguised through the use of NCTs, as in Example 13-12.

Example 13-12. Bach, Passacaglia in C Minor

Textural reduction

The members of the vii°⁷ usually move in the same ways when the chord is inverted as they do when it is in root position, and our discussion of the optionally doubled 3rd still applies (for example, see the first chord in Ex. 13-12 above). The vii°$^6_5$ (Ex. 13-13a) usually is followed by i⁶, because resolution to the root position tonic creates unequal 5ths involving the bass (review p. 78). The vii°$^4_3$ (Ex. 13-13b) moves smoothly to the i⁶; occasionally found is vii°$^4_3$-i, which is similar to the vii°$^4_3$-I cadence discussed in connection with Example 13-7. The vii°$^4_2$ (Ex. 13-13c) is generally followed by V⁷ or by a cadential or passing i$^6_4$.

Example 13-13.

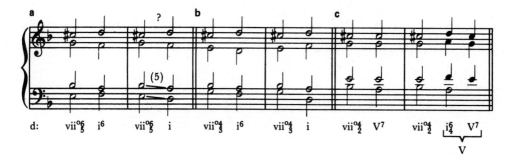

A vii°⁴₃ in chorale texture is seen in Example 13-14, where it resolves to a i⁶ with a doubled 3rd. An alternate analysis would eliminate two of the chords that occur in the same measure with the vii°⁴₃—the ii°⁶₅ and the ii°⁷—by regarding the A4s as suspensions. It would not be equally good to analyze the G♯4s as lower neighbors, thereby eliminating the vii°⁴₃ and the vii°⁶, because that analysis turns up an unconvincing progression: ii°⁶₅-i⁶-ii°⁷-i.

Example 13-14.   Bach, "Als Jesus Christus in der Nacht"

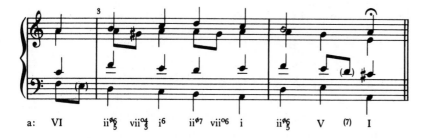

You may have noticed that Example 13-14 ends with a major tonic triad. In the Baroque period it was not at all uncommon to end a phrase or a composition in the minor mode in this way. This device, known as the *Picardy third,* is discussed further in Chapter 21.

CHECKPOINT

1. The most frequently used diatonic seventh chord is the V^7. Which one ranks second in frequency?

2. What tones of a seventh chord should not be omitted?

3. The 7th of a diatonic seventh chord resolves (up/down) by (step/leap).

4. Which types of seventh chords are found on $\hat{2}$ and $\hat{7}$ in major and minor? Which forms in minor are the most common?

5. The ii^7 tends to be followed by ____ , the $vii^{ø7}$ by ____ .

6. Which chord discussed in this chapter contains two tritones?

7. The natural tendency of the +4 is to resolve (inward/outward) by step, while the °5 resolves (inward/outward) by step.

8. Try to recall the implications of the preceding question in connection with the vii^{o7} chord.

SELF-TEST 13-1

(Answers begin on page 571.)

A. Notate the following chords. Use accidentals, not key signatures.

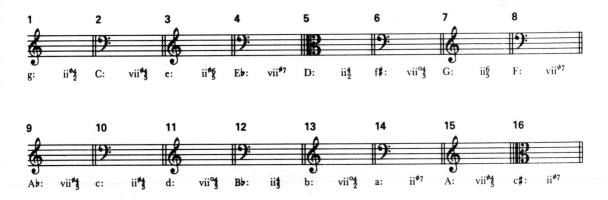

B. Analyze the following chords. Be sure your symbols indicate chord quality and inversion.

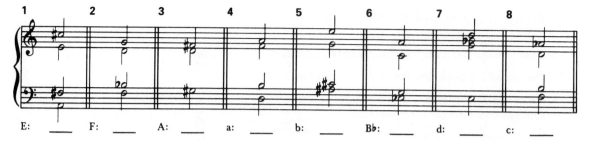

E: ___   F: ___   A: ___   a: ___   b: ___   Bb: ___   d: ___   c: ___

C. Analyze the chords and NCTs in the following excerpts. Whenever you encounter a ii⁷ (ii⁰⁷) or vii⁰⁷ (vii⁰⁷) chord, discuss the voice leading into and out of the chord.

   1. Each numbered blank indicates where a chord is to be analyzed. In many cases it would be equally valid to analyze the "chords" as NCTs.

   Bach, "Gib dich zufrieden und sei stille"

   2. Again, the chords are numbered. Also, the "real" bass notes of chords 1-3 are circled.

   Mozart, Piano Sonata K. 284, III, Var. 5

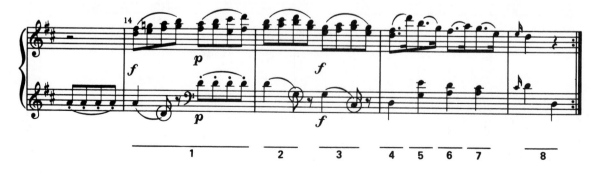

3. Trace the predominant rhythmic idea in this excerpt.

Schubert, *Aufenthalt*

Rau - schen - der Strom, brau - sen - der Wald,
star - ren - der Fels mein Auf - ent - halt,

4. The melody notes on beat 2 of each odd-numbered measure are NCTs. Try to make a reduction that would show the simple model of which this excerpt is an elaboration. What is the meaning of the asterisks in mm. 9 and 15?

Chopin, Mazurka Op. 33, No. 3

D. Notate, introduce, and resolve the specified chords. Each chord 7th is to be approached as a suspension, as a neighbor, or as a passing tone, as specified. Include key signatures and roman numerals.

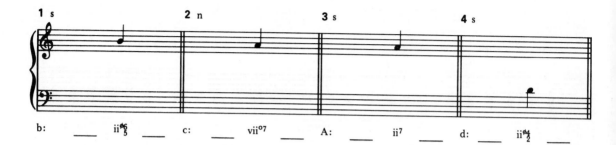

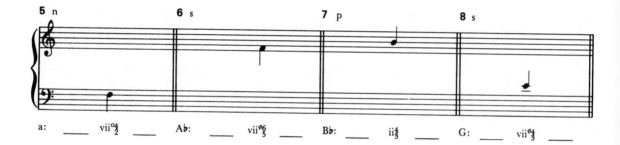

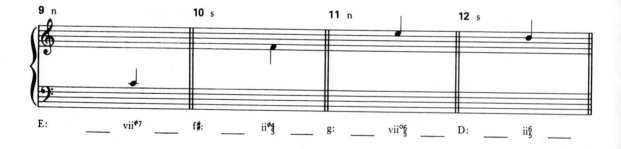

E. Analyze the chords called for by this figured bass, analyzing in D major throughout. Then add two upper treble-clef parts conforming to those chords. Note: This trio would actually be performed by four musicians: two violinists, someone playing the bass line (probably a cellist), and a keyboard player realizing the figured bass. (The numerals 3 and 5 call for root position triads.)

Corelli, Trio Sonata Op. 3, No. 2, II

EXERCISE 13-1. See Workbook.

CHAPTER FOURTEEN

OTHER DIATONIC SEVENTH CHORDS

THE IV⁷ CHORD

The diatonic subdominant seventh chord is found in the forms shown in Example 14-1.

Example 14-1.

Like the subdominant triad, the subdominant seventh moves to V (or vii°⁶), often passing through some form of the ii chord on the way. The resolution to ii⁷ (possibly inverted) is especially easy to handle, because only the 7th needs to move. This is illustrated in Example 14-2.

Example 14-2.

When iv⁷ moves directly to V, parallel 5ths may result if the 7th of the chord is placed above the 3rd (Ex. 14-3a). This can be corrected through the use of a cadential six-four (Ex. 14-3b) or by doubling the 5th of the V chord (Ex. 14-3c). The solutions illustrated in Examples 14-3d and 14-3e, while less commonly used, are also acceptable. Bach's solution in Example 13-12 (p. 217) is especially elaborate. His voice leading combines elements of Examples 14-3a and 14-3b and ornaments the result with a number of NCTs.

Example 14-3.

Otherwise, the voice leading to or from the root position or inverted subdominant seventh is smooth and offers no new problems. An interesting example is quoted on the next page. While the treatment of the IV^M7 in Example 14-4 is conventional, the rest of the progression is not. Approximately half of the chord successions would have to be called *exceptional* or *nonfunctional*. Especially unusual are the chords setting the words "Gebete, darinnen," ending with the chord labeled ♭VII. This is a "borrowed" chord, the subject of Chapter 21. The textural reduction, which shows only the soprano and the bass, explains the ♭VII as coming about through the sequential treatment of five-note motives in the outer voices. The notes belonging to each appearance of one of the motives are notated as half notes and are beamed to each other.

Example 14-4. Brahms, "Der englische Gruss," Op. 22, No. 1

in ih - rem Ge - be - te, dar - in - nen, dar - in - nen sie rang.

Eb: V   IV   V   vi   ii   iii   IV   ♭VII   V $\frac{4}{2}$ I⁶   IVᴹ⁷   V ⁷   I

Textural reduction

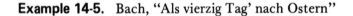

The subdominant seventh in minor with a raised $\hat{6}$ (see Ex. 14-1) has the same sound as that of a dominant seventh chord, but it does not have a dominant function. Instead, it results from ascending motion toward the leading tone ($\uparrow\hat{6}$-$\uparrow\hat{7}$-$\hat{1}$), as in the Bach example below (Ex. 14-5). This phrase is especially interesting in that it contains subdominant chords using both $\uparrow\hat{6}$ and $\downarrow\hat{6}$ and dominant chords using both $\uparrow\hat{7}$ and $\downarrow\hat{7}$.

Example 14-5. Bach, "Als vierzig Tag' nach Ostern"

e: i   6 $\frac{5}{3}$ V⁶ $\frac{5}{3}$ i   IV$\frac{6}{5}$ V⁶   i   v⁶   iv⁶   V

THE VI⁷ CHORD

The submediant seventh is found in three forms (Ex. 14-6).

Example 14-6.

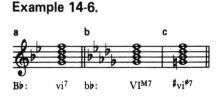

Bb: vi⁷   bb: VI^M7   #vi^ø7

Like their parent triads, the vi⁷ and the VI^M7 typically move toward V, usually passing through subdominant or supertonic chords, or both, on the way. The resolutions to IV and ii are not difficult, and some of the possibilities are illustrated in Example 14-7.

Example 14-7.

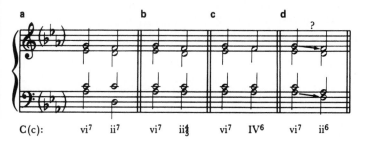

C(c):   vi⁷   ii⁷   vi⁷   ii⁴₃   vi⁷   IV⁶   vi⁷   ii⁶

If a root position vi⁷ or VI^M7 moves to a root position V, parallel 5ths are apt to result, as in Example 14-8a. In major this problem can be avoided by moving to V⁶ or V⁶₅, as in Example 14-8c.

Example 14-8.

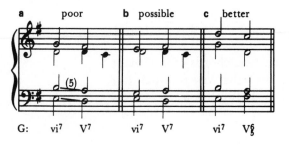

G: vi⁷   V⁷   vi⁷   V⁷   vi⁷   V⁶₃

Of course, in a freer texture, voice leading is a less critical problem. In Example 14-9 parallel 5ths are seen in the vi⁷-ii⁷ progression. Notice also the unresolved 7th in the last cadence.

Example 14-9. Chopin, Ballade Op. 38

In minor, when the root of the submediant seventh moves up by step to $\hat{7}$, the $\hat{6}$ must be raised in order to avoid the interval of a +2. The chord that results when $\hat{6}$ is raised is a half-diminished seventh: ♯vi^{ø7}. The origin of this chord is illustrated in Example 14-10.

Example 14-10.

The ♯vi^{ø7} usually serves as a passing chord between two chords of dominant function (V or vii°). It moves most smoothly to the otherwise unusual root position vii°, as in Example 14-11, but it can move to V$^6_5$ if $\hat{1}$ leaps to $\hat{5}$ (as in Ex. 14-10b).

Example 14-11. Bach, "Warum betrübst du dich, mein Herz"

a: i   V (♯₄♯₂) i⁶ V ♯vi⁰⁷ vii° i   V

THE I⁷ CHORD

The tonic seventh chord in its diatonic form is a M⁷ chord in a major key (Ex. 14-12a) and a m⁷ chord in a minor key (Ex. 14-12b). The minor-major seventh chord in minor (Ex. 14-12c), while possible, is quite rare in the tonal tradition, although it is used freely in jazz.

Example 14-12.

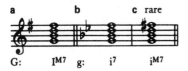

G: IM7   g: i7   iM7

Adding a 7th to the tonic triad obviously deprives it of tonal stability. Rather than being a harmonic goal or resting place, the tonic seventh is an active chord that demands resolution. It tends to move to a IV, or sometimes to a ii or vi, any of which might also contain a 7th. The chord of resolution must be one that contains $\hat{6}$ so that the chord 7th ($\hat{7}$) can resolve down to it. Some possibilities are illustrated in Example 14-13.

Example 14-13.

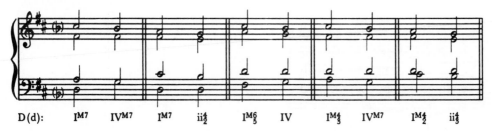

D(d):   IM7   IVM7   IM7   ii♯₂   IM⁶₅   IV   IM⁴₃   IVM7   IM⁴₂   ii♯₃

While the tonic seventh is by no means a frequently encountered sonority, it can be very effective when handled well. Two examples from Schumann's *Album for the Young* appear below, with the 7th approached as a passing tone in each case. In both cases the chord 7th could be analyzed as a NCT, as is frequently the case with seventh chords. The decision to analyze a tone as a 7th will be influenced by such factors as its relative duration (Ex. 14-14) or its suspension into the next chord (Ex. 14-15). The textural reduction of Example 14-14 shows that the chord 7ths resolve down by step, even in this fairly free texture (see the bracketed notes). In the roman numeral analysis "V$^4_3$/V" represents a secondary dominant, which will be discussed in Chapter 16.

Example 14-14. Schumann, "Mignon," Op. 68, No. 35

Example 14-15. Schumann, "Spring Song," Op. 68, No. 15

THE III⁷ CHORD

The diatonic mediant seventh chord takes the forms illustrated in Example 14-16. The first two chords in Example 14-16 (the other is rarely used) occur most often in sequences of seventh chords.

Example 14-16.

A typical instance of such a sequence is seen in Example 14-17. The music shown is played by the string orchestra, while the soloists have a somewhat embellished version. The iii⁷ usually progresses to vi⁽⁷⁾, as here, but it may also be followed by a IV chord.

Example 14-17. Corelli, Concerto Grosso Op. 6, No. 3, V

SEVENTH CHORDS AND THE CIRCLE-OF-FIFTHS SEQUENCE

As we explained in Chapter 6, the usual harmonic functions of most diatonic chords are closely related to the circle-of-fifths sequence. It is not surprising, then, that this is one of the most commonly used sequential patterns (it can still be heard occasionally in popular music). If the chords used in a circle-of-fifths sequence are seventh chords, certain voice-leading conventions are almost always followed.

If the seventh chords are in root position in a four-part texture, complete chords will alternate with incomplete chords (5th omitted). If you look back at the iv⁷ in Example 14-17, you will see that all notes of the chord are present, while the VII⁷ that follows omits the 5th (**F**). This alternation between complete and incomplete chords continues through the V⁷ chord. There is no other satisfactory way to handle the voice leading in this situation, as you can prove to yourself easily enough.

If the seventh chords are inverted in a four-part texture, either ⁶₅ chords will alternate with ⁴₂ chords, or ⁴₃ chords will alternate with 7 (root position) chords. All chords will be complete. These two situations are illustrated in Example 14-18.

Example 14-18.

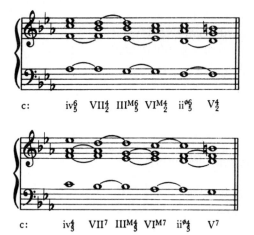

c: iv⁶₅   VII⁴₂   IIIᴹ⁶₅   VIᴹ⁴₂   ii°⁶₅   V⁴₂

c: iv⁴₃   VII⁷   IIIᴹ⁴₃   VIᴹ⁷   ii°⁴₃   V⁷

In three-part textures, a circle-of-fifths sequence will usually be in root position. A root position circle-of-fifths sequence in a three-part texture was illustrated in Example 6-7 (p. 98), although a fourth part is actually contributed by the accompaniment. The relevant part of that example is shown in reduction below, every chord omitting the 5th.

Example 14-19.

SUMMARY

Some seventeen different seventh chords have been discussed in this chapter and the preceding one. Rather than trying to memorize the typical resolutions of these chords, we suggest that you simply remember and apply these principles:

1. The function of a triad is not changed by the addition of a 7th. Since, for example, iv tends to progress to ii° or V, you may assume that iv⁷ has these same tendencies. Exception: the tonic becomes an active chord instead of a stable harmonic goal.

2. Smooth approach to the 7th of the chord is a feature of many, but not all, passages employing diatonic seventh chords.

3. Chord 7ths almost always resolve down by step. It follows, therefore, that the chord of resolution must contain the note to which the 7th will resolve. The resolution is sometimes delayed, as in iv⁷-i$^{6}_{4}$-V, or, in rare cases, simply not employed.

4. In minor, the movement of the individual lines usually conforms to the melodic minor scale. Because of this, more seventh-chord types are possible in minor than in major.

5. In a circle-of-fifths progression of root position seventh chords in four parts, incomplete and complete chords must be used in alternation.

SELF-TEST 14-1
(Answers begin on page 576.)

A. Notate the following chords. Use accidentals, not key signatures.

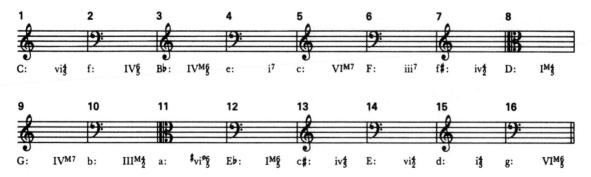

B. Analyze the following chords. Be sure your symbols indicate chord quality and inversion.

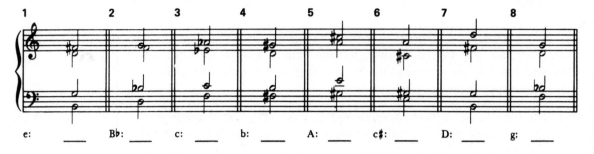

C. Analyze chords and NCTs in the excerpts below. Comment on the voice leading involving any of the chords discussed in this chapter.

1. What spacing "rules" are broken in this excerpt? Why do you suppose this was done?

Bach, "Nun ruhen alle Wälder"

2. Analyze two chords on beat 3 of the first measure.

Bach, "Warum sollt' ich mich denn grämen"

G:

3. A _____ progression occupies most of this excerpt. The seventh chords

in this three-part texture each lack a _____ . If you were to add a fourth voice
beginning on F4, how would it proceed? (Do not label NCTs in this exercise.)

Mozart, Sonata K. 533, III

D. Notate, introduce, and resolve the specified chords. Each chord 7th is to be approached
as a suspension, as a neighbor, or as a passing tone, as indicated. Include key signatures
and roman numerals.

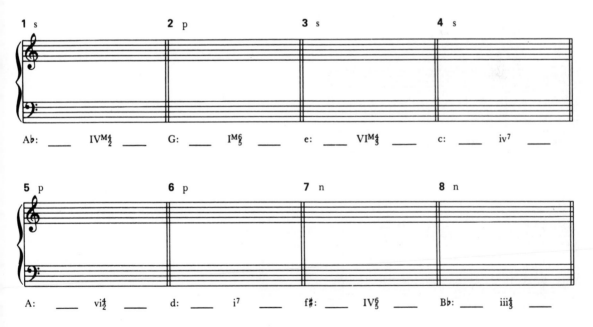

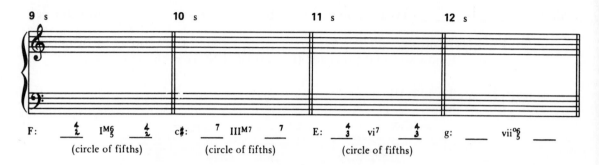

F: $\overset{4}{\underset{2}{}}$ I^M$\overset{6}{\underset{5}{}}$ $\overset{4}{\underset{2}{}}$ c♯: $\overset{7}{}$ III^{M7} $\overset{7}{}$ E: $\overset{4}{\underset{3}{}}$ vi⁷ $\overset{4}{\underset{3}{}}$ g: ___ vii°$\overset{6}{\underset{5}{}}$ ___

(circle of fifths)   (circle of fifths)   (circle of fifths)

E. Add a top voice to create a three-part texture.

d: i   iv⁷   VII   III^{M7}   VI   vii°$\overset{6}{\underset{5}{}}$ i⁶   V   i

F. Analyze the chords specified by each figured bass, and make a harmonization for four-part chorus.

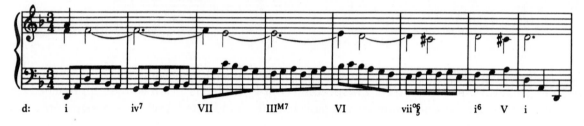

EXERCISE 14-1. See Workbook.

CHAPTER FIFTEEN

LEVELS OF HARMONY

ENGLISH GRAMMAR AND TONAL HARMONY

Reviewing a little English grammar will help us make a point about tonal harmony. Consider this sentence:

The chef carefully prepared a very memorable dinner.

Much of the meaning of the sentence is conveyed by its most essential parts, the subject and the predicate, which would appear in unmodified form as follows:

chef prepared dinner

While this telegraphic style is not elegant, it does get the idea of the sentence across, just as would a I-V-I progression. The other words in the sentence flesh it out and help describe the subject and predicate. The whole sentence can be diagramed to show the function of each word.

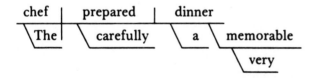

The grammar of tonal harmony has some similarities to spoken language, but it is not quite so well understood. While we might draw an analogy between chord functions and parts of speech, no one has devised a system of diagraming harmony as precisely as English sentences.

LEVELS OF HARMONY

Play this phrase (Ex. 15-1) slowly.

Example 15-1. Haydn, Sonata No. 33, II

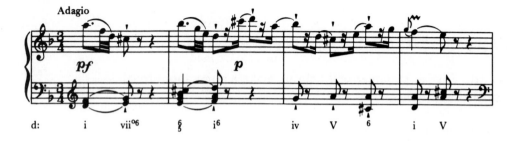

The basic tonal motion of this phrase, the skeletal subject and predicate, is made up of the i-V progression formed by the chords that begin and end the phrase. But how do the other chords *function?* How do we evaluate their relative importance? The roman numerals give us a hint, but more analysis is required. One way to approach such an analysis is to try to hear the chords as originating at different levels: some levels are rather fundamental to the structure, others are more ornamental.

Play the first two measures again. One way to hear this fragment is as an arpeggiation from i to i⁶ that is filled in by the vii°⁶₅ (or vii°⁶-vii°⁶₅). We might diagram these relationships on different levels as follows.

$$
\begin{array}{ccccc}
\text{i} & - & - & - & - \\
\text{i} & - & - & - & \text{i}^6 \\
\text{i} & - & \text{vii}^{o6}_{5} & - & \text{i}^6 \\
\end{array}
$$

The second part of the phrase is more involved. The V chord predominates, but the iv is an important dominant preparation. The root position i serves not as the goal of the phrase but as part of the prolongation of the V chord. Least important of all is the V⁶, which leads to (and depends upon) the i chord. These relationships might be summarized this way.

```
 -  -  V  -  -  -  -  -
iv  -  V  -  -  -  -  -
iv  -  V  -  -  -  i  -  V
iv  -  V  -  V⁶ -  i  -  V
```

When we put the two halves of the phrase together, the diagram should show i and V as the most significant chords, with the iv coming in at the next level. The function of every other chord in the phrase must also be made clear.

```
i  -  -  -  -  -  -  -  V  -  -  -  -  -
i  -  -  -  -  -  iv  -  V  -  -  -  -  -
i  -  -  -  i⁶  -  iv  -  V  -  -  -  -  -
i  - vii°⁶₅ - i⁶  -  iv  -  V  -  -  -  i  -  V
i  - vii°⁶₅ - i⁶  -  iv  -  V  - V⁶ -  i  -  V
```

Are there other ways to hear this phrase? Certainly. But we have gone a step beyond mere chord labeling in showing how a listener or performer might interpret this passage.

   While Example 15-1 is incomplete in the sense that it ends with a HC, Example 15-2 contains a parallel period with complete harmonic motion away from I and back again.

Example 15-2.   Haydn, Sonata No. 35, III

C: I   V⁴₂   I⁶   V⁶₃   I   V   I   V⁴₂   I⁶   IV   V⁷   I

This excerpt can be seen as an elaboration of the progression presented in Example 15-3.

Example 15-3.

I				V	I	V⁷	I

The other chords in Example 15-2 include a dominant preparation (IV), arpeggiations (I⁶), and chords that fill in the arpeggiations (V⁴₂ and V⁶₅). The chord functions might be diagramed as follows.

I -   -   -   -   -   -   -   -   - V - I -   -   -   -   -   -   - V⁷ - I

I -   -   -   -   -   -   -   -   - V - I -   -   -   -   - IV - V⁷ - I

I -   -   - I⁶ -   -   - I - V - I -   -   - I⁶ - IV - V⁷ - I

I - V⁴₂ - I⁶ - V⁶₅ - I - V - I - V⁴₂ - I⁶ - IV - V⁷ - I

This kind of analysis is much more subjective than sentence diagraming is, yet it is important that the analyst consider the function of each chord, even if several interpretations are possible. In a levels analysis the highest level will usually include only the I chord that occurs near the beginning of the phrase and the V or V-I that ends it. The next level will often include the ii or IV preceding the last V. Other chords that sometimes seem to be more significant than those surrounding them include these.

Arpeggiations of important chords

Root position I and V chords

Goals of stepwise bass lines

Tonicized chords (to be discussed in Chapters 16-17)

Chords of longer duration

SOME METHODS OF HARMONIC EMBELLISHMENT

Various methods are used to expand upon the simple progression that serves as the background of a passage. Some of them have been seen in Examples 15-1 and 15-2. The simplest of all is *octave displacement* (see m. 6 of Ex. 15-2, soprano and bass). More interesting is *arpeggiation* (mm. 1-2 of Exx. 15-1 and 15-2), which can itself be embellished. Most often used to embellish arpeggiations are *passing chords* (mm. 1-2 of Ex. 15-1), although *appoggiatura chords* (m. 1 of Ex. 15-2) are also used. Another method is the *neighbor chord*, two of which are illustrated in Example 15-4.

Example 15-4.

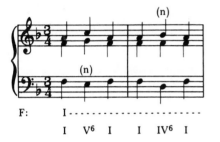

A familiar form of harmonic embellishment is the six-four chord (review Chapter 9). You will recall that many triads in second inversion serve as passing chords or as embellishments of tonic or dominant chords, while others come about as arpeggiations. Strong dominant preparation chords (usually ii or IV) are in a class by themselves. They often occur at metrically stressed points, and they are frequently embellished. In many cases you may feel they rank with or just below the fundamental I and V chords in significance. The importance of these chords is reflected in their early appearance on the levels diagrams we have presented so far in this chapter.

EXAMPLES FROM A CHORALE

The chorale harmonization is a good source for the study of levels of harmony because it presents a large number of chords in a short space of time. Since most chorales modulate (change key) or contain tonicizations (see Chapters 16-17), we will have to restrict ourselves in this chapter, for the most part, to excerpts. The remainder of the examples in this chapter are drawn from Bach's harmonization of "Nun ruhen alle Wälder."

Example 15-5 shows the first phrase of the chorale. This phrase is obviously "about" the I chord, which appears in root position three times and occupies four of the eight beats in the example.

Example 15-5. Bach, "Nun ruhen alle Wälder"

A♭: I IV vii°⁶ I   IVM⁶₅ V⁶₅ I

There is no root position V, a weaker V⁶₅ being used at the cadence. It can be heard as a neighbor chord to the I (Ex. 15-6).

Example 15-6.

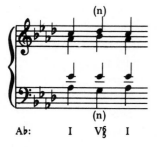

A♭: I V⁶₅ I

The preparation for the V⁶₅ is provided by the IVM⁶₅ that precedes it. So far, our levels might be shown as

I – – – – – – – – – – – –
I – – – – – – – – – V⁶₅ – I
I – – – – – – IVM⁶₅ – V⁶₅ – I

The vii^{o6} that appears early in the phrase is a weak form of dominant harmony. Like the V$_5^6$, it can be heard as a neighbor chord (Ex. 15-7).

Example 15-7.

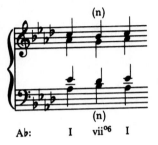

A♭:   I   vii^{o6} I

The vii^{o6} is preceded by its own dominant preparation, a root position IV, which gives us this reading of the phrase.

```
I  -  -  -  -  -  -  -  -  -  -  -  -
I  -  -  -  -  -  -  -  -  -  V⁶₅ -  I
I  -  -  -  -  -  -  IVᴹ⁶₅ -  V⁶₅ -  I
I  -  -  -  vii°⁶ -  I  -  IVᴹ⁶₅ -  V⁶₅ -  I
I  -  IV  -  vii°⁶ -  I  -  IVᴹ⁶₅ -  V⁶₅ -  I
```

The third phrase of the chorale (Ex. 15-8) is essentially a I-V progression.

Example 15-8. Bach, "Nun ruhen alle Wälder"

A♭:   V$_2^4$ I^6 vii^{o6} I   6   V

We choose the root position I as the "original" version, with the arpeggiations embellishing it, as in Example 15-9.

Example 15-9.

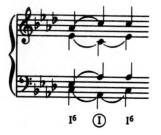

Since this phrase has no dominant preparation, the only chords left to account for are the relatively weak V_2^4 and vii^{o6} chords that embellish the tonic harmony.

$$
\begin{array}{ccccccccccc}
- & - & - & - & - & - & I & - & - & - & V \\
- & - & I^6 & - & - & - & I & - & I^6 & - & V \\
V_2^4 & - & I^6 & - & vii^{o6} & - & I & - & I^6 & - & V \\
\end{array}
$$

The last phrase of the chorale (Ex. 15-10) is an embellished I-V7-I progression.

Example 15-10.   Bach, "Nun ruhen alle Wälder"

The V7 is prepared by a IVM7 and by a weaker IV6, as diagramed below.

$$
\begin{array}{ccccccccc}
I & - & - & - & - & - & V^7 & - & I \\
I & - & - & - & IV^{M7} & - & V^7 & - & I \\
I & - & IV^6 & - & IV^{M7} & - & V^7 & - & I \\
\end{array}
$$

The other three chords serve as an *anacrusis* (upbeat) to the first I chord and are added one at a time to the levels analysis.

$$- \quad - \quad - \quad - \quad V_5^6 \quad - \quad I \quad - \quad IV^6 \quad - \quad IV^{M7} \quad - \quad V^7 \quad - \quad I$$

$$- \quad - \quad vi^7 \quad - \quad V_5^6 \quad - \quad I \quad - \quad IV^6 \quad - \quad IV^{M7} \quad - \quad V^7 \quad - \quad I$$

$$iii \quad - \quad vi^7 \quad - \quad V_5^6 \quad - \quad I \quad - \quad IV^6 \quad - \quad IV^{M7} \quad - \quad V^7 \quad - \quad I$$

CONCLUSION

The concepts presented in this chapter are by no means original, but this kind of analysis of harmonic levels is not widely used. For this reason it will not be pursued systematically throughout the text. Instead, the idea of harmonic layers is introduced here to encourage the reader to understand that, although each chord may be labeled with its own roman numeral, all chords are *not* equally important. In fact, not all chords with the same label (all V's, all I's), have identical uses. Some serve as starting points, some as goals, others as connectors, and so on. These fascinating and complicated relationships are what the grammar of tonal harmony is all about.

SELF-TEST 15-1
(Answers begin on page 579.)

Analysis.

1. Label the chords and do a levels analysis. What kind of NCT is the A4 in the soprano?

Bach, "Ich freue mich in dir"

A:

2. This exercise and the next one are two different harmonizations by Handel of the same melody. Label the chords and do a levels analysis.

Handel, "Wenn mein Stündlein vorhanden est"

Bb:

3. Label the chords and do a levels analysis. What progression in this excerpt is relatively unusual?

Handel, "Wenn mein Stündlein vorhanden est"

Bb:

4. Label the chords and do a levels analysis. What is the form of this excerpt? What kind of NCT is the C5 in m. 8?

Schumann, "Poor Orphan Child," Op. 68, No. 6

EXERCISE 15-1. See Workbook.

PART FOUR

CHROMATICISM 1

CHAPTER SIXTEEN

SECONDARY FUNCTIONS 1

CHROMATICISM AND ALTERED CHORDS

The term *chromaticism* refers to the use of pitches foreign to the key of the passage. The only chromaticism we have discussed so far involves chromatic non-chord tones. For instance, Example 16-1 contains several notes not found in the B♭ major scale, but all of them are non-chord tones.

Example 16-1. Haydn, Quartet Op. 64, No. 3, I

Some people use the term *nonessential chromaticism* to describe the use of chromatically altered tones as NCTs. *Essential chromaticism* refers to the use of tones from outside the scale as members of chords. Such chords are called *altered chords*.

SECONDARY FUNCTIONS

By far the most common sort of altered chord in tonal music is the *secondary function*. A chord whose function belongs more closely to a key other than the main key of the passage is called a secondary function. Listen to Example 16-2, paying special attention to the ending. Although the two-part texture means that incomplete chords will have to be used, it is clear that the F♯4 in m. 7 is not a NCT. In fact, the last two chords are D and G, and they sound like V-I in the key of G.

Example 16-2.   Haydn, Symphony No. 94, II

If our ears were to lose track of the original tonic at this point, or if the music were to continue in the key of G, we would analyze this as a change of key. However, since we still hear the G chord as a V, and since the next phrase is a repeat of the first one, we label the G chord as V and call the D chord a *V of V* (the symbol is V/V). We say that the D chord has *tonicized* the G chord, has given it special emphasis, but that a change of tonic has not taken place.

Most secondary functions are either secondary dominants (*V of* and *V⁷ of*) or secondary leading tone chords (*vii° of, vii°⁷ of,* and *vii⌀⁷ of*).

SECONDARY DOMINANT CHORDS

Since tonic triads are always major or minor, it makes sense that only major and minor triads can be tonicized by secondary dominants. This means that you would not expect to find V/ii° in minor or V/vii° in either major or minor. All other diatonic chords (other than I, of course) may be tonicized by secondary dominants. The chart that follows illustrates the possibilities in F major.

SECONDARY DOMINANTS IN MAJOR

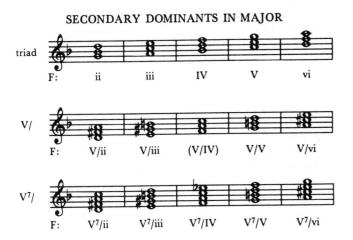

Only one of these chords, V/IV, is identical to a diatonic chord in F. Because V/IV sounds like I, composers most often use V⁷/IV instead of V/IV to make the secondary function clear.

The secondary dominants in d minor are illustrated in the chart below. Here three chords are identical to diatonic chords in d minor. The V/III (= VII) and the V⁷/III (= VII⁷) are both usable, even though they are not altered chords, since VII and VII⁷ usually function as dominants of III anyway. The V/VI, however, would usually be analyzed as III instead of as a secondary dominant.

SECONDARY DOMINANTS IN MINOR

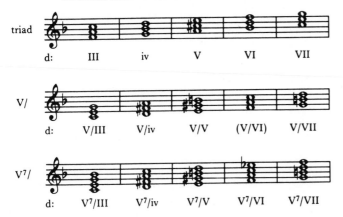

The major or minor triad that is tonicized by a secondary dominant may occur with its 7th, or the tonicized chord may itself be altered to become a secondary dominant. This means, for example, that any of the following progressions might be encountered.

$$V^7/ii\text{-}ii \qquad\qquad V^7/ii\text{-}V/V$$
$$V^7/ii\text{-}ii^7 \qquad\qquad V^7/ii\text{-}V^7/V$$

SPELLING SECONDARY DOMINANTS

There are three steps involved in spelling a secondary dominant.

1. Find the root of the chord that is to be tonicized.

2. Go up a P5.

3. Using that note as the root, spell a major triad (for V of) or a major-minor seventh chord (for V^7 of).

For example, to spell a V/vi in E♭, the steps are the following (Ex. 16-3).

1. The root of vi in E♭ is C.

2. A P5 above C is G.

3. A major triad on G is G/B♮/D.

Example 16-3.

E♭:   vi   P5↑   V/vi

Or, to spell a V^7/V in b minor (Ex. 16-4),

1. The root of V in b is F♯.

2. A P5 above F♯ is C♯.

3. A Mm^7 on C♯ is C♯/E♯/G♯/B.

Example 16-4.

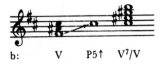

b: V   P5↑   V⁷/V

RECOGNIZING SECONDARY DOMINANTS

If you encounter an altered chord in a passage, there is a good chance that it will be a secondary dominant. These steps will work in most cases.

1. Is it a major triad or major-minor seventh chord? If not, it is not a secondary dominant.

2. Find the note a P5 below the root of the altered chord.

3. Would the diatonic triad built on that note be a major or minor triad? If so, the altered chord is a secondary dominant.

SELF-TEST 16-1
(Answers begin on page 581.)

A. Review how to spell secondary dominants (p. 252). Then notate these secondary dominants in the specified inversions. Include key signatures.

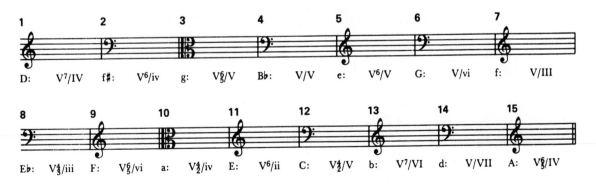

1   2   3   4   5   6   7
D: V⁷/IV   f♯:   V⁶/iv   g: V⁶₅/V   B♭:   V/V   e: V⁶/V   G: V/vi   f: V/III

8   9   10   11   12   13   14   15
E♭:   V⁴₃/iii   F: V⁶₅/vi   a: V⁴₂/iv   E: V⁶/ii   C: V⁴₂/V   b: V⁷/VI   d: V/VII   A: V⁶₅/IV

B. Label any chord that might be a secondary dominant according to the steps outlined on page 253. Label all others with an *X*.

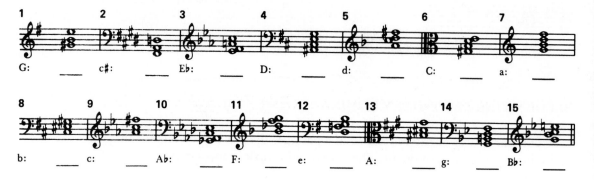

G: _____   c#: _____   Eb: _____   D: _____   d: _____   C: _____   a: _____

b: _____   c: _____   Ab: _____   F: _____   e: _____   A: _____   g: _____   Bb: _____

EXERCISE 16-1. See Workbook.

SECONDARY DOMINANTS IN CONTEXT

Secondary dominants generally resolve just as primary dominants do. That is, a V$_5^6$/V in C will resolve the same way as V$_5^6$ would in the key of G (Ex. 16-5a). The only difference is that sometimes the chord that the secondary dominant resolves to contains a 7th. In that case, the leading tone slides down a half step to become the 7th of the chord of resolution (Ex. 16-5b). Notice that complete seventh chords alternate with incomplete ones in Example 16-5c. This part-writing principle should be familiar to you from the discussion of circle-of-fifths sequences in Chapter 14 (pp. 231-232).

Example 16-5.

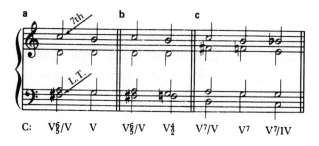

C: V$_5^6$/V   V   V$_5^6$/V   V$_2^4$ V^7/V   V^7 V^7/IV

The V^7/V is the most frequently encountered secondary dominant. In Example 16-6 the V is delayed by a cadential six-four. This is not an irregular resolution of the V^7/V, since, as we know, the I$^6_4$-V together stands for V.

Example 16-6. Schumann, *Noveletten,* Op. 21, No. 1

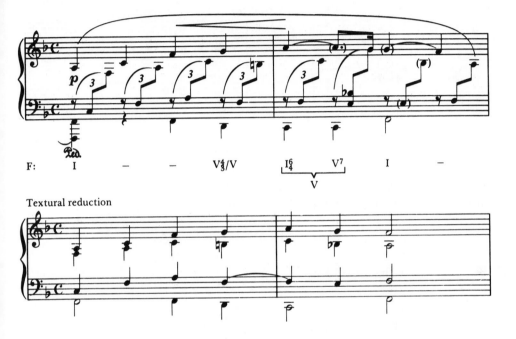

Textural reduction

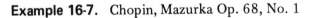

In our discussion of Example 16-5b above, we pointed out that the leading tone of the secondary dominant will move down by half step if the chord that follows contains a 7th. This is illustrated in Example 16-7.

Example 16-7. Chopin, Mazurka Op. 68, No. 1

The common deceptive progression V⁽⁷⁾-vi is often given added impetus by inserting a dominant of vi between the V and the vi, as in Example 16-8.

Example 16-8.   Schumann, *Eintritt*, Op. 82, No. 1

The V⁷/IV, which is an altered tonic chord, offers yet another way to resolve a V chord deceptively. This is seen in Example 16-9. Notice also the stepwise bass line.

Example 16-9.   Tchaikovsky, Trio Op. 50, II

A much less smooth introduction to a V⁷/IV is seen in Example 16-10. Here we see the ending of a phrase that concludes with a deceptive cadence (m. 24). All parts then immediately leap to C♮, which is ♭$\hat{7}$, to state the three-note motive that began the piece. This example also illustrates the V/ii.

Example 16-10. Haydn, Quartet Op. 20, No. 4, I

Examples of dominants of iii in major are not frequently encountered, since the iii itself is the least often used diatonic triad. However, the III in minor, which represents the relative major key, is very often tonicized. Play through Example 16-11, and then compare it to the simple sequence below it. This circle-of-fifths sequence is the background of many passages of tonal music.

Example 16-11. Bach, French Suite No. 1, Minuet II

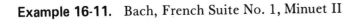

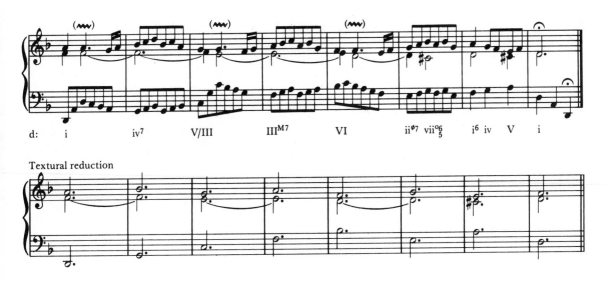

Textural reduction

SELF-TEST 16-2
(Answers begin on page 581.)

A. Analysis.

  1. Analyze with roman numerals. Find the sequence and enclose it in brackets. Although the voice leading is conventional throughout most of this excerpt, parallel 5ths do occur. Find them. Be sure to play this example so that you can appreciate the effect of the last four measures.

  Schumann, *Papillons,* Op. 2, No. 12

2. Label the chords and NCTs.

Schubert, Symphony in B♭, II

3. Analyze chords and NCTs. To what extent is this example sequential? If you play the first half of m. 1 as a chord, you will discover that there are seven different parts in the texture. To what extent are some of these voices doubling another voice at the octave? Except for this, are there any parallel 8ves to be found?

Schuman, *Romanze,* Op. 28, No. 1

4. Analyze chords and NCTs. To what extent is this example sequential?

Mozart, Violin Sonata K. 481, II

5. Analyze chords and NCTs. Treat the second and fifth eighth notes of m. 5-8 and 13-16 as NCTs. How many phrases do you hear in this excerpt? If there are two phrases, what can the form be called? What if there are four phrases? Is there a sequence in this excerpt?

Mendelssohn, Quartet Op. 44, No. 3, II

6. Analyze chords and NCTs, but ignore the grace notes for the purpose of your analysis. Study the four voices that accompany the melody. Do they follow conventional voice-leading principles? What about the melody? Does it contribute an independent fifth voice, or is it sometimes doubling an accompanying line?

Schumann, *Arabesque,* Op. 18

B. For each of the following problems, first analyze the given chord. Next, find a smooth way to lead into the chord. While there are many possibilities, it will often work to use a chord whose root is a P5 above the root of the secondary dominant. Experiment with other relationships also. Then resolve each chord properly, taking special care with the leading tone and the 7th resolutions. Analyze all chords.

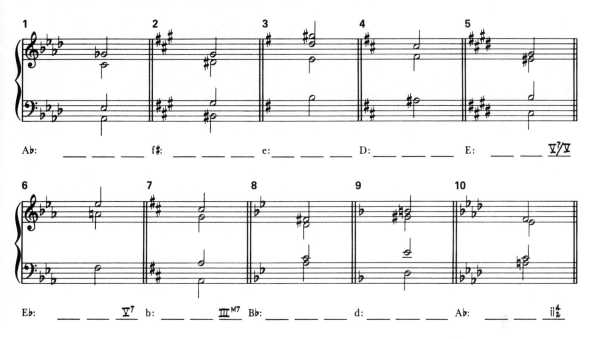

C. Below each note list the secondary V and V⁷ chords that could harmonize that note. You may find it helpful to refer to the charts on page 251.

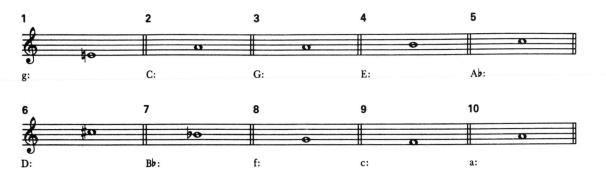

D. Provide roman numerals to show how the first note could be harmonized as a secondary dominant. The second note should be harmonized by the tonicized chord.

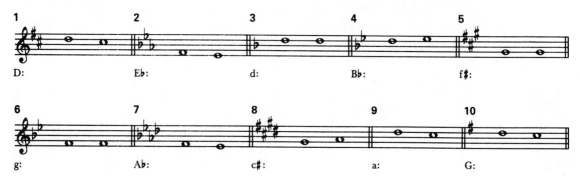

E. Harmonize each chorale phrase for SATB chorus. Include one or more secondary dominants in each phrase and activate the texture with some NCTs. Note that the key of the phrase does not always agree with the key signature.

F. Analyze the harmonies specified by each figured bass, and make a setting for SATB chorus.

1

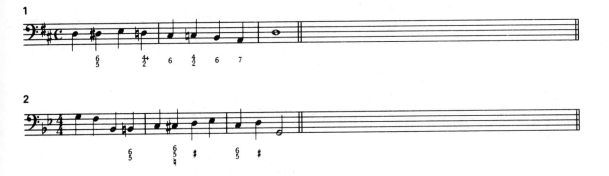

EXERCISE 16-2.   See Workbook.

CHAPTER SEVENTEEN

SECONDARY FUNCTIONS 2

SECONDARY LEADING-TONE CHORDS

The $V^{(7)}$ and vii$^{o(7)}$ chords have similar functions in tonal music (review pp. 102-103), the main difference being that $V^{(7)}$, which contains a P5 above the root, sounds like a more substantial sonority. The same generalizations hold true for secondary functions, which means that any chord that can be tonicized by a $V^{(7)}$ can also be tonicized by a vii$^{o(7)}$.

One small complication arises when a leading-tone seventh chord (as opposed to a leading-tone *triad*) is used as a secondary function. Should the resulting chord be a vii$^{o}7/$ or a vii$^{\phi}7/$? Almost all examples follow these principles:

1. If the triad to be tonicized is minor, use vii$^{o}7/$.

2. If the triad to be tonicized is major, use either vii$^{\phi}7/$ or vii$^{o}7/$,
   although the fully diminished version appears to be used more often.

The tables below list all of the secondary leading-tone chords in major and minor. While all of these chords are theoretically possible, leading-tone chords of ii, IV, iv, V, and vi are more common than the others. One chord, the vii^{o}/III in minor, is identical to a diatonic triad (ii^{o}), and the vii$^{\phi}7/$III is identical to a diatonic seventh chord (ii$^{\phi}7$). The functions of these chords can be made clear only by the context. You may also notice that there is no vii$^{\phi}7/$V in the minor mode, even though the V chord is major. This is because the key that V represents is drawn from the natural minor, which means that the key of the dominant in minor is a minor key. For this reason, vii$^{\phi}7/$V is not used in minor.

SECONDARY LEADING-TONE CHORDS IN MAJOR

SPELLING SECONDARY LEADING-TONE CHORDS

The procedure for spelling secondary leading-tone chords is not difficult and can be summarized as follows.

1. Find the root of the chord that is to be tonicized.

2. Go down a m2.

3. Using that note as the root, spell a diminished triad (for vii° of), a diminished seventh chord (for vii°7 of), or a half-diminished seventh chord (for vii⁰⁷ of).

For example, to spell a vii°7/vi in E♭,

1. The root of vi in E♭ is C.

2. A m2 below C is B.

3. A °7 chord on B is B/D/F/A♭.

RECOGNIZING SECONDARY LEADING-TONE CHORDS

If you find an altered chord in a passage and it is not a V⁽⁷⁾/, there is a good chance it will be a secondary leading-tone chord. These steps will work in most cases.

1. Is the chord a diminished triad or a diminished seventh or half-diminished seventh chord? If not, it is not a secondary leading-tone chord.

2. Find the note a m2 above the root of the altered chord.

3. Would a diatonic triad built on that note be a major or minor triad? If so, the altered chord is a secondary leading-tone chord.

SELF-TEST 17-1
(Answers begin on page 589.)

A. Review how to spell secondary leading-tone chords (p. 268). Then notate these secondary leading-tone chords in the specified inversion. Include key signatures.

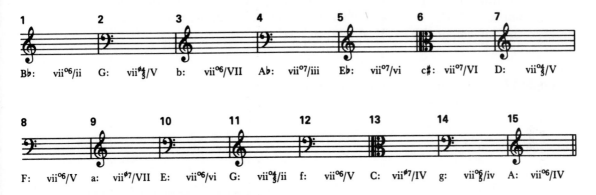

Bb: vii°6/ii   G: vii°♯4/3/V   b: vii°6/VII   Ab: vii°7/iii   Eb: vii°7/vi   c♯: vii°7/VI   D: vii°4/3/V

F: vii°6/V   a: vii°♯7/VII   E: vii°6/vi   G: vii°4/3/ii   f: vii°6/V   C: vii°♯7/IV   g: vii°6/5/iv   A: vii°6/IV

B. Label any chord that would be a secondary leading-tone chord according to the steps outlined on page 268. Label all others with an *X*.

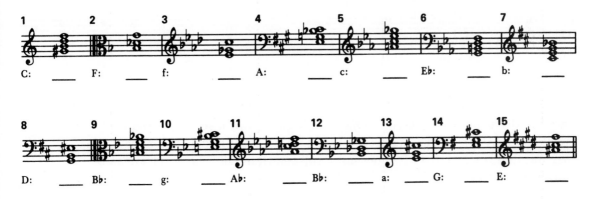

C: _____   F: _____   f: _____   A: _____   c: _____   Eb: _____   b: _____

D: _____   Bb: _____   g: _____   Ab: _____   Bb: _____   a: _____   G: _____   E: _____

EXERCISE 17-1.   See Workbook.

SECONDARY LEADING-TONE CHORDS IN CONTEXT

Secondary leading-tone chords resolve in the same way as do primary leading-tone chords—leading tone up, 7th down—but be careful not to double $\hat{7}$ in resolving a vii°7/V or a vii⌀7/V. Smooth voice leading is usually, but not always, a feature of the progressions. A few examples will give you the idea.

In Example 17-1, Haydn uses a vii⌀7/V after a IV chord in order to add impetus to the movement toward V.

Example 17-1. Haydn, Symphony No. 53, II

C: vi   IV   vii⌀7/V   V $^6_4$ I⁶   vi   ii⁶   V   I

Later in the same work, Haydn signals the beginning of a section based on the V chord by use of a dramatic vii°6/V (Ex. 17-2). The prolonged dominant that was first reached in m. 23 does not resolve until m. 38. The horns sound a m7 lower than written.

Example 17-2. Haydn, Symphony No. 53, III

A vii°$^4_3$/iv and a vii°$^4_2$ of V both appear in Example 17-3. There is a cadential six-four in m. 67, but there is not a real modulation to F♯ here. You can prove this for yourself by playing through the example. You will almost certainly hear the last chord as V, not I.

Example 17-3. Schumann, "Die feindlichen Brüder," Op. 49, No. 2

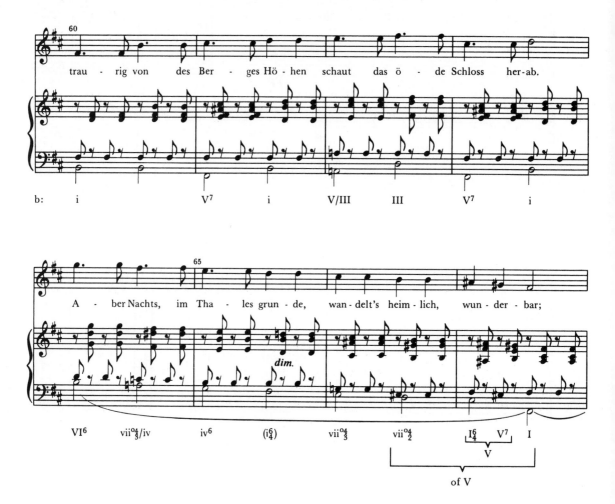

We noted on page 256 that the V$^{(7)}$-vi deceptive progression is often embellished by inserting a V$^{(7)}$/vi between the V and the vi. Even more common is the V-vii°^{7}/vi-vi progression. Example 17-4 illustrates yet another possibility. Here the cadential I$^6_4$ in m. 2 is followed not by V but by the vii°^{7}/vi. We still hear it as a deceptive progression, but the V chord is only implied.

Example 17-4.   Schumann, "Herberge," Op. 82, No. 6

Example 17-5 is interesting in several respects. Notice that the V$^6_5$/V in m. 41 resolves not to a V, as expected, but to a V$^4_3$/IV (we have chosen the A in m. 43 as the bass of the V$^4_3$/IV). This and other unexpected resolutions of secondary functions will be discussed more fully later in this chapter. The V$^4_3$/IV itself resolves normally, as do the vii°$^4_3$/ii and the vii°$^6_5$/ii, except for some liberties taken with the viola part.

Example 17-5.   Beethoven, Symphony No. 2, Op. 36, I

SEQUENCES INVOLVING SECONDARY FUNCTIONS

Sequential patterns often use secondary functions. One that is especially common is the circle-of-fifths sequence, but with one or more secondary functions (V/ or vii°/) substituting for one or more of the diatonic chords.

Below is a short circle-of-fifths sequence, with possible substitutions shown for the first three chords.

Diatonic circle of fifths in C	$e^7(iii^7)$	- $a^7(vi^7)$	- $d^7(ii^7)$	- $G^7(V^7)$ - C(I)
V^7/substitutes	$E^7(V^7/vi)$	- $A^7(V^7/ii)$	- $D^7(V^7/V)$	
vii°7/substitutes	$g\sharp^{°7}(vii^{°7}/vi)$	- $c\sharp^{°7}(vii^{°7}/ii)$	- $f\sharp^{°7}(vii^{°7}/V)$	

By choosing one chord from each of the first three columns in the chart above, we can make up some variations on the circle-of-fifths progression.

Diatonic version	e^7	- a^7	- d^7	- G^7	- C
Variation	E^7	- a^7	- D^7	- G^7	- C
Variation	E^7	- $c\sharp^{°7}$	- d^7	- G^7	- C
Variation	$g\sharp^{°7}$	- A^7	- $f\sharp^{°7}$	- G^7	- C

When a series of major-minor seventh chords is used in a circle-of-fifths sequence, certain voice-leading problems come up. For one thing, as you learned on page 254, each leading tone will resolve down by chromatic half step to become the 7th of the next major-minor seventh chord. Also, as you may recall from page 232, if the chords are in root position in a four-part texture, incomplete seventh chords must alternate with complete seventh chords. These points are illustrated in Example 17-6.

Example 17-6.

Bb: V⁷/vi   V⁷/ii   V⁷/V   V⁷   V⁷/IV

The voice leading in Example 17-6 is the precise voice leading Mozart uses in Example 17-7. However, he goes a step "too far," to an E♭⁷ in m. 58, implying a resolution to A♭. A change of key from B♭ to A♭ would be quite unexpected here. For five measures Mozart prolongs the suspense, until the E♭ in the bass is finally bent up to E♮, creating a vii°7/V in B♭. This leads back to a PAC in B♭. Notice also the A♭⁶₄ chords (pedal six-fours) that occur in mm. 58-61, adding to the listener's anticipation of A♭ as a goal. In studying this example, remember that the basses on the bottom staff sound an octave lower than written.

Example 17-7. Mozart, Symphony No. 40, K. 550, I

DECEPTIVE RESOLUTIONS OF SECONDARY FUNCTIONS

While you will find that most secondary V$^{(7)}$ and vii$^{o(7)}$ chords resolve as expected, you may encounter many interesting exceptions. One that is especially common is the resolution of a V^7/ up to the vi (or VI) of the chord that was being tonicized. For instance, in the key of C:

Chords	D^7	e
Analysis	V^7/V	vi/V
		(iii)

A beautiful example of a deceptive resolution occurs at the end of one of Schumann's songs (Ex. 17-8). Notice that the seventh of the vii^{o7}/V in m. 26 is spelled enharmonically (G♯ instead of A♭) because it is going to ascend to the A before resolving to the G in the V chord. (Incidentally, does the beginning of Ex. 17-8 remind you of a familiar Christmas carol?)

Example 17-8. Schumann, "Auf dem Rhein," Op. 51, No. 4

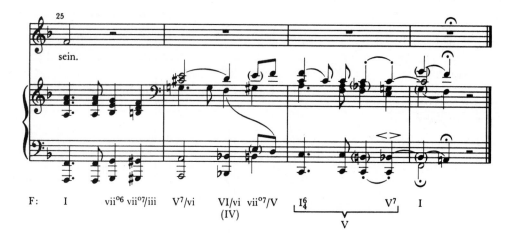

Another kind of deceptive resolution was seen in Example 17-5, above, in which a V$^6_5$/V was followed by a V$^4_3$/IV. One of the reasons this progression "works" here is that it features smooth voice leading, summarized in Example 17-9a. Even smoother is the connection between two dominant seventh chords a m3 apart (Ex. 17-9b and 17-9c) or, surprisingly, a tritone apart

(Ex. 17-9d). If you play through Examples 17-9b, c, and d, you will probably find them convincing, even though it may be hard to imagine at this point how some of these progressions could occur in tonal music.

Example 17-9.

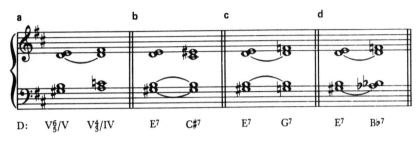

OTHER SECONDARY FUNCTIONS

We have discussed secondary dominants, secondary leading-tone chords, and, in the preceding section, secondary submediants. Other secondary functions do occur, but much less commonly. We tend to hear a change of key when we encounter several chords that are drawing our attention away from the original tonic. But a short progression of chords will generally not be enough to accomplish a change of key, and it is in such passages that other secondary functions occasionally occur.

Listen to Example 17-10. While one could argue in favor of a quick change of key to C in mm. 69-70, it is unlikely that we would really lose track of G as the tonal center so quickly. In this case, IV^6/IV would seem to be a better analysis than IV^6 in the key of C.

Example 17-10. Mozart, Sonata K. 545, II

SUMMARY OF SECONDARY FUNCTIONS

A chord whose function belongs more closely to a key other than the main key of a passage is called a *secondary function* (p. 250). A commonly encountered type is the *secondary dominant,* which may be a major-minor seventh chord or a major triad (p. 251). Also frequently found is the *secondary leading-tone chord,* which may be a diminished triad, diminished seventh chord, or a half-diminished seventh chord (pp. 266-267). Other secondary functions, such as IV/IV, are possible but rare (pp. 281-282). Secondary dominants and leading-tone chords often appear in *sequences* (pp. 276-279), and *deceptive resolutions* of secondary functions do occur (pp. 280-281).

SELF-TEST 17-2
(Answers begin on page 589.)

A. Analysis.

1. Label chords and NCTs.

Bach, "Warum betrübst du dich, mein Herz"

2. Label chords and NCTs. Review pages 276-279, then find two circle-of-fifths progressions that contain more than three chords. Remember that a leading-tone chord may substitute for a chord in the circle of fifths.

Haydn, Sonata No. 43, Minuetto I

3. Label chords and NCTs. Remember that the bass notes continue sounding until the pedal is lifted. The last eighth note in the melody is a rather unusual NCT. Discuss how it might be analyzed.

Mendelssohn, *Song without Words,* Op. 102, No. 1

4. Label chords and NCTs. Analyze the chords in m. 47 in two ways: one in the key of F, one in some key suggested in m. 46.

Mozart, Sonata K. 333, I

5. Label chords and NCTs. Explain why this excerpt is not a period. Do not include the grace notes in your analysis.

Mozart, Violin Sonata K. 379, I

6. Label the chords with roman numerals. Label NCTs in the bassoon part only. Analyze the chords from the middle of m. 88 to the middle of m. 90 in some key other than B♭. Bracket the longest circle-of-fifths progression you can find.

Mozart, Bassoon Concerto K. 191, I

B. For each of these problems, first analyze and resolve the given chord, being especially careful with the chord 7th and the leading tone. Then find a smooth way to lead into the given chord. Analyze all chords.

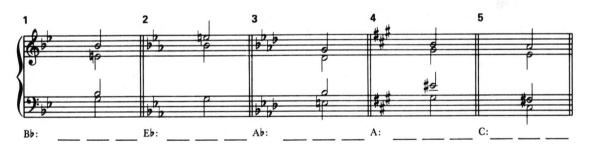

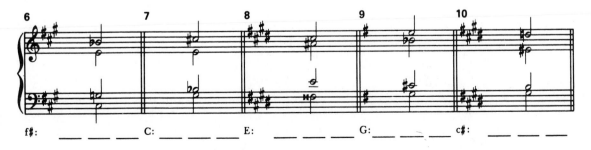

C. Harmonize each of these chorale phrases for SATB chorus. Include at least one secondary leading-tone chord or incorporate some other aspect discussed in this chapter in each harmonization.

1

e:

2

A:

3

b:

D. Analyze the harmonies specified by each figured bass, then make an arrangement of each for SATB chorus.

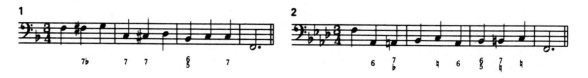

1

7♭   7   7   6̸5   7

2

6 7♭ ♮ 6 6̸5 7♮ ♮

EXERCISE 17-2. See Workbook.

CHAPTER EIGHTEEN

MODULATIONS USING DIATONIC COMMON CHORDS

MODULATION AND CHANGE OF KEY

Almost all compositions from the tonal era begin and end in the same key. Sometimes the *mode* will be changed, usually from minor to major, but the *keynote* (tonic note) remains the same. A piece that begins in c minor and ends in C major is still in C. Even multimovement works begin and end in the same key if the movements are intended to be performed together as a unit. (An interesting exception to this is the song cycle.) The principle also holds for single movements from multimovement works (sonatas, symphonies, song cycles, and so on), although the interior movements will often be in different keys. We will use the term *change of key* for such situations, as in, "There is a change of key from C major in the first movement to F major in the second movement."

Modulation is another matter. A modulation is a shift of tonal center that takes place *within* an individual movement. For while a tonal work or movement begins and ends in the same key, other tonalities generally will be hinted at, referred to, or even strongly established. The longer the work, the more time is likely to be devoted to tonalities other than the tonic and the more keys are likely to be touched upon.

The tonal structure of a composition is closely related to its overall form. For example, a Classical piano sonata might have the following tonal structure. The crooked arrows represent modulations and roman numerals represent other keys in relation to the tonic.

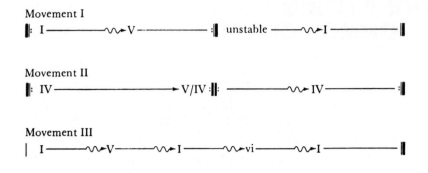

MODULATION AND TONICIZATION

The line between modulation and tonicization (using secondary functions—V/V and so forth) is not clearly defined in tonal music, nor is it meant to be. One listener may find that a very short passage tonicizing a new tonality is enough to make a convincing modulation. For instance, you may have heard some of the excerpts in Chapters 16 and 17 as modulations, while other listeners might not have. Listen to Example 18-1. At the end of the excerpt, do you hear C or A as tonic? You could analyze this passage as *tonicizing* C or as *modulating* to C major. The difference in the analyses would not be an important one. There is no right or wrong here—there are just the interpretations of different listeners.

Example 18-1.   Beethoven, Symphony No. 7, Op. 92, II

It seems clear, however, that composers have always hoped the sophisticated listener (surely a minority of the audience) would manage to follow the modulations aurally. If not, many important effects would be lost. For example, if a composer has brought back a tune in another key when we had expected it to return in tonic, the composer expects us to be surprised. Otherwise, why bother? The fact that such effects may be lost on many listeners should not keep us from trying to appreciate what the composer is doing.

KEY RELATIONSHIPS

Two keys that sound the same but that are spelled differently are called *enharmonically equivalent keys.* C♯ major and D♭ major are enharmonically equivalent. If a composer for some reason respells C♯ as D♭, no modulation has occurred, since the keynote is unchanged.

If a major key and a minor key have the same tonic note, they are called *parallel keys.* The parallel minor of C major is c minor. Since parallel keys share the same tonic, we do not use the term modulation when talking about movement from one key to its parallel. The term *change of mode* (or mutation) is used instead.

If a major key and a minor key share the same key signature, they are called *relative keys.* The relative minor of C major is a minor. The term modulation *is* appropriate here, because movement from one tonic to another is involved. Modulations between relative keys are common, especially from minor to relative major.

Most modulations in tonal music are between *closely related keys.* Two keys are said to be closely related if there is a difference of no more than one sharp or flat in their key signatures. Since this definition applies to both major and minor keys, it includes the relative major or minor key, where there is no difference at all in the key signatures. Here are the keys closely related to C major and c minor.

Starting Key: C major		
1♯	G	e
0♯, 0♭	ⒸC	a
1♭	F	d

Starting Key: c minor		
2♭	g	B♭
3♭	Ⓒc	E♭
4♭	f	A♭

Another way to find the keys closely related to some starting key is to take the keys represented by the tonic, subdominant, and dominant triads and their relatives. In minor use the natural minor scale in determining the closely related keys.

Starting Key: C major		
Dominant	G	e
Tonic	Ⓒ	a
Subdominant	F	d

Starting Key: c minor		
Dominant	g	B♭
Tonic	ⓒ	E♭
Subdominant	f	A♭

Still another method is to take the keys represented by the diatonic major and minor triads (only) of the home key. Again, use natural minor for the minor keys. The diatonic major and minor triads are also those that can be tonicized by secondary dominant or secondary leading-tone chords.

Starting Key: C Major   Starting Key: C Minor

Ⓒ d e F G a (dim.)   ⓒ (dim.) E♭ f g A♭ B♭

If you compare the three pairs of tables above, you will see that each approach yields the same result. There are always five keys closely related to the starting key. Use whichever method seems easiest to you.

All key relationships that are not enharmonic, parallel, relative, or closely related are called *foreign relationships,* and such pairs of keys are said to be *distantly related.* Some relationships are more foreign than others. Often we describe foreign key relationships in terms of simpler relationships used in the composition. Thus a modulation from C major to D major might be described as a modulation to the dominant of the dominant; one from C major to E♭ major might be called a modulation to the relative major of the parallel minor.

CHECKPOINT

1. Is movement from E major to e minor a modulation? Explain. If not, what is it called? What about a♯ minor to b♭ minor?

2. Compare and contrast *modulation* and *change of key*.

3. Name the five kinds of key relationships (discussed on pp. 292-293).

4. Describe three ways to find the five keys closely related to some starting key.

SELF-TEST 18-1
(Answers begin on page 596.)

A. Name the relative key in each case.

1. D ____   2. b♭ ____   3. f♯ ____   4. C♭ ____   5. F ____

6. d♯ ____   7. E ____   8. f ____   9. E♭ ____   10. g♯ ____

B. Name all the closely related keys to the given key. Be sure to use upper case for major, lower case for minor.

1. B♭: ____ ____ ____ ____ ____

2. D♭: ____ ____ ____ ____ ____

3. c: ____ ____ ____ ____ ____

4. a♯: ____ ____ ____ ____ ____

5. c♯: ____ ____ ____ ____ ____

6. A: ____ ____ ____ ____ ____

C. Name the relationship in each case (enharmonically equivalent, parallel, relative and closely related, closely related, or foreign).

1. G/f _____   6. C♭/G♭ _____

2. B/E _____   7. d/D _____

3. a♯/b♭ _____   8. E♭/D♭ _____

4. c/A♭ _____   9. B♭/g _____

5. f♯/A _____   10. c♯/F♯ _____

EXERCISE 18-1. See Workbook.

COMMON-CHORD MODULATION

Most modulations are made smoother by using one or more chords that are common to both keys. This common chord (or chords) serves as a hinge or pivot linking the two tonalities. In the diagram below, the shaded rectangle represents the common chord in a modulation from B♭ to F.

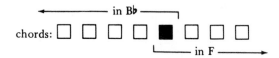

While any pair of closely related keys will have at least one diatonic triad in common, this is not always the case with most foreign key relationships. Modulation to a foreign key often requires the use of an altered chord as a common chord; techniques for such modulations are presented in Chapter 19.

To discover the potential common chords between two keys, simply run through the diatonic triads found in the first key to see if they also occur in the second key. For example, there are four triads in common between B♭ and F.

First key, B♭	I	ii	iii	IV	V	vi	vii°
Triads in B♭	B♭	c	d	E♭	F	g	a°
Triads in F	B♭	C	d	e°	F	g	a
Second key, F	IV	V	vi	vii°	I	ii	iii

In minor keys, we usually consider the chord types commonly found on each scale degree: i, ii°, III, iv, V, VI, vii°. This yields two common chords between B♭ major and c minor.

First key, B♭	I	ii	iii	IV	V	vi	vii°
Triads in B♭	B♭	c	d	E♭	F	g	a°
Triads in c	b°	c	d°	E♭	f	G	A♭
Second key, c	vii°	i	ii°	III	iv	V	VI

Less frequently, other chords that occur in minor, such as IV and v, are used as common chords. Example 18-2 illustrates a modulation from B♭ major to c minor, using the ii in B♭ as the common chord. Notice the symbol used to show the common chord modulation.

Example 18-2.

When you are composing a modulation, you will find that the V or vii° in either key is often the least successful choice as common chord. As Example 18-3a illustrates, such a modulation can sound too abrupt. The modulation will be smoother if the V-I progression is delayed by several chords, especially through the use of a deceptive progression, a cadential six-four, or both, as in Example 18-3b.

Example 18-3.

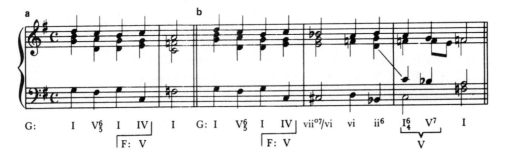

The smooth voice leading in the outer voices of Example 18-3b also contributes to making this modulation to a foreign key convincing and successful.

ANALYZING COMMON-CHORD MODULATION

In analyzing modulations, the procedure to follow is this.

1. Listen to the passage carefully.

2. Find the first chord that seems to be functioning more naturally in the second key than in the first one. (This step is often open to differing interpretations.)

3. Back up one chord. If there is a diatonic common chord, it should be in this position.

In Example 18-4 the C^7 chord at the end of m. 13 functions as V_2^4 in F, but only as a secondary dominant in d. This is the chord that signals the modulation. Backing up one chord to the beginning of the measure brings us to the common chord, B♭ (VI = IV).

Example 18-4. Tchaikovsky, Mazurka Op. 39, No. 10

Example 18-4 is "recomposed" in Example 18-5 to illustrate the fact that the common chord itself does not signal the modulation but just smooths it out. In Example 18-5 the B♭ chord is followed not by a modulation to F but by a cadence in d.

Example 18-5.

The i-III modulation (as in Ex. 18-4) is a very common one. It can be found in most pieces in minor. In major keys the most common modulation is I-V. Example 18-6 illustrates a I-V modulation in a two-part texture. The g♯ diminished triad (or incomplete E⁷) functions more naturally in A than in E and is preceded by the common chord.

Example 18-6.   Haydn, Symphony No. 73, I

Incidentally, you may hear some of the examples and exercises in this chapter as tonicizations instead of true modulations. Analyze them as modulations anyway for practice in locating common chords.

While I-V and i-III are the most frequently encountered modulations, all other closely related modulations do occur. In Example 18-7 the tonality moves briefly from I to iii. Notice that there is no change of key signature here. Indeed, the key signature of the main tonality is usually maintained throughout the work, no matter how many modulations occur.

Example 18-7.   Dvořák, Quartet Op. 51, IV

SELF-TEST 18-2

(Answers begin on page 596.)

A. Analysis.

1. Label chords and NCTs. Try inserting a secondary function before beat 4 of m. 1. What effect does this have on the modulation?

Bach, "Es ist das Heil uns kommen her"

2. Label chords and NCTs. Why is it unlikely that Bach was thinking of the sonority on the last eighth of m. 7 as a seventh chord?

Bach, "Jesu, Jesu, du bist mein"

3. Label the chords with roman numerals. Find an example of (a) sequence and (b) repetition.

Schubert, "Frühlingssehnsucht"

4. Label chords and NCTs. Remember this is an excerpt; don't be fooled by the key signature.

Schubert, "Am Feierabend," Op. 25, No. 5

5. Label chords and NCTs. Find the longest circle-of-fifths harmonic progression in the excerpt. To what extent does that progression generate a sequence in the melody and bass lines?

Schumann, "Freisinn," Op. 25, No. 2

gel - ten!   Bleibt in eu - ren Hüt - ten, eu - ren

Zel - ten! Und ich rei - te froh in al - le Fer - ne,   ü - ber

mei - ner Mü - tze nur die Ster - ne.

B. Fill in the name of the new key on the second line of each exercise.

1. $B\flat$: I   V   I ii^6 V   vi |

   ___ : ii V_3^4 I V^7 I

2. $f\sharp$: i   V   VI iv^6 |

   ___ : ii^6 V   vi   IV   V   I

3. d: i V_5^6/iv iv V_2^4 i^6 |

   ___ : iv^6 (i_4^6) $ii_5^{\varnothing 6}$ V_2^4 i^6 $vii^{\circ 6}$ i

4. A: I   V   vi ii^6 |

   ___ : iv^6 $ii^{\circ 6}$ i_4^6 V   i

   V

5. $E\flat$: I V_3^4 I^6 IV |

   ___ : I $vii^{\circ 6}$ I^6 V_2^4 I^6 ii^6 V   I

C. List the diatonic triads that could serve as common chords between each pair of keys. In minor keys, assume the usual chord qualities: i, ii°, III, iv, V, VI, vii°.

Example: First key: C: I   iii   V   vi
           Triads: C   e   G   a
           Second key: G: IV   vi   I   ii

1. First key, $A\flat$:

   Triads:

   Second key, $D\flat$:

2. First key, c:

   Triads:

   Second key, f:

3. First key, a:

   Triads:

   Second key, F:

4. First key, G:

Triads:

Second key, D:

5. First key, c♯:

Triads:

Second key, E:

6. First key, D:

Triads:

Second key, f♯:

D. Make choral settings of Part B progressions 1 (SATB) and 2 (SAB). Activate the texture with NCTs and/or arpeggiations. Arrange the metric structure so that the last chord comes on a strong beat.

E. Harmonize the following chorale tune for SATB chorus. The first phrase should modulate to V; the second should return to I.

F. Analyze the chords specified by this figured bass, then make an arrangement for SATB chorus.

EXERCISE 18-2.   See Workbook.

CHAPTER NINETEEN

SOME OTHER MODULATORY TECHNIQUES

ALTERED CHORDS AS COMMON CHORDS

In Chapter 18 we discussed modulations using chords that are diatonic in both keys as common chords. While diatonic common-chord modulation is probably the most frequently used modulatory technique, there are many others. This chapter will present a few of them.

In Chapter 18 we listed a three-step procedure for the analysis of modulations. These steps bear repeating here.

1. Listen to the passage carefully.

2. Find the first chord that seems to be functioning more naturally in the second key than in the first one.

3. Back up one chord. If there is a diatonic common chord, it should be in this position.

The phrase "if there is a diatonic common chord" may have suggested to you that altered chords may sometimes be used as common chords. For example, consider the modulation represented below:

Key of G: ⟶

...D⁷ G a A⁷ D...

Key of D: ⟶

Here the first chord that functions more naturally in D than in G is the A⁷ (V⁷ in D). But the a minor triad that precedes it cannot serve as a common chord, since it makes no sense in the context of D major. Instead, the A⁷ is itself the common chord, functioning as V⁷/V in G. This modulation is illustrated in Example 19-1.

Example 19-1. Beethoven, Sonata Op. 14, No. 2, I

G: V$^4_3$ I^6 ii^6 V$^6_5$/V   I

D: V$^6_5$

Secondary V$^{(7)}$ and vii$^{o(7)}$ chords can be used as common chords. The chord might be a secondary function in the first key, in the second key, or in both keys. Sometimes the secondary function coincides with the *point of modulation* (the first chord in the new key), as in Example 19-1, while at other times the secondary function precedes it.

A number of other altered chords, to be discussed in Chapters 21 and 22, frequently serve as the common chord in a modulation, as examples in those chapters will illustrate. An additional common chord technique involving enharmonic reinterpretation of the common chord is the principal topic of Chapter 25.

SEQUENTIAL MODULATION

It is not uncommon for a modulation to come about through the use of a sequence. This is a simple device: the composer merely states something at one pitch level and then states it again immediately at another pitch level. But the modulating sequence, instead of being diatonic, tonicizes a different pitch. Often a common chord could be analyzed in such a modulation, but the sequence is equally important in establishing the new tonal center.

Example 19-2 is a clear instance of a sequential modulation. The first phrase, in C major, is transposed with little change up to d minor to create the second phrase. Sequences up by step are very frequently encountered.

Example 19-2. Schubert, Sonata in E Major, III

While the sequential motion in Example 19-2 is up by step, that in Example 19-3 is down by step, from C major to B♭ major. Because descent by step juxtaposes foreign keys, modulating sequences of this type are not found as often.

Example 19-3. Beethoven, Sonata Op. 53, I

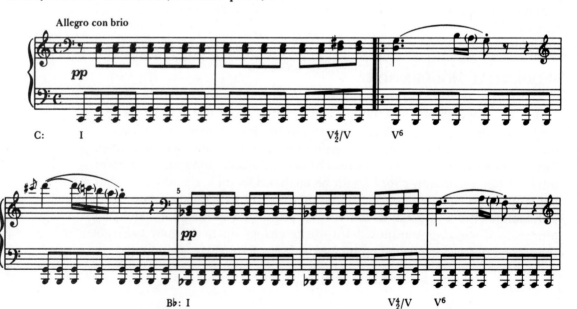

Keep in mind that many sequential modulations are of short duration and might more properly be called tonicizations. Both Example 19-2 and 19-3 return to the first key immediately after the sequence.

Another common pattern for sequential modulation is the circle of fifths. The circle-of-fifths sequences we have studied so far have been diatonic (such as vi-ii-V-I), with occasional secondary functions thrown in. But the circle of fifths can be used to get from one key to another. In Example 19-4 Haydn moves from B major to C major through the progression B-E-A-D-G-C, each chord except the last becoming a V^7 of the chord that follows. The sequence could have been stopped earlier, or it could have been carried past C to F, Bb, and so on, options that are basically open in any sequential modulation.

Example 19-4. Haydn, Quartet Op. 3, No. 3, IV

MODULATION BY COMMON TONE

In some modulations the hinge between the two keys is not a common chord but a common tone. Unlike the common-chord modulation, where the progression usually makes the modulation smooth and undramatic, common-tone modulations often announce themselves clearly to the listener by isolating the common tone. This is the case in Example 19-5, where the note F♯ joins the keys of b minor and D major.

Example 19-5. Mozart, Fantasia K. 475

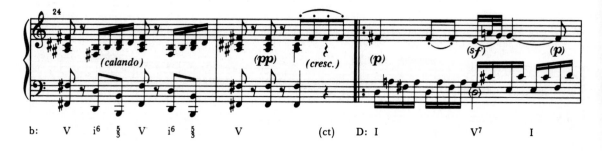

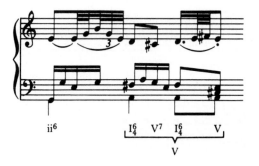

Even more dramatic is Example 19-6, which occurs at the end of the slow introduction to Beethoven's Symphony No. 4. Here an A links a pianissimo V in d minor with a fortissimo V⁷ in B♭ major.

Example 19-6. Beethoven, Symphony No. 4, Op. 60, I

d: V   (ct)   B♭: V⁷

The two chords linked by the common tone in a common-tone modulation usually exhibit a *chromatic mediant relationship,* which has the following characteristics.

1. The roots of the chords are a m3 or M3 apart. Sometimes the m3 or M3 is spelled enharmonically.

2. They are either both major triads or both minor triads (or, in the case of seventh chords, the triad portions of the chords are both major or both minor).

Some examples of chromatic mediant relationships are illustrated in Example 19-7.

Example 19-7.

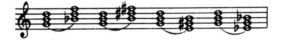

The chromatic mediant relationships that were used by Mozart and Beethoven in Examples 19-5 and 19-6 are shown in Example 19-8.

Example 19-8.

In both the Mozart and the Beethoven examples the two keys involved were closely related. But the chromatic mediant relationship used in common-tone modulations makes it easy to modulate to foreign keys as well. In Example 19-9 Brahms connects a V_5^6/iv in g minor (or V_5^6 in c minor) to a I in B major by the common tone B. Notice that in this case the common tone appears not in the melody, but in the bass.

Example 19-9.   Brahms, Ballade in G Minor, Op. 118, No. 3

MONOPHONIC MODULATION

Sometimes a modulation is carried out by a single vocal or instrumental line. This is done by introducing and emphasizing the tones that are found in the second key but not in the first. While harmonies are more or less clearly implied in a monophonic modulation, it is often better just to label the keys, as we have done in Example 19-10.

Example 19-10. Mozart, Sonata K. 576, II

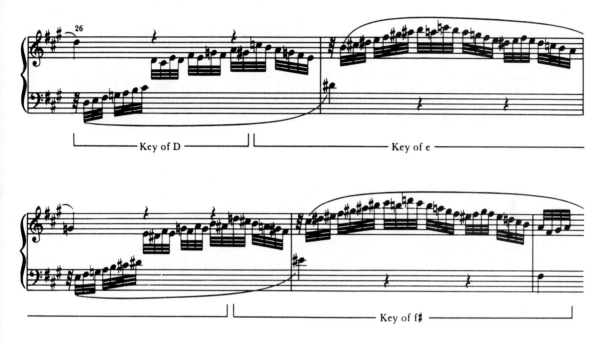

This passage is also sequential, but it is not an example of a sequential modulation. The pattern in mm. 26-27 (D to e) is moved up a step (e to f♯), but the modulation is not caused by the sequence itself.

DIRECT MODULATION

Sometimes modulations occur without any attempt to smooth them over through the use of common chords or common tones. Such modulations most frequently occur between phrases, so this kind of direct modulation is often called a *phrase modulation.* A typical example from a chorale appears in Example 19-11.

Example 19-11. Bach, "Für Freuden, lasst uns springen"

g: V

Bb: I

Most phrase modulations could also be analyzed as common chord or common-tone modulations, or both, as is the case here: the I in Bb could be analyzed as a III in g minor, while the D4 in the tenor provides a common tone between the V in g minor and the I in Bb major. Such analyses are not incorrect, but we prefer the term "phrase modulation" because it more accurately reflects the way we hear this excerpt—as one phrase ending in g minor and another beginning in Bb major, with little effort being made to bridge the gap.

Some direct modulations occur *within* the phrase. However, this kind of modulation is not frequently encountered, and you should try to eliminate all of the other possibilities for explaining the modulation before labeling it as a direct modulation.

Example 19-12 shows a textural reduction of the kind of difficult modulatory passage that you may occasionally encounter. Play through the example slowly (you will definitely need to hear the example), observing the analysis below.

Example 19-12. Mozart, Fantasia K. 475, mm. 6-16 (simplified)

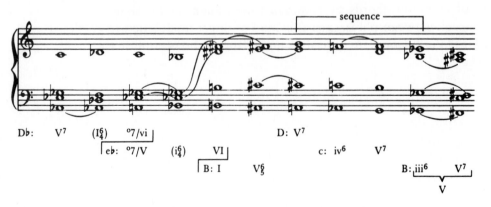

The first two tonicizations (these are too short to be called modulations), Db→eb and eb→B, are achieved by common chords. Next a short sequence hints at D major (or minor) and c minor. The key of B then emerges as the goal of the passage. In a larger sense, the sequence connects the V$^6_5$ in B to the root position V^7 in B, which makes the sequence somewhat less important harmonically than the rest of the passage. The fleeting tonicizations of D and c would be considered direct, since no other reasonable explanation is available.

SUMMARY

While diatonic common-chord modulations are the type most frequently encountered, other kinds of modulations do exist. Some of them are listed here.

1. Altered chords as common chords. The common chord is V$^{(7)}$/ or vii$^{o(7)}$/ in one or both keys (pp. 306-307). Other possibilities for common chords will be introduced in later chapters.

2. Sequential modulation. Transposition of a pattern causes the change in tonal center (pp. 307-309).

3. Modulation by common tone. The chords joined by the common tone usually exhibit a chromatic mediant relationship (pp. 310-314).

4. Monophonic modulation. A single line establishes a new tonal center (pp. 314-315).

5. Direct modulation. The usual type is the phrase modulation, in which the next phrase simply begins in another key (pp. 315-317).

Modulatory techniques often overlap. For example, a monophonic modulation might also be sequential, or a phrase modulation might also be analyzed in terms of common chords.

SELF-TEST 19-1
(Answers begin on page 603.)

A. Analysis.

   1. Analyze chords and NCTs. In addition, label the approach to the 7th of each seventh chord (review p. 206).

   Bach, "Die Nacht ist kommen"

   2. First write the root and quality of each chord below the music. Show the two occurrences of the sequential pattern. What key is implied before the double bar? After it? The first chord operating more naturally in the second key occurs right after the double bar. Could the preceding chord serve as a common chord? Label the chords with roman numerals, showing the common-chord modulation. Explain how the common-tone technique is also a factor in this modulation. To what extent is this progression a circle-of-fifths progression?

   Schumann, "Warum?" Op. 12, No. 3

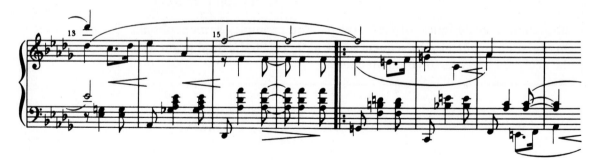

3. In this excerpt mm. 10-12 and 17-19 are all in the same key. Label the chords in those measures with roman numerals. Label the chords in mm. 13-16 with roman numerals in another key. Listen to mm. 11-14. How is the second key achieved? The return to the first key comes with the last chord in m. 16. What would be the best way to describe this kind of modulation?

Schubert, "Der Wegweiser," Op. 89, No. 20

4. Name the two keys established in this excerpt. How is the modulation accomplished? What is the relationship between the two keys?

Mozart, Symphony No. 41, K. 551, I

B. Analyze the harmonies implied by the soprano-bass framework below. Then add alto and tenor parts. Identify the modulatory technique used.

C. Follow the same instructions as for Part B, but enliven the texture with NCTs and arpeggiations.

g:

EXERCISE 19-1. See Workbook.

CHAPTER TWENTY

BINARY AND TERNARY FORMS

FORMAL TERMINOLOGY

In Chapter 8 you learned the terminology of period forms—such terms as *phrase, contrasting period*, and *parallel double period*. These terms are widely used and have generally accepted meanings. The terms we introduce in this chapter are also widely used, but writers on musical form disagree on some important aspects of their meanings. In addition, some writers recognize and name subcategories and modifications of the formal types discussed in this chapter. While our approach attempts to find a common ground among the various systems, you should be aware that any book on musical form that you might read will disagree with our definitions to some extent.

BINARY FORMS

The word *binary* has to do with the concept of twoness. You are probably familiar with binary arithmetic, in which only two digits are used. In music a *binary form* is one that consists of two approximately equivalent sections. "Approximately equivalent" means that we would not use the term binary for a piece just because it has an introduction; the introduction is obviously not equivalent to the main body of the work.

Periods and double periods are binary forms, but we do not usually use the term binary for them, either, because a term like parallel period is more informative. But in Example 20-1 we see a familiar tune whose four phrases do not add up to a double period.

Example 20-1. "Greensleeves"

A diagram of the phrase structure reveals two parallel periods.

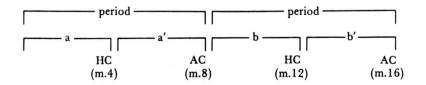

While the structure is not a double period (because of the two authentic cadences), it is a binary form. Furthermore, "Greensleeves" is in *sectional* binary form, because the first part ends with tonic harmony. If the first part of a binary form ends with something other than a tonic triad in the *main key* of the form, it is called a *continuous* binary form. The distinction between sectional and continuous forms is an important one, involving tonal independence in the first case and large-scale tonal drive in the second.

Example 20-2 illustrates a continuous binary form, since the first section ends in the relative major.

Example 20-2. Handel, *Royal Fireworks Music*, Bourrée

Notice in this example the reference in mm. 15-17 to the opening measures. This is not a clearly stated return of the opening material, so the example is not in ABA form. Instead, like most binary examples, it lies somewhere between AA′ and AB, the second section containing elements both of contrast and continuation. This is also true of "Greensleeves," (Ex. 20-1) where the endings of phrases 3 and 4 were identical to the endings of phrases 1 and 2.

The Handel example (Ex. 20-2) repeats each of the two sections exactly. Repetition does not usually change our formal analysis. The bourrée is a continuous binary form whether both, one, or no repeats are taken. However, movements or themes that consist of two repeated sections are so commonly encountered that a special term, *two-reprise,* is often used for them. To be thorough, then, we would say that Example 20-2 is a two-reprise continuous binary form. Incidentally, composers sometimes write out the repeats instead of using repeat signs, but we would still use the term two-reprise. Schumann and Chopin were especially fond of writing out repeats.

TERNARY FORMS

The idea of statement-contrast-return, symbolized as ABA, is an important one in musical form. The ABA or *ternary form* is capable of providing the structure for anything from a short theme to a lengthy movement of a sonata or symphony. The B section of a ternary form can provide contrast with the A sections by using different melodic material, texture, tonality, or some combination of these.

The minuet from an early Haydn keyboard sonata is seen in Example 20-3. Notice that this example is a two-reprise structure, that part one ends on the dominant (m. 8), and that all of part one returns (mm. 17-24), with an adjustment of the cadence to allow an ending on the tonic triad. Therefore, this minuet is an example of two-reprise continuous ternary form.

Example 20-3. Haydn, Sonata No. 11, III, Minuet

In short ternary forms the B section often is clearly based upon the A material. This was true of the Haydn minuet throughout the B part, but especially in the first few measures. The next example is the trio that completes the movement begun in Example 20-3. Again there is a two-reprise structure, but here the A section ends in tonic (m. 10). The B part (mm. 11-19) is based upon the A material, but some of the figures are inverted (compare mm. 1-2 with mm. 11-12), and it is in the key of the relative major. The return of A at m. 20 is quite obvious to the listener, although this A section is slightly longer than the original and considerably varied, and even includes some of the inverted figures from B. The form is two-reprise sectional ternary.

Example 20-4.   Haydn, Sonata No. 11, III, Trio

Menuet Da Capo

As with most minuets and trios, Haydn's minuet (Ex. 20-3) is played both before and after the trio (Ex. 20-4), so that the entire movement is itself a sectional ternary form.

At first glance, Example 20-5 may appear to be a five-part form.

$$\|: A :\| \quad B \quad A' \quad B \quad A'$$

But we see upon closer inspection that Schumann has only written out the second repeat of a two-reprise continuous ternary form.

$$\|: A :\|: B \quad A' :\|$$
$$ V$$

Example 20-5. Schumann, "Melody," Op. 68, No. 1

Many "standard" American popular songs are in sectional ternary form with the first A section repeated ("The Lady Is a Tramp," "Moonlight in Vermont," etc.).

ROUNDED BINARY FORMS

Frequently the last part of what appears to be a ternary form returns only half of the first A section.

$$A \quad B \quad \tfrac{1}{2}A$$

The term that some writers use for this frequently encountered form is *rounded binary*. Often the phrase structure of a sectional rounded binary example will be:

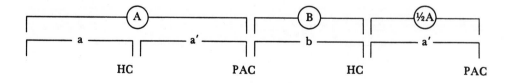

This is the form of many traditional tunes, such as "Oh, Susannah" (Ex. 20-6).

Example 20-6. "Oh, Susannah"

A more difficult example of rounded binary is seen in Example 20-7. The overall form is still AB½A, but the phrase structure involves several tonicizations.

A
┌─ a ─┐ ┌─ a' ─┐ ┌─ b ─┐ ┌─ c ─┐ ┆ B ┌─ d ─┐ ┌─ e ─┐ ½A ┌─ b ─┐ ┌─ c ─┐
g: HC   g: DC   Eb: IAC   Bb: PAC   F: IAC   Bb: HC   Eb: IAC   Bb: PAC
(m.4)   (m.8)   (m.10)   (m.13)   (m.17)   (m.21)   (m.23)   (m.26)

Since the A section ends with the tonic triad, this, like "Oh, Susannah," is a sectional rounded binary form.

Example 20-7. Brahms, "Ruf zur Maria," Op. 22, No. 5

Eb: IAC   Bb: PAC

Notice that "Ruf zur Maria" is not a two-reprise form, since only the first part is repeated. The form AAB, which this resembles, is a very old musical form called *bar form*. Perhaps AAB½A, as in "Ruf zur Maria," could be called a rounded bar form, but we will use sectional rounded binary instead.

OTHER FORMAL DESIGNS

Binary and ternary forms, especially the latter, provide the structure for many pieces and movements from multimovement works. The typical minuet and trio, for example, is sectional ternary, because the minuet is played both before and after the trio.

A   B   A

Minuet   Trio   Minuet

The minuet itself is generally a two-reprise ternary or a two-reprise rounded binary, as is the trio.

Slow movements are also often in ternary form. For example, the second movement from Brahms's Symphony No. 1 is in ternary form. It makes use of *transitions,* which are passages that connect different themes or tonal centers, and a *coda,* which is a special concluding section.

Section	A	trans.	B	trans.	A	Coda
Tonality	E (I)	mod.	c# (vi)	mod.	E (I)	E (I)
Measures	1-27	28-38	39-57	57-66	67-100	101-28

Many other musical forms are beyond the scope of this text, but two of the more important forms will be discussed briefly here.

Sonata form (or sonata-allegro form) is usually found as the first movement of a sonata, string quartet, symphony, or similar work, although other movements may also be in sonata form. Early examples of sonata form resemble two-reprise continuous ternary form.

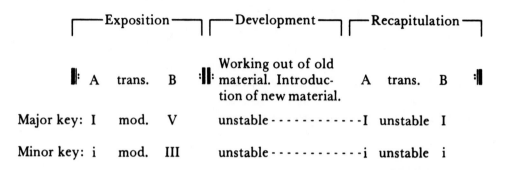

The A and B in the diagram stand for themes or groups of themes that appear in different keys in the exposition but in tonic in the recapitulation. The repeats are seen less often in nineteenth-century music than in eighteenth-century music, while lengthy introductions and codas are more commonly found. The number of themes presented in the two key areas also tends to be larger in the later music.

Rondo form is found most frequently as the final movement of a sonata, string quartet, or symphony, although slow movements are also sometimes in rondo form. There are three common types.

Five-part rondo	A	B	A	C	A		
	I	V	I	x	I		
Five-part rondo (variant)	A	B	A	B	A		
	I	V	I	?	I		
Seven-part rondo	A	B	A	C	A	B	A
	I	V	I	x	I	I	I

The *x* in the diagrams above symbolizes some key other than I or V, while ? means that a number of common possibilities exist.

<hr>

SUMMARY

Below is a list of some of the terms introduced in this chapter. If the meaning of any of them is unclear to you, read the indicated pages again.

Pages	Terms
323-326	Binary; sectional; continuous; two-reprise
326-330	Ternary
330-333	Rounded binary; bar form
333-335	Transition; coda; sonata; rondo

<hr>

SELF-TEST 20-1
(Answers begin on page 605.)

A. Sing "America" ("My Country, 'Tis of Thee"), then diagram its phrase structure. Include measure numbers and cadence types in your diagram. What is the form?

B. Diagram the piece below down to the phrase level and name the form. Assume there is a HC in m. 12, although there are other ways to hear this. Also, complete the following exercises.

1. Explain the G♮4's in m. 1 and m. 2.

2. If there were a modulation at the end of the first section (most people hear it as a tonicization), where would the common chord be?

3. Can you relate mm. 9-12 to anything in mm. 1-4?

4. Find a 9-8 suspension with change of bass.

5. Find consecutive octaves by contrary motion.

Beethoven, Bagatelle, Op. 119, No. 4

C. Diagram this trio down to the phrase level and name the form. Assume the phrases are four measures long. Also, complete these exercises.

1. The violas double what part (until m. 39)?

2. Explain the C#5 in m. 36.

3. Find parallel 5ths between the outer voices.

Mozart, Symphony K. 97, III

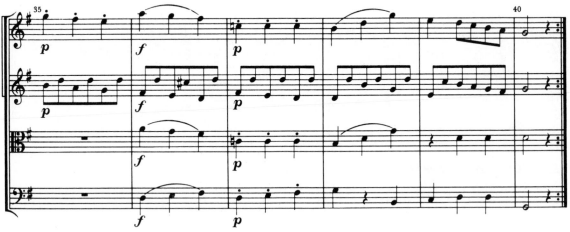

D. Diagram this piece down to the phrase level and name the form. Assume that all phrases are four measures in length, except for an eight-measure phrase in m. 9-16. Also, complete these exercises.

1. Discuss the choice of keys (tonicizations) in this piece.

2. Label the chords in mm. 17-24. Assume the modulation back to f♯ is a phrase modulation.

3. Find a disguised set of parallel 5ths in the same measures.

4. What about this piece is reminiscent of two-reprise form?

Schumann, *Album Leaf,* Op. 99, No. 1

EXERCISE 20-1. See Workbook.

CHROMATICISM 2

CHAPTER TWENTY-ONE

MODE MIXTURE

INTRODUCTION

The term *mode mixture* refers to the use of tones from one mode (*mode* here refers to the major and minor modes) in a passage that is predominantly in the other mode. Usually the mixture involves coloring a passage in the major mode with notes from its parallel minor. Mode mixture often serves an expressive purpose, and it is a frequently encountered source of altered chords. Other terms used for mode mixture are *borrowed chords* and *mutation*.

BORROWED CHORDS IN MINOR

Some writers feel that the use of raised $\hat{6}$ and $\hat{7}$ in minor is an example of mode mixture. According to that view, every V, for example, is borrowed from major, which makes mode mixture in minor a very common occurrence. Our approach is that scale degrees $\hat{6}$ and $\hat{7}$ each have two versions (review pp. 56-58), which means that the raised $\hat{3}$ is the only scale degree that can be borrowed in a minor key.

As it happens, there is a chord frequently borrowed from major that contains the raised $\hat{3}$, and that chord is the major tonic triad itself. The raised $\hat{3}$ in the tonic triad is called the *Picardy third,* and it was used to end most compositions in minor from the early 1500s until around 1750. A typical use of the Picardy third is seen in Example 21-1. Notice that the upper-case roman numeral I is enough to indicate the mode mixture. It is not necessary to add any explanatory note in the analysis. The voice leading in this example is worth examining, especially the descending tenor line and the alto part, which actually contains two lines. The textural reduction shows a simplification of the texture.

Example 21-1. Bach, "Helft mir Gottes Güte preisen"

b: i V VI i⁶ ii⁰⁶₅ V⁷ V⁷/iv iv⁶₄ I

Textural reduction

The idea of the Picardy third is sometimes used on a very large scale. For instance, Beethoven's Symphony No. 5 begins in c minor, but the main key of the last movement is C major.

THE USE OF ♭6̂ IN MAJOR

Borrowing ♭6̂ from the parallel minor creates four borrowed chords that are frequently used: vii°⁷, ii°, ii°⁷, and iv. Example 21-2 illustrates these in the key of A major. Notice that the roman numerals are identical to those used in minor.

Example 21-2.

A: vii°⁷ ii° ii°⁷ iv

The vii°7 is actually a more useful chord than the viiø7, since parallel 5ths are never a problem in its resolution. The vii°7 chord is one of the primary motivic elements in Example 21-3, where it is accented each time it occurs. Although the ♭6̂, F♭, is in an inner voice, it forms the beginning of an important line begun in the first phrase and completed in the second: F♭-E♭-D♭ | F♭-E♭-D♭-C. Notice also the nice effect created by the V-ii-V in m. 15.

Example 21-3.   Chopin, Mazurka Op. 17, No. 3

Incidentally, you will recall that either viiø7/ or vii°7/ may be used to tonicize a major triad (review p. 266). We can now understand that the use of vii°7 of a major triad is an example of *secondary mode mixture.** The vii°7/V in Example 21-3 illustrates this, the C♭ being the ♭6̂ "borrowed" from E♭ minor.

Frequently the vii°7 does not resolve directly to I but is followed instead by V7. Only one voice needs to move to accomplish this, as Example 21-4 illustrates.

---

*Some theorists use "secondary mode mixture" in an entirely different sense, as in CM/Cm-E♭M/E♭m.

Example 21-4.

G: vii°$^4_3$ V$^4_2$

The borrowed iv is frequently used in first inversion as part of a stepwise descending bass line, as in Example 21-5. The imitation between soprano and tenor in mm. 4-5 and the soaring tenor line in mm. 5-6 are among the many points to appreciate in this beautiful phrase.

Example 21-5. Bach, "Herzliebster Jesu, was hast du"

g: V   i   ii°^{6}

B♭: vii°^{6} I V$^4_2$/IV   IV^6 iv^6 I$^6_4$ vii°^{7}/V   V ^{7} I

The borrowed ii^{ø7} is probably used more often than the borrowed ii° because of the added direction provided by the 7th. Example 21-6 is typical.

Example 21-6. Bach, "Christus, der ist mein Leben"

F: I   vii°^{6} I^6 ii$^{ø6}_5$ V^7 I

In general, ♭$\hat6$ in vii°^{7}, iv, or ii$^{°(ø7)}$ moves down by half step to $\hat5$. It is often also approached by step, either from ♮$\hat6$ or from $\hat5$.

OTHER BORROWED CHORDS IN MAJOR

The most frequently encountered examples of mode mixture in major are the vii°7, iv, and ii°⁽ᶲ⁷⁾ chords. The only others that occur with any frequency are shown in Example 21-7. Notice that the symbols for the borrowed submediant and mediant triads are preceded by a flat to show that the root is lowered. Use the flat in your analysis regardless of the actual accidental found in the notation, which might be a natural, flat, or double flat, depending upon the key.

Example 21-7.

A: i   ᵇVI   ᵇIII

While vii°7, iv, and ii°⁽ᶲ⁷⁾ are often found alone in major-mode passages, the minor tonic triad frequently occurs in longer passages in the parallel minor. In Example 21-8 the minor mode takes over in m. 31, and major is not reestablished until the arrival of the D♮ in m. 36. Notice that this is *not* a modulation, since B♭ is the tonal center throughout. This example also illustrates the ♭VI, preceded here by its secondary dominant. The ♭VI is sometimes used with dramatic effect in deceptive cadences: V ♭VI. The V⁺⁶₅/IV in Example 21-8 is an augmented dominant, which will be discussed in a later chapter.

Example 21-8. Haydn, Quartet Op. 9, No. 2, I

B♭:   I   6   V⁺⁶₅/IV   IV   vii°7/V

The ♭III is by no means a frequently used chord. In Example 21-9 the ♭III is preceded by its secondary dominant and followed by a borrowed vii°⁷. The sonorities in mm. 26-27 with C and C♯ in the bass are passing chords that connect the V⁷ to the V⁶₅ (see the textural reduction). These chords do not require roman numerals.

Example 21-9. Schumann, "Ein Jüngling liebt ein Mädchen," Op. 48, No. 11

Textural reduction

CHECKPOINT

1. What is the name for the raised $\hat{3}$ in the tonic triad in the minor mode?

2. Show the chord symbols for the borrowed chords in major discussed in this chapter.

3. To what does *secondary mode mixture* refer?

4. How does $\flat\hat{6}$ most often proceed: up by step, down by step, or down by leap?

MODULATIONS INVOLVING MODE MIXTURE

Mode mixture is often employed as a signal to the listener that a modulation is taking place. In Example 21-10 a modulation from C to G occurs. In m. 42 Mozart uses an a^7 chord in third inversion. This could, of course, be a vi$^4_2$ in C. In the next measure the 5th of the chord is lowered, creating an $a^{ø7}$. This helps to weaken our perception of C as a tonic and makes the following V$^6_5$-I progression more convincing as a modulation to G.

Example 21-10.   Mozart, Sonata K. 309, III

Mode mixture also simplifies modulation to certain foreign keys. If a passage in major slips into the parallel minor, all of the keys that are closely related to the parallel minor come within easy reach. For example, mixture in the key of E gives us access to all the keys in the chart below:

Schumann uses mixture in Example 21-11 to move to the dominant of the parallel minor: E→(e)→b.

Example 21-11. Schumann, "Liebeslied," Op. 51, No. 5

SELF-TEST 21-1
(Answers begin on page 606.)

A. Notate the following chords in the specified inversions. Include key signatures.

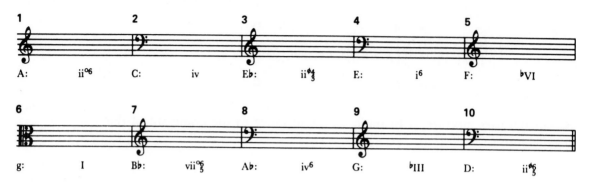

1 A: ii°6
2 C: iv
3 Eb: ii°$^{\sharp 4}_{3}$
4 E: i6
5 F: bVI

6 g: I
7 Bb: vii°$^{6}_{5}$
8 Ab: iv6
9 G: bIII
10 D: ii$^{\sharp 6}_{5}$

B. Label the following chords. Include inversion symbols.

1 F: ____
2 A: ____
3 Ab: ____
4 C: ____
5 D: ____

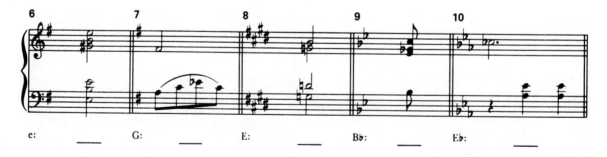

6 e: ____
7 G: ____
8 E: ____
9 Bb: ____
10 Eb: ____

C. Analysis.

1. Label chords and NCTs. Circle the roman numerals of any borrowed chords.

Bach, "Warum sollt' ich mich denn grämen"

G:

2. Label the chords, circling the roman numerals of any borrowed chords.

Schubert, Fantasy Op. 15

C:

3. Label the chords, circling the roman numerals of any borrowed chords. Which part is doubling the violas in mm. 47-51? The horn in D sounds a m7 lower than written.

Haydn, Symphony No. 73, I

4. Label the chords, circling the roman numerals of any borrowed chords. Discuss any diminished seventh chords that occur in terms of the resolution of their tritones.

Schubert, Symphony in B♭, I

5. In this remarkable excerpt, Beethoven manages to modulate from a♭ minor to D major, a tritone away. Explain how he accomplishes this (it is not necessary to label every chord in the excerpt).

Beethoven, Sonata Op. 26, III

D. Part writing. Analyze the chords implied by the soprano-bass framework. Then fill in alto and tenor parts. Be sure to use the specified mode mixture.

1. Include a vii°7.

2. Include a ii°$^6_5$.

E. Analyze the chords specified by this figured bass, then make an arrangement for SATB chorus.

EXERCISE 21-1. See Workbook.

CHAPTER TWENTY-TWO

THE NEAPOLITAN CHORD

INTRODUCTION

While the I-V-I progression is the basic organizing force in tonal harmony, much of the foreground harmonic interest in a tonal passage may be provided by the ways in which the dominant is approached. One of the more colorful chords that can be used to precede the dominant is the Neapolitan.

The *Neapolitan chord* derives its name from an important group of eighteenth-century opera composers who were associated with the city of Naples. While the composers of the "Neapolitan school" frequently used this chord in their music, they did not originate it but inherited it from earlier composers. Nevertheless, the term Neapolitan has survived, and we will make use of it and its abbreviation, N. Simply stated, the Neapolitan triad is a *major triad* constructed upon the *lowered second scale degree*. One accidental is required to spell the Neapolitan in a minor key and two in a major key, as is illustrated in Example 22-1.

Example 22-1.

CONVENTIONAL USE OF THE NEAPOLITAN

The Neapolitan is usually found in the minor mode and in first inversion. In fact, the first inversion is so typical that the Neapolitan triad is often referred to as the *Neapolitan sixth chord*. Example 22-2 illustrates several contexts in which the N⁶ is commonly found. At the piano, establish the key of e minor and play through the example so you will become familiar with the distinctive sound of the N⁶.

Example 22-2.

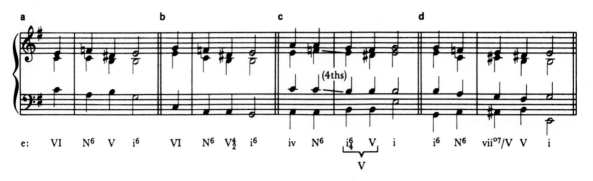

Example 22-2 illustrates several characteristics of the N^6.

1. When a tone is doubled, it is usually the 3rd of the N^6.

2. The N^6 moves to V (or i^6_4-V), but vii°7/V may appear between the N^6 and the V. The N^6 would usually not be followed by iv or ii°.

3. The $♭\hat{2}$ (the root of the N^6) moves down, especially when it appears in the melody. Its goal is the leading tone, which lies at the unusual interval of a °3 below $♭\hat{2}$ (see the soprano lines in Exx. 22-2a and 22-2b). But the °3 is filled in by the tonic pitch when the N^6 moves first to i^6_4 or vii°7/V (Exx. 22-2c and 22-2d).

4. When the N^6 moves to i^6_4, as in Example 22-2c, parallel 4ths should be used to avoid parallel 5ths. Parallel 5ths would be created in Example 22-2c by transposing the alto line an octave lower.

5. The N^6, like the unaltered ii°6, is usually preceded by VI, iv, or i.

Example 22-3 illustrates the N^6 in a three-part texture. Notice the leap in the tenor voice from A3 to E4 to provide the 3rd for the i^6_4 chord. The textural reduction brings out the stepwise ascent in the bass from $\hat{1}$ up to $\hat{5}$.

Example 22-3. Haydn, Sonata No. 36, I

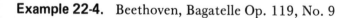

Textural reduction

In Example 22-4 the N^6 appears in a more complicated keyboard texture. Both Neapolitans in the example proceed directly to V. In the resolution of the first N^6, the interval of a $°3$ in the melody is filled in by a supermetrical passing tone (the A5). Notice that the freer treatment of the inner parts allows the $♭\hat{2}$ (B♭3) in the left hand to move upward to $♮\hat{2}$. This does not disturb the listener, whose attention is drawn to the resolution of the more significant B♭5 in the melody.

Example 22-4. Beethoven, Bagatelle Op. 119, No. 9

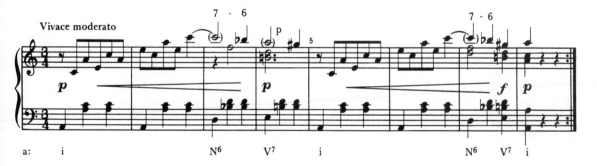

OTHER USES OF THE NEAPOLITAN

The Neapolitan is usually employed in first inversion in the minor mode, and it usually moves toward V. However, several other contexts for the Neapolitan may be encountered.

1. The Neapolitan may appear in root position (N) or, rarely, in second inversion (N_4^6). In both cases, the bass will probably be doubled in a four-part texture.

2. The Neapolitan may occur in the major mode.

3. The Neapolitan may be tonicized. This may take the form of a single chord (such as V^7/N), or it might be a genuine modulation to the key of the Neapolitan. In some cases VI may function as V/N.

4. In a modulation the common chord may be a Neapolitan in either key. Foreign key relationships might be involved in such a modulation.

5. The Neapolitan may, on occasion, serve a function other than that of a pre-dominant chord.

6. In rare instances, the Neapolitan may include a 7th (N^{M7}).

The examples below illustrate most of these uses of the Neapolitan.

Both a V^7/N and a root position Neapolitan occur in Example 22-5. Notice the tritone root relationship between the N and V chords.

Example 22-5. Chopin, Mazurka Op. 7, No. 2

In Example 22-6 Brahms uses the N^6 in a major key. However, he does prepare for the N^6 by using a borrowed iv chord. Incidentally, the I_4^6 in m. 21 is a cadential six-four that is interrupted for a measure and a half, only to return in m. 24.

Example 22-6.   Brahms, "Dein Herzlein mild," Op. 62, No. 4

Example 22-7 begins in A major and ends in a♭ minor (although neither key signature agrees with that analysis). The I⁶ chord before the double bar is enharmonically the same as a B♭♭ major triad, which is the Neapolitan in a♭. It then moves normally to i⁶₄-V in a♭.

Example 22-7.   Schubert, *Moment Musical*, Op. 94, No. 6

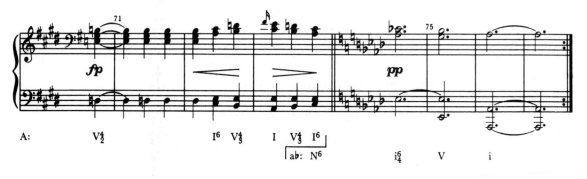

The chord in m. 108 of Example 22-8 contains all the notes of a Neapolitan chord, but it does not move to V. Instead, as the textural reduction shows, the N⁶ serves as a neighbor chord to the i⁶ that appears on either side of it.

Example 22-8. Mozart, Sonata K. 310, I

a: i⁶   N⁶

i⁶   ii⁰⁷   V⁷   i

Textural reduction

i⁶ . . . . ii⁰⁷ V   i
        (N⁶)

SELF-TEST 22-1
(Answers begin on page 609.)

A. Label each chord. Include inversion symbols, if any.

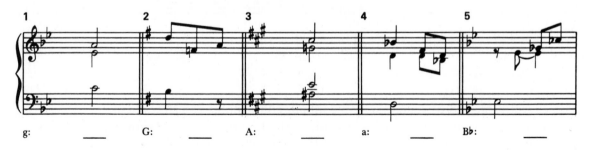

g: ___   G: ___   A: ___   a: ___   B♭:   ___

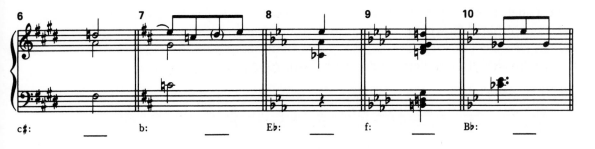

B. Notate each chord. Include key signatures.

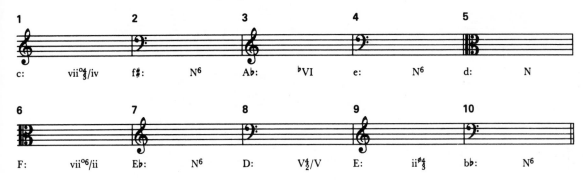

C. Analysis.

1. Label chords with appropriate symbols. Try to think of two interpretations of the first chord in m. 16.

Haydn, Sonata No. 37, II

2. Label chords and NCTs. The form of this excerpt is a (parallel/contrasting) (period/double period), with a two-measure introduction.

Schubert, "Der Müller und der Bach," Op. 25, No. 19

3. Label chords and NCTs. Assume that the F4 in m. 11 is a chord tone. Omit inversion symbols, because the bass has the melody in this example.

Chopin, Prelude Op. 28, No. 6

4. This excerpt from a well-known Mozart sonata begins in a minor and ends in F, with the first chord in m. 41 serving as the common chord. Label all the chords.

Mozart, Sonata K. 545, I

D. For each exercise provide the correct key signature and notate the specified chords preceding and following the N⁶. Use the given three- or four-part texture in each case.

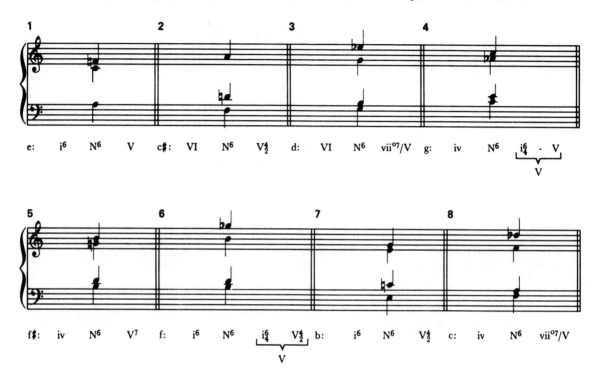

E. Analyze the harmonies implied by the soprano-bass framework. Then fill in inner voices to make a four-part texture. Each excerpt should include a Neapolitan chord.

F. Analyze the harmonies specified by this figured bass, then make a setting for four-part chorus. It does contain a modulation.

G. Make a setting of the following progression in d minor for three-part chorus. Then make another setting in b minor for four-part chorus. Arrange the rhythm and meter so that the final chord comes on a strong beat.

i V⁶ V⁴₂/iv iv⁶ V V⁴₂/N N⁶ V⁴₂ i⁶ vii°⁶ i V

EXERCISE 22-1. See Workbook.

CHAPTER TWENTY-THREE

AUGMENTED SIXTH CHORDS 1

THE INTERVAL OF THE AUGMENTED SIXTH

One way to emphasize a tone is to approach it by a half step, either from above or from below. In Examples 23-1a and 23-1b the dominant in g minor is approached by half steps. Approaching the dominant by half steps from above *and* below at the same time makes for an even stronger approach to the dominant, which is illustrated in Example 23-1c. You will notice that the two approaching tones form a vertical interval of an *augmented 6th*. This method of approaching the dominant distinguishes a whole category of chords called *augmented sixth chords*.

Example 23-1.

The characteristic elements of most augmented sixth chords are those illustrated in Example 23-1c.

1. The chord being approached is the V chord.
2. The minor-mode $\hat{6}$ (chromatically lowered if in a major key) appears in the bass.
3. The $\sharp\hat{4}$ is in an upper part.

The interval of an $^+6$ formed by these pitches is enharmonically equivalent to a m7, but the difference between the effect of the $^+6$ and that of the m7 is easily detected by the ear. The m7 tends to resolve as in Example 23-2a, the $^+6$ as in Example 23-2b. Play both parts of Example 23-2, and notice the contrast in the effect of these two intervals.

Example 23-2.

In a two-part texture the augmented sixth chord appears as in Examples 23-1c and 23-2b. The analytical symbol to be used is simply +6. Notice that the numeral is an arabic +6 and not a roman +VI.

The interval of the +6 usually resolves outward by half step, following the tendencies of the tones to lead to the dominant. Less commonly, the top pitch of the +6 may descend chromatically to produce the 7th of a V⁷. This generally occurs only in +6 chords that have three or more pitch classes (see below), with the top pitch of the +6 interval in an inner part.

For the reasons mentioned above, the +6 chord is among the strongest of all approaches to the dominant, and it generally moves directly to V (or i⁶₄-V). It is frequently used just after a modulation to make it clear to the listener that a modulation has, in fact, occurred. Like the N⁶, the +6 originated in the minor mode, but it was soon found to be equally useful in major keys. When used in major keys, it is often preceded by mode mixture.

THE ITALIAN AUGMENTED SIXTH CHORD

In most cases +6 chords contain more than two pitch classes. When a third pitch class is included, it is usually the tonic pitch. This combination of tones is referred to as an *Italian augmented sixth chord* (It⁺⁶), which is illustrated in Example 23-3. This geographical term, like the others we will be using, has no historical authenticity—it is simply a convenient and traditional label.

Example 23-3.

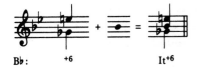

Bb: +6   It⁺⁶

The It⁺⁶, like any other +6 chord, resolves to V or I§-V. In a four-part texture the tonic pitch is doubled. Typical resolutions are shown in Example 23-4.

Example 23-4.

Example 23-5 includes an illustration of the It⁺⁶ in a three-part texture. Most of the excerpt consists of parallel 6ths (soprano and bass) surrounding a tonic pedal (alto). Notice that the bass reaches $\hat{5}$ four times, with different harmony in each case.

Example 23-5. Mozart, *The Magic Flute*, K. 620, Overture (piano reduction)

THE FRENCH AUGMENTED SIXTH CHORD

There are two common +6 chords that contain four pitch classes, and both of them may be thought of as It⁺⁶ chords with one pitch added. If the added tone is $\hat{2}$, the sonority is referred to as a *French augmented sixth chord* (Fr⁺⁶), which is shown in Example 23-6.

Example 23-6.

c: +6   It⁺⁶   Fr⁺⁶

The Fr⁺⁶ works best in four-part or free textures. Typical resolutions are illustrated in Example 23-7.

Example 23-7.

bb: Fr⁺⁶   V   i   Fr⁺⁶   i⁶₄   V   i
                                              V

In Example 23-8 a Fr⁺⁶ provides the harmonic color for the climax of an entire movement. At this point, in m. 38, Beethoven shifts to a seven-part texture, which explains why #$\hat{4}$ is doubled. In the following measure there is a sudden return to *piano* and a thinner texture, with the note of resolution ($\hat{5}$) appearing only in the bass. Notice that the bass and "tenor" move in parallel 3rds throughout.

Example 23-8. Beethoven, Sonata Op. 10, No. 3, III

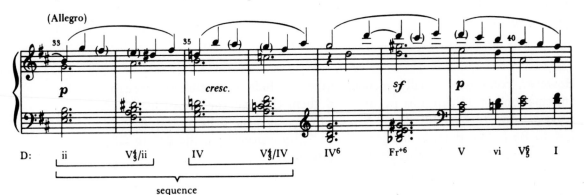

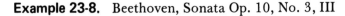

THE GERMAN AUGMENTED SIXTH CHORD

The other common +6 chord that contains four pitch classes is the *German augmented sixth chord* (Ger+6, not G6). It may be thought of as an It+6 with the addition of a minor-mode $\hat{3}$ (chromatically lowered if in a major key). The Ger+6 is shown in Example 23-9.

Example 23-9.

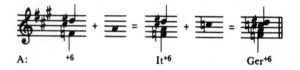

A: +6   It+6   Ger+6

As with any +6 chord, the usual resolutions of the Ger+6 are to V and to i$^6_4$-V. When the Ger+6 moves directly to V, parallel 5ths are apt to result, as in Example 23-10. Because the ear is distracted by the resolution of the interval of the +6, the parallels are not so objectionable here, and they may occasionally be encountered.

Example 23-10.

g: Ger+6   V

However, composers usually manage either to hide the parallels through anticipations or suspensions or to avoid them through the use of leaps or arpeggiations. In Example 23-11 Mozart first avoids the 5ths by leaping the E♭4 to B3 (a °4), then, in the second Ger+6, by arpeggiating the B♭3 to G3 before the resolution, turning the Ger+6 into an It+6.

Example 23-11. Mozart, Quartet K. 173, I

c: i   Ger⁺⁶   V   g: i   Ger⁺⁶   V

A simpler resolution to the problem of the parallels is to delay the V through the use of a cadential six-four, as in Example 23-12.

Example 23-12.

g: Ger⁺⁶   I⁶₄ V   i   G: Ger⁺⁶   I⁶₄ V   I   G: Ger⁺⁶   I⁶₄ V   I
                V   V   V

You may have noticed that the last Ger⁺⁶ in Example 23-12 is spelled differently from the others, although it sounds the same (A♯= B♭). This is a fairly common enharmonic spelling of the Ger⁺⁶, used in the major mode only, when the Ger⁺⁶ is going to I⁶₄. The reason for its use is more for the eye than for the ear: A♯ to B♮ looks more reasonable than B♭ to B♮, since we expect raised notes to ascend and lowered ones to descend.

Enharmonic spellings are also involved when we compare the Ger⁺⁶ with the V⁷/N. The listener can tell the Ger⁺⁶ from a dominant seventh chord only by its resolution, a feature that can lead to some interesting modulations (to be discussed in Chapter 25). For instance, the Ger⁺⁶ in m. 33 of Example 23-13 sounds like a V⁷/N (a D♭⁷), especially since it is preceded by a N⁶. The resolution to V⁷ is needed before its function is clear to us. Notice also that the ♯$\hat{4}$ (B♮3) moves down chromatically to ♮$\hat{4}$ (B♭3) to provide the 7th of the V⁷ chord.

Example 23-13. Beethoven, Quartet Op. 18, No. 1, II

F: V/vi   vi   ii   V⁷   ♭VI
                                                                   (V/N)

N⁶   Ger⁺⁶   V⁷   I
            (V⁷/N)

SELF-TEST 23-1

(Answers begin on page 612.)

A. Label each chord, using inversion symbols where appropriate.

B. Notate each chord in close position. Augmented sixth chords should be in their customary
bass position (♭6 in the bass). Include key signatures.

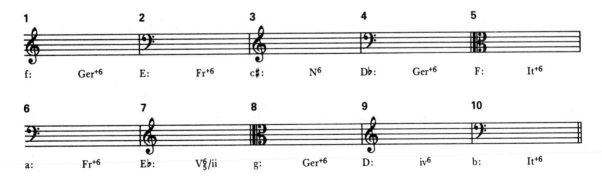

C. Label the chords in each excerpt below. Also, discuss the details of the resolution of each +6 chord. Do #$\hat{4}$ and b$\hat{6}$ follow their expected resolutions to $\hat{5}$? How are parallel 5ths avoided in the Ger^{+6} resolution(s)?

1. This excerpt modulates.

Haydn, Quartet Op. 64, No. 2, III

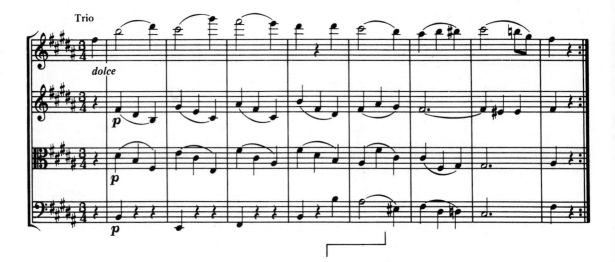

2. This sixteen-measure excerpt is an elaborated i-V progression. The chords in mm. 15, 17, and 19 are already labeled.

Mozart, Piano Concerto K. 491, I

3. In this excerpt find an example of a chromatic passing tone.

Haydn, Quartet Op. 20, No. 5, I

4. The two excerpts below are from the same song.

Beethoven, "Die Ehre Gottes aus der Natur," Op. 48, No. 4

D. Supply the missing voices for each fragment below. All but exercise 5 are four-part textures.

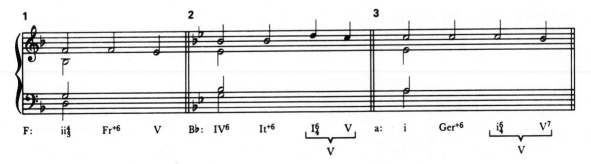

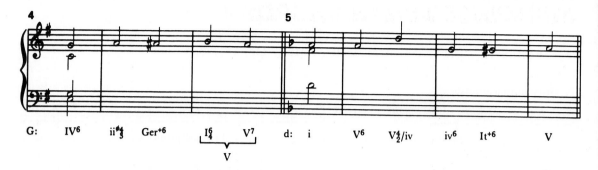

G: IV⁶   ii⁴₃   Ger⁺⁶   I⁶₄   V⁷   d: i   V⁶   V⁴₂/iv   iv⁶   It⁺⁶   V

V

E. Analyze the harmonies implied by this soprano-bass framework, and try to include a Fr⁺⁶ and an example of mode mixture in your harmonization. Then complete the piano texture by filling in two inner parts in the treble-clef staff, following good voice-leading procedures.

F. Analyze the chords specified by this figured bass, then make an arrangement for SATB chorus.

EXERCISE 23-1. See Workbook.

CHAPTER TWENTY-FOUR

AUGMENTED SIXTH CHORDS 2

INTRODUCTION

Chapter 23 presented augmented sixth chords as they usually occur in tonal music: with ($\flat$)$\hat{6}$ in the bass, $\sharp\hat{4}$ in some upper part, and resolving outward to form a P8 on $\hat{5}$, which serves as the root of a V chord. Augmented sixth chords are sometimes used in other ways, however, including these:

1. A chord member other than ($\flat$)$\hat{6}$ may be used as the bass note.

2. The interval of the $^+6$ may be created by scale degrees other than ($\flat$)$\hat{6}$ and $\sharp\hat{4}$ in order to lead to some scale degree other than $\hat{5}$.

3. The interval of the $^+6$ may expand to the 3rd or the 5th of a chord instead of to its root.

4. The augmented sixth chord may not be one of the three commonly encountered types.

These four possibilities are discussed in more detail in the following sections. The list is organized according to frequency of occurrence, which means that you would rarely encounter the uses listed toward the bottom.

OTHER BASS POSITIONS

We have not yet discussed what pitch serves as the root of an augmented sixth chord. The reason for this is that the augmented sixth chord is a linear sonority that *has no root*. One can arrange the notes of a Fr^{+6} to resemble an altered ii$^{\circ 7}$, and the It^{+6} and Ger^{+6} sonorities can be likened to altered iv^7 chords. Indeed, many theorists prefer to use modified roman numerals as a convenient way to represent augmented sixth chords. Still, these chords are rootless; they have only a most common bass position, that position having the ($\flat$)$\hat{6}$ in the bass.

Although the minor-mode $\hat{6}$ usually constitutes the bass of an $^+6$ chord, other bass positions do occur, especially in music of the Romantic period.

Generally, the voice leading will be identical or similar to that found in the standard resolutions discussed in Chapter 23, but the interval of the +6 will often be inverted to become a °3. The most common of the various possibilities is that with $\sharp\hat{4}$ in the bass, as in Example 24-1. Notice also the enharmonic spelling of the Ger⁺⁶.

Example 24-1. Brahms, "Ruf zur Maria," Op. 22, No. 5

The only other bass position that occurs with any frequency is that with the tonic pitch in the bass, as in Example 24-2.

Example 24-2. Brahms, Symphony No. 1, Op. 68, II (piano reduction)

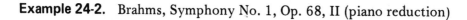

Because +6 chords have no root and therefore technically cannot be inverted, it is not necessary to show the bass position of the chord in the analytical symbol. Just use It⁺⁶, or whatever is appropriate, regardless of the bass position.

RESOLUTIONS TO OTHER SCALE DEGREES

As we have shown, the interval of the +6 is usually created by the half steps above and below $\hat{5}$. Especially in the Romantic period, this same principle is occasionally applied to other scale degrees as well. In such cases we will employ analytical symbols similar to those used with secondary functions to indicate that the +6 is embellishing some scale degree other than the dominant. The +6 chords we have presented so far have all embellished the dominant, and we could have used symbols like Fr⁺⁶/V for these chords. However, we have followed the custom of symbolizing Fr⁺⁶/V as Fr⁺⁶. But when the +6 embellishes some scale degree other than $\hat{5}$, we will make this clear by using the method shown in Example 24-3.

Example 24-3.

C: +6/I   +6/ii   +6/iii   etc.

In order to spell or recognize the various +6 types in these contexts, you will have to be familiar with the intervallic structure of the three kinds of augmented sixth chord. In Example 24-4, +6 chords embellishing $\hat{1}$ are formed by transposing the intervals from the more familiar +6/V spellings.

Example 24-4.

C: It⁺⁶   It⁺⁶/I   Fr⁺⁶   Fr⁺⁶/I   Ger⁺⁶   Ger⁺⁶/I

The Ger⁺⁶/I-I cadence in Example 24-5 comes at the very end of a song, following a more conventional V⁴₃-I cadence a few measures earlier.

Example 24-5. Chausson, *Sérénade italienne*, Op. 2, No. 5

B: I   Ger⁺⁶/I   I

Often when an augmented sixth chord resolves to something other than V, the chord that it resolves to is a secondary dominant. In that case, it is probably better to show the analysis in relationship to the chord being tonicized. For instance, the chord in m. 44 of Example 24-6 could be analyzed as an It⁺⁶/vi, but it is better understood as part of a tonicization of F minor (ii).

Example 24-6. Mozart, Sonata K. 457, I

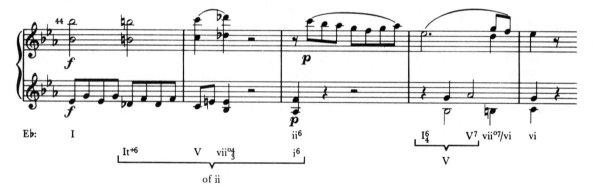

RESOLUTIONS TO OTHER CHORD MEMBERS

In all of the resolutions discussed so far, the interval of the +6 (or °3) has resolved to the root of the next chord (which was sometimes ornamented with a cadential six-four chord). Much less common is the resolution of the +6 or °3 to the 3rd of a chord (as in Ex. 24-7a) or to the 5th of a chord (Ex. 24-7b). Such a use of the augmented sixth sonority is very different from those discussed so far. To signify this, the chord symbol is placed in brackets. It is important to realize that Examples 24-7b and 24-7c have little in common, even though they both show identically spelled Ger⁺⁶ chords

followed by tonic triads. The tonic triad in Example 24-7b is in the relatively stable six-three position, while the tonic triad in Example 24-7c is a cadential six-four standing for the root position dominant that follows.

Example 24-7.

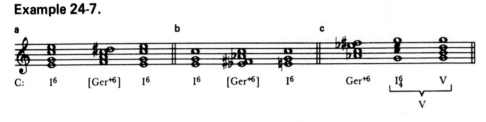

An example of a Ger^{+6} resolving to the 5th of a I chord is seen in Example
24-8. The textural reduction shows that the voice leading is very smooth. Be
sure to listen to both versions.

Example 24-8. Chopin, Nocturne Op. 55, No. 2

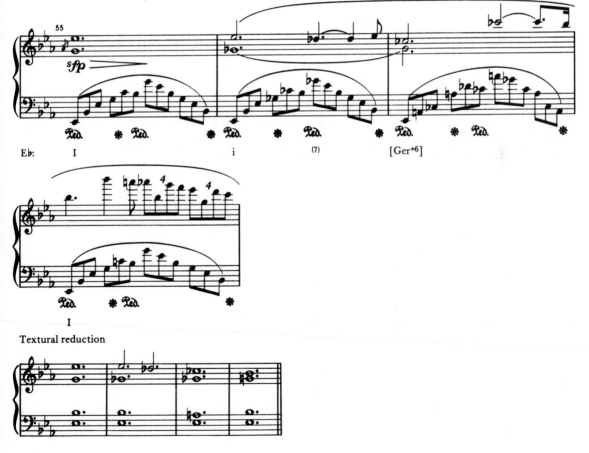

Textural reduction

OTHER TYPES OF AUGMENTED SIXTH CHORDS

Only rarely will you encounter an augmented sixth chord that is not one of the three standard types: Italian, French, or German. When you do encounter such a sonority, the symbol +6 will suffice to show the characteristic interval found in the chord. One such chord is seen in Example 24-9. Here the +6 sonority resembles a Fr+6, but the D♭ would have to be a D♮ for it to be a Fr+6.

Example 24-9. Strauss, *Till Eulenspiegel's Merry Pranks*, Op. 24 (piano reduction)

The +6 symbol may also be used for what is actually a very common occurrence—the use of two or three augmented sixth sonorities within the span of a single +6 interval. In Example 24-10 the pitches of all three types of augmented sixth chord appear in m. 15. In such cases the symbol +6 would seem to be a good solution, although you could label the sonority that has the longest duration (Ger+6) or the sonority that appears last (It+6) in Example 24-10.

Example 24-10. Mozart, Symphony No. 40, K. 550, I (piano reduction)

SELF-TEST 24-1
(Answers begin on page 615.)

A. Label the following chords.

d: _____ _____   e: _____ _____   c#: _____ _____   F: _____ _____   D: _____ _____

bb: _____ _____   c: _____ _____   Ab: _____ _____   A: _____ _____   g: _____ _____

B. Analysis.

   1. Label the chords in this short excerpt.

   Brahms, Quartet No. 2, Op. 51, No. 2, III

c:

2. Label the chords in this excerpt.

Tchaikovsky, "The Witch," Op. 39, No. 20

3. This is the ending of one of Schumann's better known songs. What national anthem is hinted at in the vocal part? Notice also the contrast between the diatonic setting of the text and the more chromatic codetta that ends the song. Label chords and NCTs.

Schumann, "Die beiden Grenadiere," Op. 49, No. 1

Kai - ser, den Kai - ser zu schü - tzen!"

EXERCISE 24-1. See Workbook.

CHAPTER TWENTY-FIVE

ENHARMONIC SPELLINGS AND ENHARMONIC MODULATIONS

ENHARMONIC SPELLINGS

Enharmonic spellings are used by composers for a variety of reasons. One reason is to indicate clearly the direction in which a pitch will move. For example, consider the viiº7/V in Example 25-1a. When the viiº7/V moves to the cadential I⁶₄, there is nowhere for the A♭ to go but up to A♮. This motion looks a little more sensible when the A♭ is spelled as G♯, as it is in Example 25-1b, but the aural result with any fixed-pitch instrument is the same. This new spelling changes the chord visually from a b°7 to a g♯°7, but it does not change its function or the analysis. Of course, when the viiº7/V moves directly to V, as in Example 25-1c, the A♭ spelling poses no problem, since the seventh resolves immediately downward to the G.

Example 25-1.

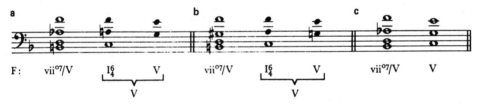

If you turn back to an earlier excerpt (Ex. 17-8 on p. 280), you will see an illustration of the enharmonically spelled viiº7/V, voiced exactly as in Example 25-1b, above. Very similar to the enharmonically spelled viiº7/V is the enharmonically spelled Ger⁺6 chord (review Ex. 23-12 on p. 373). Notice that both involve the respelled ♭3̂/♯2̂ preceding a I⁶₄ in the major mode.

Another reason for enharmonic spellings is the desire on the part of the composer to make things easier for the performer. This is presumably the case in Example 25-2, which changes briefly from A♭ to a♭ (mode mixture), then reaches F♭ (VI of a♭) before returning to A♭. In the F♭ portion (mm. 89-92) the viola and second violin are notated enharmonically in the key of E, perhaps to make their tremolos easier to read.

Example 25-2.   Mendelssohn, Quartet Op. 80, IV

Instead of enharmonically spelling only some of the parts, as Mendelssohn did in the example above, composers usually respell the key entirely. In Schubert's String Trio there is a modulation from B♭ to G♭ (♭VI), which then changes by mode mixture into g♭ minor. In order to avoid this awkward key (the key signature would contain nine flats!), Schubert quite reasonably notates it in f♯ minor. The harmonic skeleton of this passage is shown in Example 25-3.

Example 25-3. Schubert, String Trio D. 581 (textural reduction)

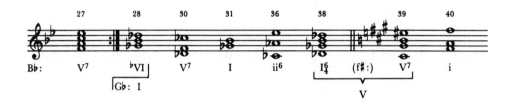

Examples of enharmonically spelled keys abound in nineteenth-century music. Schubert's Impromptu contains a passage with the following tonal structure: E♭-e♭-c♭, the last being spelled as b minor. The e♭-c♭ portion of that passage is given as Example 25-4.

Example 25-4. Schubert, Impromptu Op. 90, No. 2

Composers will often—but not always—change the key signature in situations such as this. Otherwise, they will use whatever accidentals are required. In either case, the enharmonically spelled key is an example of enharmonic spelling for convenience, and the listener is entirely unaware of the enharmonic spelling. Enharmonic spelling for convenience is *not* the same as enharmonic modulation, which is a much more interesting topic and which is the subject of the rest of this chapter.

ENHARMONIC REINTERPRETATION

The enharmonic spelling discussed so far in this chapter is intended primarily for the eye, not the ear. But there are four sonorities used in tonal music that can be reinterpreted enharmonically *in a different key* (not in enharmonic keys, like Gb and F#), and the listener can hear this reinterpretation when these chords resolve.

One such sonority is the major-minor seventh, which can serve either as a V[7] or as a Ger[+6] (Ex. 25-5a). Another is the diminished seventh chord, where any tone can serve as the leading tone (Ex. 25-5b). The other two possibilities are the augmented triad (Ex. 25-5c) and the Fr[+6] chord (Ex. 25-5d), although these chords are rarely reinterpreted enharmonically.

Example 25-5.

a

Db: V[7]   c: Ger[+6]

b

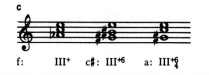

a: vii°[7]   f#: vii°$^6_5$ eb: vii°$^4_3$ c: vii°$^4_2$

c

f: III[+]   c#: III[+6]   a: III[+]$^6_4$

d

C: Fr[+6]   F#: Fr[+6]

The implications of all of this are that when the listener hears a major-minor seventh or diminished seventh sonority, certain expectations will probably arise (such as, "This chord will resolve as a V^7 in D♭"), only to be pleasantly thwarted on occasion by an equally logical enharmonic reinterpretation (such as, in this case, a Ger^{+6} in C). This process, which is often reserved for especially dramatic spots in a composition, is known as *enharmonic modulation*.

CHECKPOINT

1. Contrast enharmonic spelling for convenience and enharmonic modulation.

2. Make up a key scheme starting with B♭ that might result in enharmonic spelling for the convenience of the performer.

3. What four sonorities can be reinterpreted enharmonically so that they occur in different keys?

4. Which two of these four sonorities are commonly used enharmonically in tonal music?

ENHARMONIC MODULATIONS USING THE MAJOR-MINOR SEVENTH SONORITY

The term *enharmonic modulation* is used to refer to a modulation in which the common chord is reinterpreted enharmonically in order to fit into the second key. The actual spelling of the chord is not important—it might be spelled as it would appear in the first key, or in the second key, or even in both if it occurs more than once. What is important is that the common chord can be *heard* as a sensible chord in both keys.

The person listening to Example 25-6 probably expects the fourth chord to resolve as a V^7/IV in A♭, as it does in the top staff. But the possibility exists that it may be enharmonically reinterpreted as a Ger^{+6} in c minor, as seen on the bottom staff. This reinterpretation results in an enharmonic modulation from A♭ to c. Play Example 25-6 several times, comparing the effect of the two resolutions of the major-minor seventh sonority.

Example 25-6.

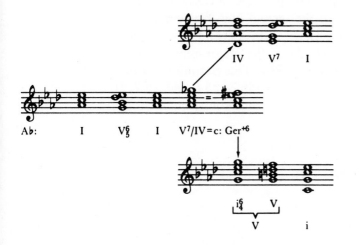

The last chord in m. 41 of Example 25-7 sounds like a G^7 chord. Since the tonality at this point is G, the listener probably expects the next measure to begin with a C chord (IV in G). Instead, the G^7 is treated and spelled as a Ger^{+6} in B major.

Example 25-7. Schubert, "Der Neugierige," Op. 25, No. 6

Any V[7] chord or secondary V[7] in the first key can be reinterpreted as a
Ger[+6] chord in the new key. The reverse is also possible—a Ger[+6] in the first
key can become a V[7] or secondary V[7] in the second key. However, in the
majority of cases the common chord is a Ger[+6] in the second key, presumably because of its more dramatic effect. Also, the major-minor seventh
chord in the first key seems most often to be a V[7]/IV. This common relationship, V[7]/IV becoming Ger[+6], was illustrated in Examples 25-6 and 25-7. It
would also be possible to use an It[+6] as the enharmonic equivalent of an incomplete V[7], but this is not often encountered.

ENHARMONIC MODULATIONS USING THE
DIMINISHED SEVENTH CHORD

Surprisingly, the diminished seventh chord is not used as frequently as
the major-minor seventh chord in enharmonic modulations, even though any
diminished seventh chord can lead in four directions, compared to the two
possible with the major-minor seventh (see Ex. 25-5). The top staff of Example 25-8 shows four resolutions of the same diminished seventh sonority.
The bottom staff is similar, except that the diminished seventh chord in each
case is followed by a V[7] before the resolution to tonic. Both methods—vii°[7]-I
and vii°[7]-V[7]-I—are used in enharmonic modulations. You should play through
Example 25-8 to familiarize yourself with the sound of these resolutions.

Example 25-8.

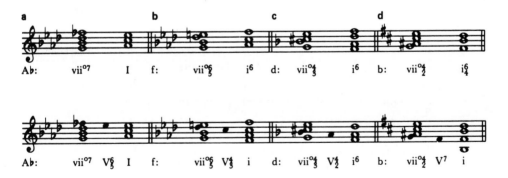

Example 25-9 is from the end of the first part of a movement by Haydn. The movement begins in f minor and modulates to A♭, the relative major. Because the composer is going to repeat the entire first section, he must modulate back to f minor before the repeat. Haydn prepares for the modulation in mm. 46-47 by using a g°7 chord (vii°7 in A♭), just as in the top staff of Example 25-8a. In the first ending, however, he uses the same sonority, respelled as vii°$\frac{6}{5}$ in f, and resolves it as in the bottom staff of Example 25-8b, bringing us back to f minor for the repeat.

Example 25-9. Haydn, Quartet Op. 20, No. 5, I

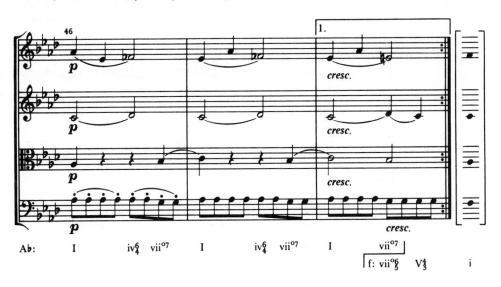

Example 25-10 begins and ends in A major. A c♯°7 chord appears in m. 140, but the listener probably hears it as an a♯°7, which is a vii°$\frac{6}{5}$/ii in A major (vii°7/IV would be another possibility). But Beethoven treats this chord as a vii°$\frac{4}{2}$ in F, the c♯ in the bass really acting like a d♭. This is similar to the bottom staff of Example 25-8b. When this same chord recurs in m. 145, it *sounds* like a vii°7/vi in F, because it follows V and seems to imply a V-vii°7/vi-vi deceptive progression. Instead, it is treated (and notated) as an a♯°7, a vii°7/ii in A major.

Example 25-10.   Beethoven, Sonata Op. 2, No. 2, IV

A: I   V$_3^4$ I^6 V^6 I   IV^6

I$_4^6$ _____ V ____ $_2^4$ | I^6 vii$^{o6}_5$/ii |

_____V_____   F: vii$^{o4}_2$ _____ V^7

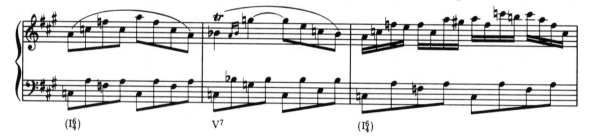

(I$_4^6$)   V^7 (I$_4^6$)

V^7 ^{o7}/vi | ii^6 I$_4^6$ V^7 I

        A: $^{o6}_5$/ii | _____V_____

Textural reduction

The textural reduction that appears below Example 27-10 is worth studying. Play it and listen to it, paying special attention to the bass line. You will find that mm. 140-45 constitute a harmonic digression, keeping the C♯ in m. 139 from reaching its goal, D, until m. 146. The entire example is a parallel period, the second phrase being expanded from four to ten measures by means of the passage that tonicizes F. This is indicated by the dotted phrase mark in the example.

SELF-TEST 25-1

(Answers begin on page 616.)

A. Analyze the given chord. Then show any possible enharmonic reinterpretation(s) of that chord, keeping the same key signature. Each enharmonic reinterpretation should involve a new key, not just an enharmonically equivalent key (such as g♯ and a♭). Number 1 is given as an example.

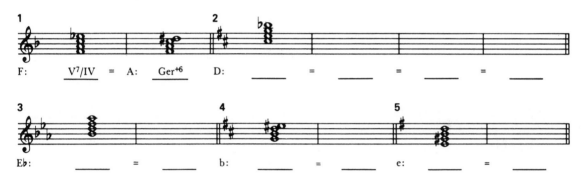

B. Each of the following short examples contains an enharmonic modulation. Analyze each example *after* playing it slowly at the piano and listening for the point of modulation. Do not try to analyze these examples without hearing them.

C. Analysis. Be sure to play as much of each excerpt at the piano as you can, simplifying the texture as necessary.

1. This excerpt begins in Gb and ends in bb minor, although Bb major is the eventual goal. Label all of the chords. Can you relate the F-Gb-F figure in the last measure to anything that has happened earlier? That is, does it remind you of any other figure heard in this excerpt?

Beethoven, "Adelaide," Op. 46

A - bend - lüft - chen im zar - ten Lau - be flü - stern, Sil - ber - glöck - chen des Mais im Gra - se

säu-seln, Wel-len rau-schen und Nach-ti-gal-len flö-ten, und Nach-ti-gal-len flö - ten:

2. This excerpt begins in D♭ and ends in A. A is enharmonic with what flat key? How does that key relate to D♭? Is this an example of an enharmonic modulation? Explain. If you were going to analyze this modulation as a common-chord modulation, which would be the common chord? What other modulatory technique discussed in Chapter 19 could be used to explain this modulation? Note: The chords in this excerpt can all be analyzed by reference only to the lower staff.

Chopin, Nocturne Op. 27, No. 2

3. This excerpt begins and ends in c minor. Label all of the chords. This passage really represents an extended V-i cadence in c minor. An important role in extending the passage is played by the pitch class F#/Gb. Make a list of all of the chords containing F#/Gb and their locations.

Beethoven, Sonata Op. 10, No. 1, III

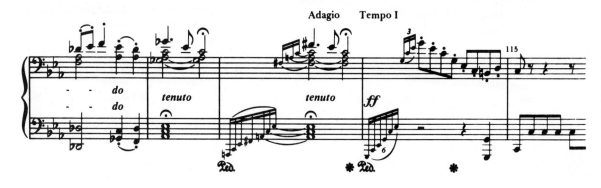

4. This passage begins in C and ends in E, although the eventual goal is the key of A.
Label all chords in this excerpt. Is there an important pitch class in this excerpt similar
to the F#/Gb in the previous passage? If so, which one do you think it is and why?

Schubert, Quartet Op. 125, No. 2, II

EXERCISE 25-1. See Workbook.

CHAPTER TWENTY-SIX

FURTHER ELEMENTS OF THE HARMONIC VOCABULARY

INTRODUCTION

Tonal harmony, on the surface a simple and natural musical phenomenon, is in reality a very complex and variable set of relationships. Many people have devoted years to the study of tonal harmony and to the almost limitless number of musical structures for which it has provided the foundation. It surely represents one of the highest achievements of Western art and intellect.

Because the subject is so complex, we have been concerned throughout this text with those harmonic events in tonal music that could be thought of as the basic vocabulary of the system—those events that occur with a relatively high degree of frequency. This chapter deals with a few details which are perhaps less fundamental but which, nevertheless, deserve attention. But, of course, even with this chapter we will not completely exhaust the harmonic vocabulary. The variations in detail and exceptions to the norms found in tonal music are too numerous to codify; in fact, it is doubtful that they ever will be codified. This complexity is one of the really fascinating aspects of tonal music, an aspect you can look forward to exploring in your further study of the literature.

THE DOMINANT WITH A SUBSTITUTED 6TH

You may be familiar with the concept of added-note chords, such as the triad with an added 6th. Such chords were not really a standard part of the vocabulary of Western music before impressionism, but they were recognized as a possibility long before that time. For example, Jean Philippe Rameau (1683-1764), an influential French theorist and composer, considered the first chord in Example 26-1 to be a IV chord with an added 6th. Although you might prefer to label it as a ii$^6_5$, that approach does not explain the unresolved 7th (B♭3). Whichever analysis you choose, the cadence is plagal (review p. 131).

Example 26-1.

Bb: IV^{add6} I
        (ii$^6_5$)

While triads with added 6ths are not characteristic of most tonal music, the dominant chord with a *substituted 6th* is not uncommon, especially in the nineteenth century. In this case, the 6th above the root is substituted for the 5th, which does not appear. If you play the three cadences in Example 26-2, you will find that they have a similar effect. The first one, of course, is a familiar form of the perfect authentic cadence. Example 26-2b incorporates an escape tone that embellishes the 5th of the V chord. In Example 26-2c the A4 appears in place of the 5th—it is a substituted 6th (V^{subs}_{6th}). You may have noticed that the V^{subs}_{6th} contains the same scale degrees as those found in a iii^6 chord, but the function is clearly dominant. To analyze the cadence in Example 26-2c as iii^6-I would certainly be an error.

Example 26-2.

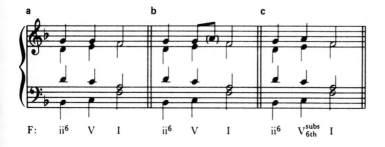

F: ii^6 V   I   ii^6 V   I   ii^6 V^{subs}_{6th} I

Example 26-3 contains an illustration of the V^{subs}_{6th}. Notice that the E5, the pitch that would have been the 5th of the V chord, appears immediately before the F$\sharp$5. The V$^{\text{subs}}_{\text{6th}}$ is usually prepared in this manner, which leads some theorists to analyze the V$^{\text{subs}}_{\text{6th}}$ as a V chord with a metrical escape tone. Either approach is acceptable.

Example 26-3. Haydn, Symphony No. 101, IV

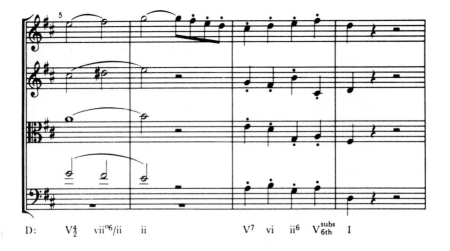

D: V$^4_2$ vii^{o6}/ii   ii   V^7 vi   ii^6 V$^{\text{subs}}_{\text{6th}}$ I

Example 26-4 is strikingly similar to the previous example, but it is in the minor mode. Notice again the preparation of the 6th.

Example 26-4. Schumann, "Folk Song," Op. 68, No. 9

d: i^6 vii^{o6} V^7 VI   ii$^{\o6}_5$ V$^{\text{subs}}_{\text{6th}}$ i

The substituted 6th may appear in connection with the dominant triad, as in the examples above, or with the V^7, as in Example 26-5.

Example 26-5. Schumann, *Humoresque*, Op. 20

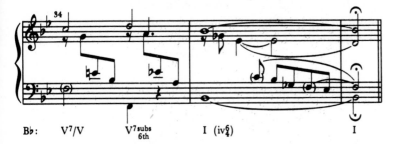

B♭:   V⁷/V   V⁷subs   I (iv⁶₄)   I
                 6th

The V_{6th}^{subs} and V_{6th}^{7subs} are usually found in root position with the substituted 6th in the top voice, and the 6th is always voiced higher than the 7th in the V_{6th}^{7subs}. The 6th resolves by leaping down to the tonic pitch.

THE DOMINANT WITH RAISED 5TH

When the 5th of a V or V⁷ is chromatically raised, the sonority that results is either an augmented triad (V⁺) or an augmented minor-seventh chord (V⁺⁷). This alteration is useful in that the raised 5th creates a leading tone to the 3rd of the tonic triad. The leading-tone effect would not be present if the tonic triad were minor, and for this reason the augmented dominant is not found resolving to a minor triad. These concepts are illustrated in Example 26-6.

Example 26-6.

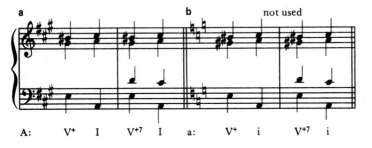

A: V⁺   I   V⁺⁷   I   a: V⁺   i   V⁺⁷   i

Notice that the V⁺⁷ may contain the interval of an +6, depending upon the voicing (between the soprano and tenor in Ex. 26-6a). Try not to confuse this altered dominant, whether in root position or inversion, with more conventional +6 chords.

Most instances of V⁺ and V⁺⁷ find the augmented dominant preceded by its diatonic form, which means that the #$\hat{2}$ could also be analyzed as a chromatic passing tone. The C#5 in Example 26-7 is a chromatic passing tone, but at the same time it creates a V⁺⁷ for a duration of four eighth notes.

Example 26-7.   Beethoven, Symphony No. 9, Op. 125, III (strings)

The V⁺ and V⁺⁷ in the major mode are enharmonic with the V$_{6th}^{subs}$ and V$_{6th}^{7subs}$ in the minor mode, as Example 26-8 illustrates. The resolutions are quite different, however: the raised 5th of the V⁺ moves up by half step to $\hat{3}$ (Ex. 26-8a), while the substituted 6th of the V$_{6th}^{subs}$ leaps down to $\hat{1}$ (Ex. 26-8b).

Example 26-8.

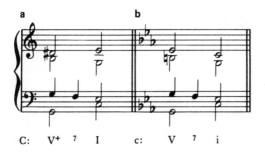

Example 26-9 begins with a V chord in the key of C♯, and the chord eventually resolves to a I, enharmonically spelled as D♭. In the second measure of the example, the E4 would appear to create a V^{7subs}_{6th}, but if you play the example, you will hear that the E4 is really a D𝄪4, and the chord is a $G♯^{+7}$ (compare Ex. 26-8a). Chopin used this enharmonic spelling for the convenience of the performer, who would rather read G♯-E-F in the soprano than G♯-D𝄪-F.

Example 26-9. Chopin, Nocturne Op. 48, No. 2

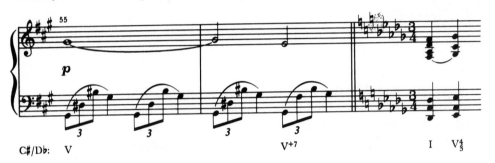

Secondary dominants may also appear in augmented form. Most common are the V^+/IV and the V^{+7}/IV, as in Example 26-10.

Example 26-10. Haydn, Quartet Op. 9, No. 2, I

NINTH, ELEVENTH, AND THIRTEENTH CHORDS

Just as superimposed 3rds produce triads and seventh chords, continuation of that process yields ninth, eleventh, and thirteenth chords (which is not to say that this is the manner in which these sonorities evolved historically). These chords are shown in Example 26-11.

Example 26-11.

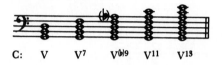

C: V   V⁷   V⁽ᵇ⁾⁹   V¹¹   V¹³

Interesting as these chords may be, the triad and the seventh chord were really the standard fare of music in the eighteenth and nineteenth centuries. True elevenths and thirteenths are rare before impressionism. Ninths occur throughout the tonal era, but the 9th of the chord often can be analyzed as an NCT and usually disappears before the chord resolves. The most common way to resolve the 9th is to slip down a step to double the root of the V⁷. This is what happens in Example 26-12, where the minor-mode 9th, F♭5, moves down by step to E♭5, the root of the V⁷.

Example 26-12. Beethoven, Sonata Op. 2, No. 1, I

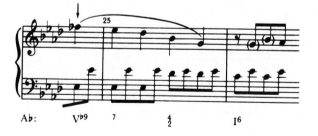

A♭:   V♭9   7   4   I⁶
                               2

Another possibility, illustrated in Example 26-13, is to arpeggiate from the 9th of the chord down to the 7th.

Example 26-13. Beethoven, Quartet Op. 59, No. 2, III (piano reduction)

Certainly, examples may be found of ninth chords that maintain the quality of a ninth chord right up to the resolution, at which point the 9th resolves down by step. This is illustrated in Example 26-14, where the 9th, Cb4, resolves to Bb3 in the next chord. The minor ninth quality is used here as secondary mode mixture: the diatonic V^{b9} in eb. Notice also the V^7 in m. 193, which could be analyzed as a V$^{7\text{subs}}_{6\text{th}}$.

Example 26-14. Schumann, *Humoresque*, Op. 20

All of the examples of ninth chords cited so far have been dominant ninths. Although dominant ninths are the most commonly encountered, other ninth chords do occur. Example 26-15 contains a clear instance of a iv^9.

Example 26-15.   Schumann, *Scheherazade*, Op. 68, No. 32

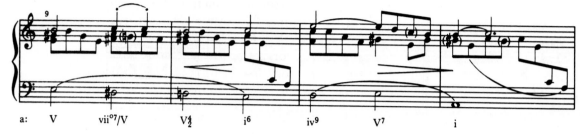

a: V   viiº7/V   V$^4_2$ i^6 iv^9 V^7 i

The symbols used in the analysis of ninth chords are not standardized. The easiest approach is to let the roman numeral reflect the triad type, with the *9* simply appended to it. Inversions of ninth chords are not as common as inversions of triads and seventh chords. Moreover, the figured bass symbols for inversions of ninth chords are too cumbersome to be practicable. A useful, if unscientific, solution is to give in parentheses the figures used for inversions of seventh chords: V^9($^6_5$), and so on. This will not work in the case of a ninth chord in fourth inversion, but the fourth inversion is very uncommon.

THE COMMON-TONE DIMINISHED SEVENTH CHORD

Most diminished seventh chords function as leading-tone sevenths of tonic or of some other chord within the tonality. While the enharmonic potential of the diminished seventh chord is occasionally exploited in enharmonic modulation, the resolution of the chord generally clarifies its function.

However, there is a diminished seventh chord usage that does not conform to the usual pattern. In this case, the diminished seventh chord progresses to a major triad or dominant seventh chord, the *root* of which is the *same* as one of the notes of the º7 chord. In Example 26-16, G5, the 7th of the a$\sharp$º7, is retained to become the root of the next chord. It is obvious that the a$\sharp$º7 is not a leading-tone 7th of the G^6 or the G$^6_5$. We refer to a diminished seventh chord used in this way as a *common-tone diminished seventh* (ctº7). Remember that the tone in common is the root of the major triad or dominant seventh chord.

Example 26-16.

a$\sharp$ º7   G^6 a$\sharp$ º7   G$^6_5$

The function of a ct°7 is simply one of embellishment, and we put its analytical symbol in parentheses to indicate its weak harmonic function. A ct°7 can be used to embellish any major triad or dominant seventh chord, but it is most often found progressing to I in major or V(7) in major or minor. Most often the ct°7 has a distinctly nonessential flavor, acting as a neighbor chord (Exx. 26-17a and 26-17b) or as a passing chord (Ex. 26-17c). Notice the smooth voice leading in all the parts. Because the ct°7 has no theoretical root, no inversions should be indicated when labeling ct°7 chords.

Example 26-17.

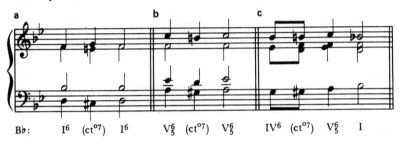

Bb: I⁶   (ct°⁷)   I⁶   V⁶₅   (ct°⁷)   V⁶₅   IV⁶   (ct°⁷)   V⁶₅   I

Example 26-18 illustrates the ct°⁷-I progression interpolated between a pedal IV⁶₄ and its resolution back to I. The textural reduction of the accompaniment shows that the only significant harmonic event here is the presentation of the tonic triad. The V⁴₃ consists only of neighbor tones on a weak beat, while the IV⁶₄ and ct°⁷ in combination form a double neighbor group figure in the inner voices.

Example 26-18.   Mozart, Sonata K. 545, II

G: I   V⁴₃   I   (IV⁶₄)   (ct°⁷)   I

Textural reduction

The ct°7 in Example 26-19 serves as a passing chord between the tonally more significant tonic and dominant chords. The tone in common between the ct°7 and the V$^4_3$ is the G5 in the melody.

Example 26-19. Brahms, Symphony No. 1, Op. 68, I (strings)

The ct°7 that embellishes I is usually spelled as a ♯ii°7 and that which embellishes V as a ♯vi°7, as in Example 26-17. However, enharmonic spellings are frequently found. In Example 26-19 Brahms spells the ct°7 embellishing V as a ♯i°7 so that the viola line would read C-B♭-B♮ instead of C-A♯-B♮. In Example 26-20 he spells the ct°7 embellishing I as a ♯iv°7 in order to clarify the F-A♭-F arpeggiation in the melody (instead of F-G♯-F).

One feature of the theme that begins in Example 26-20 is extensive use of mode mixture, and the A♭ introduces this technique more clearly than G♯ would have. This marvelous theme should be studied in its entirety (mm. 1-15), using a recording and a full score. You will discover not only mode mixture, but additional ct°7 chords, other altered chords, and polymeter (the aural effect of two or more different meters occurring at the same time). Motivic relationships are also of interest. For example, compare the melody in mm. 1-3 with the bass in mm. 3-5. Incidentally, the inner voices of this example have been included only to clarify the harmonies—they do not indicate Brahms's actual voice leading, which is too complicated for a piano reduction.

Example 26-20. Brahms, Symphony No. 3, Op. 90, I (simplified texture)

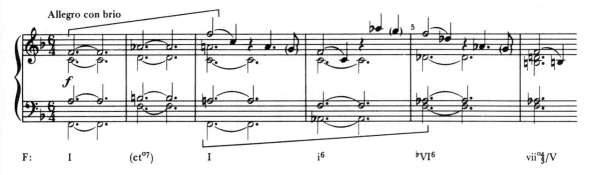

It is easy to confuse the vii°7/V with the ct°7 that embellishes the tonic, because they are enharmonically equivalent and both are sometimes spelled enharmonically (review Chapter 25, p. 392). This is especially clear in the preceding example, where the ct°7 is spelled as a vii°7/V (b°7). You should have no trouble if you will keep the following in mind:

Chord following the °7 chord:	*Should be analyzed as:*
I or I⁶	ct°7
V or I⁶₄	vii°7/V

In Example 26-21 Schumann spells the chord on the second beat of m. 15 as a d♯°7, a ct°7 of I, but its resolution to I⁶₄-V⁹ requires an analysis as a vii°7/V. The texture of this example is quite complex and features imitation between the soprano and alto parts.

Example 26-21. Schumann, "Lento espressivo," Op. 68, No. 21

SIMULTANEITIES

We know that some chords in a passage have more of an embellishing function than other chords do. This was discussed in Chapter 15 and also in relationship to passing six-four chords, parallel sixth chords, and others. Sometimes the traditional label for an embellishing chord (that is, V, ii, and so on) seems particularly meaningless, and we might use the term *simultaneity* for such a sonority to distinguish it from a traditional *chord*. A frequently encountered example is the diminished seventh sonority fulfilling a passing function.

Consider Example 26-22. It employs a tonic pedal throughout. The chord roots and sonority types are these:

Roots: Db G / A D / E Eb / Ab   / Db

Types: M °7 / °7 °7 / °7 ø7 / Dom7 / M

But the real "chords" in this progression are

D :   I   ii^{ø7} V^7 I

The diminished seventh chords are better understood as *simultaneities*—traditional sonorities used in nontraditional ways. Here the chromatically descending sonorities serve not as vii°7 or ct°7 chords, but as passing chords connecting the I to the ii^{ø7}. While these diminished seventh chords could be analyzed as a circle-of-fifths sequence (review pp. 276-279), it is unlikely that we would hear them that way, so we do not use roman numerals in their analysis.

Example 26-22. Chopin, Nocturne Op. 27, No. 2

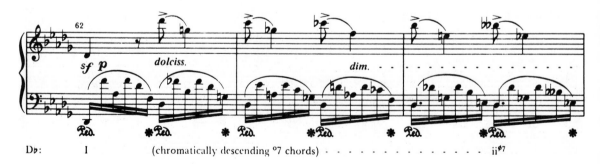

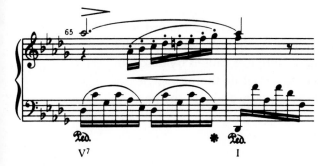

V⁷   I

Example 26-23 is more complicated, and you should play through it several times before reading further. The phrase is in g minor, and it consists entirely of traditional sonorities. The NCTs, if there are any, are difficult to identify. The roots of the sonorities are labeled, with alternative analyses shown in two cases.

Example 26-23. Schumann, "Das verlassne Mägdelein," Op. 64, No. 2

Two of the sonorities in this example are meaningless in the g minor context in which they occur: the B♭m in m. 2 and the It⁺⁶ over the C♭4 in m. 4. If we assume that these are simultaneities fulfilling a passing function, the phrase begins to make more sense. The analysis would be as follows:

$$\text{i} \quad \text{ii}^{\o6}_{4} \quad | \quad \text{vii}^{\o4}_{2} \quad \text{i}^{6}_{4} \quad | \quad \text{IV}^{7} \quad \text{ii}^{\o6} \quad | \quad \text{vii}^{\o4}_{3} \quad \text{i}^{6}$$
$$\phantom{\text{i}} \quad \text{or VI} \qquad\qquad | \qquad\qquad\quad | \qquad\quad \text{or iv} \quad\quad |$$

Now we can hear the phrase in two segments, each ending with a vii°⁷-i progression, the first one being a weaker progression because the i chord is in six-four position. The only oddity in the phrase is the IV⁷, which usually comes about through ascending melodic minor. Here it is caused by descending chromaticism in the alto line. An interesting detail of the passage is the imitation of the alto and bass in mm. 1-2 by the soprano and alto in mm. 3-4.

COLORISTIC CHORD SUCCESSIONS

Another way that a fundamental chord progression may be embellished is through the use of unexpected root movements to chords foreign to the key. Example 26-24 consists of an enormous I-V⁷-I final cadence in C major, with the approach to the V⁷ dramatized by a colorful series of unexpected chords. They do not seem to imply any tonicization or to function in a traditional sense in any key. In the analysis we simply indicate the root and sonority type of each chord.

Example 26-24. Liszt, *Orpheus* (reduction)

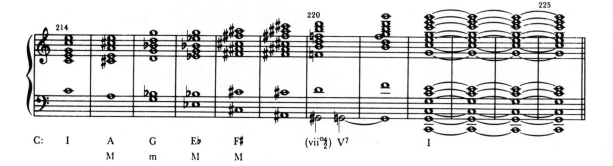

Coloristic successions often involve *chromatic mediant* relationships. Two triads are said to exhibit a chromatic mediant relationship if they are both major or both minor and their roots are a 3rd apart. In Example 26-24 the C to A and E♭ to F♯ relationships are both chromatic mediants. Even more distant is the *doubly-chromatic mediant* relationship. In this case, the chords are of *opposite* mode (major/minor), have roots a 3rd apart, and share *no* common tones. Examples would be C to a♭ and C to e♭.

SUMMARY

This chapter has been concerned with the following six topics:

1. *The dominant with a substituted 6th.* This is a V or V^7 chord in which the 6th above the root ($\hat{3}$) appears instead of the 5th ($\hat{2}$). The 6th is usually approached by ascending step and left by descending leap: $\hat{2}$-$\hat{3}$-$\hat{1}$.

2. *The dominant with raised 5th.* Augmented dominants (V$^+$ and V^{+7}) are not uncommon in the major mode. The raised 5th (#$\hat{2}$) leads to the 3rd of the I chord. Secondary dominants may also be augmented.

3. *Ninth, eleventh, and thirteenth chords.* Of these, only the ninth chord occurs with any frequency before the twentieth century. Most often the 9th of the chord disappears before the chord resolves. Otherwise, it resolves down by step.

4. *The common-tone diminished seventh chord.* This chord has a tone in common with the root of the chord it embellishes. It usually embellishes either I (in which case it will probably be spelled as a #ii^{o7}) or V (spelled as a #vi^{o7}). Enharmonic spellings do occur.

5. *Simultaneities.* This term is sometimes applied to traditional sonorities (diminished seventh chords, for example) handled in a nontraditional fashion. Roman numerals are inappropriate for simultaneities.

6. *Coloristic chord successions.* This refers to the unexpected and nontraditional use of chords foreign to the key. We do not include here, of course, an unexpected secondary dominant, or a Neapolitan, for example.

SELF-TEST 26-1

(Answers begin on page 618.)

A. In each exercise below, analyze the given chord. Then notate the specified chord in such a way that it leads smoothly into the given chord with acceptable voice leading. Some of the problems use a five-part texture for simpler voice leading.

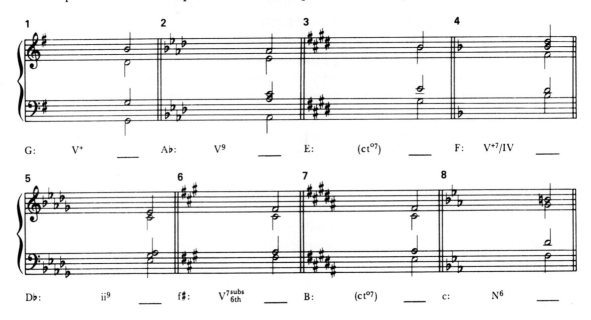

B. Analysis. Throughout this section, highlight (using arrows, and so on) any occurrences of the chords discussed in this chapter.

1. Label chords and NCTs, analyzing in B♭ throughout. Two simple means of extending a musical idea are repetition and sequence: show where they occur in this example.

Beethoven, "Adelaide," Op. 46

2. This excerpt is in E throughout. What bass notes are implied in the second half of m. 90 and m. 94? The chord in mm. 96-97 appears to be unrelated to the chord in m. 98. Can you think of a better explanation? Label all chords.

Schumann, "Aus alten Märchen," Op. 48, No. 15

3. Label the chords in this excerpt, which modulates from E to A. The clarinets are in A and the horns are in E, but the harmonic analysis can be carried out by studying only the nontransposing instruments.

Beethoven, Symphony No. 7, Op. 92, II

4. This example is one of the thirteen short pieces that comprise Schumann's *Kinder-szenen* (*Scenes of Childhood*). While it could be analyzed entirely in F, your analysis should somehow reflect the strong tonicizations of C, g, and d. How can the reharmonization heard in the last three measures be related to the rest of the piece? Label chords and NCTs throughout, except for measures that are exactly the same as earlier measures. What is the best name for the form of this piece?

Schumann, "Träumerei," Op. 15, No. 7

5. This famous song has been the subject of several contradictory analyses. Phrase 1 (mm. 1-4) offers no problems; label the chords with roman numerals. The second chord in m. 4 is a simultaneity, as are most of the chords in phrase 2 (mm. 5-12). Label the roots of any simultaneities in mm. 5-8. Most of the seventh chords are passing simultaneities rather than true chords. How can you tell? What interval used in parallel motion forms the basis for mm. 5-8? Label the chords in mm. 9-12.

Schumann, "Ich grolle nicht," Op. 48, No. 7

EXERCISE 26-1. See Workbook.

PART SIX

LATE ROMANTICISM AND THE TWENTIETH CENTURY

CHAPTER TWENTY-SEVEN

TONAL HARMONY IN THE LATE NINETEENTH CENTURY

INTRODUCTION

The forces that ultimately led to the breakdown of the tonal system may be viewed as the logical extension of the direction in which music had been developing since the beginning of the nineteenth century. In attempting to identify which characteristics of the transitional period eventually opened the door onto the new horizons of the twentieth century, we would certainly note the increasing prevalence of contrapuntal writing, the systematic blurring of essential harmonies by means of longer, stronger nonharmonic tones, the more rapid rate of change from one transient tonality to another, the tendency to avoid dominant-to-tonic cadences for longer periods of time, and frequently, the total avoidance of any clear definition of a principal key center until well along into the work. We might also note that melody was gradually released from its traditional harmonic associations, with the result that melodic and harmonic successions began to exist in their own coloristic right.

Consider Example 27-1.

Example 27-1.   Dvořák, Symphony Op. 95 (*From the New World*), II (piano reduction)

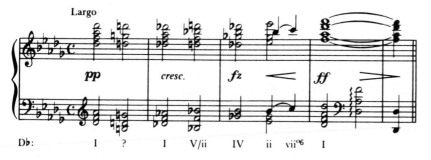

The G major chord that follows the tonic of D♭ totally defies any attempt at functional analysis. The B♭ chord in the second measure might be heard as V/ii, but its subsequent movement to IV seems to refute that implication. The final authentic cadence in D♭, which closes the movement, is satisfying; yet it seems to emerge from a "nonprogression."

The period in which such practices became most pervasive lies roughly within the last two decades of the nineteenth century and the first two of the twentieth. Often referred to as the *post-Romantic era,* it is an elusive and intriguing epoch in many ways. Surely the trends that it spawned tended to develop in distinctly different directions as the twentieth century unfolded.

Of course, not all practices of the post-Romantic era were revolutionary. We have already encountered passages in the music of Mozart and Beethoven, even Bach, that defy tonal analysis, either written or aural. By the close of the nineteenth century, however, we find that this description applies to the greater part of the literature, as opposed to representing an occasional anachronistic curiosity.

Other developments that should be mentioned in passing include the expansion and modification of many of the accepted large forms, as seen in the symphonies of Bruckner and Mahler, the monumental music dramas of Wagner, and the tone poems of composers such as Liszt and Sibelius. When we are dealing with the concept of standard form, to be sure, we must note that the life cycle of any new musical venture is typically characterized by its introduction, gradual acceptance, standardization, and shortly thereafter, rapid fall into disfavor through excessive use. Nowhere in Western musical history, however, may this process be observed more clearly than in the brief but turbulent span that preceded the dawn of the twentieth century.

Very much in evidence is an increasing emphasis on the dramatic and programmatic aspects of concert music. This trend may have inspired a spirit of nationalism on the part of numerous composers. Most notable among them are the so-called Russian Five: Cui, Balakirev, Borodin, Moussorgsky, and Rimsky-Korsakov. Much of their music is rich in historical allusion as well as in references to Russian folk legends. These five were by no means an isolated geographic phenomenon; other composers who drew upon the heritage of their native lands include Edward McDowell (United States), Sir Edward Elgar (England), Jan Sibelius (Finland), Edward Grieg (Norway), and Antonin Dvořák (Bohemia), to name but a few. This reawakening of national awareness proved to be profoundly significant in its influence upon the ensuing diversity of musical style. While it is not within the scope of this brief chapter for us to deal with the aspects of structural evolution and nationalism cited above, it is nonetheless useful to recall that they were taking place more or less simultaneously with the technical details we will discuss here.

COUNTERPOINT

While we will treat various elements of the post-Romantic style separately, you will notice that they are in a sense inseparable. Excessive melodic chromaticism will unavoidably affect harmonic movement; irregular resolutions must inevitably influence linear movement. Perhaps the dominant characteristic of this music is the prevalence of contrapuntal manipulation, particularly of supporting voices. Since these voices tend to be chromatically inflected and to move independently of the principal voice (if there is a principal voice), the individual harmonies and, hence, any clear sense of harmonic progression are blurred.

Richard Wagner is generally considered to have been the most influential single figure in the late Romantic era, particularly in the sense that his compositional procedures seem to provide the most obvious link between the mid-nineteenth century and the ultimate development of the twelve-tone system, to be discussed in Chapter 28.

The Prelude to *Tristan und Isolde* illustrates how moving lines may serve to obscure, or even misrepresent, vertical harmonies.

Example 27-2. Wagner, *Tristan und Isolde,* Prelude (piano reduction)

The sonority found on the first beat of m. 2 suggests an $F^{\emptyset 7}$ chord (enharmonically spelled). Yet before this chord is allowed to function in any way, the G♯ resolves to A, creating a Fr^{+6} chord that seems to suggest the key of A. The ultimate conclusion of the phrase in m. 3 confirms the tonal center of A by means of its dominant; we are, however, uncertain whether to expect a major or minor tonic. The voice leading in this example is worthy of mention. Notice the following points:

1. The bass line of mm. 2-3 echoes the alto of m. 1.

2. The soprano line beginning at m. 2 represents an *exact mirror* of the alto in mm. 1-3.

3. The tenor line mirrors, in reverse, the first and last pitches of the soprano line.

The Prelude then continues as follows (Ex. 27-3).

Example 27-3. Wagner, *Tristan und Isolde,* Prelude (piano reduction)

Although the opening leap of B to G♯ appears to confirm A as tonal center, it serves instead as the link to a sequential passage that leads first to a half cadence in the key of C, and finally, to a reiterated half cadence in E. Of future significance here is the fact that we find these keys (A, C, and E) subsequently serving as important tonal regions throughout the Prelude. It should also be noted that the exceedingly slow tempo at which this piece is to be performed tends to further obscure the sense of harmonic direction.

Contrapuntal interplay between voices may also serve to prolong a single harmony. Let us examine the opening eight measures of Brahms's Symphony No. 1. The violins, along with the cellos, present the principal theme, shown below (Ex. 27-4).

Example 27-4.   Brahms, Symphony No. 1, Op. 68, I (first violins)

Notice the syncopated, irregular character of the melodic line. Notice also the use of both natural and raised submediant, leading to the subtonic pitch of B♭, which is used exclusively in place of the leading tone. Besides B♮, the other chromatic pitches not heard in this ascending scale are those most typically associated with tonicization, E and F♯ (the leading tones to iv and V respectively). The E finally appears in m. 8, followed immediately by F♯, leading to V.

Example 27-5 shows a reduction of the voice leading in this passage. Keep in mind that the inner voices are doubled in various octaves by the entire woodwind choir, as well as by the violas, creating unusually powerful two-voiced activity.

Example 27-5. Brahms, Symphony No. 1, Op. 68, I (reduction)

The first vertical sonority following the opening octave is a C[7] chord that avoids the confirmation of either major or minor. The texture is that of a duet between the principal melody and the accompanying voices, which move in parallel 3rds, all above a tonic pedal. The syncopation of the melody and its irregular treatment of tendency tones render any attempt at roman numeral analysis meaningless and, in fact, preclude any sense of forward harmonic motion. Yet the inexorable logic of the contrary motion between the two lines, pitted against the insistence of the tonic pedal, creates a sense of drama and mounting tension that could hardly be heightened by harmonic means.

SEQUENCE

We have observed the manner in which sequential treatment serves to facilitate movement among mediant-related keys in Example 27-3. The device of sequence proves equally serviceable in homophonic passages,* particularly in the harmonization of unwieldy melodies. In Example 27-6 we find a melody, consisting of a chromatic scale, that is used to embellish the progression V-I in B♭ major.

Example 27-6. Tchaikovsky, *Nutcracker Suite,* Op. 71a, Overture
(piano reduction)

Although we have pointed out similar examples of passing harmonies in earlier examples, you will notice that this succession of chord roots (indicated by pop symbols) is strictly parallel. Yet the contrary motion inherent in the sequence pattern creates a sense of intense harmonic activity. Still another example in which sequential activity—in this case, a more extended pattern—serves to "legitimize" nontraditional relationships may be seen in the passage from *Scheherazade,* a tone poem by Rimsky-Korsakov.

*Passages in which a single melodic line (as opposed to the juxtaposition of multiple melodies found in contrapuntal writing) is harmonized, either with block chords, or by means of a more elaborate accompaniment.

Example 27-7.   Rimsky-Korsakov, *Scheherazade* (piano reduction)

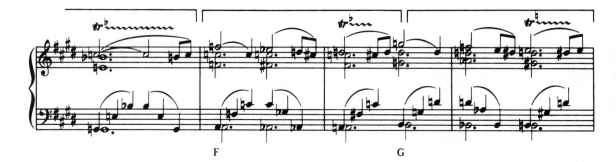

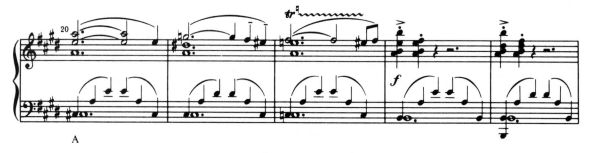

This passage, found near the beginning of the work, establishes the key of
E major. The excerpt quoted here opens with C♯ major harmony, suggesting
V/ii. The sequence that begins in the third measure of the excerpt moves
through a series of tonicizations a whole step apart, from C♯ to A, and ultimately leads to a half cadence on B. Of interest is the second chord of the

sequence, which vaguely suggests an +6. This sonority, which embellishes the third chord of the pattern (V⁷ of the following tonal area) also shares a common tritone with it. The smoothness of the sequential movement renders convincing the somewhat tenuous relationship between the series of chords thus tonicized (C♯-E♭-F-G-A) and the overall tonality of E major.

Perhaps the quintessence of a chromatically saturated sequential succession is the *omnibus,* a coloristic series of chords used to harmonize nonfunctional bass movement. For example, in the music of Liszt and Chopin we frequently encounter this phenomenon:

B♭:   V⁷   V⁶₅   V⁷

Although it would perhaps be possible to analyze the chords interpolated between root position V⁷ and V⁶₅ as tending to tonicize c minor (Ger⁺⁶-i⁶₄-Ger⁺⁶), the bravura tempo at which such passages are normally performed will more likely suggest extended V⁷ harmony with chromatic passing tones in bass and soprano. The omnibus may also serve to harmonize a descending bass line as shown in Example 27-8.

Example 27-8. Omnibus

c⁶₄   a⁶₄   f♯⁶₄   e♭⁶₄   c⁶₄

You will notice that only one voice at a time is moving in contrary motion to the bass, and that this function is passed back and forth between soprano, alto, and tenor. Notice, too, that the minor triads found as every third chord bear a mediant relationship to one another.

SHIFTING KEYS

The examples we have looked at thus far, including the omnibus, bear one important resemblance to one another: they can all, if broken down into sufficiently small components, be analyzed in terms of functional relationships. The descending form of the omnibus, for example, responds believably to the following analysis.

$$i^6_4$$
$$ii^6_4 \quad \text{passing} \quad ^{+6} \quad V^7$$
$$\text{Ger}^{+6} \quad i^6_4$$
$$ii^6_4 \quad \text{passing} \quad ^{+6} \quad V^7$$
$$\text{Ger}^{+6} \quad \text{etc.}$$

At any point we might logically discontinue the sequence by means of a functional progression from any of its members to tonic harmony. Increasingly, however, late nineteenth-century music features chord relationships that do not correspond to traditional root movement. Look, for example, at the following music by Liszt.

Example 27-9. Liszt, Polonaise No. 2

The key of a minor, which has until now been clearly established (typically, as we have noted before, by means of a tonic chord embellished through nonessential +6 harmony), is suddenly interrupted by the appearance of f minor. While the ear can easily accommodate the pitches F and C in a minor, the flatted tonic is a jarring occurrence, and it instantly raises doubts about the solidity of the previous key center, without suggesting a new one. The subsequent movement to Db (which, in retrospect, labels the f minor chord as a V_{6th}^{subs}) is quickly eradicated by the return of a minor.

The relationship of Db major to a minor is an interesting one; if we respell the Db as C♯ (since the ear will indeed process these chords as being related by 3rd rather than by °4) we note a *double chromatic mediant* relationship. Examining a reduction of this chord succession, we may summarize the relationship as follows: two triads of *contrasting* quality (minor to major, or vice versa) whose roots are located a 3rd apart.

Occasionally, as in this example, a M3 may be respelled as a °4 for the sake of convenience. The movement between them will, of necessity, involve two chromatic inflections, as opposed to the previously encountered *chromatic mediant* (one chromatic inflection and one common tone, triads matching in quality) or the *diatonic mediant* (no chromatic inflections, two common tones, triads contrasting in quality). The possibilities for double chromatic mediant relationship to A are as follows:

a minor to C♯ major or F♯ major

A major to c minor or f minor

The chief significance of this chord movement lies in the incompatibility of the two sonorities, in terms of a single diatonic key, and thus in the assurance of a startling tonal shift.

The next example, by Wagner, a modulation from Gb to F (although, as is typical of the music of Wagner, the F never appears in the form of a consonant triad), shows a key shift accomplished essentially by linear means. The tonality changes from m. 5 to m. 6, when the $F^{ø7}$, representing vii°7, is chromatically inflected to become a $B^{ø7}$, suggesting vii°7/V in the new key.

Note the tritone root relationship that exists between these two chords; note, too, the smoothness of the contrapuntal motion. Once again the linear distraction provided by the moving inner parts, with their pervasive nonchord tones, continues to propel the harmonic motion forward, though at the same time defying the listener's prediction of the eventual tonal outcome.

Example 27-10. Wagner, *Tristan und Isolde,* Act II, Scene 2
(piano-vocal score)

TREATMENT OF DOMINANT HARMONY

Certainly the single structural bulwark upon which the traditional tonal system rests is most aptly represented by the inviolability of the V-I progression. Rudolph Reti summed up this concept rather succinctly when he observed, in *Tonality in Modern Music:* *

> In fact the scheme I - x - V - I symbolizes, though naturally in a very summarizing way, the harmonic course of any composition from the Classical period. This *x*, usually appearing as a progression of chords, as a whole series, constitutes, as it were, the actual "music" within the scheme, which through the annexed formula V-I, is made into a unit, a group, or even a whole piece.

Inevitably, then, when this traditional relationship is tampered with, the ensuing musical result, despite surface consonance, represents a significant historical digression.

In the following example a chain of major-minor seventh chords, each suggesting a dominant function but forced to resolve deceptively, creates a strikingly parallel, and hence nontonal, effect.

Example 27-11.   Brahms, Symphony No. 4, Op. 98, IV (piano reduction)

Brahms has heightened the natural ambiguity of this brief passage still further by means of alternating registral displacement. In the following passage by Fauré, who is frequently mentioned as the most obvious predecessor of

---

*Rudolph Reti, *Tonality in Modern Music* (New York: Collier Books, 1962), p. 28. (Originally published as *Tonality-Atonality-Pantonality*.) Used by permission of Hutchinson Publishing Group Limited, London, England.

Debussy, we note V⁷ sonorities, moving coloristically in parallel motion with no pretense of harmonic function, arriving finally at a brief but satisfying tonicization of E♭ (Ex. 27-12).

Example 27-12.   Fauré, "L'hiver a cessé," Op. 61, No. 9

We have seen a tendency on the part of post-Romantic composers to delay, or obscure, or both, the resolution of dominant to tonic. This process may be observed in the opening measures of Brahms's Violin Sonata in d minor (Ex. 27-13).

Example 27-13. Brahms, Violin Sonata No. 3, Op. 108, I

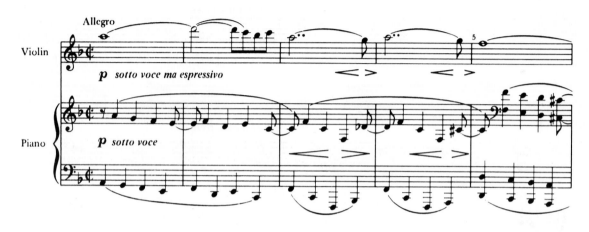

Although the movement opens with d minor harmony, the first actual harmonic motion, in m. 3, leads to the mediant, suggesting relative major, while mm. 7 and 8 strongly suggest subtonic (C), though perhaps in a V/III function. The first rhythmically significant cadence, in m. 11, falls on dominant harmony. After extended chromatic hovering about V, the key shifts almost imperceptibly (by means of sequence) to a minor, leading to a cadence on a minor. Though we might logically hear the final A major chord of the cadence as a preparation for a return to tonic, our expectations are thwarted, as we are hurried off, if only briefly, to F and the beginning of a transition section that ultimately establishes the relative major as the second key area—but without a single authentic cadence having been heard in the original key.

EXPANDED TONALITY

The process of avoiding confirmation of tonic may sometimes be carried so far that the listener is never entirely sure of the primary tonal center of the piece. Examine Example 27-14.

Example 27-14. Wolf, "Herr, was trägt der Boden"

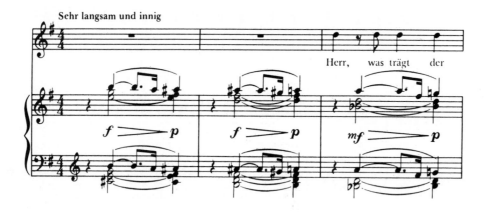

Actually, the opening measures might lead us to expect eventual resolution to b minor as tonic, although the key signature contradicts this. However, m. 2 negates the leading tone of A♯, and m. 3 with its g minor sonority all but destroys any previous expectations. In m. 4 (minor v?), m. 5 (iv⁶), and m. 6 (V⁷) we are brought seemingly back to b minor, only to be abruptly jarred by the d minor interruption of m. 7. (Note the double chromatic mediant root relationship between d minor and the preceding F♯⁷ chord.) It is not until the final measures of the piece (Ex. 27-15) that E (albeit E major) is at last allowed to serve as tonal center of gravity.

Example 27-15. Wolf, "Herr, was trägt der Boden"

Even here we note a certain ambiguity suggested by the tonicization of the Neapolitan (m. 25), the harmonic enigma of the A♯/B♭, and the final attempt to hold back tonic by means of a deceptive cadence in m. 26. Still, the very functional root movement leading to the end (C♯-F♯-B-E) seems to compensate for the unexpectedness of this tonal goal.

Our final nineteenth-century example, by Mahler, also serves to illustrate the principle of what has aptly been described as *nonconcentric tonality;* that is to say: a change of tonal center between the opening and closing of a work or movement. The terms *concentric* or *centric* are sometimes employed to designate the common tonal practice in which opening and closing keys are in agreement, providing a tonal framework for the composition. Example 27-16 illustrates a striking departure from that tradition.

Example 27-16.   Mahler, *Kindertotenlieder,* No. 2

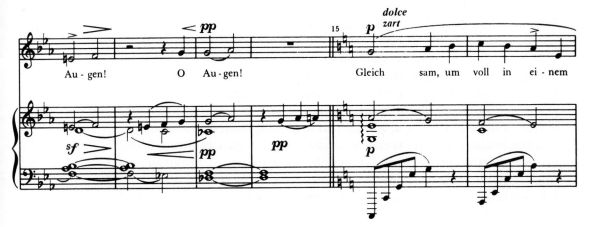

The opening measures suggest g minor, despite the key signature, which more logically would point to c minor. It is worthy of mention, in light of our preceding comments regarding the traditional inviolability of the dominant, that in both this example and the preceding one by Wolf, the "wrong key" heard at the outset is, in fact, serving as a *minor* dominant for what ultimately proves to be the intended tonic. Let us note, too, that the tonicizing process for g minor takes place by means of Neapolitan and ⁺6 sonorities, which are much prized in post-Romantic music, since they provide linear support with a minimum of functional root movement. Interestingly, at the point at which the music seems to move away from tonic toward the expected dominant, the tonality appears to be shifting toward E♭ (mm. 10-12).

Mahler's systematic manipulation of tendency tones within the established key is particularly crafty. As you play through the example, note the G♮ in m. 13 (which our ear perceives as $\hat{3}$ in E♭, moving on to A♭, its expected destination). In the meantime, however, the bass E♭, which our ear has interpreted as a tonic passing tone headed for the leading tone of D♮, moves instead to D♭, and suddenly we find ourselves expecting a resolution to G♭ major, the soprano G♮ having been transformed into a leading tone to the supertonic. Yet before this is allowed to happen, our expectations are once again thwarted as the D♭⁷ in m. 14 is treated unexpectedly as an ⁺6 chord and drops to C major, while the passing tone A♮, seeming to drive upward, resigns itself to function as a suspended submediant in C.

SUMMARY

It is possible to identify a number of developments that took place during the approximately forty-year period comprising the post-Romantic age. For one, we note a resurgence of interest in contrapuntal manipulation, particularly insofar as it serves to obscure harmonic rhythm and tonality; the sequence was increasingly used as a means of creating relationships between seemingly disparate musical elements or, in one of its more traditional functions, as a means of prolonging a single tonality. Composers began to lean toward less conventional key relationships, particularly ones that confound functional analysis. The means for establishing a key became coloristic rather than functional. Increased use of the augmented sixth chord for this purpose became commonplace. Irregular treatment of dominant harmony and a lessening of control by any single key as an organizing factor also represent a significant departure from earlier tonal styles.

As we have mentioned, an investigation of larger formal practices is not, unfortunately, within the scope of this brief chapter. If you wish to gain a more accurate understanding of this transitional period, you will need to study large musical structures; you will also need to gain some familiarity with the striking political, sociological, and philosophical movements that characterized the era.

EXERCISE 27-1. See Workbook.

CHAPTER TWENTY-EIGHT

AN INTRODUCTION TO TWENTIETH-CENTURY PRACTICES

INTRODUCTION

As the traditional tonal system was being stretched to, and even beyond, its furthermost limits, composers became aware of the growing need for alternative means of musical organization. Elements that seemed to lend themselves to modification were scale, chord structure, harmonic succession, rhythm and meter, and overall musical texture. The early experiments that took place seemed to lead along two somewhat different paths: one, an extension of the principles of ultrachromaticism; the other, a reaction against chromatic excess.

Throughout the unfolding of the twentieth century, we find each of these paths themselves branching off in various directions, creating a vast array of musical styles, philosophies, and practices. In some instances, one may observe the gradual overlapping of seemingly disparate patterns of musical thought. Worthy of note is the relative speed with which this has taken place, especially in comparison with stylistic developments of the Common Practice period.* The richness and diversity of today's musical experience present problems for any musician attempting to synthesize, codify, or define the prevailing trends in twentieth-century music, even as that very century draws to a close. This chapter will serve primarily as an overview of certain historically significant events which ultimately resulted in the definition of today's cultural environment. It may also provide a springboard for continued study and analysis.

IMPRESSIONISM

Debussy, whose music represents a move away from the chromaticism characteristic of the post-Romantic era, is considered by many to have made some of the most significant contributions to the evolution of early twentieth-

---

*A term sometimes used to designate the time span from c. 1650-1900, during which Western music composition was based on the principles of tonal harmony.

century musical thinking. His compositional style reveals departures from previous practices which, though easily accessible to the tonally-oriented ear, clearly defy traditional tonal expectations.

You will notice the clear suggestion of G♭ major in Example 28-1.

Example 28-1. Debussy, "La Fille aux cheveux de lin," from *Preludes,* Book I

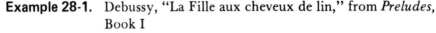

But notice, too, the nontraditional procedures he employs.

1. The opening measures outline an e♭⁷ chord, whose function is far from obvious.

2. The first cadence leading to tonic is plagal and thus avoids functional use of the leading tone.

3. The progression beginning in m. 5, with its predominance of mediant relationships, serves to render the G♭ tonic still more elusive.

In general, the most revealing aspects of earlier twentieth-century music may be discovered through an examination of the treatment of tonality: does the piece seem to have a tonal center or centers? If so, how is tonality accomplished? If not, how is it avoided? The answers to these questions will do a great deal to shed light upon a composer's style and musical inclinations.

SCALES

One reaction to the chromatic saturation of the late nineteenth century was a renewed interest in the church modes, given below (Ex. 28-2). The simplest way to represent each of the modes is by using the pitches of the C major scale, but with a pitch other than C serving as tonic or *final* for each mode.

Example 28-2.

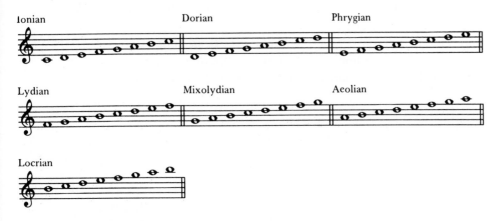

If we compare the modes directly to major and minor scales (Ex. 28-3), we find that the Ionian and Aeolian modes are identical to the major and natural minor scales, respectively, and that the remaining modes (except Locrian) may be likened either to a major scale or to a natural minor scale with one alteration.

Example 28-3.

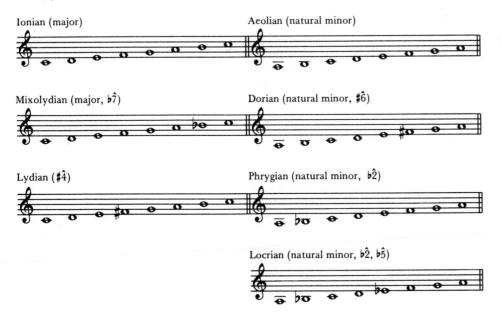

The Locrian mode, which requires two accidentals compared to minor and which lacks a true dominant, occurs less frequently as a basis for musical composition.

The modes may also be arranged as shown below, in decreasing relative order of "brightness," that is, according to the number of major or augmented intervals above the final. For comparison each mode in Example 28-4 is built on C.

Example 28-4.

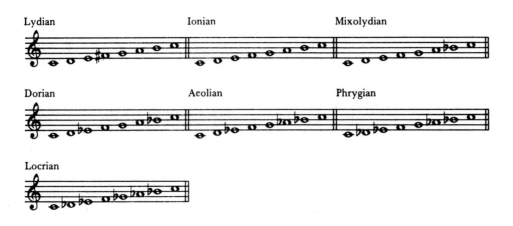

A scale Debussy particularly favored is the Lydian-Mixolydian, or $\sharp\hat{4}$, $\flat\hat{7}$ scale. This hybrid collection of pitches may well have resulted from the juxtaposition of two major-minor seventh chords with roots a whole step apart, as indicated by the brackets in Example 28-5.

Example 28-5.

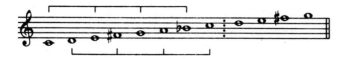

You will notice, given the presence of both B♭ and F♯, that it would be impossible to realize this scalar pattern using only the white keys of the piano. Just as each of the diatonic modes possesses unique color characteristics, the scale discussed above may be made to sound quite different with different pitches serving as "tonic." For example, beginning on D will result in a major scale with a ♭6̂ and ♭7̂. Likewise, beginning on A will yield a Phrygian/Dorian pattern (a minor with ♭2̂ and ♯6̂). When G is used, an ascending melodic minor scale is created.

When we start this scale on the note B♭, the resulting pattern begins with five pitches in whole tone relationship to one another. For this reason, you may occasionally see the designation *4+1,* indicating that this type of scale may be arranged so as to consist of four whole steps, separated by a half step from the one remaining whole step, as follows:

$$B♭ - C - D - E - F♯ - G - A - B♭$$

Accordingly, the white key scale could be designated *3+2* when arranged as follows:

$$F - G - A - B - C - D - E - F$$

Obviously the nonspecific nature of these labels would be useful only to distinguish between the two scalar patterns used, say, in a passage which contains no clear tonal center.

Example 28-6 shows this scale resulting from the canonic mirroring of two voices.

Example 28-6. Bartók, "Subject and Reflection," *Mikrokosmos* No. 141

The *pentatonic,* or five-note, scale has played a significant role in music, particularly non-Western music, for centuries. Although the term pentatonic literally denotes any collection of five pitches, the two forms of the scale shown in Example 28-7 tend to be encountered the most frequently in the literature.

Example 28-7.

Diatonic (Anhemitonic)   Hirajoshi

There are no half steps or tritones in the diatonic pentatonic, which may be likened to the pattern of the black keys on the piano. Any one of its five pitches may be made to serve as tonic by means of reiteration and metric accent. The effect of the scale is likely to be harmonically static, however, particularly if its use is prolonged. For this reason, a composer will seldom use the pentatonic scale as the basis for a composition of any length.

Debussy's use of the diatonic pentatonic scale is illustrated in Example 28-8.

Example 28-8. Debussy, "Nuages," from *Nocturnes* (piano reduction)

Used by permission of Edward B. Marks Music Company.

The pentatonic tune, appearing in octaves, centers around F♯ and is harmonized by d♯ minor and G♯ major sonorities. To the traditional ear, this might possibly suggest ii-V in C♯ major, or perhaps a D♯ Dorian key center. At no point in the piece, however, is either C♯ or D♯ permitted to function decisively as tonic.

The pitch collections we have discussed so far bear a clear resemblance to scales or fragments of scales associated with the diatonic system. Composers have also, however, made extensive use of *artificial* or *synthetic scales*. One of the most prominent of these, the *whole-tone scale,* composed entirely of major 2nds, was also a favorite of Debussy's. This scale is used in Example 28-9. It is of interest to note that "Voiles," the closing section of which appears below, is composed in ABA structure, the B section being based exclusively on the pentatonic scale.

Example 28-9. Debussy, "Voiles," from *Preludes,* Book I

Like the pentatonic scale, the whole-tone scale possesses several structural limitations, since it contains basically only three intervals: the major 2nd, the major 3rd, and the tritone (along with their inversions). Its symmetry and its total lack of perfect intervals (and hence of major or minor triads) bestows upon it an elusive, tonally ambiguous quality that has proved attractive to many composers. The vertical sonorities that may result from whole-tone simultaneities are often referred to as *whole-tone chords.* (The Fr^{+6} chord, though used in tonal contexts, may be structurally derived from the whole-tone scale.)

The *mystic scale,* so-called because it consists of pitches from Scriabin's "mystic chord," is shown below in Example 28-10.

Example 28-10.   Mystic Scale and Mystic Chord

You will notice that, except for the presence of the pitch A, the scale corresponds to a five-note segment of the whole-tone scale. For that reason, some authors have referred to this as the "almost whole-tone" scale.

The available variety of synthetic scales is, obviously, limited only by the composer's imagination. We shall mention here only two additional ones that are interesting because of their symmetrical structure: the *octatonic* or *diminished scale,* derived from the superimposition of two diminished seventh chords at the interval of a half or whole step, and the *half step-minor 3rd scale,* derived from the juxtaposition of two augmented triads at the interval of the half step.

Example 28-11.

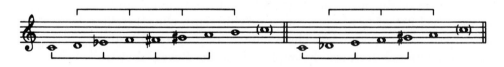

The octatonic scale can, in some instances, suggest modal combinations, although it is infrequently used for that purpose. It may be found with some regularity in the music of the Russian Five, as well as that of their immediate successors.

The *dodecaphonic,* or twelve-note, scale may serve as the basis of a composition that suggests a tonal center, although its use will be strictly nonfunctional. The term dodecaphonic is used in place of its seemingly synonymous counterpart, chromatic, so as to avoid any implication of functional tendency tones (the significance of $\sharp\hat{6}$ versus $\flat\hat{7}$, and so on). Example 28-12 illustrates the use of this scale.

Example 28-12. Kennan, Prelude No. 1

The opening four measures make use of all twelve pitch classes; yet through the bass position and reiteration of the note F, we are made aware of its function as tonal center.

CHORD STRUCTURE

One obvious extension of the post-Romantic tradition of tertian harmony is found in the increased use of ninth, eleventh, and thirteenth chords (tall chords) on the part of some composers. These chords may occur in both functional and nonfunctional settings. Example 28-13 by Ravel, shown below, illustrates a coloristic use of tall chords in the sense that traditional rules of resolution fail to apply. Notice the clear sense of root movement in mm. 1-3, as indicated in the analysis. The texture of succeeding measures continues to employ tall chords, created through the scalewise motion of the bass line. The effect of this passage is to prolong the sense of C as tonal center until the music slips unobtrusively into G in m. 7 of the excerpt, again employing a functional bass line.

Example 28-13. Ravel, "Rigaudon," from *Le Tombeau de Couperin*

As has been noted in Chapter 26, tall chords are created through the stacking of major and minor 3rds. The most frequently encountered of these are shown below with lead sheet symbols. Although widely differing labeling systems exist, those given in Example 28-14 are generally considered to be standard.

Example 28-14.

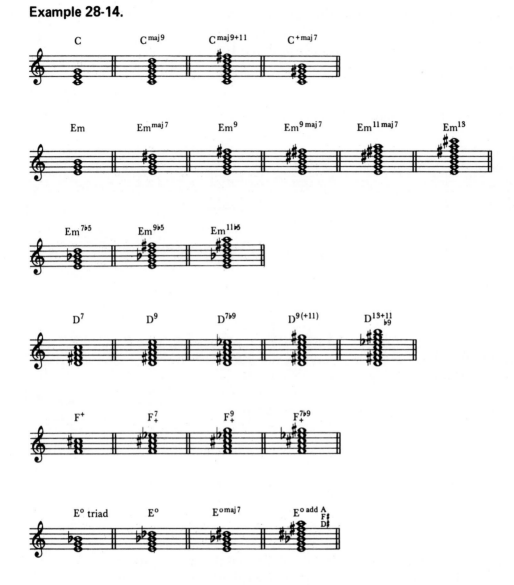

Frequently, in the interests of lightening up the texture and achieving greater flexibility, a composer may omit some components of a tall chord, such as the 5th or the 11th. Depending on the context, this omission may tend to alter the listener's perception of the basic chord structure. Play the three chords of Example 28-15.

Example 28-15.

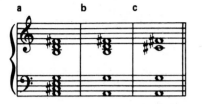

Example 28-15a is clearly a thirteenth chord. If we interpret the root A as being a dominant, we can see that all pitches of the D major scale are being sounded. This adds a certain heaviness to the sonority, which a composer might prefer to avoid. The omission of the 3rd and 5th of the chord, as shown in Example 28-15b, does little to alter our perception of the sonority. In Example 28-15c, however, when we systematically omit the 5th, 9th, and 11th, we might interpret the sonority as a V^{7subs}_{6th}, or we might even hear the F♯ as a nonharmonic tone. The "correct" interpretation is obviously dependent not only on the previous musical experience that the listener brings to it, but also on the context in which the chord occurs. For example, a popular song arrangement that features almost exclusively tall tertian sonorities will logically suggest analyzing such a chord as a thirteenth chord.

Yet another extended tertian harmony is the *polychord*—superimposed triads—several versions of which are shown in Example 28-16.

Example 28-16.

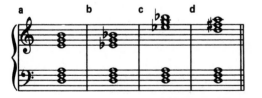

In Example 28-16a the diatonic relationship of the pitches might well suggest a chord of the thirteenth. Example 28-16b might still be perceived as a d minor ninth chord with upper extensions, but the chromatic inflection of the upper triad is far more likely to suggest two independent triads with their roots a m9 apart. This effect is greatly enhanced by the separation occurring in Example 28-16c between the two sets of pitches. The sonority occurring in Example 28-16d is often referred to as a *split-third chord*, as it represents both major and minor quality built on the same root.

Now play Example 28-17 which is polychordal.

Example 28-17. Schuman, *Three-Score Set*, No. 2

The independent movement of two chord streams contributes to the impression of two independent harmonic lines, despite the obvious rhythmic homogeneity of the passage. At the same time, we perceive no clear tonality, as opposed to two distinct key centers. When several key centers are heard at the same time—which occurs considerably less frequently than polychordality—we refer to *bitonality* or *polytonality*. In order for the listener to perceive duality of key, it is necessary for the harmonic motion of each key to be relatively uncomplicated and very diatonic. Bitonality is illustrated in Example 28-18.

Example 28-18. Bartók, "Playsong," *Mikrokosmos* No. 105

While we may theorize about the possibility of three or more independent and simultaneous tonal centers, as suggested by the term polytonality, we would nonetheless be hard pressed to locate examples of literature in which this tonal multiplicity is perceptible at the aural level.

Another modification of the traditional tertian system of chord construction may be found in the use of the *added-note chord,* as shown in Example 28-19.

Example 28-19. Grieg, "Wedding Day at Troldhaugen," Op. 65, No. 6

The circled chord in the preceding example would according to traditional analysis be interpreted as a b⁷ in first inversion. In the context of the extremely static D major harmony, however, especially with the doubling of the A, we find the ear being forced to acknowledge D as chord root; B thus becomes an added 6th. The added-note chord will frequently feature either a 2nd (or 9th) or 4th above the chord root. The latter is particularly likely to occur in jazz arrangements.

This points out an interesting aspect of sonorities found in twentieth-century composition. Whereas in the tonal system the pitches of a tertian triad or seventh chord may be perceived as a discrete and identifiable unit, despite doubling, inversion, and even the presence of non-chord tones, the aural effect of sonorities in a less traditional setting is far more dependent on doubling, spacing, and arrangement in general.

Example 28-20 shows five possible arrangements of the pitches of a pentatonic scale. As you play each of the five, you will probably hear in turn:

1. a major triad with added 6th and 2nd

2. a stack of perfect 5ths

3. a 4th-rich sonority

4. an implied V^9 with suspension

5. a tone cluster (chord built from 2nds)

Example 28-20.

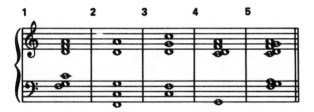

It may well have been the intervallic "accidents" occurring as the result of tall stacks of 3rds that suggested to composers the possibility of experimenting with other intervals for constructing chords. The P5 and its inversion, the P4, seem particularly well suited to avoiding any commitment to traditional major or minor implications. Example 28-21 illustrates the use of chords built in 5ths.

Example 28-21. Debussy, "La Cathédrale engloutie," from *Preludes*, Book I

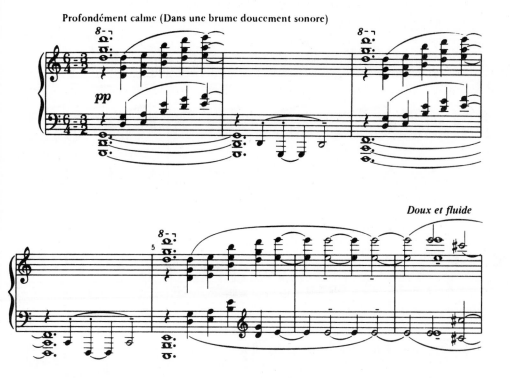

Except for the moving bass line, the pitches used adhere strictly to the diatonic pentatonic scale (G-A-B-D-E). If we view the pentatonic scale in terms of its derivation from stacked 5ths (G-D-A-E-B), this interdependence of scale and chords seems almost inevitable.

An example of predominantly *quartal* harmony (based on 4ths) may be observed in Example 28-22.

Example 28-22. Hindemith, Flute Sonata, II

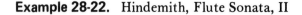

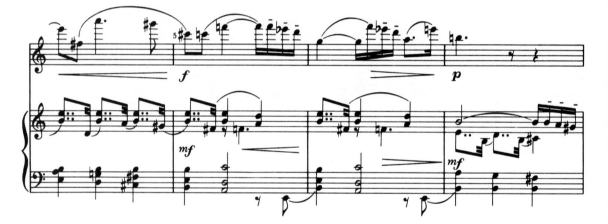

Notice how the sense of B as tonal center is maintained by the bass line which consists of a descending Dorian scale based on B, as well as frequent reference to F♯ by the solo flute.

The use of 2nds as a method of chord construction also proved attractive to many composers. Example 28-23 illustrates Bartók's use of *secundal* harmony.

Example 28-23. Bartók, "Free Variations," *Mikrokosmos* No. 140

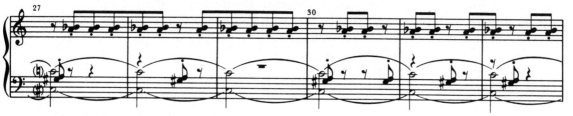

Any collection of three or more pitches in secundal relationship may correctly be referred to as a *tone cluster*. The term was coined by the American composer Henry Cowell, whose early experiments called for pianists to play certain passages with fists, palms, and, frequently, the entire forearm. Example 28-24, an excerpt from *The Tides of Manaunaun*, illustrates this technique. The sonorities thus created are powerful and richly programmatic.

Example 28-24. Cowell, *The Tides of Manaunaun*

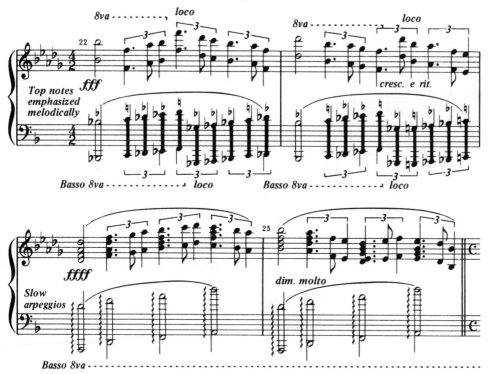

The concept of cluster chords, especially when used in conjunction with the rich timbral palette of an orchestra or chamber group, has continued to prove extremely useful for composers in the latter half of the twentieth century and will be further explored in this chapter.

PARALLELISM

You may have noticed by now that the treatment of texture plays a significant role in our perception of twentieth-century music. The instrumental timbre, the structure of the chords, the doublings, the vertical spacing, the melodic construction, and the method of movement from one musical event to another—all of these aspects contribute significantly to our impression of the piece as having a tonal center or not.

One of the earliest indications of a break with traditional procedures of harmonic progression was the use of *parallelism.* In some forms, of course, parallelism has been known before the twentieth century; you have already been exposed to parallel sixth chords in a tonal context, as illustrated in Example 28-25.

Example 28-25.

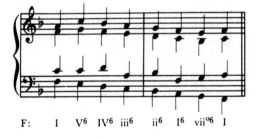

F: I   V⁶ IV⁶ iii⁶   ii⁶ I⁶ vii°⁶ I

Even in this diatonic, triadic progression, the ear experiences at least a brief confusion in the space between the beginning and the ending tonic chords, due to the sliding effect produced by parallel movement between the outer voices.

Even more challenging to the ear is Debussy's use of parallel movement of dominant seventh chords, contrasted in the intervening measure with parallel movement of augmented triads (Ex. 28-26). The term *planing*, essentially synonymous with parallelism, is frequently used to describe this device when it occurs in twentieth-century music—perhaps to avoid the pejorative connotations of the formerly used term.

Example 28-26. Debussy, "Nuages," from *Nocturnes* (piano reduction)

Used by permission of Edward B. Marks Music Company.

Following the first beat of mm. 61 and 63 the melody outlines the pitches of a dominant ninth chord on A♭, enharmonically respelled for convenience. The planing observed in this example is referred to as strict, since the vertical intervals remain unchanged. This type of parallel motion will inevitably require a substantial number of accidentals, since such consistent chord quality does not normally occur within a diatonic key; as a result, the feeling of tonal center will be unclear. In contrast, diatonic planing involves parallel movement of vertical sonorities whose quality is determined by the prevailing diatonic scale. Example 28-27 shows parallel triads used to harmonize a chantlike melody in C.

Example 28-27.   Debussy, "La Cathédrale engloutie," from *Preludes,* Book I

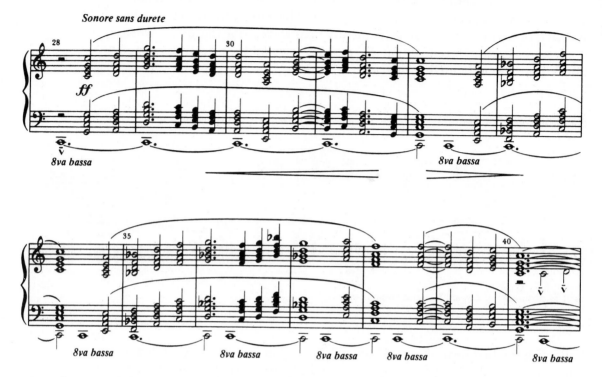

The pedal on C and the rhythmic emphasis on C, E, and G all serve to maintain a strong sense of C as tonal center of gravity. Notice, however, that Bb is substituted for B♮ in the melodic line in order to maintain the consonant quality of major and minor triads. Although the Bb could suggest a Mixolydian scale on C, the previous establishment of C major causes us instead to hear merely a brief tonicization of the subdominant.

We occasionally encounter parallel chord movement that can be explained neither by consistency of chord type nor by the limitations of a single scale. Such a passage is shown in Example 28-28.

Example 28-28.   Debussy, "Fêtes," from *Nocturnes* (piano reduction)

Used by permission of Edward B. Marks Music Company.

In this case, the composer's aim is harmonization of the upper fourth of the chromatic scale below A (A-G♯-G-F♯-F-E). This descending line is further enhanced by the secondary line (C♯-B-B♭-A-A♭) which doubles it in 3rds. The concluding A♭ might be considered a misspelled leading tone in A. This seems especially plausible when we encounter a recurrence of this material in the closing section of the work (Ex. 28-29), harmonized to sound almost functional in the key of A. Here the juxtaposition of A♭ against B♭ clearly suggests an +6, serving as a means of tonicization.

Example 28-29.   Debussy, "Fêtes," from *Nocturnes* (piano reduction)

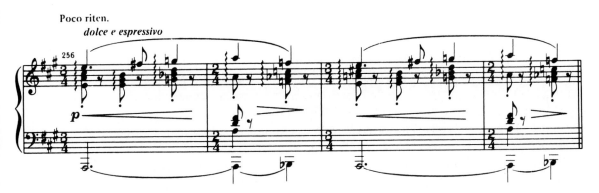

Used by permission of Edward B. Marks Music Company.

Obviously, the principle of parallelism may be applied to other structures, such as quintal and quartal chords, as well as to simple melodic doubling at intervals other than the traditional octave.

The second movement of Bartók's *Concerto for Orchestra* provides us with a virtual catalogue of doublings. The movement opens with a duet for bassoons doubled at the 6th, as illustrated in Example 28-30.

Example 28-30.   Bartók, *Concerto for Orchestra,* II (reduction)

This is followed by a passage featuring new material for oboes (Ex. 28-31), doubled at the m3 with an occasional M3.

Example 28-31.   Bartók, *Concerto for Orchestra,* II (reduction)

Following a brief transition by the strings, the work continues with other pairs of instruments: clarinets doubled at the m7, flutes doubled at the P5, and trumpets playing parallel major 2nds. If you are not yet familiar with this masterpiece of orchestral literature, you should make an effort to listen to it in its entirety.

PANDIATONICISM

The technique of *pandiatonicism* represents an attempt to equalize the seven pitches of the diatonic scale so that no single pitch is heard as tonic. The texture of pandiatonic passages tends to be contrapuntal, while individual lines are likely to be somewhat angular. Example 28-32 is a typical pandiatonic passage.

Example 28-32. Stravinsky, "Danse russe," from *Petrouchka* (piano reduction)

Used by permission of Edward B. Marks Music Company.

Using C, the lowest pitch, as a reference point, we discover the excerpt to be based on a $\sharp\hat{4}$, $\flat\hat{7}$ scale; yet at no point is the ear permitted to accept C as tonic. In this instance the designation *4+1* scale might prove useful. In another example from the same ballet (Ex. 28-33), E♭ seems to serve as a kind of tonal center.

Example 28-33.   Stravinsky, "The Masqueraders," from *Petrouchka*

SET THEORY

Music of the post-Romantic period remained sufficiently tonal to yield, albeit imperfectly, to traditional methods of study and analysis. As composers moved farther and farther from conventions of the Common Practice period, however, it became increasingly clear that previously employed analytical procedures were inadequate to deal with the new harmonic and tonal language.

Early attempts to address this problem came, in many cases, from composers grappling with these issues in their own work. Two of the most notable of these, Paul Hindemith and Howard Hanson, sought to clarify and codify new materials and means of organization, and to relate these resources to broader musical principles.

Hindemith's goal was to formulate an acoustic basis for consonance and dissonance, and thus to discover extensions to traditional practice that could be derived, or at least defended, through "natural musical laws." His theories attempted to define levels of harmonic tension, and are perhaps most illuminating when applied to music which retains a clear allegiance to principles of tonality.

Hanson, on the other hand, sought to explore and catalogue all possible pitch relationships within the tempered scale.

Investigation of music based on a chromatic pitch collection offers unique problems to the analyst. Much atonal music employs intricate systems of pitch organization which require precise analytical language. It was to address this need that the procedures of *set theory* were developed. Although mathematical set theories have existed for some time, Allen Forte is generally recognized as having first codified and refined this system for use by musicians in *The Structure of Atonal Music.* *

The term *set* applies to any collection of pitches. For the purposes of this system, each pitch class may be designated by a number as follows.

C	C♯/D♭	D	D♯/E♭	E	F	F♯/G♭	G	G♯/A♭	A	A♯/B♭	B
0	1	2	3	4	5	6	7	8	9	10	11

Thus the sonority shown in Example 28-34 may be seen to consist of the pitch numbers 10, 4, and 5.

---

*Allen Forte, *The Structure of Atonal Music* (New Haven: Yale University Press, 1973).

Example 28-34.

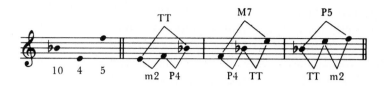

Having defined the pitch contents, it is then appropriate to designate a "normal" or consistently used order for the set. If this is not done, the six possibilities for arrangement [4,5,10; 5,4,10; 4,10,5; 5,10,4; 10,4,5; or 10,5,4] would render the analytical method confusing and impractical. *Normal order* for a set requires two conditions.

1. The interval framing the set must be the smallest possible.

2. Pitch numbers must appear in ascending order, from left to right.

Given these conditions, we may correctly conclude that the normal order for these three pitches is [4,5,10]. Since it is a three-note set or *trichord,* we may also designate it as being of *cardinality three.*

As we examine the various positions of the set [4,5,10] as illustrated in Example 28-34, we find that the requirements for normal order have been fully satisfied.

Example 28-35 illustrates yet another trichord which contains the pitches 1, 2, and 8.

Example 28-35.

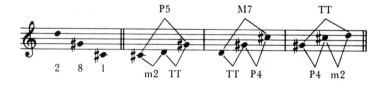

Normal order for this set might logically seem to be [1,2,8], yet upon closer examination, we find that it does not satisfy condition 1 which requires the smallest possible interval between the outer pitches of the set. The position

[8,1,2] is the only arrangement which will fulfill this condition. This seeming discrepancy may be explained if we consider 0 to be the *modulus* from which numbering begins over again. (Were this not the case, then the *octave* C would logically become 13, C♯ would become 14, etc.) Thus, by adding 12 to each of the numbers *above* zero—that is, 1 and 2—we arrive at the "expanded" values of [8,13,14], thus proving that condition 2 has been met. Similarly, if we were to transpose the pitches of the preceding example up a m3 as shown below

the normal order of [7,8,1] would be obtained by adding 12 to the digit beyond zero—that is, 1 + 12 becomes the equivalent of 13 for purposes of transposition.

Intervals, like pitches, may be assigned numerical values according to size, as shown below:

Interval	Number	Interval	Number
m2	1	P5	7
M2	2	m6	8
m3	3	M6	9
M3	4	m7	10
P4	5	M7	11
TT	6	P8	12

You will note that in each case, the numerical value corresponds to the number of half steps which comprise the interval.

As you compare the trichords discussed in the previous two examples, you will notice a similarity of intervallic content, despite the nonconformity of pitch content or shape. In order to demonstrate this equivalence, we must reduce each of the two intervals to its *prime form*. This requires two operations; the first of these requires the reduction of the twelve discrete intervals to six *interval classes*. The following chart summarizes the content of each class.

Interval class	Interval
1	m2 (1)
	M7 (11)
2	M2 (2)
	m7 (10)
3	m3 (3)
	M6 (9)
4	M3 (4)
	m6 (8)
5	P4 (5)
	P5 (7)
6	TT (6)

Note that the class of any interval larger than 6 may be obtained by subtracting the value of the larger integer from 12.

Finally, we arrive at the prime form by listing the order of intervals from smallest to largest, beginning with zero. This requires that we read the original trichord from left to right and the subsequent one from right to left, in order that the half step may be the first interval represented. Thus we discover that both trichords share the prime form of [0,1,6].

The *interval content* of this set would be expressed as a series of numbers, or *vector*, showing the number of times each interval class is represented in the sonority. The vector for the trichord above would be represented as follows:

$$\langle 1, \quad 0, \quad 0, \quad 0, \quad 1, \quad 1 \rangle$$
Interval classes: 1 2 3 4 5 6

We see that the system of set theory provides a logical and consistent mechanism for determination of (1) pitch content, (2) interval content, and (3) fundamental classification for any sonority. For this reason it has proved to be enormously useful to today's theorists as they seek to discover underlying motivic patterns in atonal works. Obviously it is not within the scope of this chapter to explore the various applications of this system in any depth. The reader wishing a more complete discussion is referred to *Basic Atonal Theory* by John Rahn.*

*John Rahn, *Basic Atonal Theory* (New York: Longman, Inc., 1980).

THE TWELVE-TONE TECHNIQUE

The procedure for composing with twelve tones is perhaps the most methodically revolutionary technique of the twentieth century. It was developed by Arnold Schoenberg, who, after a number of years of composing in the post-Romantic style, became intrigued with the concept of *atonality,* that is, the systematic avoidance of permitting any single pitch to sound as tonal center.

Even before Schoenberg had organized his ideas into an actual method of composition, certain procedures were operational in his music, such as the following.

1. Avoidance of the 8ve, either as melodic component or harmonic interval

2. Avoidance of traditional pitch collections, that is, any that might suggest major or minor triads, and hence, a tonic

3. Avoidance of more than three successive pitches that might be identified with the same diatonic scale

4. Use of wide-ranging and extremely disjunct melodies

The *Klavierstücke,* Op. 11, composed by Schoenberg a number of years before his twelve-tone system had been codified, illustrate the application of some of these constructs. Example 28-36 shows the opening measures of the first of the three pieces.

Example 28-36. Schoenberg, *Klavierstücke,* Op. 11, No. 1

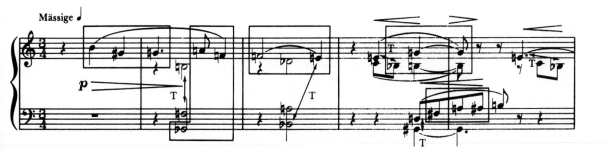

The tritone is prevalent as a vertical interval, and the composer makes extensive use of the three-note cell [0,1,4] that opens the work. The lush, Romantic texture of the piano writing is indicative of Schoenberg's close spiritual ties with the preceding era.

The principles mentioned above continued to hold true in much of Schoenberg's twelve-tone music, as well as in that of his early followers, especially Webern and Berg. His system was designed to methodically equalize all pitches of the dodecaphonic scale by the following means:

1. A twelve-tone composition is to be based on an arrangement or series of the twelve pitches that is determined by the composer. This arrangement is the *tone row* or *set.*

2. No pitch may be repeated until all other pitches have been sounded. There is one exception to this restriction: a pitch may be repeated immediately after it is heard. Repetition may also occur within the context of a trill or tremolo figure.

3. The tone row may, within the confines of the system, legitimately be used in retrograde (reversed order), inversion (mirroring of each interval), or retrograde inversion (reverse order of the mirrored form), as shown below in Webern's row that forms the basis for his Symphony Op. 21 (Ex. 28-27).

Example 28-37. Webern, Row forms of Symphony Op. 21

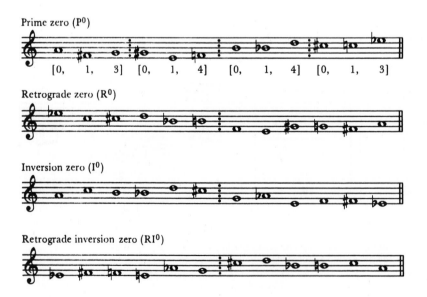

Prime zero (P⁰)

[0, 1, 3] [0, 1, 4] [0, 1, 4] [0, 1, 3]

Retrograde zero (R⁰)

Inversion zero (I⁰)

Retrograde inversion zero (RI⁰)

Note the consistency and symmetry of arrangement in the trichords which comprise the row. [0,1,3] begins and ends the set, while two versions of [0,1,4] appear in the middle.

Any one of these forms may be transposed to begin at any pitch level; thus the process may yield up to forty-eight versions of the row (in most instances). It is important to remember that the original series of pitches is in no way comparable to the theme of a theme and variations. While the intervallic arrangement of the row may tend to bring about the recurrence of melodic and harmonic cells, tremendous variety results from the rhythmic manipulation and octave displacement typically found in early twelve-tone works.

When you examine a twelve-tone composition, it is helpful to have immediate access to the forty-eight possible forms of the series. This is most conveniently obtained by use of a *matrix* or *Babbitt square* (sometimes called a *magic square*), illustrated in Example 28-38 with the original or prime form of the series of Example 28-37 shown as its top row of pitches. The inversion zero form is laid out in the first vertical column, from top to bottom. This is accomplished by inverting or mirroring the intervals in P^0, that is, A-F♯ (M6 up) inverts to A-C (M6 down). F♯-G (m2) equates with C-B. The symmetry of this operation may be viewed in the following diagram in which the note A serves as the axis of involution.

B C A F♯ G

Example 28-38.

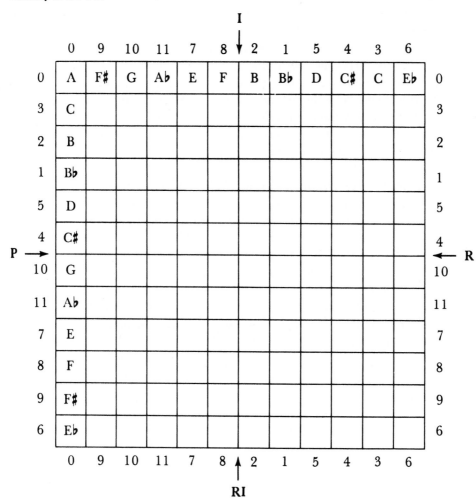

Using this method, we find that the interval which begins each prime row form will be a M6. Thus A-F♯ will be followed by C-A, then B-G♯(A♭), etc.

Index numbers on each side of the matrix designate levels of transposition, arranged in ascending chromatic order from zero. The P⁰ set, for example, transposed up a M3 to begin on C♯, would be designated as P⁴. You will note that the index number reflects, in each case, the number of half steps contained within the interval of transposition. The retrograde P⁴ would be labeled as R⁴ and would begin on G. When correctly done, the sum of the index numbers for a prime form and its inversion should equal 12—that is, P,3 + I,9; P,2 + I,10, etc. Likewise, RI,3 will correspond with R,9, etc.

We should mention here that the actual procedure for labeling set forms tends to vary somewhat, depending on the theorist cited. In the writings of earlier twelve-tone composers, we find the term *original* used in place of prime. The inevitable confusion arising between the letter "o" (original) and the numeral "0" (zero) may have prompted the change in terminology.

Example 28-39.

	I												
	0	9	10	11	7	8	2	1	5	4	3	6	
0	A	F♯	G	Ab	E	F	B	Bb	D	C♯	C	Eb	0
3	C	A	Bb	B	G	Ab	D	C♯	F	E	Eb	F♯	3
2	B	Ab	A	Bb	F♯	G	C♯	C	E	Eb	D	F	2
1	Bb	G	Ab	A	F	F♯	C	B	Eb	D	C♯	E	1
5	D	B	C	C♯	A	Bb	E	Eb	G	F♯	F	Ab	5
4	C♯	Bb	B	C	Ab	A	Eb	D	F♯	F	E	G	4
10	G	E	F	F♯	D	Eb	A	Ab	C	B	Bb	C♯	10
11	Ab	F	F♯	G	Eb	E	Bb	A	C♯	C	B	D	11
7	E	C♯	D	Eb	B	C	F♯	F	A	Ab	G	Bb	7
8	F	D	Eb	E	C	C♯	G	F♯	Bb	A	Ab	B	8
9	F♯	Eb	E	F	C♯	D	Ab	G	B	Bb	A	C	9
6	Eb	C	C♯	D	Bb	B	F	E	Ab	G	F♯	A	6
	0	9	10	11	7	8	2	1	5	4	3	6	

P →   ← R

RI

Precise intervallic spellings are unnecessary; for example, the half-step transposition of D-F may be represented by E♭-F♯, since the music under discussion is not governed by traditional rules of consonance and dissonance. It is advisable, however, to strive for consistency: always choose F♯ rather than G♭, for example, or vice versa.

The construction of the Op. 21 pitch set is an interesting one from many standpoints. Each half of the row is made up of adjacent pitches of the chromatic scale. In addition the second *hexachord* (set of six pitches) represents the retrograde of the first. Upon comparing R^6 (the retrograde of the row, transposed up a $^o5$), we discover that it is identical with P^0. We may then assume that for each transposition of the prime set, there is a matching retrograde pattern; likewise, for each inversion, there will be a matching retrograde inversion form.

This built-in correlation between set forms will, of necessity, reduce the available pitch series to twenty-four possibilities, rather than the usual forty-eight. The term *combinatoriality* is often used to describe this feature. The distinguishing property of a combinatorial set is its capability of generating a number of hexachords that are mutually exclusive, that is, in which no pitches are duplicated.

The availability of complementary hexachords will often play an important role in a composer's choice of particular set forms and will tend to bring about maximum structural cohesion in a work. To be sure, not all combinatorial rows exhibit the intricate symmetrical relationships found in Webern's. An exhaustive discussion of combinatoriality is better suited to advanced study in serial techniques than to this introductory chapter. If you would like to pursue these topics further, you should look into the writings of George Perle or Milton Babbitt.

Certain rows, such as those of Example 28-40, have achieved a certain reknown, by virtue of their having formed the basis for well-known serial compositions.

Example 28-40.

Berg, Tone row for Violin Concerto

Dallapiccola, Tone row for *Quaderno musicale di Annalibera*

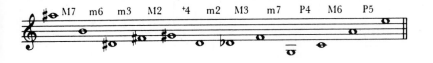

These rows illustrate the care composers lavished on the melodic and harmonic possibilities of the original set. The predominance of the 3rd in the Berg row, for example, plays an important role in bringing about an almost triadic texture within the body of the work. Also in the Berg row, pitches 1, 3, 5, and 7 of the series (bracketed) represent the open strings of the violin, while the last four pitches, which comprise a segment of a whole-tone scale, represent the opening notes of "Es ist genug," the Bach chorale prominently featured in the last movement. The second example, from Dallapiccola's *Quaderno musicale di Annalibera,* illustrates an all-interval set, in which eleven different intervals make up the series.

Example 28-41 illustrates two processes, both of which occur with some frequency in atonal music. The first is the atomization of the melodic line, a process known as *pointillism.* The second is the deliberate juxtaposition of minute melodic fragments of contrasting timbre and register; this compositional device, in which melody is in a sense created by the rapid shifting of tone colors, is referred to as *Klangfarbenmelodie,* or, literally, "sound color melody," and it is a concept that continues to fascinate many composers in the second half of the twentieth century. As you listen to a recording of this work, it may be helpful to try to suspend previously studied tonal listening habits.

Example 28-41. Webern, Concerto Op. 24

This composition, like most compositions by Webern, lends itself to analysis of set types. Notice the consistency of use of [0,1,2] and [0,1,4] trichords, several of which are labeled.

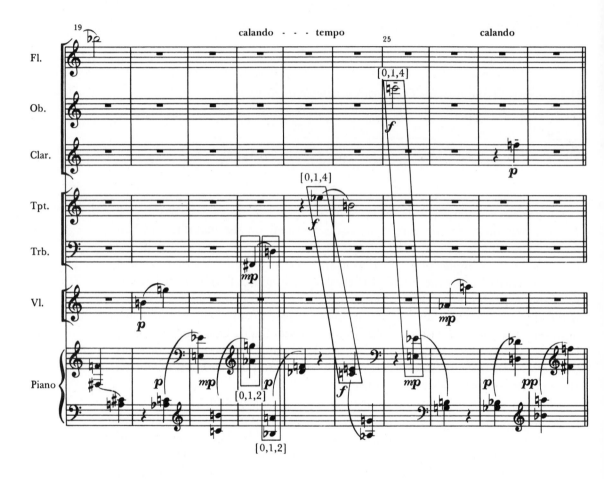

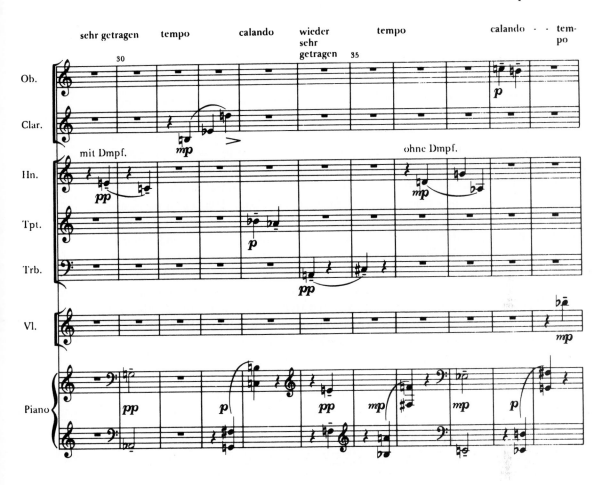

We should also mention here that the twelve-tone procedure, while conceived specifically as a systematic means for avoiding (or rather, for providing alternatives to) tonality, has been adapted by later composers as an effective means for organizing more tonally oriented music. The row may even be employed as a quasi-pandiatonic procedure. Stravinsky, for example, makes use of a twenty-eight-note series for the variations found in the second movement of his Sonata for Two Pianos and a five-note set for *In Memoriam Dylan Thomas,* consisting of the pitch series E-E♭-C-C♯-D.

TOTAL SERIALIZATION

Inevitably, as composers became fascinated with the concept of ordering pitches, there evolved a keen interest in ordering other parameters of a piece, such as rhythm, dynamics, and articulation. The term *serialization,* which earlier in the twentieth century had been considered by some to be synonymous with *twelve-tone method,* came to denote the process whereby such aspects of music as the subdivisions of the beat, dynamic level of individual pitches, and in the case of instrumental music, choice of timbre, were decided on by means of a predetermined rhythmic, dynamic, and/or timbral series. It is sometimes referred to as *integral serialism.* Two composers associated with the origins of this practice are Anton Webern, whose fascination with the problem of ordering we have already observed, and Olivier Messiaen, whose 1949 piano etude, *Mode de valeurs et d'intensités,* exerted a profound influence upon his pupil, Pierre Boulez. Example 28-42 shows the Messiaen pitch set, along with its rhythmic, dynamic, registral, and attack characteristics, while Example 28-43 illustrates the set used by Boulez in *Structures.* We perceive Boulez's debt to his teacher in the fact that the pitch set used is identical to Series I of the Messiaen piece.

Example 28-42. Messiaen, Set forms for *Mode de valeurs et d'intensités*

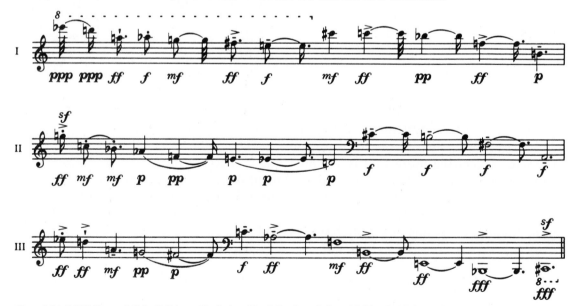

Example 28-43. Boulez, Set forms for *Structures,* Ia

	1	2	3	4	5	6	7	8	9	10	11	12
Notes (P⁰)	E♭	D	A	A♭	G	F♯	E	C♯	C	B♭	F	B
Durations	♪	♪	♪.	♪	♪♪	♪.	♪..	♩	♩♪	♩♪	♩♪.	♩.
Dynamics	*pppp*	*ppp*	*pp*	*p*	*quasi p*	*mp*	*mf*	*quasi f*	*f*	*ff*	*fff*	*ffff*
Mode of Attack	>	>.	•		normal	⌢.	'	*sfz* ∧	>̣		..	⌢

On the introductory page of *Mode de valeurs,* Messiaen explains that he has employed a thirty-six-pitch series (that is, three separate pitch sets, each of which is assigned to a specific register of the piano) and twelve methods of attack as follows:

$$
\begin{array}{cccccccccccc}
> & ' & • & - & ⌢ & >̣ & >̣ & >̣ & ⌢.. & \overset{sf}{>} & \overset{sf}{>̣} & \text{``normal'', no sign}\\
1 & 2 & 3 & 4 & 5 & 6 & 7 & 8 & 9 & 10 & 11 & 12
\end{array}
$$

He notes that there are seven dynamic levels ranging from *ppp* to *fff,* while the register is to a certain extent controlled by the pitch series being used. Thus no two appearances of the same pitch class will be identical.

Example 28-44 shows the beginning of the Messiaen work. Clearly the range of dynamic shading called for presents a singular challenge in pianistic control and a still more formidable challenge to even the most sophisticated listener.

Example 28-44. Messiaen, *Mode de valeurs et d'intensités*

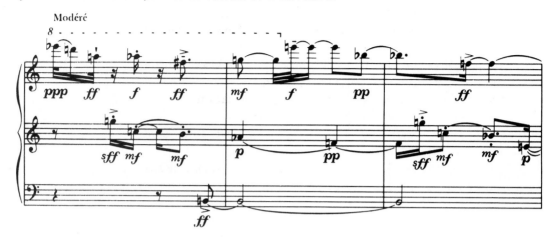

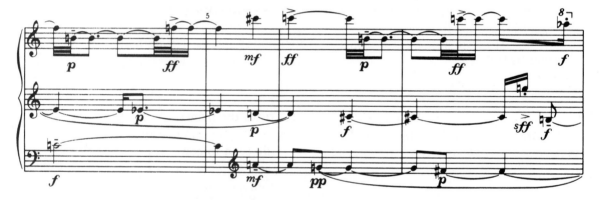

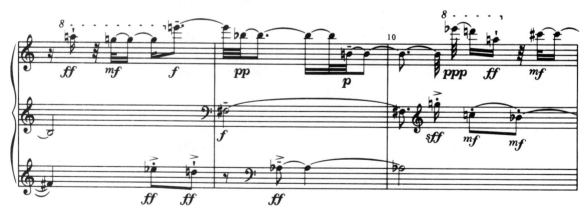

As you might imagine, the mathematical possibilities for systematic ordering or reordering of sets are virtually limitless, and they continue to present a fascinating avenue of exploration for many composers as well as a challenge for speculative theorists. The term *stochastic music* refers to music composed through computer-generated choices, based on the laws of probability. This procedure, which has been used by LeHaren Hiller and Iannis Xenakis, may be viewed as the ultimate extension of total serialization.

There is a striking similarity between two seemingly contradictory compositional processes—namely, the effort to achieve total control and the effort to abdicate control entirely through chance or aleatory procedures. Both these processes reflect a composer's desire to break free from conscious aural choice, thereby discovering sounds or effects that might not otherwise occur to him or her. Later in the chapter we will turn our attention to various aspects of aleatoric composition. First, however, we will discuss some experiments in rhythm and meter that preceded the move toward *multiparametric serialization* (the serialization of several aspects of a composition, as we have just discussed).

RHYTHM AND METER

Because the study of pitch associations constitutes the primary bulwark of the traditional tonal system, it would seem reasonable that most attempts to establish alternative systems of organization would tend to concentrate on that area. Nonetheless, the mainstream of early twentieth-century composition saw significant innovations in the areas of rhythm and meter, procedures that impart a distinctive twentieth-century flavor to the music involved.

Primarily, these efforts lay in escaping from the established norm of regularly recurring pulses subdivided into groupings of two or three. Various methods have been employed to this end, with an enormous variety of results. Perhaps the most common of these is that of asymmetric meter such as $\frac{5}{4}$ or $\frac{7}{8}$, or a composite meter such as $\frac{3+3+2}{8}$, which we encounter frequently in the music of Bartók. These are used to provide what we might describe as a "regular irregularity" in that the groupings in a $\frac{5}{4}$ piece are likely to occur consistently as either **2+3** or **3+2**. When these two groupings alternate, however, the effect becomes one of considerably more unpredictability. A composer may achieve this desired irregularity by cross accentuation, as seen in Example 28-45.

Example 28-45. Copland, *Billy the Kid*, "Mexican Dance and Finale"
(piano reduction)

A composer may achieve much the same aural effect by the use of rapidly changing meter signatures—a process known as *mixed meter*. This technique is illustrated in Example 28-46, where we also observe irregular subdivision of the $\frac{5}{8}$ measures.

Example 28-46. Adler, "Capriccio"

Both these procedures provide the listener with a sense of intense rhythmic activity coupled with constantly shifting metric accentuation. Since the effect upon the listener is one of unequal groupings of subdivisions being added together, the process is sometimes referred to as *additive* rhythm.

The term *polyrhythm* has been coined to denote a musical texture in which the listener is made aware of multiple rhythmic streams or layers in operation simultaneously, each responding to an independently recurring metric accent. In some instances the listener may be unaware of the presence of any downbeats in the texture. In the following example from *Le Sacre du printemps,* four different ostinato-like patterns occur simultaneously. The aural effect thus created is one of a hovering, static sound mass, almost hypnotic in quality.

Example 28-47.   Stravinsky, *Le Sacre du printemps* (piano reduction)

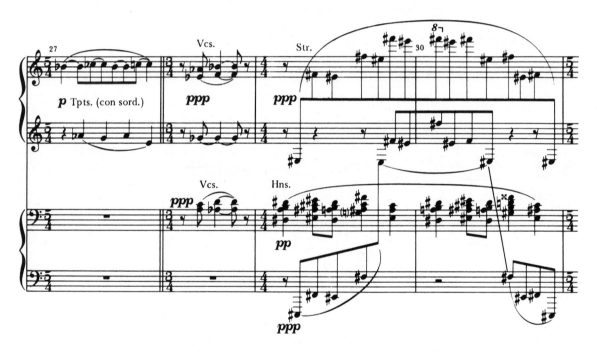

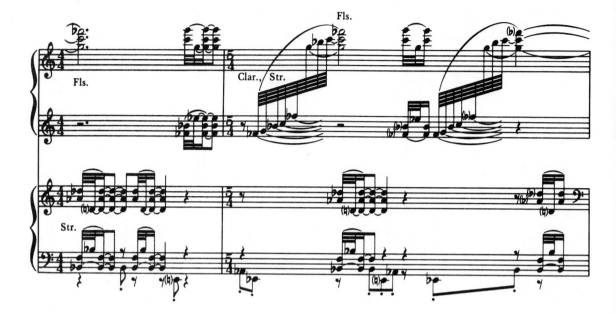

The term *polyrhythm* is sometimes confused with another term in common usage, *polymeter.* We use the former to denote the aural phenomenon of simultaneous rhythmic streams, and the latter to refer to the notation of two or more meters at once. It is possible for a passage to be polyrhythmic and polymetric at the same time, as shown in Example 28-48.

Example 28-48. Stravinsky, "Danse de la foire," from *Petrouchka* (piano reduction)

Used by permission of Edward B. Marks Music Company.

The effect of this passage upon the listener may imply a total lack of bar lines. He or she is rather aware of a constant triplet background against which seemingly spontaneous bursts of rhythmic activity occur. You should keep in mind that *Petrouchka,* which we most often hear performed in the concert hall, was first composed as a ballet score. In this particular scene, the conflicting musical events represent specific actions taking place on the stage.

The system of *metric modulation,* developed by Elliott Carter, represents yet another form of rhythmic experimentation, namely, an intense focus on, and exploitation of, minute mathematical relationships as a means of precisely controlling the flow of the music. In Example 28-49, we see the duple pulse being systematically stretched, through the interpolation of added sub-beats, from ♩ = 126 to ♩ = 72. Fourteen measures later, we find that the quarter-note beat has been compressed to a value of 90, through the use of sixteenth-note quintuplet subdivisions, from which the subsequent "normal" sixteenth-note subdivision derives its duration.

Example 28-49. Carter, Fantasy for Woodwind Quartet

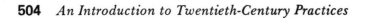
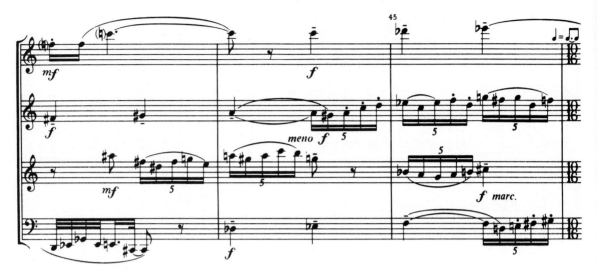

Because of the complexity of this procedure and the rapid shift of the rhythmic groupings involved, the listener's perception tends to be one of little or no feeling of pulse, although recurring rhythmic cells may be noted.

The final rhythmic concept we will present is that of *added value,* which is not to be confused with *additive rhythm,* mentioned earlier. Like metric modulation, this process—developed largely by Olivier Messiaen and described at length in his book, *The Technique of My Musical Language*—creates rhythmic irregularity through the addition of a note, a dot, a tie, or a rest to what otherwise appears to be a perfectly regular rhythmic pattern. For example, consider the following grouping:

This figure might be transformed in any of the following ways, to mention but a few of what are almost limitless possibilities:

Messiaen himself admits to a fondness for the subtleties of Indian rhythms, and we see abundant evidence of this in much of his music. Example 28-50 shows the principles of added value in operation.

Example 28-50. Messiaen, "Dance of Fury for Seven Trumpets," from
Quartet for the End of Time

The opening two measures, except for one sixteenth beat, would fit a $\frac{4}{4}$ framework. The third measure contains one eighth-note value too many, while the fourth measure has been lengthened by three sixteenths. As the movement proceeds, any comparison with a time signature becomes pointless; in fact, the listener would have difficulty perceiving an implied regular meter even at the beginning.

ALEATORY OR CHANCE MUSIC

Aleatory refers to music in which various elements of a composition are, in varying degrees, determined by chance. While the term is essentially a twentieth-century addition to the vocabulary of music, the idea of chance is by no means new to the realities of musical performance. Composers have long been at the mercy of poor performers, inadequate instruments, cough-racked audiences, and imprecise musical notation. We can also mention the time-honored practice of improvisation, encompassing the Baroque continuo part, the realization of a Classical concerto cadenza, and certainly the virtuoso group improvisation associated with jazz.

The application of *chance* to music composition may manifest itself in one of two ways: the overall plan of the piece may be precisely notated, with specific details left either to the performer or to chance, or the compositional process itself may be indeterminate. The best-known, and perhaps the earliest, advocate of indeterminacy as a valid approach to music performance and composition is the American John Cage. His *Imaginary Landscape for 12 Radios* is a model of precise notation. Each pair of twenty-four performers is furnished with a radio and an individual part, on which is indicated tuning, volume, and tone control. There is, in addition, a conductor equipped with a stopwatch. Obviously, despite the precision of performance instructions, every performance will differ greatly from every other one, dependent upon geographic location and time of day. A performance in New York City, for example, will always be a totally different experience than one in Omaha, Nebraska (where the premiere performance took place in 1951).

The piece with which Cage is most widely identified may well be the one entitled *4'33"*. The first performance took place at Woodstock, New York, on August 29, 1952, and featured David Tudor, a pianist and longtime professional associate of Cage. The piece consisted at that time of three movements, the beginnings of which were indicated by the closing of the keyboard lid; the opening of the keyboard lid signaled the end of each movement. For the duration of each movement (33", 2'40", and 1'20" respectively), the pianist remained motionless on stage. The published score of the piece consists of a single page, and gives the playing instructions "Tacet" for each movement. It further specifies that the work is "playable" by any instrument or instrumental ensemble, and that it may last any length of time. The chief importance of this seemingly tongue-in-cheek work, whose aural effect relies entirely upon miscellaneous noises occurring in the concert hall, lies in the obligation it places upon the listener to incorporate what would normally be disturbing noises (a cough, the hiss of a radiator, the rustling of a program, a plane passing overhead) into the framework of a musical experience.

Cage's pioneer efforts inspired a host of followers, and the result was an incredible diversity of musical endeavor. The length to which Cage disciples have carried his original ideas may be seen in a group of pieces by Max Neuhaus, composed between 1966 and 1968. The set comprises six sound-oriented compositions, specifically designed for a situation other than that of the concert hall. The first of these, "Listen," specifies that the audience, who arrive expecting a concert or lecture, are to be put on a bus, have their hands stamped with the word "Listen," and then driven through an existing sound environment. One such "performance," for example, took place in the Consolidated Edison Power Station at Fourteenth Street and Avenue D in New York City. "Drive-In Music," the fifth piece in the group, is designed for people in automobiles. The original score consists of a street map of a small area in Buffalo, New York, designating the streets along which the listener is to drive. At various locations along the route, radio transmitters, which may be heard only through an AM radio, are mounted on telephone poles or trees. Their broadcast areas are designed to overlap, so that at any given time the listener is hearing a combination of signals. Since the actual "music" heard by the concertgoer is subject to such a multitude of fluctuations, brought about not only by the choice of sounds (which might range anywhere from noise to snippets of classical repertoire), but also by the weather, speed of travel, engine noise, and so on, we simply cannot conceptualize or describe the resulting musical effect without having experienced it. The last piece in the group, "Telephone Access," requires active participation in the composition process by the listener, who is instructed to dial a specific long distance number. Upon reaching the number, which is hooked into an electronic sound system, the caller pronounces individual words that are then transformed into electronic sounds and immediately played back over the phone line.

Compositions such as those just described tend, of necessity, to be notated either by means of specific verbal instructions, or in a graphic manner. The earliest use of graphic notation was often viewed as a means of saving the composer tedious hours of copying, while providing a more dramatic and descriptive representation of his or her musical intent to the performer. But the unique notational requirements of some types of aleatoric music spawned an interest in the artistic layout of the score itself, even in the case of music intended for performance by traditional instruments.

One such example, scored for solo piano and showing a great deal of pitch and rhythm detail, is illustrated in Example 28-51, by George Crumb.

Example 28-51. Crumb, "The Magic Circle of Infinity," from *Makrokosmos I*

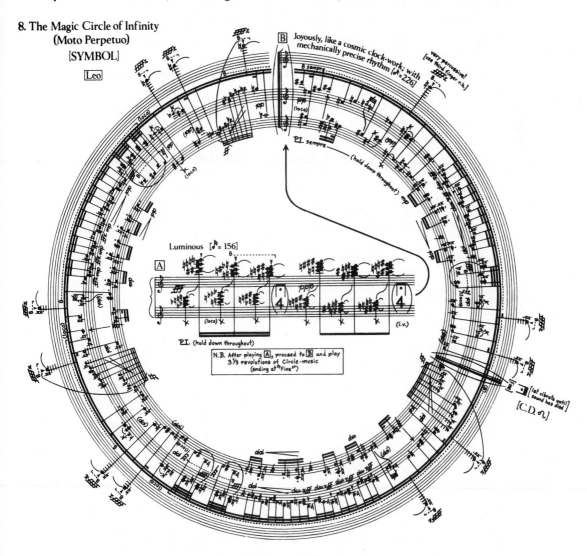

The concept of *phase* or *process* music may be seen as a logical extension of the aleatoric procedure. Use of this terminology is generally credited to Steve Reich, who introduced the technique in a 1965 tape piece, *It's Gonna Rain,* and later applied it to an instrumental work, *Piano Phase* (1967). Phase music consists of the constant repetition, over an extended period of time, of a given number of musical elements by an ensemble which may or may not be precisely specified. The musical segments are most often performed in a predetermined order; the unique property of this music results from the indeterminacy of the time lapse between each event, thus causing the instruments to move in and out of "phase" with each other as the music progresses. *Piano Phase* consists of thirty-two musical fragments, to be played either by two pianos or two marimbas.

The instructions and first page of the score of *Piano Phase* are given below in Example 28-52.

In "Music as a Gradual Process," taken from his book of essays, *Writings about Music,* Reich articulates the type of thinking that led to this procedure:

> I do not mean the process of composition, but rather pieces of music that are, literally, processes. The distinctive thing about musical processes is that they determine all the note-to-note (sound-to-sound) details and the over all form simultaneously. (Think of a round or infinite canon.) I am interested in perceptible processes. I want to be able to hear the process happening throughout the sounding music. To facilitate closely detailed listening a musical process should happen extremely gradually.
>
> Performing and listening to a gradual musical process resembles: pulling back a swing, releasing it, and observing it gradually come to rest; turning over an hour glass and watching the sand slowly run through to the bottom; placing your feet in the sand by the ocean's edge and watching, feeling, and listening to the waves gradually bury them.*

*Steve Reich, *Writings about Music* (Halifax: The Press of the Nova Scotia College of Art and Design, 1974), p. 9.

Example 28-52. Reich, *Piano Phase*

Directions for Performance

Repeats

The number of repeats of each bar is not fixed but may vary more or less within the limits appearing at each bar. Generally speaking a number of repeats more than the minimum and less than the maximum should be aimed for. The point throughout, however, is not to count repeats, but to listen to the two voice relationship and as you hear it clearly and have absorbed it, move on to the next bar.

Duration

Although duration may obviously vary, experience has shown that it should be about 20 minutes.

Performance

The first performer starts at bar 1 and, after about 4 to 8 repeats, the second gradually fades in, in unison, at bar 2. After about 12 to 18 repeats getting into a comfortable and stable unison, the second performer gradually increases his or her tempo very slightly and begins to move very slowly ahead of the first until, after about 4 to 16 repeats, he or she is one sixteenth note ahead, as shown at bar 3. This relationship is then held steadily for about 16 to 24 repeats as outlined above. The dotted lines indicate this gradual movement of the second performer and the consequent shift of phase relation between both performers. This process of gradual phase shifting and then holding the new stable relationship is continued with the second pianist becoming an eighth (bar 4), a dotted eighth (bar 5), a quarter note (bar 6), etc. ahead of the first performer until he or she passes through all twelve relationships and returns to unison at bar 14. The second performer then gradually fades out and the first continues alone at bar 15. The first performer changes the basic pattern at bar 16 and the second performer gradually fades in with still another pattern at bar 17. The second performer again very slowly increases his or her tempo and slowly moves ahead and out of phase until he or she arrives one sixteenth note ahead as shown at bar 18. This relationship is then held steadily as before. After moving through all eight relationships in this way the second performer returns to his or her starting point at bar 25. The first performer then gradually fades out and the second performer continues alone at bar 26. The second performer changes the basic pattern at bar 27 and the first fades in, in unison, at bar 28. The second performer again slowly increases his or her tempo and moves ahead and out of phase as before until he or she returns to unison at bar 32. After several repeats in unison one performer nods his or her head on the downbeat and, after 4 repeats, both performers end together.

Rehearsal

When first rehearsing the piece it may be useful for the first performer to play bar 1 and keep on repeating it while the second performer tries to enter directly at bar 3 exactly one sixteenth note ahead *without trying to phase there*. After listening to this two voice relationship for a while the second performer should stop, join the first performer in unison and only then try to increase very slightly his or her tempo so that he or she gradually moves one sixteenth note ahead into bar 3. This approach of first jumping in directly to bar 3, 4, 5, etc., listening to it and only then trying to phase into it is based on the principle that *hearing* what it sounds like to be 1, 2 or more sixteenth notes ahead will then enable the performer to phase there without increasing tempo too much and passing into a further bar, or phasing ahead a bit and then sliding back to where one started. Several rehearsals spread over several weeks before performance will help produce smooth phase movements and the tendency to phase too quickly from one bar to the next will be overcome allowing performers to spend due time – the slower the better – in the gradual shifts of phase between bars.

Instruments

When two pianos are used they should be as identical as possible. The lids should both be open or removed. The pianos should be arranged as follows:

AUDIENCE

When two marimbas are used they should be as identical as possible. Soft rubber mallets are suggested. *The piece may be played an octave lower than written, when played on marimbas.* The marimbas may be moderately amplified by conventional microphones if the hall holds more than 200 people. The marimbas should be arranged as follows:

AUDIENCE

Used by permission of the composer and Universal Edition (London) Ltd.

piano phase

for two pianos
or two marimbas*

steve reich

♩. = ca. 72

Repeat each bar approximately number of times written. / Jeder Takt soll approximativ wiederholt werden entsprechend der angegebenen Anzahl. / Répétez chaque mesure à peu près le nombre de fois indiqué.

hold tempo 1 / Tempo 1 fortsetzen / tenir le tempo 1.

* The piece may be played an octave lower than written, when played on marimbas. / Wenn Marimbas verwendet werden, kann das Stück eine Oktave tiefer als notiert gespielt werden. / La pièce pourra être jouée à l'octave inférieure quand elle est exécutée par des marimbas.

a.v.s. = accelerando very slightly. / sehr geringfügiges accelerando. / très légèrement accelerando.

Used by permission of the composer and Universal Edition (London) Ltd.

In addition to Reich, both Phil Glass and Terry Riley have used this approach, which is sometimes referred to as *minimalism* because of the extreme economy of means which it represents.

Terry Riley's *In C* (1964) is composed of fifty-three melodic fragments, to be played in order and in tempo by an ensemble. The group may consist of any number of players, and may comprise any instrumental combination. Each player decides for himself or herself (1) when to enter and (2) whether, and how often, to repeat each fragment. Pulse is maintained by a pianist playing steady eighth notes on the top two C's of a grand piano. The aesthetic effect of a performance, which in some cases may extend beyond an hour, depends in large part upon the attitude and expectation brought to it by the listener. Although essentially static when compared with more traditional compositional procedures, the subtle counterpoint and shifting pitch colors of the texture can be compelling, even hypnotic.

TEXTURE AND EXPANDED INSTRUMENTAL RESOURCES

We have seen the increasingly important role played by texture in the evolution of twentieth-century musical thought. One reason for this lies in its capability to provide a convincing means of musical organization free from the traditional conventions of key and chord. Even in the relatively conservative textural style of Debussy we find an unusual preponderance of unaccompanied, angular melodies, figuration independent of functional considerations, and vertical sonorities used solely for the sake of color.

As composers turned their attention to further explorations of texture, changes occurred not only in the performance demands placed on players of traditional instruments, but also in the structure and size of ensembles. The massive orchestral forces favored by Berlioz and Mahler gave way to a renewed interest in chamber groups. Stravinsky's interest in nontraditional groupings of instruments did a great deal to legitimize the concept of a smaller, more heterogeneous instrumental body. His *L'Histoire du soldat* (1918), scored for clarinet, bassoon, horn, trombone, percussion, violin, and bass, became a model of innovative procedure which many composers chose to follow. Featured along with the varied instrumental forces found in this work was the aspect of theatre music; it includes a part for narrator, as well as speaking roles for one or more characters and specific directions for stage movement and dance (possibly indicative of Stravinsky's intense and continuing interest in music for the ballet).

Other methods of exploiting the coloristic properties of traditional instruments proved attractive to later composers. We have already noted Henry Cowell's experimentation with tone clusters on the piano in the 1920s. Another early work by Cowell, entitled *The Banshee,* calls for the performer to play inside the instrument. Effects created by plucking the strings or drawing the finger or fingernail across the length of the string are eerie, and reminiscent of the legendary figure of Irish folklore for which the piece is named.

The use of "prepared piano" is generally associated with John Cage. It calls for the pianist to place objects on or between the strings to create harmonics, as well as exotic timbres. The score might also call for strings to be damped with felt or pieces of rubber. In many cases the altered pitch and timbral characteristics produce a sound suggestive of a percussion ensemble.

The role of percussion has been greatly expanded in the twentieth century. One of the earliest landmarks in this field is Edgar Varèse's *Ionisation,* composed in 1931. This work calls for thirteen musicians to play a total of thirty-seven percussion instruments, including, in addition to the standard battery, two sirens, bongos, guiros, slapsticks, Chinese blocks in three registers, maracas, and a number of less usual instruments. Despite the presence of chimes, celesta, and piano (all of which are saved exclusively for the Finale), the piece is essentially a study in non-pitched sonorities; its novelty has perhaps never been surpassed.

American composers, including John Cage and Lou Harrison, have experimented extensively with new percussive effects and music for percussion ensembles. Nontraditional instruments and techniques include brake drums and bowing of mallet instruments. In many cases, these composers have modeled their works on Eastern traditions, such as the gamelan. Also interested in oriental music and philosophy is American Harry Partch, known primarily as the inventor of new percussion instruments.

An important work, composed in 1960, *Threnody for the Victims of Hiroshima* by Krzysztof Penderecki, represents a striking departure from the conventional use of string sonorities. Although other composers had experimented with this medium, *Threnody* is generally considered a landmark work in the literature. Examine Example 28-53, a page from the score of this work.

Example 28-53.   Penderecki, *Threnody for the Victims of Hiroshima*

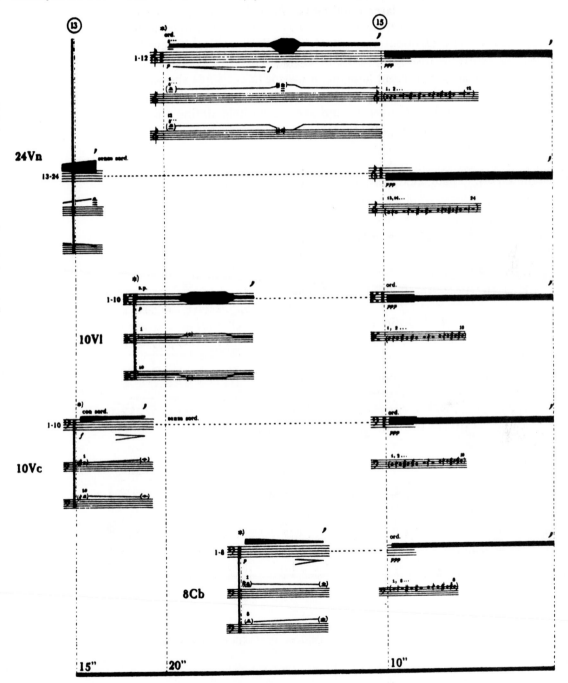

The cluster effect, shown graphically in the score, involves very specific pitch indications on each player's individual part. For rhythmic direction, the performers must obviously rely heavily on cues from the conductor. This example shows the traditional concept of "chord" or vertical "event" being replaced by a shifting, iridescent fabric of sound.

Another passage, taken from later in the work (Ex. 28-54) shows the use of what we might term "noise" brought about through nontraditional use of the fifty-two stringed instruments, and serving to help define the overall formal structure of the work.

Example 28-54. Penderecki, *Threnody for the Victims of Hiroshima*

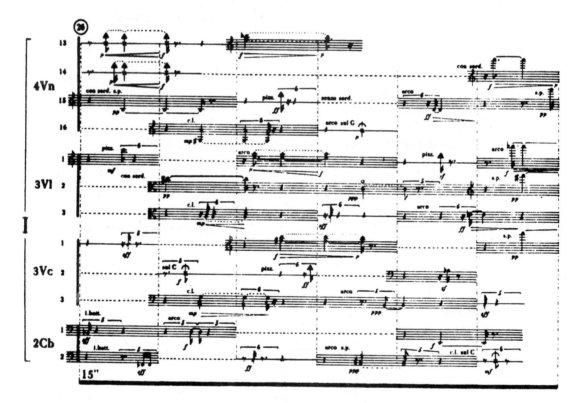

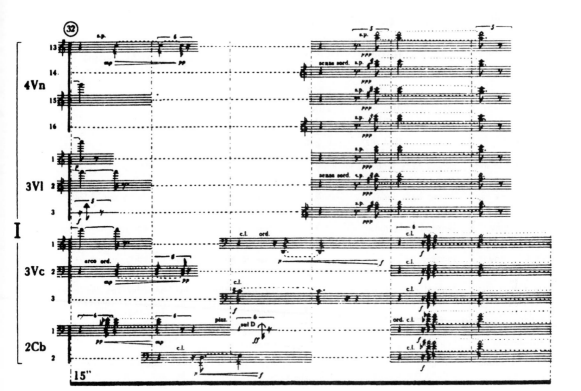

The symbols used in this excerpt are explained in an introductory page to the score, shown in Example 28-55.

Example 28-55. Penderecki, *Threnody for the Victims of Hiroshima*

SKRÓTY I SYMBOLE	ABBREVIATIONS AND SYMBOLS		SIGNES D'ABREVIA-TION ET SYMBOLES	ABKÜRZUNGEN UND SYMBOLE
ordinario		ord.		
sul ponticello		s. p.		
sul tasto		s. t.		
col legno		c. l.		
legno battuto		l. batt.		
podwyższenie o ¼ tonu	raised by ¼ tone	⇞	hausse la note d'un quart de ton	Erhöhung um ¼ Ton
podwyższenie o ¾ tonu	raised by ¾ tone	⇞	hausse la note de trois quarts de ton	Erhöhung um ¾ Ton
obniżenie o ¼ tonu	lowered by ¼ tone	♭	abaisse la note d'un quart de ton	Erniedrigung um ¼ Ton
obniżenie o ¾ tonu	lowered by ¾ tone	⅃	abaisse la note de trois quarts de ton	Erniedrigung um ¾ Ton
najwyższy dźwięk instrumentu (wysokość nieokreślona)	highest note of the instrument (indefinite pitch)	▲	le son le plus aigu de l'instrument (hauteur indéterminée)	höchster Ton des Instrumentes (unbestimmte Tonhöhe)
grać między podstawkiem i strunnikiem	play between bridge and tailpiece	↑	jouer entre le chevalet et le cordier	zwischen Steg und Saitenhalter spielen
arpeggio na 4 strunach za podstawkiem	arpeggio on 4 strings behind the bridge	 ⇟⫰	arpège sur 4 cordes entre le chevalet et le cordier	Arpeggio zwischen Steg und Saitenhalter (4 Saiten)
grać na strunniku (arco)	play on tailpiece (arco)	⊥	jouer sur le cordier (arco)	auf dem Saitenhalter spielen (arco)
grać na podstawku	play on bridge	⊤	jouer sur le chevalet	auf dem Steg spielen
efekt perkusyjny: uderzać w górną płytę skrzypiec łabką lub czubkami palców	percussion effect: strike the upper sounding board of the violin with the nut or the finger-tips	∮	effet de percussion: frapper la table de dessus du violon avec le talon de l'archet ou avec les bouts des doigt	Schlagzeugeffekt: mit dem Frosch oder mit Fingerspitze die Decke schlagen
kilka nieregularnych zmian smyczka	several irregular changes of bow	⊓ ∨	plusieurs changements d'archet irréguliers	mehrere unregelmäßige Bogenwechsel
molto vibrato	molto vibrato	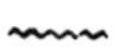 ∿∿∿	molto vibrato	molto vibrato
bardzo wolne vibrato w obrębie ćwierćtonu, uzyskane przez przesuwanie palca	very slow vibrato with a ¼ tone frequency difference produced by sliding the finger	 ∿∿	vibrato très lent à interval d'un quart de ton par le déplacement du doigt	sehr langsames Vibrato mit ¼ - Ton-Frequenzdifferenz durch Fingerverschiebung
bardzo szybkie i nierytmizowane tremolo	very rapid not rhythmicized tremolo	⚡	trémolo très rapide, mais sans rythme précis	sehr schnelles, nicht rhytmisiertes Tremolo

The composer Georgy Lygeti is also widely recognized for compositions which feature sustained chromatic clusters. His *Atmospheres* for orchestra (1961) and *Volumnia* for organ (1961-62) both served as models for subsequent composers.

Wind instruments have been subjected to a number of unusual techniques, including multiphonics (the production of more than one pitch at a time on a single instrument, using various means); blowing or humming into a disengaged mouthpiece; speaking into or playing the instrument without its mouthpiece; percussive effects created by tapping on or fingering the instrument; and others. Example 28-56 shows special performance instructions and two pages of score taken from *Ultra Mensuram*. This work, composed by William Penn in 1971, combines traditional and nontraditional techniques to produce both pitched and non-pitched sonorities. Note the unusual scoring which calls for three brass quintets. Like many of today's chamber combinations, this work requires a conductor for performance.

Example 28-56. Penn, *Ultra Mensuram* (Performance directions and first two pages of score.)

SPECIAL SIGNS

1) Blow air through instrument.

2) Blow air through instrument and abruptly stop the flow of air with the tongue.

3) Blow air through instrument and clatter keys.

4) "Kiss" mouthpiece.

5) Clatter keys (valves), or any kind of exterior metal noise. Loosen valve caps.

6) ↓ Any note in the extreme low register of the instrument.

↑ Any note in the extreme high register of the instrument.

 Trill on any note in the extreme low register of the instrument.

Gliss from low note to any indeterminate higher pitch.

NOTE: All of the notes at the extreme registers (↑ and ↓) of the instrument must be played with a good, full sound. For example, ↑ means the highest note possible that can also be played *fff*.

↓ for trumpets and horns will probably be best achieved by using just the lower lip.

7) For group C only—the expansion of the 2 parallel lines indicates a crescendo; the contraction indicates a decrescendo; the above would be played : *pp* < >

8) The beams indicate an accelerando of the note group.

The beams indicate a ritardando of the note group.

The beams indicate an accelerando followed by a ritardando of the note group.

The beams indicate a ritardando followed by an accelerando of the note group.

 etc. In non-metered sections, the "slash" indicates as fast as possible.

9) ▬ ▬ ▬ Repeat the preceding material--with variation when possible.

10) ∿∿∿ Continue in a similar manner.

11) Indicates the duration of the tone, proportionate to the length of the line. Breathe at random when the duration of the tone is too long to be sustained in one breath.

12) · ⋰⋱ From ① to ③ only: palm hits mouthpiece. From ③ on, free staccato playing.

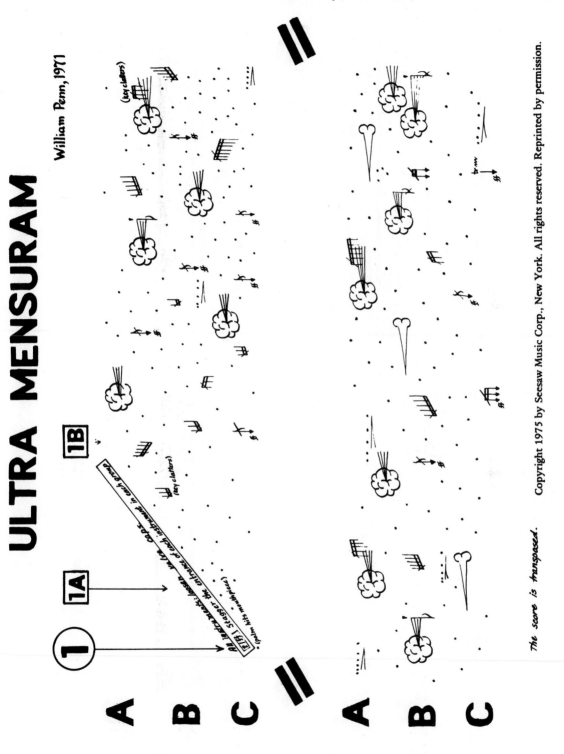

ULTRA MENSURAM

William Penn, 1971

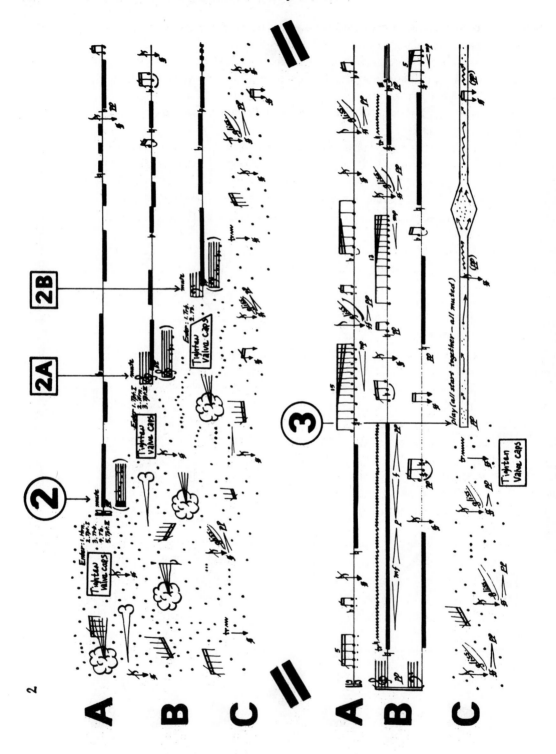

In terms of vocal effects, the technique of *sprechstimme,* a cross between singing and dramatic declamation, was used by Schoenberg in *Pierrot Lunaire* (1912), a work which calls for reciter accompanied by an ensemble consisting of five instrumentalists. The effect has been widely used since then, as have techniques of whistling, whispering, clucking, cooing, and laughing. Composers such as Penderecki, Stockhausen, and Oliveros have employed these sounds on a wide scale.

Further exploration of coloristic possibilities has resulted from the gradual incorporation of jazz techniques into concert literature. Besides its unique harmonic language, jazz represents a characteristic and readily identifiable approach to instrumentation. This frequently involves electric guitar, electric bass, keyboard synthesizers (to be discussed later), and extensive use of contact microphones.

Finally, one may occasionally find objects such as wine glasses pressed into musical service in the works of Crumb, Schwantner, and others.

ELECTRONIC MUSIC

Inevitably, with the mounting interest in coloristic effects, the possibilities for electronic sound generation began to be investigated more closely. The earliest instruments to have practical applications were developed in the 1920s and included the theremin, the trautonium, and the ondes martenot. All three instruments made use of electronic oscillators as tone generators; they differed only in the manner by which the performer played the instrument. The theremin enjoyed a period of renewed interest in 1945 when employed by Miklos Rozsa in the films *Spellbound* and *Lost Weekend.*

Toward the midpoint of the century technical developments in the tape recorder resulted in the growing popularity of *musique concrète,* in which natural sounds—such as a voice, an instrument, or the ticking of a clock—were first recorded, then subjected to modification by means of altered playback speed, reversed tape direction, fragmentation and splicing of the tape, creation of a tape loop, echo effect, and other timbral manipulations. In 1948 Pierre Schaeffer, who is generally credited with introducing the above term, presented a concert featuring *musique concrète* exclusively over French radio.

Although the distinction may not be apparent to the listener, the term *electronic music,* strictly speaking, refers to music generated synthetically by means of an oscillator. The tones thus obtained may be precisely controlled for frequency, amplitude, and waveform. Types of sound waves produced by these generators included the "sine wave" (a sound without overtones, suggestive of an open flute); the "sawtooth wave" (a jagged, nasal tone which contains all overtones); and the "rectangular" or "square wave" (pitch containing only odd-numbered harmonics). The "white noise" generator produces a "hissing" sound, composed of all the audible frequencies at random amplitudes. These basic sounds were then subject to modification by means of amplifiers, filters, modulators, equalizers, sequencers, and reverberation units.

It was the development of synthesizers around the midpoint of the twentieth century that allowed the composer freedom to generate and combine sounds without the former need for laborious splicing and mixing of tape. Edgar Varèse's *Poème Électronique,* performed at the Brussels World's Fair in 1958, was created directly on magnetic tape. It took place in a pavilion designed by Le Corbusier and specified the installation of four hundred loudspeakers which filled the curved space of the pavilion with continuous waves of sound. The *Poème* was accompanied by a series of film projections which interacted randomly with the music. The visual and sonic synthesis of this extraordinary work evoked reactions ranging from wild enthusiasm to stark terror among its audience.

The subsequent introduction of modular synthesizers, marketed under trade names of Moog, Buchla, and ARP, offered a wide palette of new sounds. An interesting offshoot of this development may be found in the "Switched-On-Bach" series: a realization of several of the Bach Brandenburg Concerti and other orchestral works. Other synthesized adaptations of standard repertoire followed suit and achieved widespread, if brief, popularity.

The inevitable loss of drama in performances of purely electronic music was found by many composers to be an unacceptable trade-off. This spawned efforts to combine live performers and taped sound. Composers who experimented with this form of collaboration included Bruno Maderna, Vladimir Ussachevsky, Otto Luening, and Milton Babbitt. Champions of indeterminacy, such as John Cage, found that the theatrical possibilities of this combination were well-suited to their musical philosophies. More recent composers especially well-known for their work in this medium include Mario David-owsky and Jacob Druckman. Davidowsky's eight *Synchronisms* for various solo instruments and tape, along with Druckman's series of compositions entitled *Animus* for tape and trombone, voice/percussion, and clarinet re-spectively, have become part of the standard contemporary recital literature for these instruments. In some instances, the collaboration calls for the per-former to play into a tape recorder. The sounds thus generated are electron-ically modified and played back, providing an improvisatory partnership. In other cases, pre-recorded music by the solo instrument is combined on tape with electronic or concrete sounds. The final product may be the result either of strict control on the part of the composer, or may represent processes of indeterminacy.

Recent and critically significant newcomers on the scene include the digi-tal synthesizers, such as the Yamaha DX series, and various sound sampling devices. The Yamaha has long been the mainstay of many popular music groups, not only because of its wide variety of timbres, but also because of its portability. Its essential unit is a digital oscillator which enables the com-poser to control the various parameters of a musical sound, creating new colors as well as simulating those of acoustic instruments with amazing ac-curacy. The Yamaha and other models also make available a certain number of pre-set tone combinations.

It was the introduction of MIDI (Musical Instrument Digital Interface) that virtually revolutionized the field of electronic music. This process was originally conceived as a means whereby the keyboard of one synthesizer could be made to drive the sound generators of another. MIDI makes possible the use of audio processors, drum machines, and even the control of multiple computers by a single performer. It can expedite changes in key velocity, pitch bend, and modulation; units are also available which notate a piece of music as it is being played or composed. Through the use of a *sequencer,* a digital recorder which stores "sequences" of musical information rather than actual sounds, a composer may significantly modify the timbre, tempo, or texture of a previously encoded piece.

Sampling machines include the Ensoniq Mirage, the Emulator II (or EMU), and the Kurzweil. These instruments have the capability of recording and storing precise information concerning a given sound. The actual "sampling" involves the encoding of an analog signal by reading its level at precisely spaced intervals of time. The sound thus encoded may then be reproduced, either singly or in combination with other material. The sample of, for example, a C major chord performed by the Boston Symphony, may be reproduced at various pitch or volume levels and subsequently modified.

The implications of these developments for performing musicians are virtually incalculable, particularly in the field of commercial music (advertising, film and TV scores). Whereas this field of endeavor has traditionally involved the services of a composer, studio musicians, a copyist, recording engineer, and editor (to name but a few), we now have the situation in which the composer in one of the new direct-to-digital studios can accomplish all the above functions in a matter of hours. The final result is, in some cases, indistinguishable from its complex and expensive acoustic counterpart.

The student wishing to learn more about developments in this area is referred to *Foundations of Computer Music,* edited by Roads and Strawn.*

Accompanying the continuing strides occurring in the realm of technology, there seems to be a tendency on the part of some composers to pay homage to earlier musical sources. Composers such as George Rochberg, Peter Maxwell Davies, and Luciano Berio have, especially in later works, borrowed extensively from pre-existing materials, as well as earlier musical styles. These references may take the form of clearly recognizable themes from Common Practice composition, folk literature, or plainchant. An interesting example is found in George Crumb's *Makrokosmos I* (cited earlier in this chapter on page 509) in which Section II of the work (entitled "Gemini") is interspersed with partial quotations of Chopin's *Fantasie Impromptu.* An earlier section (No. 6) makes use of a quasi-pentatonic hymn tune, "Will There Be Any Stars in My Crown?" In both instances, the borrowed material forms the basis for many of the composer's pitch and motivic choices. The eclectic style which results may be described as a new language, but one whose traditional roots are unmistakable.

Another interesting phenomenon may be found in the lessening of lines of demarcation between jazz and popular styles, and the so-called "serious" or concert music. Not only has the contemporary jazz idiom become more stylistically allied with its academic counterpart, but major composers are increasingly inclined to incorporate clearly recognizable jazz idioms into their concert works.

Foundations of Computer Music, edited by Roads and Strawn (Cambridge, Mass.: The MIT Press, 1985).

SUMMARY AND FORWARD LOOK

We have observed that the early twentieth century was characterized by a curious dichotomy: on the one hand, an extension of post-Romantic tendencies, while on the other, a conscious (at times almost militant) attempt to establish a totally new musical language. Composers in both camps succeeded in developing distinctly new methods of expression that were clearly indigenous to their age. This early ambivalence has continued to manifest itself in the continuing diversity of musical language.

Although this chapter has not discussed commercial or popular music in depth, we should perhaps mention that these genres alone have maintained strict allegiance to the conventions of tonality, at least up until the mid-twentieth century. Some observers cite this exception as evidence that as the twentieth century progressed, a rift was gradually widening between composers of serious music and the public taste.

No one at present can know just how future historians will regard our era and evaluate the primary direction of our musical culture. Surely no component of musical style—pitch, harmony, rhythm, texture, form—has remained untouched by the stylistic explosion that marked the turn of the century. Yet as the century draws to a close, there seems to be an attempt by many to draw from earlier developments rather than to strike out on totally individual and innovative paths. We can see, in some cases, a fusion of trends that at one time seemed headed in opposite directions. The idea of serialism, for example, which was conceived as a systematic means of escape from the deeply entrenched conventions of tonality, has indeed been pressed into the service of what we hear as very tonal music. Recent efforts in electronic music frequently reflect a consolidation of ideas of color and movement from very early in the century. *Third stream* compositions borrow heavily from the jazz idiom, while many contemporary jazz groups perform works that are scarcely distinguishable from today's "serious" concert music. The pace of technological development has wrought profound changes upon the music profession itself. But whatever the direction we seem to be taking, it is indeed a challenging and exciting time in which to be a musician.

INSTRUMENTAL RANGES AND TRANSPOSITIONS

In this Appendix we suggest some practical ranges to assist you in composing exercises to be performed in class. These are not extreme ranges, by any means, but the extreme highs and lows of even these ranges should be used cautiously, especially with the brasses.

Instrument	*Abbreviation*	*Sounding range*	*Written range*
Flute	Fl.		Same
Oboe	Ob.		Same
B♭ Clarinet	Clar. in B♭		Treble clef, M2 higher
Bassoon	Bsn.		Same
Alto Sax	A. Sax		Treble clef, M6 higher
Tenor Sax	T. Sax		Treble clef, M9 higher

Instrument	Abbreviation	Sounding range	Written range
French Horn	Hn. in F		P5 higher
Bb Trumpet	Tpt. in Bb		Treble clef, M2 higher
Trombone	Trb.		Same
Tuba	Tuba		Same
Violin	Vl.		Same
Viola	Vla.		Same
Cello	Vc.		Same; tenor clef also used when convenient
Bass	D.B.		P8 higher

ANSWERS TO SELF-TESTS

The answers given to certain kinds of Self-Test problems must be considered to be suggested solutions, since more than one correct answer might be possible. When you have questions, consult your instructor.

CHAPTER 1

Self-Test 1-1

Part A, p. 5.

1. C1   **2.** E2   **3.** F3   **4.** B4   **5.** A5   **6.** G6   **7.** D7

Part B, p. 6.

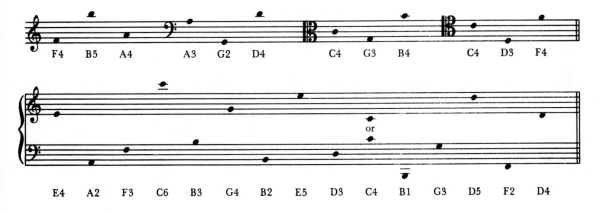

| F4 | B5 | A4 | A3 | G2 | D4 | C4 | G3 | B4 | C4 | D3 | F4 |

| E4 | A2 | F3 | C6 | B3 | G4 | B2 | E5 | D3 | C4 | B1 | G3 | D5 | F2 | D4 |

Self-Test 1-2

Part A, p. 11.

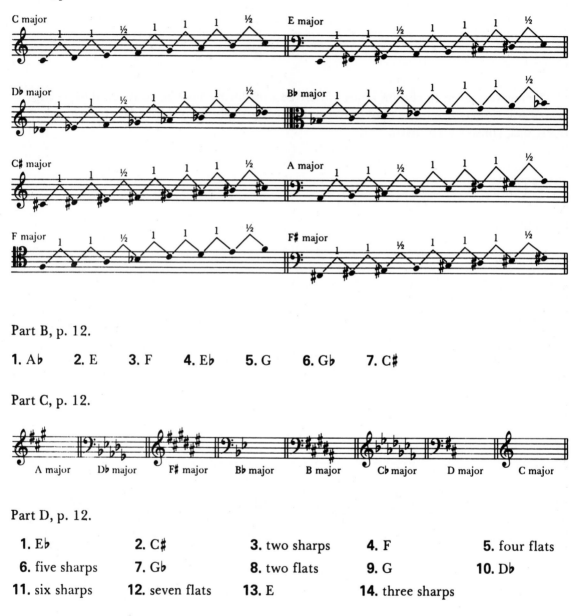

Part B, p. 12.

1. A♭   **2.** E   **3.** F   **4.** E♭   **5.** G   **6.** G♭   **7.** C♯

Part C, p. 12.

Part D, p. 12.

1. E♭	**2.** C♯	**3.** two sharps	**4.** F	**5.** four flats
6. five sharps	**7.** G♭	**8.** two flats	**9.** G	**10.** D♭
11. six sharps	**12.** seven flats	**13.** E	**14.** three sharps	

Self-Test 1-3

Part A, p. 16.

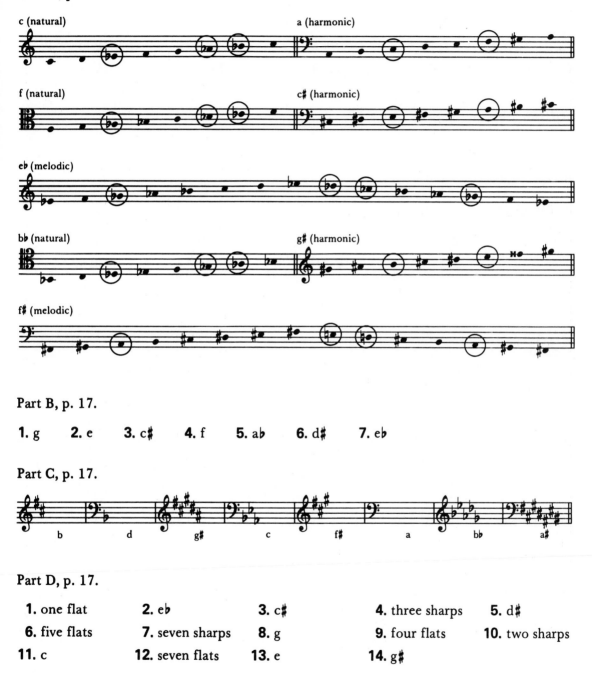

Part B, p. 17.

1. g   **2.** e   **3.** c♯   **4.** f   **5.** a♭   **6.** d♯   **7.** e♭

Part C, p. 17.

b   d   g♯   c   f♯   a   b♭   a♯

Part D, p. 17.

1. one flat   **2.** e♭   **3.** c♯   **4.** three sharps   **5.** d♯

6. five flats   **7.** seven sharps   **8.** g   **9.** four flats   **10.** two sharps

11. c   **12.** seven flats   **13.** e   **14.** g♯

Self-Test 1-4

p. 20.

1. 2	**2.** 5	**3.** 7	**4.** 1	**5.** 3
6. 4	**7.** 8	**8.** 6	**9.** 4	**10.** 2
11. 6	**12.** 7	**13.** 8	**14.** 3	**15.** 5

Self-Test 1-5

Part A, p. 22.

All are "P" except 4 and 7.

Part B, p. 22.

1. M	**2.** m	**3.** m	**4.** M	**5.** m
6. m	**7.** m	**8.** M	**9.** M	**10.** m

Part C, p. 22.

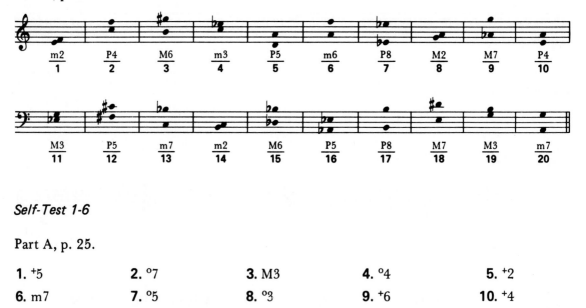

Self-Test 1-6

Part A, p. 25.

1. +5	**2.** °7	**3.** M3	**4.** °4	**5.** +2
6. m7	**7.** °5	**8.** °3	**9.** +6	**10.** +4

Part B, p. 25.

1. P5	**2.** m2	**3.** °7	**4.** m6	**5.** +4
6. M7	**7.** M3	**8.** °3		

Part C, p. 25.

Part D, p. 25.

1. m3	**2.** P1	**3.** m6	**4.** P8	**5.** M3
6. P4	**7.** m3	**8.** °5	**9.** m2	**10.** +1
11. m2	**12.** M7			

CHAPTER 2

Self-Test 2-1

Part A, p. 28.

1. 2	**2.** 4	**3.** 3	**4.** 8	**5.** 7
6. 5	**7.** 6	**8.** 4	**9.** 2	**10.** 12

Part B, p. 29.

1. triple **2.** duple (or quadruple) **3.** quadruple (or duple)
4. duple (or quadruple) **5.** triple

Part C, p. 29.

1. Bb	**2.** Ab	**3.** E	**4.** D#	**5.** E
6. B	**7.** Bb	**8.** Eb	**9.** Ab	**10.** A
11. G	**12.** G#	**13.** F	**14.** C#	**15.** C#

Self-Test 2-2

p. 30.

1. simple quadruple (or simple duple)

2. compound duple (or compound quadruple)

3. simple triple

4. simple duple (or simple quadruple)

5. compound duple (or compound quadruple)

Self-Test 2-3

Part A, p. 38.

1. simple quadruple ♩ ; ♪   **2.** ♪; $\frac{9}{8}$ **3.** simple duple; ♪; ♪

4. ♩·; $\frac{6}{4}$ **5.** simple triple; ♩; $\frac{3}{2}$ **6.** compound quadruple; ♪; $\frac{12}{16}$

Part B, p. 38.

1. 𝄾   **2.** 𝄾· (or 𝄾 𝄾)   **3.** 𝄾 𝄾 (or 𝄾 𝄾 𝄾)   **4.** 𝄾   **5.** 𝄾   **6.** 𝄾 𝄾 (or ▬)

Notice that ▬ would not be a good answer for no. 3, since this rest would obscure the beats in the measure (see pp. 35-36).

Part C, p. 38.

1. $\frac{9}{4}$ **2.** $\frac{4}{4}$ or $\frac{2}{2}$ or C or ₵   **3.** $\frac{3}{8}$ **4.** $\frac{6}{16}$ **5.** $\frac{12}{8}$ **6.** same as no. 2

Part D, p. 39.

Part E, p. 39.

1.

2.

Part F, p. 39.

1. simple duple (or quadruple); 2 (or 4) over some note value (1, 2, 4, 8, etc.)

2. compound quadruple (or duple); 12 (or 6) over some note value

3. sounds like compound duple or compound single, but notated as simple triple (see p. 34); 3 over some note value

4. simple quadruple (or duple); 4 (or 2) over some note value

5. compound duple (or quadruple); 6 (or 12) over some note value

Part G, p. 40.

1. f	**2.** G	**3.** c♯	**4.** A	**5.** B♭
6. c	**7.** D	**8.** E♭	**9.** b	**10.** F
11. g	**12.** f♯	**13.** E	**14.** A♭	

Part H, p. 40.

Part I, p. 40.

CHAPTER 3

Self-Test 3-1

Part A, p. 42.

1. bb: Bb Db F **2.** E: E G# B **3.** g°: G Bb Db **4.** f°: F Ab Cb

5. c: C Eb G **6.** D+: D F# A# **7.** A: A C# E **8.** d: D F A

9. Gb: Gb Bb Db **10.** B: B D# F# **11.** ab: Ab Cb Eb **12.** c#: C# E G#

Part B, p. 43.

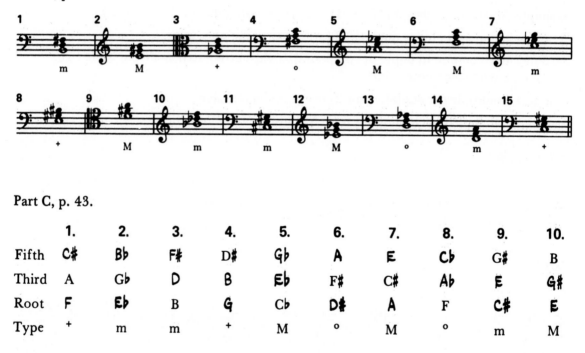

Part C, p. 43.

	1.	2.	3.	4.	5.	6.	7.	8.	9.	10.
Fifth	C#	Bb	F#	D#	Gb	A	E	Cb	G#	B
Third	A	Gb	D	B	Eb	F#	C#	Ab	E	G#
Root	F	Eb	B	G	Cb	D#	A	F	C#	E
Type	+	m	m	+	M	°	M	°	m	M

Part D, p. 43.

fifth root third fifth root fifth third third
M o m + M m M o

Self-Test 3-2

Part A, p. 45.

1. m7	**2.** M7	**3.** ⏀7	**4.** ⏀7	**5.** M7
6. ⏀7	**7.** m7	**8.** Dom 7	**9.** M7	**10.** Dom 7
11. °7	**12.** °7	**13.** Dom 7	**14.** °7	**15.** m7

Part B, p. 45.

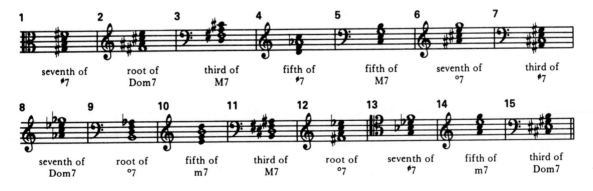

⏀7 Dom 7 M7 Dom 7 m7 ⏀7 ⏀7

°7 M7 M7 M7 m7 m7 M7 °7

Part C, p. 45.

seventh of root of third of fifth of fifth of seventh of third of
⏀7 Dom 7 M7 ⏀7 M7 °7 ⏀7

seventh of root of fifth of third of root of seventh of fifth of third of
Dom 7 °7 m7 M7 °7 ⏀7 m7 Dom 7

Self-Test 3-3

Part A, p. 50.

	3	4	5	6	7	8	9	10	11	12	13	14	15	16
Root	E	A	G#	E	C#	D	E	G	B	Eb	F#	G	E	D
Type	m7	M	°7	Dom7	m	⌀7	M7	m	⌀7	M	°7	m7	°	Dom7
Inversion symbol	$\frac{6}{5}$	6	$\frac{4}{3}$	$\frac{4}{3}$	$\frac{6}{4}$	$\frac{4}{2}$	7	6	$\frac{4}{3}$	$\frac{6}{4}$	$\frac{6}{5}$	7	6	$\frac{4}{2}$

Part B, p. 50.

           2. G M   3. C#°   4. D M   5. D#°

6. D# °7   7. B Dom7   8. E m   9. F# Dom7   10. B m

11. E M   12. A M   13. E M   14. A M

Self-Test 3-4

Part A, p. 53.

	1	2	3	4	5	6	7	8	9	10	11
Root	F	A#	E	F	B	G	C	F#	Db	C	F#
Type	m7	°7	M	m	Dom7	⌀7	M	M	Dom7	⌀7	M7
Inversion symbol	7	$\frac{6}{5}$		$\frac{6}{4}$	$\frac{4}{2}$	$\frac{6}{5}$	6	$\frac{6}{4}$	7	$\frac{4}{2}$	7

Part B, p. 54.

1. Schubert.

	1	2	3	4	5	6	7	8	9	10	11	12
Root	Db	Gb	Eb	Ab	Db	Gb	Db	Db	Ab	Bb	Ab	Db
Type	M	M	Dom7	M	M	M	M	M	M	m	Dom7	M
Inversion symbol	6		$\frac{6}{5}$		6		6		6		7	

2. Byrd.

	1	2	3	4	5	6	7
Root	F	C	F	Eb	A	Bb	F
Type	m	M	M	M	o	M	M
Inversion symbol					6		

3. Fischer.

	1	2	3	4	5	6	7	8	9	10	11	12	13
Root	E	G#	A	F	B	F	G	C	D	B	D	G	C
Type	M	o7	m	M7	ø7	M	Dom7	M	m7	o	m	Dom7	M
Inversion symbol		$\frac{4}{3}$	6	7	$\frac{4}{3}$		$\frac{4}{2}$	6	7	6		7	$\frac{6}{4}$

CHAPTER 4

Self-Test 4-1

Part A, p. 61.

1. V	**2.** iv^6	**3.** ii	**4.** III^6	**5.** ii
6. vii^o	**7.** I	**8.** ii^o	**9.** iii	**10.** vii^o
11. V$^6_4$	**12.** IV	**13.** i	**14.** vi	**15.** III$^6_4$

Part B, p. 61.

1	2	3	4	5	6	7
B: iii	c#: VI	Bb: IV	Eb: V	d#: iv	E: V	d: III
($\hat{3}$)	($\hat{6}$)	($\hat{4}$)	($\hat{5}$)	($\hat{4}$)	($\hat{5}$)	($\hat{3}$)

8	9	10	11	12	13	14	15
a#: iv	B: vii^o	A: IV	d: vii^o	Eb: V	b: V	Gb: vi	D: ii
($\hat{4}$)	($\hat{7}$)	($\hat{4}$)	($\hat{7}$)	($\hat{5}$)	($\hat{5}$)	($\hat{6}$)	($\hat{2}$)

Part C, p. 62.

1. IV	**2.** V	**3.** IV⁶	**4.** V	**5.** I⁶
6. IV	**7.** V	**8.** V	**9.** I	**10.** iii
11. IV	**12.** iii⁶	**13.** iii	**14.** IV	**15.** I
16. I	**17.** V	**18.** I	**19.** IV	**20.** IV⁶
21. I	**22.** ii	**23.** vi	**24.** vi	**25.** V
26. V	**27.** IV	**28.** vii°⁶	**29.** I	**30.** V⁶
31. I	**32.** I	**33.** V	**34.** IV	**35.** iii⁶
36. vi	**37.** iii⁶	**38.** IV	**39.** I	**40.** I
41. V	**42.** ii	**43.** iii	**44.** vi	**45.** iii⁶
46. IV	**47.** I	**48.** I		

Self-Test 4-2

Part A, p. 65.

1. iv⁷	**2.** IᴹＶ₅⁶	**3.** iii⁷	**4.** ii⌀₃⁴	**5.** VIᴹ⁷
6. IVᴹ⁷	**7.** vii⌀⁷	**8.** i⁷	**9.** vii°⁷	**10.** vi₅⁶
11. V₂⁴	**12.** V⁷	**13.** ii⌀⁷	**14.** iii₃⁴	**15.** Iᴹ⁷

Part B, p. 66.

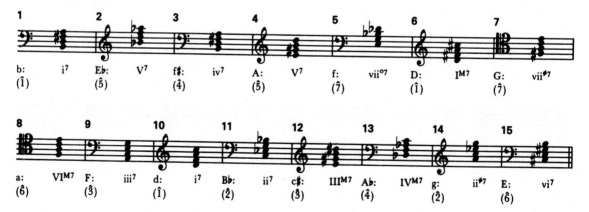

Part C, p. 66.

1. Bach.

1. I	**2.** vi	**3.** iii	**4.** IV	**5.** IV^{M7}
6. V$^4_2$	**7.** I^6	**8.** ii$^6_5$	**9.** V	**10.** I

2. Schumann.

1. I	**2.** vii^{o6}	**3.** I^6	**4.** vii^{o6}	**5.** I
6. ii$^6_5$	**7.** V	**8.** I	**9.** I	**10.** I^6
11. IV	**12.** I^6	**13.** V$^4_3$	**14.** I	**15.** V

CHAPTER 5

Self-Test 5-1

Part A, p. 71.

1.

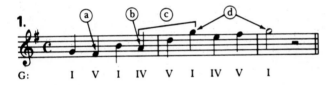

G: I   V   I   IV   V   I   IV   V   I

a. Resolve $\hat{7}$ to $\hat{1}$.
b. Not in a IV chord.
c. Two leaps should outline a triad.
d. Two focal points.

2.

B♭:   I   –   V   I   IV   V   I   V   I

a. Leap of a 7th.
b. Leap of a $^+4$.
c. Two focal points.

3.

d: i iv V i   iv V i – iv V i

a. Not in a iv chord.
b. Large leap should be preceded and followed by ascending motion.
c. Follow leap with descending motion.
d. Interval of ⁺2.

Part B, p. 72 (sample solutions).

1.

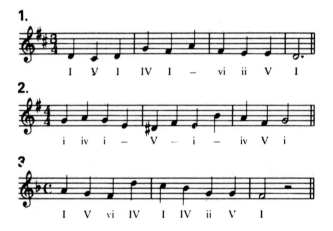

    I V I IV I – vi ii V I

2.

    i iv i – V ... i – iv V i

3.

    I V vi IV I IV ii V I

Self-Test 5-2

Part A, p. 74.

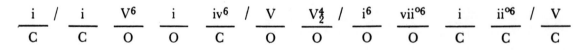

i	/	i	V⁶	i	iv⁶	/	V	V⁴₂	/	i⁶	vii°⁶	i	ii°⁶	/	V
C		C	O	O	C		O	O		O	O	C	C		C

Part B, p. 75.

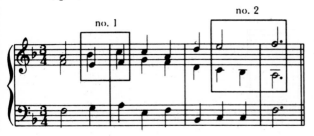

Part C, p. 75 (alternative solutions in parentheses).

Self-Test 5-3

Part A, p. 80.

The progression is G: I / IV I / V / vi V / I /
Parallel 6ths: S/A, m. 1; S/T, mm. 3-4
Parallel 3rds: S/T, mm. 1-3; S/B, m. 3

Part B, p. 81.

Part C, p. 81.

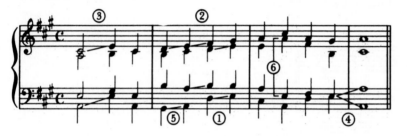

Self-Test 5-4

p. 83 (sample solutions).*

four parts

three parts

*Solutions to this and similar exercises throughout the book are sample solutions only. Many other correct solutions are possible.

Self-Test 5-5

Part A, p. 85.

d: i   iv   A: vi   ii   V   I   Bb: ii   V   I   IV

e: V   i   iv   i   F: I   IV   I   V   Bb: I   V   I   IV   I

Part B, p. 86.

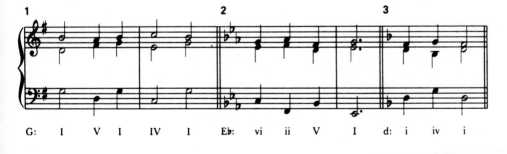

G: I   V   I   IV   I   Eb: vi   ii   V   I   d: i   iv   i

Self-Test 5-6

Part A, p. 87.

B♭:   vi IV ii V   f♯: i VI iv i   G: I iii vi ii V — I

Part B, p. 88.

A: I iii vi IV   d: i III VI iv   i   B♭: I vi IV I V   I

Self-Test 5-7

Part A, p. 90.

Part B, p. 91.

1.

E♭:   I   vi   V   I   IV   I   IV   V   —   I

2.

b: V   i   VI   iv   V   VI   iv   V   —   i

Part C, p. 91.

1.

a: i   V   i   VI   iv   V   i

2.

D: I   iii   vi   IV   V   vi   IV   ii   V   I

Self-Test 5-8

Part A, p. 92.

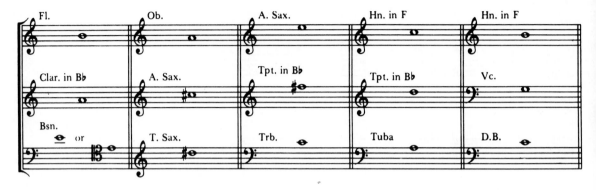

Part B, p. 93.

1.

CHAPTER 6

Self-Test 6-1

Part A, p. 106.

1. iii or V   **2.** I or ii   **3.** I or vi

4. iii or vi   **5.** ii or IV   **6.** I

Part B, p. 106.

1. ⌐V ii⌐   **2.** ⌐VII I⌐   **3.** ⌐IV iii⌐   **4.** none

Part C, p. 106.

1. Bach.   I / ⌐vi iii⌐ IV V⁷ / vi V I /

2. Vivaldi.

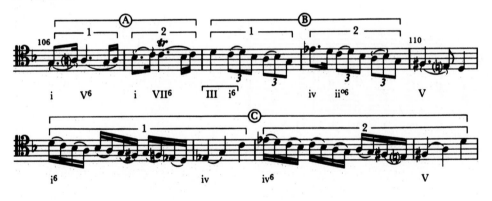

Part D, p. 108.

Part E, p. 108.

Part F, p. 109.

2. Four-part chorus (SATB)

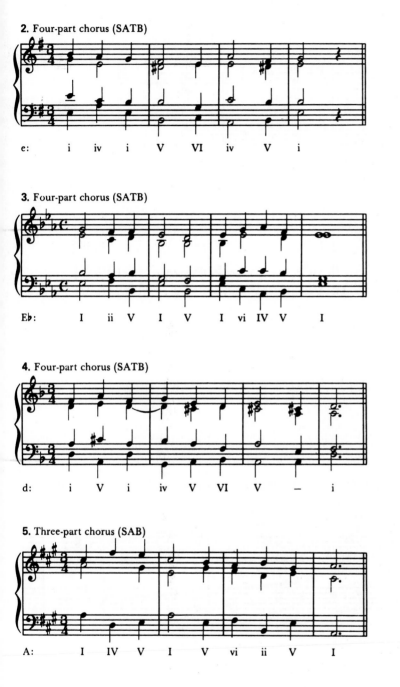

e: i iv i V VI iv V i

3. Four-part chorus (SATB)

E♭: I ii V I V I vi IV V I

4. Four-part chorus (SATB)

d: i V i iv V VI V — i

5. Three-part chorus (SAB)

A: I IV V I V vi ii V I

Part G, p. 109.

Bb: I   iii   IV   V   vi   ii   V   I   iii   vi   IV   ii   V   I

Part H, p. 110.

1. V^6_5 **2.** IV^6 **3.** iv^7 **4.** I^{M7} **5.** $ii^{ø6}_5$

6. vi^7 **7.** V^4_2 **8.** vii^{o6}_5 **9.** ii^6 **10.** V^4_3

11. iv^4_2 **12.** I^6_4 **13.** VI **14.** I^{M4}_3 **15.** V^6

CHAPTER 7

Self-Test 7-1

Part A, p. 120.

1. The voice-leading features parallel 4ths (arpeggiated in the right hand), as in Example 7-9.

2. i / iv⁷ iv⁶ V V$\frac{4}{2}$ / i⁶ vii°⁶ i i / vii°⁷ i V

The i⁶ and iv⁶ use the doubling in Example 7-10a; the vii°⁶ uses Example 7-10b.

3. / i / / V$\frac{6}{5}$ / / i / vii°⁶ or V$\frac{4}{3}$ / i⁶ ii°⁶ / V

With a little imagination, we can find most of the bass line, both forward and backward, in the melody.

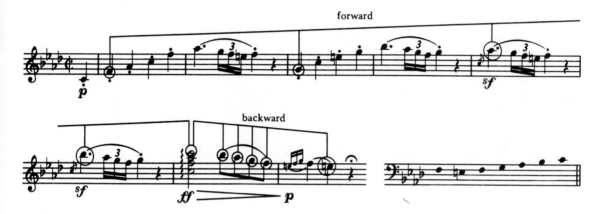

Part B, p. 122.

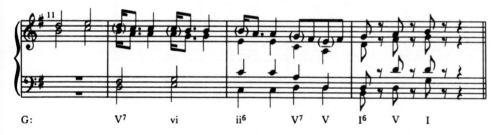

Part C, p. 122.

B♭: I 6 V   e: i V6 5/3 i   D: vi ii6 V vi

Eb: IV V I6 IV6   f#: i V6 i iv   d: i6 iv6 V i

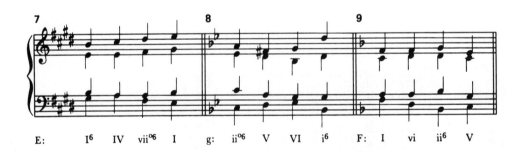

E: I6 IV vii°6 I   g: ii°6 V VI i6   F: I vi ii6 V

G: V6 V vi ii6   b: i6 ii°6 V VI   A: V I6 IV V

Part D, p. 123.

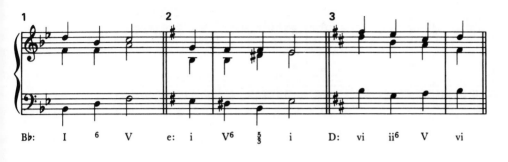

Bb: I   6   V   e: i   V⁶ ⁵₃ i   D: vi ii⁶ V vi

Eb: IV   V   I⁶ IV⁶   f#: i   V⁶ i iv   d: i⁶ iv⁶ V i

Part E, p. 123.

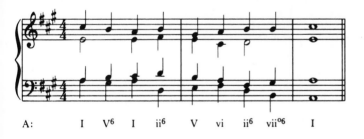

A: I V⁶ I ii⁶   V vi ii⁶ vii°⁶   I

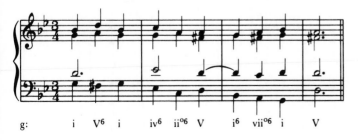

g: i V⁶ i iv⁶ ii°⁶ V   i⁶ vii°⁶ i   V

Part F, p. 124.

G: I   V⁶   vi   iii⁶   IV   ii⁶   V   (⁶₄   ⁶   ⁷)   I

Part G, p. 124.

F: I   V⁶   I   ii⁶   V   I   ⁶   V   —   I

b: i   vii°⁶   i⁶   ii°⁶   V   i⁶   i   V⁶   i   iv⁶   V   i

Part H and I, p. 125.   (Compare to Ex. 6-5 and Ex. 7-7b.)

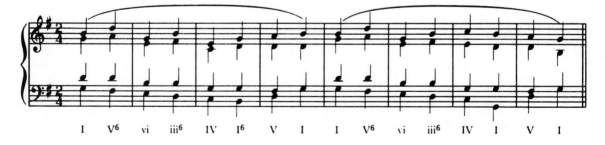

I   V⁶   vi   iii⁶   IV   I⁶   V   I   I   V⁶   vi   iii⁶   IV   I   V   I

CHAPTER 8

Self-Test 8-1

Part A, p. 144.

1. This excerpt is a repeated parallel period.

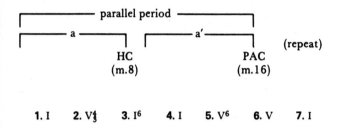

1. I   **2.** V$^4_3$ **3.** I^6 **4.** I   **5.** V^6 **6.** V   **7.** I

2. There are modified sequences in the melody in mm. 1-4, 5-6, 9-12, and 13-14.

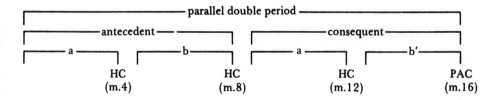

3. Since mm. 1-8 constitute a contrasting period, the whole theme can be heard as a contrasting period with a repeated and extended consequent phrase.

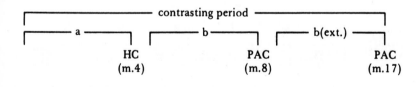

4. This excerpt is a repeated parallel period (not a double period). Octaves by contrary motion occur between melody and bass in mm. 7-8 and mm. 15-16.

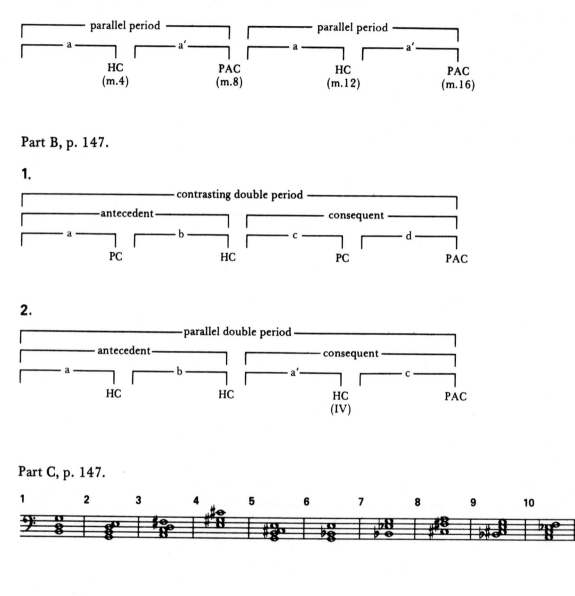

Part B, p. 147.

1.

2.

Part C, p. 147.

CHAPTER 9

Self-Test 9-1

Part A, p. 157.

1. g: i / iv$_4^6$ / – / i / vii$^{\circ6}_5$ i^6 / vii$^{\circ6}_5$ i^6 /

The iv$_4^6$ is a pedal six-four chord.

2. I V^6 / – IV^6 I$_4^6$ V^7 / I IV I /

The I$_4^6$ is a cadential six-four.

3. The I$_4^6$ in this example is also a cadential six-four.

E: IV   I^6 IV   I$_4^6$ V^7 I

                                    V

Part B, p. 158.

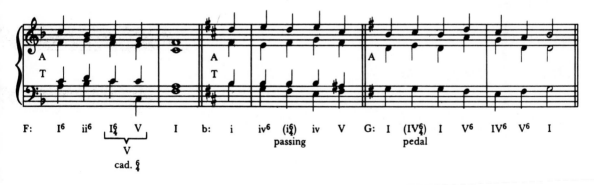

F: I^6 ii^6 I$_4^6$ V   I   b: i   iv^6 (i$_4^6$) iv   V   G: I (IV$_4^6$) I   V^6 IV^6 V^6 I

                      V   passing   pedal

           cad. $_4^6$

Part C, p. 158.

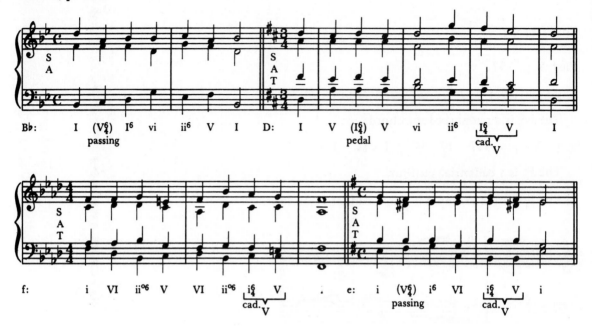

Bb: I (V⁶₂) I⁶ vi ii⁶ V I   D: I V (I⁶₄) V vi ii⁶ I⁶₄ V I
        passing   pedal   cad. V

f: i VI ii°⁶ V VI ii°⁶ i⁶₄ V . e: i (V⁶₂) i⁶ VI i⁶₄ V i
                              cad. V   passing   cad. V

CHAPTER 10

Self-Test 10-1

Part A, p. 173.

1. *Measure*   *Treble*   *Bass*

  1   p
  2   n   p
  3   7-6
  5   p
  6   p   p
  7   4-3

2. soprano: p; alto: p, p; tenor: 7-6, p, p

3. The only voice-leading problem seen in the reduction is found in m. 4, where direct 5ths (review p. 79) occur between the I and IV chords. Bach disguised these through the use of passing tones. The parallel 5ths in m. 2 are not objectionable, because the second 5th is a °5 (review p. 78). Slightly unusual is the proportion of chords with a doubled 3rd: four out of sixteen.

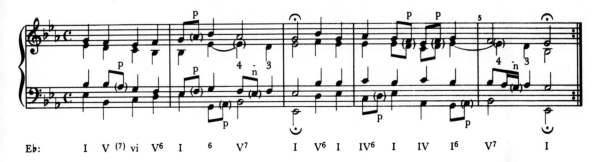

Eb: I V (7) vi V6 I   6 V7   I V6 I IV6 I IV I6 V7   I

Textural reduction

Part B, p. 174.

Part C, p. 174.

Bach, "Herr Christ, der ein'ge Gott's-Sohn"

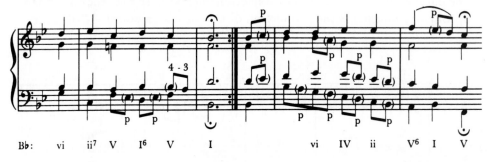

CHAPTER 11

Self-Test 11-1

Part A, p. 185.

1. m. 1: p; m. 3: p, p, app; m. 4: app, p

2. m. 24: app, app; m. 25: app, app; m. 26: app, p, p

3. m. 72: n, n; m. 74: 7-6; m. 75: 7-6, app, p; m. 76: p, p; m. 77: (melody) ant, (alto) ant

4. Notice (1) the scalar motion in all voices, inspired, of course, by the melody; (2) the incomplete IV, which contributes to the scalar motion; (3) the root position vii°, appearing here in one of its few typical usages; (4) the $\hat{7}$-$\hat{3}$ movement at the cadence—not unusual for Bach in an inner voice.

5. This is a difficult example that could be analyzed a number of ways. Notice in the reduction (1) how the vi^6 in m. 1 breaks up the parallel 5ths between alto and bass from the I chord to the ii chord; (2) the melodic sequence in mm. 1-4; (3) the parallel sixth chords in mm. 5-8 (review pp. 115-116).

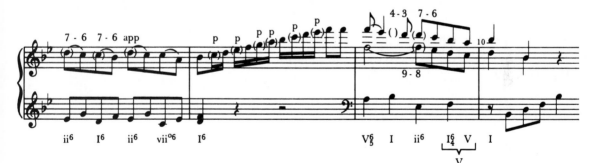

Textural reduction

Part B, p. 187.

F: I   V⁶   I   V   vi IV vii°⁶   I

Part C, p. 187.

Mozart, Sonata K. 330, III

CHAPTER 12

Self-Test 12-1

Part A, p. 199.

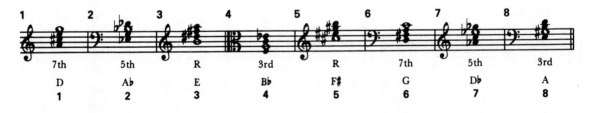

Part B, p. 199.

m. 1 V^7-vi deceptive progression. With $\hat{7}$ in an inner voice and in the major mode, it may move down to $\hat{6}$ instead of up to $\hat{1}$. The 7th resolves normally. All voices move by step.

m. 2 V^7 ornamented by a neighbor and a 4-3 suspension. The V^7 is complete, but the I is incomplete, due to the resolution of the leading tone in the alto. The 7th resolves down by step.

m. 5 Another ornamented V^7, but in this case the leading tone is frustrated, leading to a complete I chord. The 7th resolves down by step.

Part C, p. 200.

Part D, p. 200.

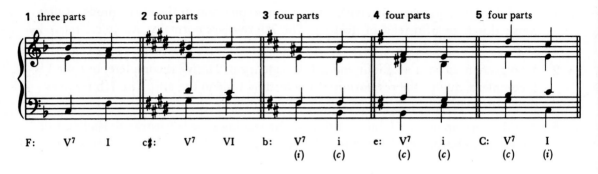

F: V⁷ I c♯: V⁷ VI b: V⁷ i e: V⁷ i C: V⁷ I
(i) (c) (c) (c) (c) (i)

Part E, p. 201.

1. Bach, "Kommt her zu mir, spricht Gottes Sohn"

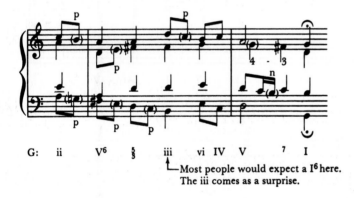

G: ii V⁶ ⁶₅ iii vi IV V ⁷ I
└─Most people would expect a I⁶ here.
The iii comes as a surprise.

2. Bach, "Jesu, der du meine Seele"

b♭: i ⁶ V ⁷ i iv⁶ ii°⁶ V ⁷ i

Part F, p. 201.

Ab: I   V⁷ vi   V⁶ V I   ii⁶ I⁶₄ V⁷   I

Self-Test 12-2

Part A, p. 208.

C: V⁶₅   e: V⁴₃   Bb: V⁴₂   G: V⁴₃   A: V⁴₂   g: V⁶₅   f♯:   V⁴₂   Ab: V⁶₅

Part B, p. 208.

1. The leading tone (G♯3) resolves up to tonic. The 7th (D3) is approached by a suspension figure and resolves down by step to $\hat{3}$.

2. The leading tone (F♯4) resolves up to $\hat{1}$. The 7th (C5) is approached by a passing tone figure and resolves down by step to $\hat{3}$.

3. There is no leading tone in this chord. The 7th (F4) is approached by an appoggiatura figure and resolves down by step to $\hat{3}$.

Part C, p. 208.

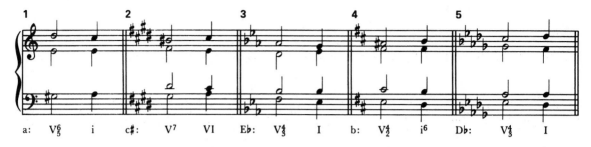

a: V⁶₅   i   c#: V⁷   VI   Eb: V⁴₃   I   b: V⁴₂   i⁶   Db: V⁴₃   I

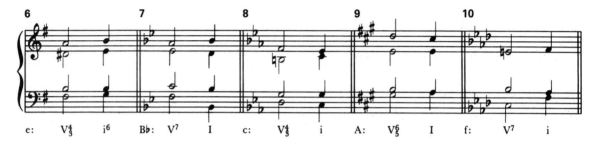

e: V⁴₃   i⁶   Bb: V⁷   I   c: V⁴₃   i   A: V⁶₅   I   f: V⁷   i

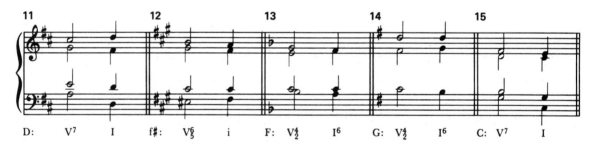

D: V⁷   I   f#: V⁶₅   i   F: V⁴₂   I⁶   G: V⁴₂   I⁶   C: V⁷   I

Part D, p. 209.

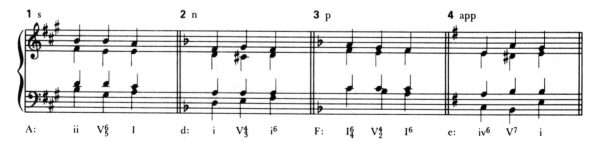

A: ii   V⁶₅   I   d: i   V⁴₃   i⁶   F: I⁶₄   V⁴₂   I⁶   e: iv⁶   V⁷   i

Part E, p. 209.

1. F	**2.** A	**3.** E♭	**4.** G, g	**5.** E
6. d	**7.** B♭	**8.** D	**9.** E, e	**10.** A♭
11. D	**12.** c♯	**13.** B♭	**14.** g	**15.** b

CHAPTER 13

Self-Test 13-1

Part A, p. 219.

g: ii$^{\flat4}_2$　　C: vii$^{\varnothing4}_3$　　e: ii$^{\varnothing6}_5$　　E♭: vii$^{\varnothing7}$　　D: ii$^4_2$　　f♯: vii$^{o4}_3$　　G: ii$^6_5$　　F: vii$^{\varnothing7}$

A♭: vii$^{\varnothing4}_3$　　c: ii$^{\varnothing4}_3$　　d: vii$^{o4}_3$　　B♭: ii$^6_5$　　b: vii$^{o4}_2$　　a: ii$^{\varnothing7}$　　A: vii$^{\varnothing4}_3$　　c♯: ii$^{\varnothing7}$

Part B, p. 220.

1. ii$^6_5$	**2.** ii$^4_2$	**3.** vii$^{\varnothing7}$	**4.** ii$^{\varnothing6}_5$	**5.** vii^{o7}
6. vii$^{\varnothing4}_3$	**7.** ii$^{\varnothing7}$	**8.** vii$^{o4}_3$		

Part C, p. 220.

1. The ii$^{\emptyset4}_{2}$ has its 7th approached as a suspension (from the previous chord tone). The large leap in the tenor (C4-F♯3) is necessary because of the motion in the upper voices. The 7th of the vii^{o7} is approached as an appoggiatura. The resolution of both tritones leads to a tonic triad with doubled 3rd. In the last complete measure notice the 5-4 suspension, which "works" because of the dissonance with the G4, and the tonic pedal under the final i-iv^7-vii^o-i progression.

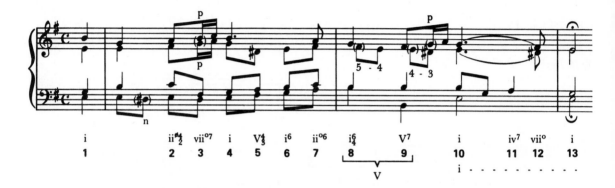

2. The 7th of the vii$^{\emptyset7}$ is approached as an appoggiatura. It is left by arpeggiation, although one could hear it as leading to the B5-A5 in the next measure.

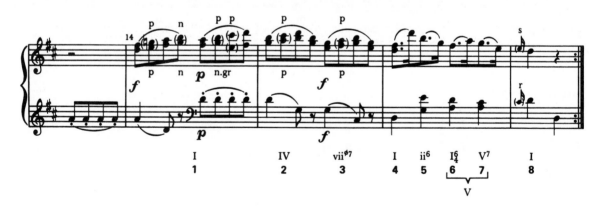

3. The 7th of the ii^{ø4}₃ is approached as a suspension. Resolution from the ii^{ø4}₃ is normal, the 7th becoming part of a 4-3 suspension. The main rhythmic motive (♩ ♪. ♪ | ♩) appears three times in the vocal part and three times in the accompaniment, alternating between the two.

4. The 7th of the ii⁷ is prepared as a suspension in another voice (the bass in the previous measure). The texture thickens to five parts before the ii⁷ resolves normally to the V⁷. The asterisks indicate when the damper pedal is to be released. The reduction helps us to appreciate Chopin's imaginative elaboration of a simple progression. Notice that the C5 in m. 15 is analyzed as a passing tone that connects B4 to D5.

Part D, p. 222.

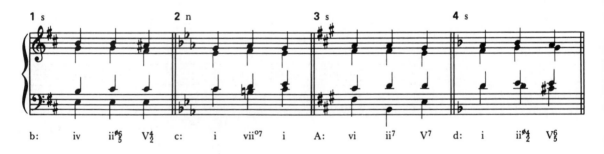

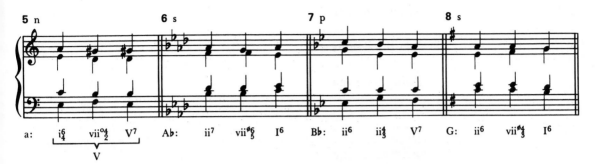

Part E, p. 223.

Corelli, Trio Sonata Op. 3, No. 2, II

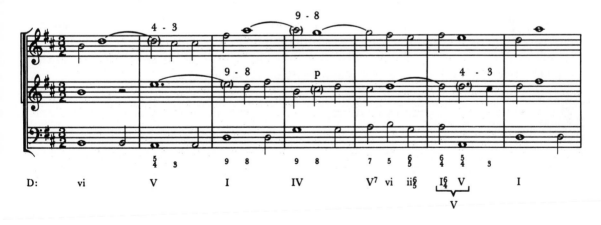

CHAPTER 14

Self-Test 14-1

Part A, p. 233.

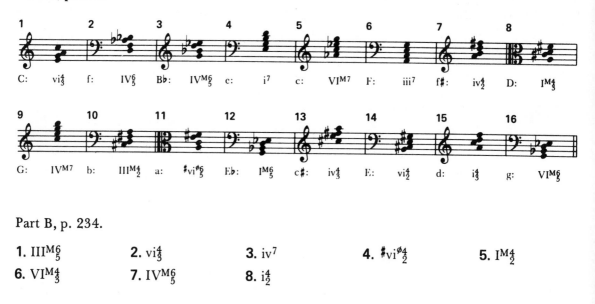

C: vi$^4_3$ f: IV$^6_5$ Bb: IVM$^6_5$ c: i^7 c: VIM^7 F: iii^7 f#: iv$^4_2$ D: IM$^4_3$

G: IVM^7 b: IIIM$^4_2$ a: #vi$^{ø6}_5$ Eb: IM$^6_5$ c#: iv$^4_3$ E: vi$^4_2$ d: i$^4_3$ g: VIM$^6_5$

Part B, p. 234.

1. IIIM$^6_5$ **2.** vi$^4_3$ **3.** iv^7 **4.** #vi$^{ø4}_2$ **5.** IM$^4_2$

6. VIM$^4_3$ **7.** IVM$^6_5$ **8.** i$^4_2$

Part C, p. 234.

1. The alto and tenor parts cross, and the soprano is more than an octave from its nearest neighbor (all of this in the second half of the first measure). This certainly could have been avoided (you might try it yourself), but at the expense of the sweeping lines in the inner voices. The 7th of the IVM$^6_5$ is approached as a suspension.

Bb: I   IV   vii^{o6} I   IVM$^6_5$ V$^6_5$ I

2. The 7th of the vi⁷ is approached as a suspension. The resolution is slightly unusual in that the ii has a doubled 3rd. But if the tenor had gone to a, the line would not have been as satisfactory, and parallel 5ths would have been formed with the alto.

G: iii   vi⁷   ii vii°⁶ I⁶   V   ⁷ I

3. Circle of fifths; 5th; it would proceed downward by step, one note per measure: F4-E♭4-D♭4-C4.

i iv⁷ / VII⁷ IIIᴹ⁷ / VIᴹ⁷ ii⌀⁷ / V⁷ i

Part D, p. 235.

A♭:   I⁶   IVMᵍ₂   vii°⁶   G: I⁶   IMⁱ   IVMᵍ₂   e: i⁶   VIMⁱ   vii°ᵍ   c: i   iv⁷   Vᵍ₂

A: vi   viⁱ₂   Vᵍ₂   d: i   i⁷   iv⁷   f♯: V⁷   IVᵍ   Vᵍ   B♭: I   iiiⁱ   vi⁷

F: V$^4_2$ IM$^6_5$ IVM$^4_2$ c♯: VII^7 III^{M7} VI^{M7} E: iii$^4_3$ vi^7 iii$^4_3$ g: ii$^{♯7}$ vii$^{o6}_5$ i^6

Part E, p. 236.

Notice the similarities between this excerpt and the one in Part C, no. 3.

Bach, French Suite No. 1, Minuet

Part F, p. 236.

1.

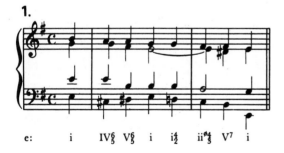

e: i   IV$^6_5$ V$^6_5$ i   i$^4_2$ ii$^{♯4}_3$ V^7 i

2.

F: I vi⁷ ii$_3^4$ V⁷   I V$_3^4$ I⁶ IV$^{M_2^4}$ ii⁷ V   I

CHAPTER 15

*Self-Test 15-1 ***

p. 245.

1. - - I - - - - - V - I

   - - I - - - ii$_5^6$ - V - I

  V⁶ - I - - - ii$_5^6$ - V - I

  V⁶ - I - IV⁶ - ii$_5^6$ - V - I

The A4 is an anticipation.

*All the levels analyses are subject to other interpretations.

2. Here are two interpretations, the first probably being the better one, since it agrees with the meter.

```
I  -   -   -   -   -  V  -   -   -   -   -   -  -  I
I  -   -   -   -   -  V  -  vi  -   -   -  V  -  I
I  -  IV⁶  -  I  -  V  -  vi  -  I⁶  -  V  -  I

I  -   -   -   -   -   -   -   -   -   -  V  -  I
I  -   -   -   -   -   -   -   -  I⁶  -  V  -  I
I  -   -   -   -  V  -   -   -  I⁶  -  V  -  I
I  -  IV⁶  -  I  -  V  -  vi  -  I⁶  -  V  -  I
```

3. The progression ii⁶-vi is relatively unusual. In fact, *retrogression* would be a better term here, since vi usually lies further away from tonic than ii⁶ does in tonal harmony.

```
I  -   -   -   -   -   -   -   -   -  V  -  I
I  -   -   -   -   -  ii⁶  -   -   -   -  V  -  I
I  -   -   -  I⁶  -  ii⁶  -   -   -   -  V  -  I
I  -  vii⁰⁶  -  I⁶  -  ii⁶  -  vi  -   -   -  V  -  I
I  -  vii⁰⁶  -  I⁶  -  ii⁶  -  vi  -  I⁶₄ - V  -  I
                                        V
```

4. The form is a parallel period. The C5 is an escape tone.

```
i  -   -   -   -   -   -   -   -   -   -  V  -  i  -   -   -   -   -   -   -   -   -   -   -  V  -  i
i  -   -   -   -   -   -   -  ii⁰⁶ -  V  -  i  -   -   -   -   -   -   -   -   -  ii⁰⁶ -  V  -  i
i  -   -   -  i  -   -   -  III  -  ii⁰⁶ -  V  -  i  -   -   -  i  -   -   -  III  -  ii⁰⁶ -  V  -  i
i  -  V  -  i  -  VII  -  III  -  ii⁰⁶ -  V  -  i  -  V  -  i  -  VII  -  III  -  ii⁰⁶ -  V  -  i
```

CHAPTER 16

Self-Test 16-1

Part A, p. 253.

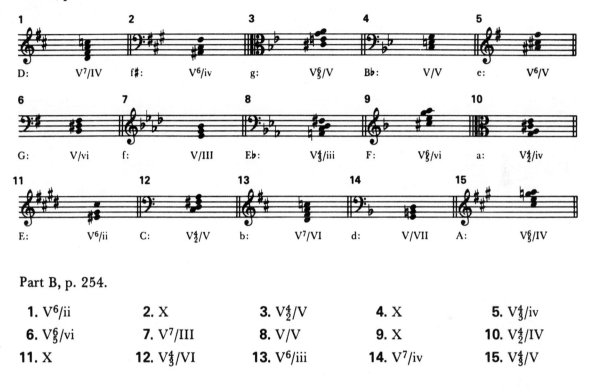

D: V^7/IV	f#: V^6/iv	g: V$^6_5$/V	B♭: V/V	e: V^6/V
G: V/vi	f: V/III	E♭: V$^4_3$/iii	F: V$^6_5$/vi	a: V$^4_2$/iv
E: V^6/ii	C: V$^4_2$/V	b: V^7/VI	d: V/VII	A: V$^6_5$/IV

Part B, p. 254.

1. V^6/ii	**2.** X	**3.** V$^4_2$/V	**4.** X	**5.** V$^4_3$/iv
6. V$^6_5$/vi	**7.** V^7/III	**8.** V/V	**9.** X	**10.** V$^4_2$/IV
11. X	**12.** V$^4_3$/VI	**13.** V^6/iii	**14.** V^7/iv	**15.** V$^4_3$/V

Self-Test 16-2

Part A, p. 258.

1.

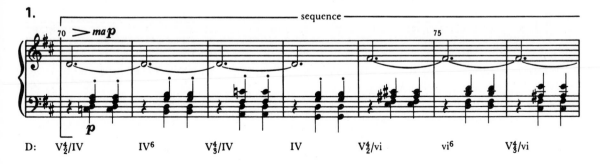

D: V$^4_2$/IV   IV^6 V$^4_3$/IV   IV   V$^4_2$/vi   vi^6 V$^4_3$/vi

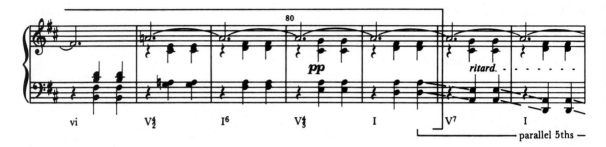

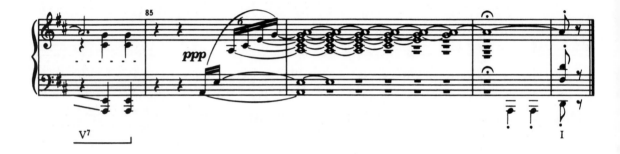

3. Mm. 1-2 return at a different pitch level in mm. 5-6. This is not really a sequence, since mm. 3-4 intervene. Counting from the bottom, parts 1 and 2 double at the octave. Part 4 doubles 7 (the melody) until the second half of m. 7. Other parallel octaves occur occasionally, as between parts 3 and 6 over the bar line from m. 2 to m. 3.

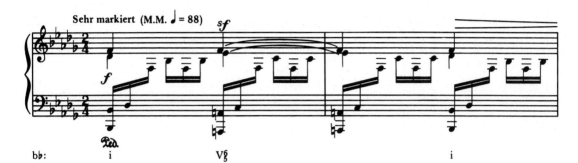

4.

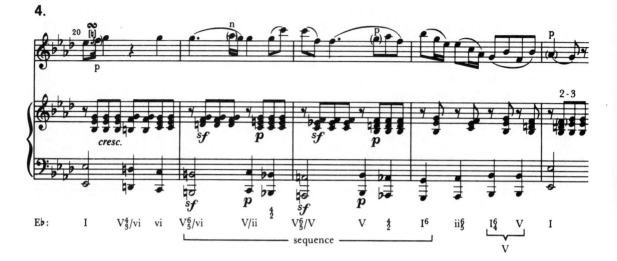

5. If you hear two phrases, the form is a period. If you hear four, it is a double period. In either case, the construction is parallel, because the phrases that begin in m. 1 and m. 9 begin similarly.

6. Yes, the four accompanying parts follow conventional voice-leading principles. The melody is an independent line for the most part, but it doubles an inner voice in mm. 2-3.

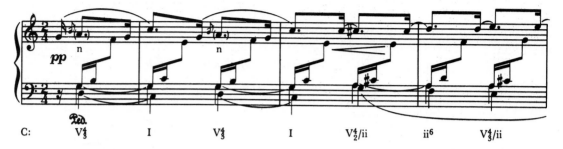

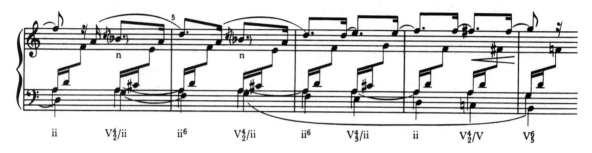

Part B, p. 263.

Part C, p. 263.

1. V$^{(7)}$/V, V$^{(7)}$/VII

2. V$^{(7)}$/ii, V$^{(7)}$/V, V^7/iii

3. V$^{(7)}$/V, V^7/vi

4. V^7/ii, V^7/IV

5. V$^{(7)}$/ii, V$^{(7)}$/vi, V^7/IV

6. V$^{(7)}$/iii, V$^{(7)}$/vi

7. V^7/IV, V^7/V

8. V$^{(7)}$/III, V$^{(7)}$/V

9. V$^{(7)}$/III, V$^{(7)}$/VII

10. V$^{(7)}$/iv, V$^{(7)}$/VII, V^7/V

Part D, p. 264.

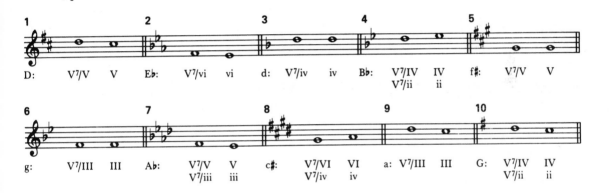

Part E, p. 264.

1. Bach, "Herzlich thut mich verlangen"

2. Bach, "Christus, der ist mein Leben"

3. Bach, "Ermuntre dich, mein schwacher Geist"

4. Bach, "Christ lag in Todesbanden"

e: i   V$^4_3$ i^6 V$^6_{(5)}$/iv   iv   V$^6_5$ V ^{7} i   e: V^6 i   V^6/III   III   V$^4_3$ i   ii$^{\varnothing 6}_5$ V^7 i

Part F, p. 265.

1.

D: I   V$^6_5$/vi   vi   V$^4_2$/V   V^6 V$^4_2$/IV   IV^6 V^7 I

2.

g: i   V/III   III   V$^6_5$/iv   iv   V$^6_5$/V   V   VI   ii$^{\varnothing 6}_5$ V   i

CHAPTER 17

Self-Test 17-1

Part A, p. 269.

Part B, p. 269.

1. vii°7/vi	**2.** X	**3.** vii°6/VI	**4.** vii°$^6_5$/IV	**5.** vii°7/VII
6. X	**7.** vii°7/III	**8.** X	**9.** vii°7/ii	**10.** vii°$^6_5$/V
11. vii°$^4_3$/V	**12.** X	**13.** vii°6/iv	**14.** vii°6/V	**15.** X

Self-Test 17-2

Part A, p. 282.

1.

2.

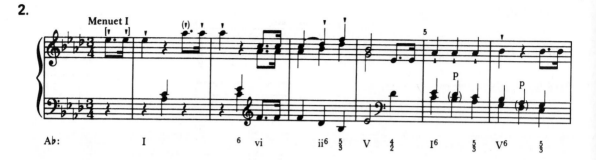

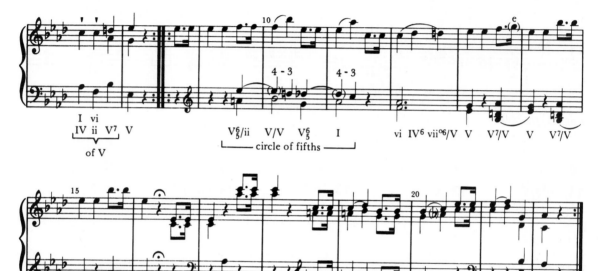

3. According to the definitions given on page 161, the G4 is an escape tone. But escape tones are usually followed by a leap in the *opposite* direction (so they seem to be escaping from a stepwise line, as in A-B-G). The G4 might be heard as part of an incomplete passing tone figure (A-G-F♯-E, with the F♯ omitted) or as an escape tone from the F♯4 that occurred a beat earlier (as F♯-G-E).

e:　　i　　　　　　　　V⁷/iv　　　　iv　　　vii°⁴₂/V　V⁷/V　V⁷

i　　　　iv　　　　　V　　⁷　i

The A5 is an ornamented 7-6 suspension.

4.

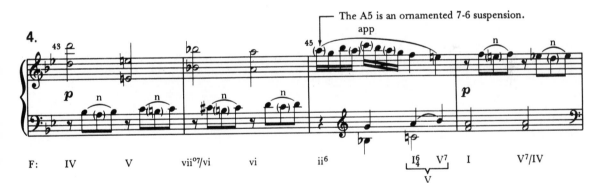

F:　IV　　　V　　　vii°⁷/vi　　vi　　　ii⁶　　　I⁶₄　V⁷　I　　V⁷/IV
　　　　　　　　　　　　　　　　　　　　　　　　　　　　V

V⁶₅/ii　　　　　ii　　　V⁶₅　　　　I　　　　V⁶₅/V　　I⁶₄　V⁷　I
V⁶₅/vi　　　　　vi　　　　　　　　　　　　　　　　　　　V
　　　　of IV

5. The excerpt is not a period, because the second cadence is not more conclusive than the first. The first cadence (m. 4) is a PAC, while the second (m. 8) is a HC.

The 5-4 suspension is marked with an exclamation point because it involves a note that is consonant with the bass resolving to one that is dissonant with the bass, exactly the reverse of the commonly accepted definition of a suspension.

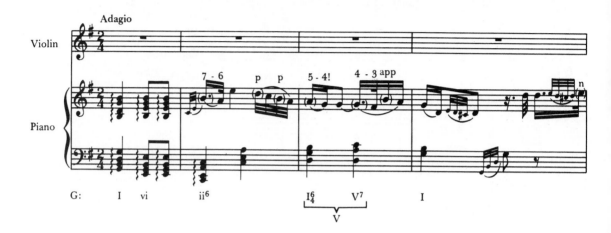

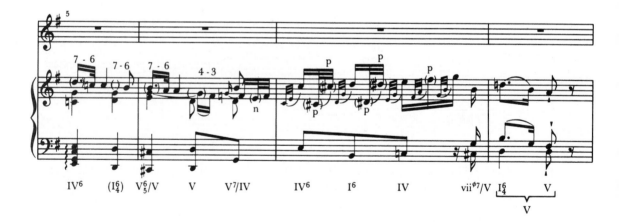

6.

Part B, p. 287.

Part C, p. 288.

1. Bach, "Du grosser Schmerzensmann"

2. Bach, "Ach Gott, wie manches Herzeleid"

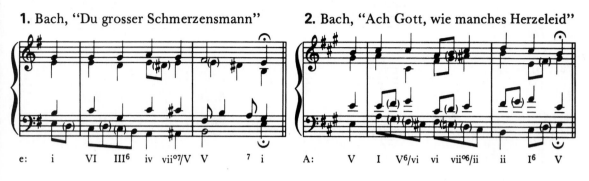

e: i VI III⁶ iv vii°⁷/V V ⁷ i

A: V I V⁶/vi vi vii°⁶/ii ii I⁶ V

3. Bach, "Ein' feste Burg ist unser Gott"

e: i III V/III V⁶₅ i V

(7)

V V⁶₅/vi vi
of III

Part D, p. 288.

F: I vii°⁷/ii ii V⁷ vii°⁷/vi vi ii⁶₅ V ⁷ I

f: i ⁶ vii°⁷/iv iv V i⁶ ii°⁶₅ vii°⁷/V V i

CHAPTER 18

Self-Test 18-1

Part A, p. 294.

1. b	**2.** D♭	**3.** A	**4.** a♭	**5.** d
6. F♯	**7.** c♯	**8.** A♭	**9.** c	**10.** B

Part B, p. 294.

1. c, d, E♭, F, g   **2.** e♭, f, G♭, A♭, b♭
3. E♭, f, g, A♭, B♭   **4.** C♯, d♯, e♯, F♯, G♯
5. E, f♯, g♯, A, B   **6.** b, c♯, D, E, f♯

Part C, p. 294.

1. foreign   **2.** closely related
3. enharmonic   **4.** closely related
5. relative and closely related **6.** closely related
7. parallel   **8.** foreign
9. relative and closely related **10.** foreign

Self-Test 18-2

Part A, p. 300.

1. The c♯° triad prepares us for the D♮. It seems to smooth out the modulation somewhat.

2. If the last chord in m. 7 were a ii$^6_5$, the 7th (E5) would resolve by step.

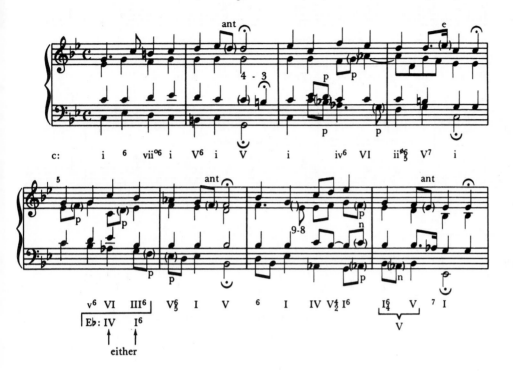

3.

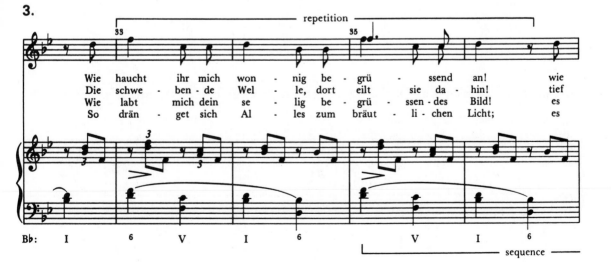

5. The outer voices in the sequence in mm. 9-11 could be heard as an elaboration of this pattern.

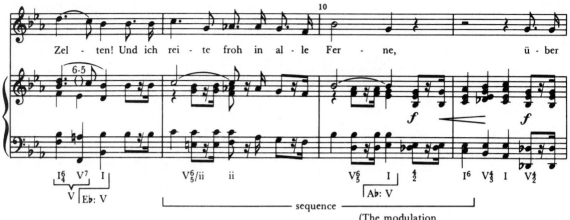

Zel - ten! Und ich rei - te froh in al - le Fer - ne, ü - ber

mei - ner Mü - tze nur die Ster - ne.

Part B, p. 304.

1. F   **2.** A   **3.** a   **4.** f♯   **5.** A♭

Part C, p. 304.

1. First key, A♭:

	I	ii	IV	vi
Triads:	A♭	b♭	D♭	f
Second key, D♭:	V	vi	I	iii

2. First key, c:

	iv	VI
Triads:	f	A♭
Second key, f:	i	III

3. First key, a:

	i	III	iv	VI
Triads:	a	C	d	F
Second key, F:	iii	V	vi	I

4. First key, G:

	I	iii	V	vi
Triads:	G	b	D	e
Second key, D:	IV	vi	I	ii

5. First key, c♯:

	i	ii°	III	iv	VI
Triads:	c♯	d♯°	E	f♯	A
Second key, E:	vi	vii°	I	ii	IV

6. First key, D:

	I	iii	V	vi
Triads:	D	f♯	A	b
Second key, f♯:	VI	i	III	iv

Part D, p. 305.

Bb: I   V   I   ii⁶   V   vi⌐ V$\frac{4}{3}$ I   V⁷   I

                                                                   ⌐F:ii

f#:   i   V   VI   iv⁶⌐ V ⁷ vi IV V   I

                                          ⌐A:ii

Part E, p. 305.

Bach, "Freu' dich sehr, o meine Seele"

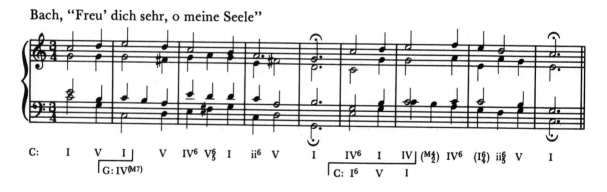

C: I   V   I⌐   V IV⁶ V$\frac{6}{5}$ I ii⁶ V   I   IV⁶   I   IV⌐(M$\frac{4}{2}$) IV⁶ (I$\frac{6}{4}$) ii$\frac{6}{5}$ V   I

            ⌐G:IV(M7)   ⌐C:I⁶ V I

Part F, p. 305.

G: I V⁶ V$\frac{4}{2}$/IV IV⁶   ii⁶⌐ vii°⁶ i V⁶ i   ⁶ ii°⁶ V⁷   i

                                 ⌐a:i⁶

CHAPTER 19

Self-Test 19-1

Part A, p. 318.

1. This modulation might also be analyzed as a phrase modulation.

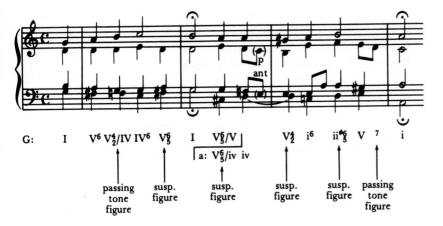

2. At least four elements combine to accomplish this modulation, and all should be taken into account.

   a. The common chord, D♭, serving as I in D♭ and VI in f.

   b. The common tone, F, linking the D♭ and G^7 chords.

   c. The two-part sequence in the "alto" part.

   d. The circle-of-fifths progression: E♭-A♭-D♭-G-C-F.

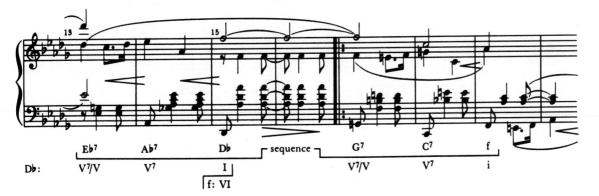

3. The modulation from g minor to f minor is sequential. The modulation back to g minor is a direct modulation.

g: i / iv⁶ / V⁷ / f: iv⁶ / V⁷ / i ⁶ V / i V g: iv / i⁶₄ V / i⁶₄ V / i

└─ sequence ─┘

4. The two keys are G major and E♭ major. A monophonic modulation is accomplished in mm. 121-123. The relationship between G and E♭ could be described in at least two ways. For one, there is a chromatic mediant relationship between the two keys (see p. 313). Also, E♭ is VI in g minor, the parallel minor of G major.

Part B, p. 321.

Part C, p. 322.

Bach, "Hilf, Herr Jesu, lass gelingen"

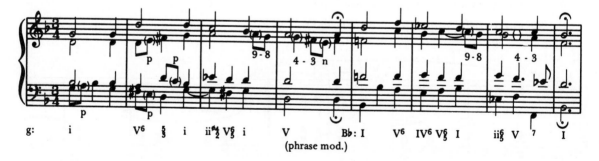

CHAPTER 20

Self-Test 20-1

Part A, p. 335.

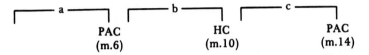

Or b and c could be considered one phrase. Either way, the form is sectional binary, unless you wish to use the term *phrase group* (review p. 142).

Part B, p. 335.

Two-reprise continuous rounded binary.

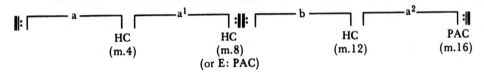

1. The first G4 is the 7th of a V⁷ of IV. The other is part of a 4-3 suspension.

2. End of m. 6: A: I = E: IV

3. The melodic figures resemble the opening motive (leap up, stepwise down), while the bass line is related to the first two bass notes.

4. m. 7, beat 3.

5. m. 7, beat 4 to m. 8, soprano and bass.

Part C, p. 336.

Two-reprise sectional binary.

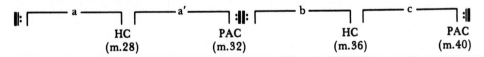

1. The first violins (or the melody) at the octave.

2. Part of a vii°6/V.

3. In mm. 4-5, perhaps explainable as occurring between phrases.

Part D, p. 338.

Continuous ternary.

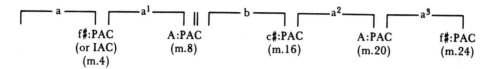

1. Schumann moves from i to the relative major (III) to the minor dominant (v), and then back the same way (III, then i). The tonicized pitch classes arpeggiate the tonic triad: F♯-A-C♯-A-F♯.

2. A: vii°⁷/ii / ii / V⁴₃/V V⁷ / I / f♯: i V / VIᴹ⁷ iv⁷ / i⁶₄ V⁷ / i / /
                                                                                                   V

3. In mm. 21-22, V-VIᴹ⁷, there are parallel 5ths between the bass and tenor. They are hidden by the anticipation (A3) in the tenor.

4. The double bar after m. 8.

CHAPTER 21

Self-Test 21-1

Part A, p. 350.

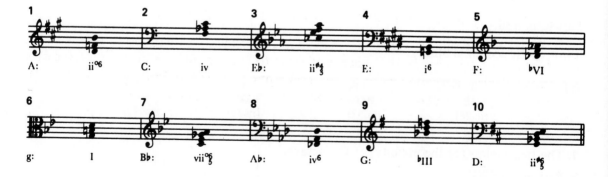

Part B, p. 350.

1. ii°⁶   **2.** iv⁶   **3.** vii°⁴₃   **4.** i   **5.** ♭VI

6. I   **7.** vii°⁶₅   **8.** ♭III   **9.** ii°⁴₂   **10.** iv

Part C, p. 351.

1.

G: I   IV   V⁴₂   I⁶   ii⌐   (iv⁶)   I⁶₄   V   I
⌐C: vi   V

2. C: V⁷ / I / IV⁶ / / I⁶ / / (ii°⁷) V⁴₃ / I⁶ vii°⁴₃/V V / (ii°⁷) V⁴₃ / I⁶ vii°⁴₃/V V /

3. The flutes double the violas in mm. 47-51.

A: V V⁴₂/ii / ii⁶ / V⁴₂ I⁶ / IVM⁴₂ ii (♭VI⁶) / V⁶₅ I ii⁶ V⁷ / vi V⁶₅/V / V⁷ / I /
                              or
                              vii°⁶

4. Mm. 5 and 6 contain diminished seventh chords. Both contain a °5 and a +4, and in both cases the tendency of the °5 to resolve inward and of the +4 to resolve outward is followed. The chords of resolution then have doubled 3rds.

B♭: I⁶ / V⁴₂ / I⁶ V / I / vii°⁷/ii ii / (vii°⁷) I / IV V⁶/V / V

5. The first modulation is from a♭ minor to its relative major, C♭, by means of the common chord in m. 5 (a♭: i = C♭: vi). A change of mode to c♭ minor follows in m. 9, notated as b minor. This change of mode simplifies the second modulation, from c♭/b to its relative major, E♭♭/D, through the common chord in m. 14 (b: iv = D: ii).

Part D, p. 355.

1.

D: I vii°7 I ii⁶₅ V⁷ vi IV I V

2.

F: I vii°7/ii ii vii°7 I ii°⁶₅ V I

Part E, p. 356.

B♭: I V⁴₂/IV IV⁶ iv⁶ I⁶₄ V⁴₂ I⁶ V I

CHAPTER 22

Self-Test 22-1

Part A, p. 362.

1. ii°⁶   **2.** vii^{ø7}/IV   **3.** vii°⁷/ii   **4.** N⁶   **5.** N⁶

6. N⁶   **7.** N   **8.** iv⁶   **9.** V$^6_5$/V   **10.** N

Part B, p. 363.

Part C, p. 363.

1. d: vii°$^6_5$ / i⁶   V$^6_5$/iv / N⁶   vii°⁷/V / i$^6_4$ V   i$^6_4$ V⁷   i$^6_4$ / V / /

                         or

                      VI⁶/iv

2. The form is a parallel period with an introduction.

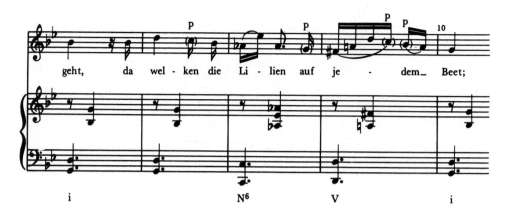

geht,   da   wel - ken die   Li - lien auf   je - dem_ Beet;

i   N⁶   V   i

3.

b: i   V⁷/N   N

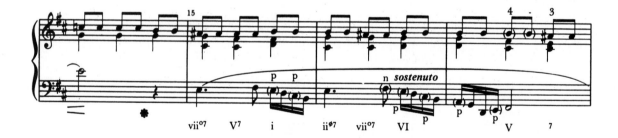

vii°⁷   V⁷   i   ii°⁷ vii°⁷   VI   V   7

4. Notice that the excerpt begins with a long circle-of-fifths sequence.

a: i⁶   iv / VII⁶   III / VI⁶   ii° / V⁶   i / N⁶ |

                   Bb: IV⁶   V⁷ / I / V⁴₃   I / IV⁶₄   I / V⁶₅   I /

Part D, p. 366.

e: i⁶ N⁶ V c♯: VI N⁶ V⁴₂ d: VI N⁶ vii°⁷/V g: iv N⁶ i⁶₄ V / V

f♯: iv N⁶ V⁷ f: i⁶ N⁶ i⁶₄ V⁴₂ / V b: i⁶ N⁶ V⁴₂ c: iv N⁶ vii°⁷/V

Part E, p. 366.

e: i N⁶ V⁷ i g: VI N⁶ i⁶₄ V / V VI f♯: i⁶ V⁶₅/iv iv N⁶ V⁴₂ i⁶

Part F, p. 367.

g: i vii°⁶ i⁶ N⁶ V⁴₂ i⁶ V⁶₃/V i⁶₄ V⁷ I
          F: ii⁶   / V

Part G, p. 367.

CHAPTER 23

Self-Test 23-1

Part A, p. 375.

1. Ger^{+6} **2.** Fr^{+6} **3.** vii^{o6}/V **4.** Ger^{+6} **5.** vii$^{o4}_{2}$

6. It^{+6} **7.** Fr^{+6} **8.** ii$^{o4}_{3}$ **9.** iv$^{6}_{5}$ **10.** It^{+6}

Part B, p. 375.

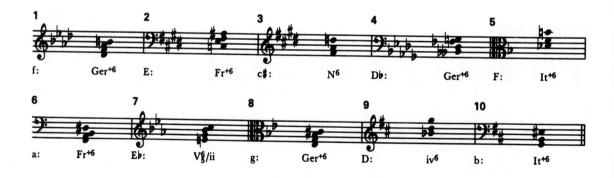

Part C, p. 376.

1. The resolution of the Fr^{+6} is ornamented with a 4-3 suspension in the second violin. The $\flat\hat{6}$ and $\sharp\hat{4}$ expand to an 8ve on $\hat{5}$.

B: I / ii^6 / V ^{7} / I / V^6 |

         | F$\sharp$: I^6 V$^6_5$ / I   IV^6 Fr^{+6} / V / I /

2. Both $\hat{6}$ and $\sharp\hat{4}$ resolve normally to the 8ve on $\hat{5}$. The parallel 5ths are avoided by arpeggiation within m. 27 in most parts. Only the horns are left with the E$\flat$ at the end of the measure, and they move by leap up to a concert G ($\hat{5}$) to avoid creating parallels with the bass (not to mention that the written B$\natural$ was almost impossible to play on an E$\flat$ valveless horn).

c: i / / VI^6 / vii$^{\circ 4}_3$/V / V^6 / vii$^{\circ 4}_3$/IV / IV^6 / vii$^{\circ 4}_2$ / (i$^6_4$) / N^6 (i$^6_4$) / vii$^{\circ 4}_2$ / (i$^6_4$) /

     N^6 (i$^6_4$) / vii$^{\circ 4}_2$ / Ger^{+6} / V /

3. The chromatic passing tone occurs at the beginning of m. 6 in the first violin. In both Ger^{+6} chords the viola has the 5th above the bass. The parallels are avoided in the first instance by leaping up to $\hat{5}$. In the second Ger^{+6} the parallels are disguised by means of a 6-5 suspension. In the first Ger^{+6} the resolution of $\sharp\hat{4}$ in the second violin is taken by the viola, allowing the violin to leap up to $\hat{2}$ (the 5th of the V chord).

f: i / vii$^{\circ 7}$ V$^6_5$ / i / iv^6 / Ger^{+6} / V   vii$^{\circ 7}$/V / V   Ger^{+6} / V / /

4. In m. 9, $\sharp\hat{4}$ moves down by half step to provide the 7th of the V^7 chord. In m. 26 $\flat\hat{6}$ and $\sharp\hat{4}$ move to an octave on $\hat{5}$.

C: I / / / / / / I   V$^6_5$ I / I$^6_4$ V / / / It^{+6} V^7 / I

                                           V

V$^4_3$ / i / It^{+6} / V / ^{7}

Part D, p. 381.

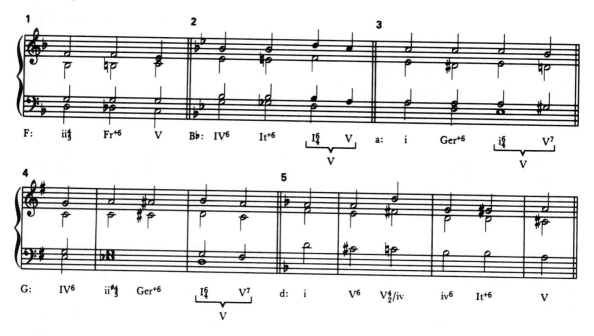

Part E, p. 382.

Part F, p. 382.

CHAPTER 24

Self-Test 24-1

Part A, p. 389.

1. Ger^{+6} V   **2.** It^{+6}/iv iv   **3.** V$^6_5$/iv iv   **4.** Ger^{+6} $\underbrace{\text{I}^6_4 \quad \text{V}^4_2}_{\text{V}}$ **5.** iv$^4_2$ V$^4_3$

6. [Ger^{+6}] i   **7.** +6 V   **8.** It^{+6} V^6 **9.** Fr^{+6}/I I   **10.** N^6 vii^{o7}/V V

Part B, p. 389.

1. e: N^6 Ger^{+6} / $\underbrace{\text{i}^6_4 \quad \text{V}^7}_{\text{V}}$ / I   **2.** e: / [Ger^{+6}] / i^6 / [Ger^{+6}] / i^6

CHAPTER 25

Self-Test 25-1

Part A, p. 401.

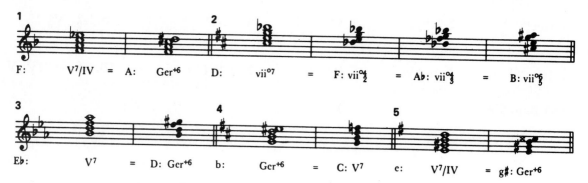

F: V^7/IV = A: Ger^{+6} D: vii°^{7} = F: vii°$^4_2$ = A♭: vii°$^4_3$ = B: vii°$^6_5$

E♭: V^7 = D: Ger^{+6} b: Ger^{+6} = C: V^7 c: V^7/IV = g♯: Ger^{+6}

Other correct answers in addition to those given above are possible. For example, the third chord in no. 2 could have been spelled and analyzed as a vii°$^4_3$ in g♯ (or G♯), or as a vii°$^4_3$/V in c♯, and so on.

Part B, p. 401.

1. E: I / vii°^{7} / I / V$^4_3$ / I^6 $^5_3$ / vii°^{7}⌐
⌐G: vii°$^4_2$ / V^7 / I / V^7 / I /

2. c: i   V$^4_2$ / i^6 ii°$^6_5$ / vii°^{7}/V⌐
⌐e: vii°$^6_5$ V$^4_3$ / i^6 / ii°$^6_5$ V^7 / i /

3. D: I   iii   IV / I^6 V$^4_3$ I   V^7/IV⌐
⌐f♯: Ger^{+6} / i$^6_4$ V ^{7} / i /

Part C, p. 402.

1. The F-G♭-F figure in m. 65 may be related to the voice line in mm. 58-62 (B♭-C♭-B♭) and to the bass in mm. 59-63 (F-G♭-F).

G♭: I / V$^6_5$ / I / V$^6_5$ / I   V^7/IV⌐
⌐b♭: Ger^{+6} / V ^{6} i ^{6} / V $^6_5$ i ^{6} / V

2. A is enharmonic with B♭♭, which is ♭VI in D♭. This is not an example of enharmonic modulation, but of respelling for convenience. The common chord between the keys could be the first chord in m. 34, which would be a ♭VI⁶ in D♭ and a I⁶ in A (or B♭♭). This might also be explained as a modulation by common tone, D♭/C♯ being the tone in common between the D♭ and A triads in mm. 33-34.

3. c: V⁷   Ger⁺⁶ / V⁶₅/V   i⁶₄ V⁷ / i /   / Ger⁺⁶ |
                                            ⌣ V   ⌜D♭: V⁷ / / / / / I V⁴₂ I⁶ /

   V⁷ / I   ii⁶ V⁶₅/V / V / I V⁴₂   I⁶ / V⁷ / vii°⁷/vi |
                                                        ⌜c: vii°⁶₅/V / i⁶₄ V / i
                                                                              ⌣ V

m. 98	c: Ger⁺⁶	m. 99	c: V⁶₅/V
mm. 102-6	c: Ger⁺⁶ = D♭: V⁷	m. 107	D♭: V⁴₂
m. 108	D♭: V⁷	m. 109	D♭: ii⁶
m. 111	D♭: V⁴₂	m. 112	D♭: V⁷
m. 113	D♭: vii°⁷/vi = c: vii°⁶₅/V		

Also note the importance of F♯/G♭ as a melodic pitch in this passage.

4. B♭/A♯ is an important pitch class in this passage. It appears melodically as the 7th of the vii°⁷/ii four times in mm. 34-41 (the first time accented), and it is used as the enharmonic hinge between the keys of C and E in m. 43.

   C: I vii°⁶₅/ii / ii⁶ /   / V⁶₅ / I   vii°⁷/ii   ii   vii°⁶₅ / I⁶   vii°⁶₅/ii   ii⁶ / ii°⁶₅ V⁴₂ /

   I⁶ i⁶ (V⁶₄) vii°⁷/ii / ii   V⁶₅ / I   V⁴₂/IV |
                                              ⌜E: Ger⁺⁶   i⁶₄ V⁷ / I V⁶₅ I / V ⁴₂ I⁶ V⁶₅ / I
                                                           ⌣ V

CHAPTER 26

Self-Test 26-1

Part A, p. 422.

G: V⁺   I   A♭: V⁹   I   E: (ct°⁷)   I⁶   F: V⁺⁷/IV   IV

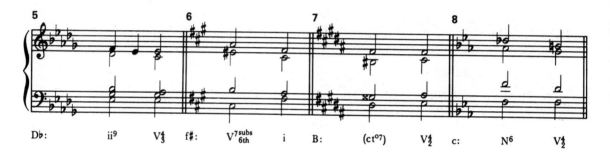

D♭:   ii⁹   V⁴₃   f♯: V⁷subs 6th   i   B: (ct°⁷)   V⁴₂   c: N⁶   V⁴₂

Part B, p. 422.

1.

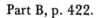

A - de - la - i - de!   A   de - la - i - de!

repetition — sequence

B♭: V⁴₂ I⁶ V⁴₃ I⁶ V⁴₂ I⁶ V⁴₃ I⁶ V⁴₂/IV IV⁶ I⁶₄ V⁴₃/IV IV⁶ V⁴₂/IV V⁺⁶/IV IV ii⁶ I⁶₄ V⁷ I

2.

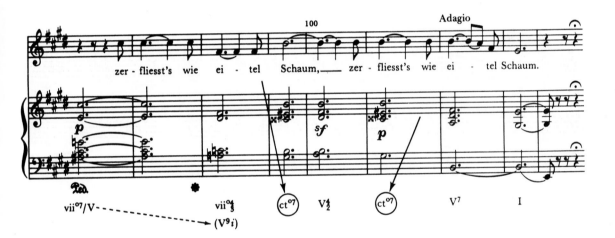

3. E: I / V⁷ / I / ⓒᵗ°⁷ / V⁴₂/IV / ⓒᵗ°⁷ / V⁴₂/IV / ⓒᵗ°⁷

A: vii°⁶₅/ii / ii⁶ / I⁶₄ V⁷ / I

V

4. The form of this piece is continuous ternary.

IV

iv⁷ (V⁹)   i   vii°⁴₃ i⁶₄   (ii°⁶₄) i⁶₄   V⁷ i⁶₄   V⁷

of vi (d)

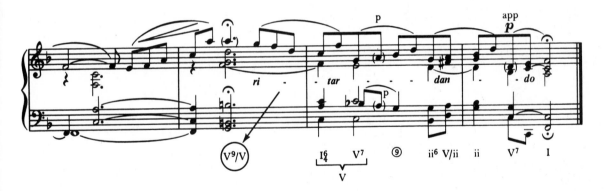

(V⁹/V)

I⁶₄   V⁷   ⑨   ii⁶ V/ii   ii   V⁷   I

V

5. I / IV⁶ ⁵₃ / ii°⁷ V⁷ / I   C / vi   C / F   A / D   F / B   ii⁴₃ / V⁷   V⁷/V /
V   IV⁶ / (ct°⁷) V⁶₅ / I

The chords in mm. 5-8 appear to be simultaneities because they do not create a logical progression and because the chord 7ths do not resolve. Parallel 10ths above the bass can be traced throughout these measures.

INDEX OF MUSIC EXAMPLES

All examples are identified by page number.

Adler, Samuel (1928-   )
  Capriccio, 497

Bach, Johann Sebastian (1685-1750)
  Chorale Preludes
    Allein Gott in der Höh' sei Ehr', 180
    Helft mir Gottes Güte preisen, 342
  Chorales
    Als Jesus Christus in der Nacht, 218
    Als vierzig Tag' nach Ostern, 105,
      226
    Befiehl du deine Wege, 128
    Christus, der ist mein Leben, 344
    Danket dem Herren, denn er ist
      sehr freundlich, 169
    Die Nacht ist kommen, 318
    Ermuntre dich, mein schwacher
      Geist, 80, 185
    Es ist das Heil uns kommen her, 300
    Für Freuden, lasst uns springen, 316
    Gib dich zufrieden und sei stille, 220
    Herzlich lieb hab' ich dich, o Herr, x
    Herzliebster Jesu, was hast du, 121,
      344
    Ich freue mich in dir, 245
    Jesu, Jesu, du bist mein, 300
    Nun lob', mein' Seel', den Herren, 66
    Nun ruhen alle Wälder, 195, 234,
      242, 243, 244
    O Ewigkeit, du Donnerwort, 89, 102
    O Herre Gott, dein göttlich Wort, 107
    Schmücke dich, o liebe Seele, 114,
      173
    Warum betrübst du dich, mein
      Herz, 229, 282
    Warum sollt' ich mich denn grämen,
      234, 351
    Wo soll ich fliehen hin, 75
  Easter Oratorio, 49, 50-51

French Suites
  No. 1, 257
  No. 2, 168
  No. 5, 124
Partita No. 2, 95-96
Passacaglia in C Minor, 217
Sinfonia No. 9, 197
Well-Tempered Clavier, Book I
  Fugue 2, 57
  Prelude 1, 212
  Prelude 10, 58
Well-Tempered Clavier, Book II
  Fugue 14, 184
  Fugue 22, 179
  Prelude 10, 127
  Prelude 12, 127
  Prelude 22, 57
Bartók, Béla (1881-1945)
  Concerto for Orchestra, 476
  Mikrokosmos
    No. 105, Playsong, 466
    No. 140, Free Variations, 471
    No. 141, Subject and Reflection,
      458
Beethoven, Ludwig van (1770-1827)
  Adelaide, Op. 46, 402-403, 422
  Bagatelles, Op. 119
    No. 4, 336
    No. 9, 359
  Die Ehre Gottes aus der Natur, Op. 48,
    No. 4, 381
  Minuet, 100
  Piano Sonatas
    Op. 2, No. 1, 121, 412
    Op. 2, No. 2, 58, 400
    Op. 10, No. 1, 404
    Op. 10, No. 3, 144, 371
    Op. 13, 145-146, 205
    Op. 14, No. 2, 307

Op. 26, 141-142, 354-355
Op. 53, 308
Op. 79, 125
String Quartets
Op. 18, No. 1, 195, 374
Op. 59, No. 1, 150
Op. 59, No. 2, 413
Symphonies
No. 2, Op. 36, 274-276
No. 4, Op. 60, 311-312
No. 6, Op. 68, 80, 132
No. 7, Op. 92, 291, 424-425
No. 9, Op. 125, 410
Violin Sonata, Op. 12, No. 1, 139
Berg, Alban (1885-1935)
Violin Concerto, 489
Boulez, Pierre (1925-)
Structures Ia, 493
Brahms, Johannes (1833-1897)
Ach lieber Herre Jesu Christ, 62-63
Ballade in G Minor, Op. 118, No. 3, 314
Dein Herzlein mild, Op. 62, No. 4, 361
Marienlieder, Op. 22
No. 1, Der englische Gruss, 226
No. 5, Ruf zur Maria, 332-333, 384
String Quartet No. 2, Op. 51, No. 2,
389
Symphonies
No. 1, Op. 68, 384, 416, 435, 436
No. 3, Op. 90, 417
No. 4, Op. 98, 444
Unsere Vater hofften auf dich, Op. 109,
No. 1, 214
Variations on a Theme by Schumann,
Op. 9, 183
Violin Sonata No. 3, Op. 108, 446-447
Byrd, William (1543-1623)
Psalm LIV, 54

Carter, Elliott (1908-)
Fantasy for Woodwind Quartet, 502-504
Chausson, Ernest (1855-1899)
Sérénade italienne, Op. 2, No. 5, 386
Chopin, Frédéric (1810-1849)
Ballade, Op. 38, 228
Mazurkas
Op. 7, No. 2, 360
Op. 17, No. 3, 343

Op. 33, No. 2, 146-147
Op. 33, No. 3, 221
Op. 68, No. 1, 255
Nocturnes
Op. 27, No. 2, 176, 403, 418-419
Op. 48, No. 2, 411
Op. 55, No. 2, 387
Prelude, Op. 28, No. 6, 364-365
Copland, Aaron (1900-)
Billy the Kid, 496
Corelli, Arcangelo (1653-1713)
Concerti Grossi, Op. 6
No. 3, 231
No. 8, 155
Trio Sonata, Op. 3, No. 2, 223
Cowell, Henry (1897-1965)
The Tides of Manaunaun, 471
Crumb, George (1929-)
Makrokosmos I, 509

Dallapiccola, Luigi (1904-1975)
Quaderno musicale di Annalibera, 489
Debussy, Claude (1862-1918)
Nocturnes
Fêtes, 475
Nuages, 459, 473
Preludes
La Cathédrale engloutie, x, 469,
474
La Fille aux cheveux de lin, 454
Voiles, 460
Dvořák, Antonín (1841-1904)
String Quartet, Op. 51, 299
Symphony, Op. 95, 213, 431
Dykes, John (1823-1876)
Holy, Holy, Holy!, 130

Fauré, Gabriel (1845-1924)
L'hiver a cessé, Op. 61, No. 9, 445
Fischer, J. C. F. (ca. 1665-1746)
Blumen-Strauss, 55

Grieg, Edvard (1843-1907)
Wedding Day at Troldhaugen, Op. 65,
No. 6, 467

Handel, Georg Frideric (1685-1759)
Messiah, 96, 103

Royal Fireworks Music, 325-326
Wenn mein Stündlein vorhanden est, 246
Haydn, Franz Joseph (1732-1809)
  Piano Sonatas
    No. 4, 129
    No. 11, 327, 328
    No. 15, 133
    No. 33, 111, 238
    No. 35, 103, 104, 177, 239
    No. 36, 359
    No. 37, 363
    No. 43, 112, 283
    No. 44, 129
    No. 45, 113
  String Quartets
    Op. 3, No. 3, 309
    Op. 9, No. 2, 345-346, 411
    Op. 20, No. 4, 257
    Op. 20, No. 5, 380, 399
    Op. 50, No. 6, 204
    Op. 64, No. 2, 376
    Op. 64, No. 3, 249
    Op. 64, No. 4, 78
    Op. 74, No. 3, 215
    Op. 76, No. 1, 196
  Symphonies
    No. 53, 270, 271
    No. 73, 298, 352-353
    No. 94, 250
    No. 101, 408
    No. 104, 116
Hindemith, Paul (1895-1963)
  Flute Sonata, 470

Kennan, Kent (1913-   )
  Prelude, 462

Liszt, Franz (1811-1886)
  Orpheus, 420
  Polonaise No. 2, 441

Mahler, Gustav (1860-1911)
  Kindertotenlieder, No. 2, 450-451
Mendelssohn, Felix (1809-1847)
  Song without Words, Op. 102, No. 1, 284

String Quartets
  Op. 44, No. 3, 261-262
  Op. 80, 393
  Symphony No. 4, Op. 90, 149
Messiaen, Olivier (1908-   )
  Mode de valeurs et d'intensités, 492, 494
  Quartet for the End of Time, 506
Mozart, Wolfgang Amadeus (1756-1791)
  An die Freude, K. 53, 134-135
  Bassoon Concerto, K. 191, 286-287
  Eine kleine Nachtmusik, K. 525, 122
  Fantasia, K. 475, 310, 316
  Magic Flute, K. 620, 370
  Piano Concerto, K. 491, 377-379
  Piano Sonatas
    K. 279, 120-121
    K. 283, 140
    K. 284, 79, 144-145, 220
    K. 309, 153, 203, 348
    K. 310, 362
    K. 330, 187
    K. 332, 180
    K. 333, 157, 186, 284-285
    K. 457, 386
    K. 533, 235
    K. 545, 281, 365, 415
    K. 570, 197
    K. 576, 315
  String Quartets
    K. 173, 373
    K. 465, 155
  Symphonies
    K. 97, 337
    K. 114, 99
    K. 550, 154, 278-279, 388
    K. 551, 163-164, 212, 320-321
  Violin Concerto, K. 271a, 151
  Violin Sonatas
    K. 377, 138
    K. 379, 285
    K. 481, 260

Pachelbel, Johann (1653-1706)
  Canon in D, 97
Penderecki, Krysztof (1933-   )
  Threnody, 515, 516-517, 518

Penn, William (1943-   )
  Ultra Mensuram, 520-522

Ravel, Maurice (1875-1937)
  Rigaudon, 463
Reich, Steve (1936-   )
  Piano Phase, 511-512
Rimsky-Korsakov, Nikolay (1844-1908)
  Scheherazade, 438

Schoenberg, Arnold (1874-1951)
  Klavierstücke, Op. 11, No. 1, 483
Schubert, Franz (1797-1828)
  Am Meer, 137
  Aufenthalt, 221
  Bardengesang, 119
  Die Schöne Müllerin, Op. 25
    No. 5, Am Feierabend, 302
    No. 6, Der Neugierige, 397
    No. 19, Der Müller und der Bach, 364
  Die Winterreise, Op. 89
    No. 11, Frühlingssehnsucht, 301
    No. 20, Der Wegweiser, 319
  Fantasy, Op. 15, 351
  Frühlingstraum, Op. 89, No. 11, 160
  Impromptu, Op. 90, No. 2, 182, 394
  Moment Musical, Op. 94, No. 6, 54,
    361
  Piano Sonata in E Major, 308
  String Quartets
    Death and the Maiden, Op. Post., 194
    Op. 125, No. 2, 405
  String Trio, D. 581, 394
  Symphony in B♭, 259, 354
Schuman, William (1910-   )
  Three-Score Set, 466
Schumann, Robert (1810-1856)
  Album for the Young, Op. 68
    No. 1, Melody, 329-330
    No. 4, Chorale, 66
    No. 6, Poor Orphan Child, 246
    No. 9, Folk Song, 130, 408
    No. 15, Spring Song, 230
    No. 17, Little Morning Wanderer,
      157, 158, 179
    No. 18, Reaper's Song, 181
    No. 21, Lento espressivo, 417

    No. 32, Scheherazade, 414
    No. 35, Mignon, 230
  Album Leaf, Op. 99, No. 1, 338
  Arabesque, Op. 18, 262
  Das verlassne Mägdelein, Op. 64, No. 2,
    419
  Dichterliebe, Op. 48
    No. 7, Ich grolle nicht, 428
    No. 11, Ein Jüngling liebt ein
      Mädchen, 347
    No. 15, Aus alten Märchen, 423
  Eintritt, Op. 82, No. 1, 256
  Freisinn, Op. 25, No. 2, 302-303
  Humoresque, Op. 20, 409, 413
  Lieder und Gesänge, Op. 51
    No. 4, Auf dem Rhein, 280
    No. 5, Liebeslied, 349
  Nachtlied, Op. 96, No. 1, 128
  Noveletten, Op. 21, No. 1, 255
  Papillons, Op. 2, No. 12, 258
  Romanze, Op. 28, No. 1, 259
  Romanzen und Balladen, Op. 49
    No. 1, Die beiden Grenadiere,
      390-391
    No. 2, Die feindlichen Brüder, 272
  Scherzo, Op. 32, 165
  Träumerei, Op. 15, No. 7, 426-427
  Waldscenen, Op. 82
    No. 1, Eintritt, 256
    No. 6, Herberge, 273
  Warum? Op. 12, No. 3, 318
Strauss, Richard (1864-1949)
  Till Eulenspiegel's Merry Pranks,
    Op. 24, 388
Stravinsky, Igor (1882-1971)
  Petrouchka, 477, 478, 501
  Le Sacre du printemps, 498-500

Tchaikovsky, Piotr I. (1840-1893)
  Children's Album, Op. 39
    No. 10, Mazurka, 297
    No. 20, The Witch, 390
  Nutcracker Suite, Op. 71a, 437
  Symphony No. 5, Op. 64, 175
  Trio, Op. 50, 256
Traditional
  Greensleeves, 324

Oh, Susannah, 331
Old One Hundredth, 74

Verdi, Giuseppe (1813-1901)
La forza del destino, 101
Vivaldi, Antonio (c. 1685-1741)
Cello Sonata in G Minor, 107-108
Concerto Grosso, Op. 3, No. 11, 98

Wagner, Richard (1813-1883)
Die Götterdämmerung, 25
Tristan und Isolde, 433, 434, 443
Webern, Anton (1883-1945)
Concerto, Op. 24, 490-491
Symphony, Op. 21, 484
Wolf, Hugo (1860-1903)
Herr, was trägt der Boden, 448-449

SUBJECT INDEX

accidental, 8
added-note chords, 406-407, 467-468
added value, 505-507
additive rhythm, 497
aleatory, 495, 507-513
altered chords, 56, 249
antecedent-consequent phrases, 136
anticipation, 161, 178-180
appoggiatura, 161, 175-177
arpeggiation, 112, 149-150, 238-244
asymmetric meter, 495
atonality, 483
augmented sixth chords, 368-369, 383
   in modulation, 395-398
   other bass positions, 383-385
   other uses, 385-387
   types
      French, 370-371, 395
      German, 372-374
      Italian, 369-370

Babbitt square, 485-488
bar form, 333
bar line, 28
Baroque, 47
beam, 35, 37
beat, 27
   division of, 30
   simple and compound, 30
binary form, 323-326
   rounded, 330-333
bitonality, 466-467
borrowed chords. *See* mode mixture
brace, 5

cadences
   authentic, 126-128, 131
   deceptive, 129, 131, 345. *See also*
      deceptive progression

   half, 129-131
   Phrygian, 129
   plagal, 130-131
cadenza, 151
cell, 484
chain of suspensions, 168
chance music, 495, 507-513
change of bass suspension, 167
change of key, 289. *See also* modulation
chorales, 69
chord sevenths. *See* seventh chords
chord structures
   close and open, 73-74
   mystic, 461
   polychord, 465-466
   quartal (quintal), 468-470
   secundal, 468, 470-472, 516-519
   tall, 462-465
   tertian, 41
   whole-tone, 460-461
chromatic mediant. *See* mediant
   relationship
chromaticism, 249
circle of fifths, 10-11, 14-15
circle-of-fifths progression, 97. *See also*
   sequence
clefs, 4-5
close structure, 73-74
cluster, 468, 471-472, 516-519
coda, 333
coloristic chord successions, 420
combinatoriality, 488
common chord (in modulation), 295-299
common tone (in modulation), 310-314
common-tone diminished seventh chord,
   414-417
composite meter, 495
conjunct, 70
contrapuntal texture, 117

counterpoint, 69, 433-436
crossed voices, 74

deceptive cadence. *See* cadence
deceptive progression, deceptive resolution, 104, 198, 256, 280-281. *See also* cadence
diatonic chord, 56
diminished seventh chord in modulation, 395-396, 398-401
direct 5ths and octaves, 79
dominant
    avoided resolution, 444-448
    with raised or lowered 5th, 409-411
    with substituted 6th, 406-409
dominant preparation, 238-244
double pedal point, 181
doubling, 82, 117-119, 156
durational symbols, 26-27, 35-37

electronic music, 523-526
eleventh chord, 412-414, 462-466
elision, 134
enharmonic spelling
    for convenience, 373, 392-395
    in modulation, 374, 395-401
    See also keys, enharmonic
escape tone, 161, 177
expanded tonality, 448-451

fifth of chord, 42
    omission of, 82, 118-119, 193-197
fifths
    consecutive, 77-78
    direct, 79
    hidden, 79
    parallel, 76-80
    unequal, 78
figured bass, 47-49, 170
focal point, 70
form, 126
free anticipation, 179-180

grand staff, 5
graphic notation, 508-509
grouplet, 36

half step, 6
harmonic progression, 69, 94-106

hexachord, 488
hidden 5ths, octaves, 79

Impressionism, 453-454
interval, 19-24
interval class, 482
inversion
    of intervals, 23-24
    of ninth chords, 414
    of a set (tone row), 484
    of seventh chords, 48
    of triads, 46-47. *See also* triad
inversion symbols, 47-49
inverted pedal point, 181

key relationships, 292-293
key signatures
    major, 9-11
    minor, 14-15
keyboard, 3
keys
    closely related, 292-293
    enharmonic, 10, 292
    foreign, 293
    parallel, 14-15, 292
    relative, 14-15, 292
Klangfarbenmelodie, 489

lead sheet symbols, 463-464
leading tone (in V^7 chord), 192-197
ledger line, 4
levels of harmony, 237-245

magic square, 485-488
matrix, 485-488
measure, 28
mediant relationship, 313-314, 420, 446
melodic bass, 149
melody, 70-71
meter, 27-28, 495-507
meter signatures, 31-35
minuet and trio, 333
mixed meter, 496-497
mode mixture, 225, 341-349. *See also* modulation
modes, 454-456
modulation, 250, 289-292
    common-tone, 310-314
    diatonic common chord, 295-299

direct, 315-317
enharmonic, 395-401
metric, 501-505
mode mixture, 348-349
monophonic, 314-315
Neapolitan common-chord, 360-362
secondary function common chord, 306-307
sequential, 307-309
motive, 132, 136
multiphonics, 519
musique concrète, 523
mutation. *See* mode mixture

nationalism, 432
Neapolitan chord, 357-362
neighbor group, 161, 177-178
neighboring tone, 161, 164-165
ninth chords, 412-414, 462-466
non-chord tone, 160-172, 175-184.
   See also neighboring tone, passing tone, etc.

octave register, 3
octaves, 3, 20
 consecutive, 77-78
 direct, 79
 hidden, 79
 parallel, 76-80
omnibus, 439-440
open structure, 73-74
ostinato, 101

pandiatonicism, 477-478
parallel intervals
 5ths, 76-80, 196, 372-373
 octaves, unisons, 76-80, 118
 other intervals, 476-477
parallel sixth chords, 115-116
parallelism, 472-477
part writing, 69, 72-90, 117-119, 156, 192-198, 202-207, 210-218, 224-233, 254-257, 270-281, 343-347, 358-362, 368-374, 383-388
passing chords, 115, 418-419
passing tone, 162-164
pedal point, 155, 161, 180-181

period, 136-142
phase music, 510-513
phrase, 132-136
 repeated, 137
phrase group, 142
phrase segment, 132-133
Picardy third, 218, 341-342
pitch, 3
pitch class, 52
plagal progression, 103. *See also* cadence, plagal
planing, 473
pointillism, 489
polychord, 465-466
polymeter, 501
polyrhythm, 498
polytonality, 466-467
pop symbols, 463-464
preparation of a suspension, 165-166
prepared piano, 514
prime form, 481-482, 485
process music, 510-513
prolongation, 238

raised 5th, 409-411
ranges
 instrumental, 92, 529-530
 vocal, 74
resolution of a suspension, 165-166
rests, 26
retardation, 161, 168-169
retrograde, 484
retrograde inversion, 484
rhythm, 26-28, 30-37, 495-507
roman numerals, 49, 59-60, 63-65
rondo form, 334-335
root, 42
 omission of, 118, 156
rounded binary form, 330-333

scale degree, 7
scale degree names, 18
scales
 dodecaphonic, 462
 4+1, 3+2, 457
 Lydian-Mixolydian, 456-458
 major, 6-9
 minor, 13-14, 56-58

modal, 454-456
mystic, 461
octatonic, 461
pentatonic, 458-459
whole-tone, 460-461
score, 72-73
secondary functions, 250
    deceptive resolutions of, 280-281
    other secondary functions, 281-282
    secondary dominant, 250-257, 360
    secondary leading-tone chords, 266-276
    sequences involving, 276-279
secundal harmony, 470-472, 516-519
sequence, 95-98, 115, 307-309, 437-440
    circle-of-fifths, 97-98, 231-232,
        276-279, 309
serialization, 483-495
    tonal or multiparametric, 492-495
set, 479, 484
set theory, 479-482
seventh chords, chromatic. *See* secondary
        functions
seventh chords, diatonic
    approach to 7th, 206-207
    resolution of 7th, 192-193, 202,
        204-205, 210
    sequences involving, 231-232
    spelling in major and minor keys, 63-65
    types, 44
    I⁷, 229-230
    II⁷, 211-213
    III⁷, 231
    IV⁷, 224-226
    V⁷, 191-198, 202-207
    VI⁷, 227-229
    VII⁷, 213-218, 342-344, 395-396,
        398-401
shifting keys, 440-443
simple time signature, 31-32
simultaneity, 418-420
six-four chord. *See* triad
sonata form, 334
spacing, 74
Sprechstimme, 523
staff, 4
stems, 36-37, 72-73
stochastic music, 495
structure, close and open, 73-74

substituted 6th, 406-409
subtonic triad, 105
suspensions, 161, 165-170
synthesizers, 524-526

tempo, 27
tendency tone, 71
ternary form, 326-330, 333
tertian, 41
textural reduction, 113
texture, 69, 117, 472, 513-523. *See also*
        counterpoint
third of chord, 42
    omission of, 156, 194, 196-197
third stream, 527
thirteenth chord, 412-414, 462-466
thorough bass. *See* figured bass
ties, 26
time signatures, 31-35
tone cluster, 471-472, 516-519
tone row, 484
tonicization, 250, 290-292
transition, 333
transposition, 10
    instrumental, 92, 529-530
triad, 39-40, 44-45
    augmented, 41, 152, 395, 409
    diminished, 41, 114
    major and minor, 41
    spelling in major and minor keys, 59-60
    I, 98-99
    II, 99-100, 104
    III, 101-102, 104, 152
    IV, 103-104
    V, 98-99, 102-104. *See also* dominant
    VI, 100-101, 104
    VII, 102-103, 105
triads in first inversion
    bass arpeggiation, 112-113
    parallel, 115-116
    part writing, 117-119
    substituted, 113-115
triads in second inversion
    bass arpeggiation, 149-150
    cadential, 103, 150-152
    melodic bass, 149-150
    part writing, 156
    passing, 152-154

pedal, 154-155, 181
tritone, 23, 193
twelve-tone technique, 483-495
two-reprise form, 326

unequal 5ths, 78
unison, 20

voice crossing, 74
voice leading. *See* part writing
voicing of chords, 73-74, 468

white noise, 524
whole step, 6

About the Authors

Stefan Kostka holds degrees in music from the University of Colorado and the University of Texas and received his Ph.D. in music theory from the University of Wisconsin. He was a member of the faculty of the Eastman School of Music from 1969 to 1973. Since that time he has been on the faculty of the University of Texas at Austin. Kostka initiated courses in computer applications in music at both the Eastman School and the University of Texas. More recently he has specialized in courses in atonal theory and contemporary styles and techniques, interests that have led to a forthcoming book, *Materials and Techniques of Twentieth-Century Music*. Kostka is active in various professional organizations and currently serves as president of the Texas Society for Music Theory.

Dorothy Payne presently serves as head of the music department and professor of theory at the University of Connecticut. A graduate of the Eastman School of Music, she has earned Bachelor's and Master's degrees in piano performance, as well as her Ph.D. in music theory. Before assuming her responsibilities at the University of Connecticut, she taught at the University of Texas at Austin, the Eastman School of Music, and Pacific Lutheran University. She has been the recipient of teaching excellence awards at both the Eastman School and the University of Texas. In addition to remaining active as a performer, Payne has presented numerous workshops on theory pedagogy at meetings of professional societies. She presently chairs the College Board's Advanced Placement Test Development Committee for Music.